Women and Revenge
in Shakespeare

Revenge with a dagger (plate 22), by Antonio Tempesta (after a design by Otto van Veen), in *Historia septem infantium de Lara* (Antwerp, 1612). © The British Museum.

Women and Revenge in Shakespeare

Gender, Genre, and Ethics

Marguerite A. Tassi

Selinsgrove: Susquehanna University Press

New hardcover printing 2012 by Susquehanna University Press
Co-published with The Rowman & Littlefield Publishing Group, Inc.
4501 Forbes Boulevard, Suite 200, Lanham, Maryland 20706
www.rowman.com

Estover Road, Plymouth PL6 7PY, United Kingdom

978-1-57591-131-1 (cloth: alk. paper)

Originally published by Associated University Presses
2010 Eastpark Boulevard
Cranbury, NJ 08512

Library of Congress Cataloging-in-Publication Data
Tassi, Marguerite A., 1965–
    Women and revenge in Shakespeare : gender, genre, and ethics / Marguerite A. Tassi.
        p.   cm.
    Includes bibliographical references and index.
    ISBN: 978-1-57591-131-1 (alk. paper)
    1. Shakespeare, William, 1564–1616—Characters—Women. 2. Revenge in literature. 3. Women in literature. I. Title.
    PR2991.T37 2011
    822.3'3—dc22

    2010038144

Printed in the United States of America

To my loving family:
Shaun, Francesca, and James

I had thought, before I began, that what I had on my hands was an almost excessively masculine tale, a saga of sexual rivalry, ambition, power, patronage, betrayal, death, revenge. But the women seem to have taken over; they marched in from the peripheries of the story to demand the inclusion of their own tragedies, histories and comedies, obliging me to couch my narrative in all manner of sinuous complexities, to see my "male" plot refracted, so to speak, through the prisms of its reverse and "female" side. It occurs to me that the women knew precisely what they were up to—that their stories explain, and even subsume, the men's.

—Salman Rushdie, *Shame*

Contents

Preface

SOME YEARS AGO, I WAS INVITED BY A MEDIEVALIST COLLEAGUE, JOHN Damon, to prepare a guest lecture on feuds in the Anglo-Saxon epic *Beowulf* for his graduate seminar. What I wished to do in that lecture was challenge a commonly held view of the feud, that the frequent eruptions of violence between clans illustrate the doom caused by revenge. It seemed to me that an anthropological approach to the text might offer significant insights into the cultural meanings of social codes and exchanges typical of an aristocratic, martial, prestate society such as we find in *Beowulf*. In particular, the function of women in the feud, often dismissed as tragically useless and exemplary of revenge's baneful effects, might be understood better. Perhaps the most troubling case of a female caught up in a feud is Queen Hildeburh, who appears in the Finnsburh episode. The anguished story of Hildeburh, a Danish princess married as a peace-weaver to the Frisian king, Finn, is a moving case-in-point of how the feud is stronger than any peace effort made between clans. She survives her son and brother who perish when violence erupts during the Danes' visit to King Finn. An unruly group among Finn's retainers reignite the Danish-Frisian feud, betraying the Danes and Finn in their efforts to maintain peace. With renewed bloodshed between clans, Hildeburh's peace-weaving inevitably fails. Her political purpose thwarted and her kin's lives lost on both natal and marital sides, Hildeburh would seem to exemplify the helpless victimization of women in a warrior society. What has she left but endless grief for her dead?

Such a conclusion, however, devalues the cultural work performed by women in Anglo-Saxon poetry and fails to attend to the epic's striking verbal clues offered in this episode. Such clues reveal a hierarchy in kinship ties, attitudes toward honor maintenance and revenge, and the potency of the female mourner's keening and management of the funeral pyre. The narrative clearly places the grieving queen at the political and "affective center" of the episode.[1] Hildeburh is introduced first by name and then by patriline as the Danish king "Hoc's daughter" (line 1076)[2] as she takes charge of the ritual lamentation of her brother and son. In his comparative ethnological study of *Beowulf*, John M. Hill has done a remarkable reading of this scene, urging readers to see how intensely purposeful Hildeburh is at the funeral pyre, where she holds court, as it were, over a funeral of terror.[3] To assume that Hildeburh is anything other than vengeance-minded and honor-bound to her natal clan and to her son is to lose sight of the cultural norms at work in the *Beowulf* poem. Furthermore, Hill points out that the kinship tie between uncle and nephew (Hildeburh's brother and son, respectively) is the most tender, most strongly felt blood connection represented in the poem's world. And this is the tie so brutally torn asunder by Finn's retainers.

Hildeburh's purpose at the funeral pyre, then, is not retrospective, as some critics assume; rather, she is urging a future revenge through her fierce lamentation. Hildeburh's vengeful spirit—her agency—is conveyed through the images of the devouring fire and the animism of the dead bodies on the pyre. The ghastly melting of heads and shooting up of blood bespeak the grieving sister-mother's bitter anger and, in their aggression, urge retribution. Her keening has the quasi-magical effect in the verse of appearing to rouse action: "the noblewoman wept, / mourned with songs. The warrior rose up" (lines 1117–18). The linguistic position of "warrior" stands ambiguously for both Hildeburh's dead and the living avenger, her brother's chief thane, Hengest, who in time *will* rise up as the agent of Hildeburh's will to avenge the Danes.

The conclusion I drew was that Hildeburh's keening perpetuates her culture's revenge ethic by inciting male kin to a just revenge. Her lamentation urges Hengest and the other visiting Danes to avenge the despicable slaying of their people. When the bloodletting is finished, King Finn is dead, and Hildeburh, still in possession of her rights as Danish royalty, sails back home with Finn's treasure to "her people" (line 1159). In the end, grim as it is, the Finnsburh episode recounts a Danish victory.

Working outside of one's area of specialty has the beneficial effect of defamiliarizing subjects that have become all too familiar. In my field of early modern English drama, one such subject is revenge, which has been treated extensively by critics and scholars for more than a century. To see revenge anew, to reopen such an old matter for reinvestigation, as I did in working on Hildeburh's function in *Beowulf,* seemed like an exciting prospect years ago when I started this book. Much to my surprise, I found that extended studies on women and revenge in Shakespeare's plays were hard to come by. Out of this neglect was born my intention to explore this subject in all of its nuances. Herein lies the promise and burden of the present book.

A number of pressing questions arose early in my investigation into Shakespeare's women: What understanding of revenge do women offer, and what relationship do they have with men who pursue revenge? Can women's revenge do ethical work? Can women exhibit a virtue in their vengeance? What can the rhetoric of revenge, the social circumstances, and the performance possibilities in drama show us about women's responses to injustice and the function of such responses in the theater?

Contemporary Western thought has long decried revenge as immoral, irrational, barbaric, and psychologically aberrant. The Christian-Stoic tradition, in particular, has suppressed and "denatured" what might be recognized as a natural moral instinct in human beings to revenge. In this tradition, revenge has been defined as the infliction of harm upon another out of anger and resentment, or the return of injury for injury. Morally speaking, this notion has fostered a sense of revenge as the return of evil for evil. Often, malicious intent, rather than just cause, is assumed in those who seek revenge, and forgiveness is held up as the rarer virtue. Today, we are the inheritors of this mind-set, which tends to color our understanding of the ethical dimension of literary revenge. For Shakespeare's contemporaries, Christian-Stoic ideas were prominent, and the conservative religious belief was that vengeance belonged solely to God and his ministers. The state and church alike upheld the authority of legally invested ministers, not the victims themselves, to execute what they perceived to be divinely sanctioned vengeance. Christians were to define their virtue through passivity, nonviolence, hope, and charity.

But copresent with the antirevenge ethic was an alternative view, barely acknowledged by critics of early modern thought, drawn from the philosophical tradition of Aristotelian-Thomistic virtue ethics. From that tradition, which would have been known to Shakespeare and his contemporaries, came the idea of a noble or virtuous vengeance. To avenge wrongdoing meant activating justice and giving the guilty party what was due, in keeping with the moral order. While ministers of justice were authorized to practice lawful revenge, individuals, as well, if acting in the name of virtue, God, and the harmed party, might claim moral authority for their actions. From classical and medieval sources, too, came ideas of revenge as a cultural practice and ethical action that maintained or restored honor. Revenge in ancient and medieval literatures is represented often as coequal with justice, reflecting societal norms, a god's will, and a moral obligation.

In Shakespeare's England, the terms *vengeance, revenge, retaliation,* and *retribution* were used somewhat interchangeably to signify punishment or repayment for an injury or wrong.[4] The concept of debt governed early modern meanings of these terms, suggesting that wrongdoers who harmed individuals, families, and communities incurred a debt that must be repaid by a sufficient punishment. Justice is the underlying concern expressed in this metaphor, for the notion of balance (as a moral and social good) is articulated here. We might recall the traditional image of Justice with her balanced scales and sword. Justice referred to a system of rewards and punishments—legal vengeance, if you will—that vindicated what was right. Sixteenth-century definitions of *revenge* included *satisfaction* as part of the emotional and psychological terrain of punishment. The old phrase "to satisfy a debt" was imaginatively transposed into the realm of revenge to articulate the kind of transaction at work here. *Revenge* also could mean *chastisement* of a wrongdoer, which stretched the notion of punishment to include verbal rebuke and other symbolic cultural actions. *Retribution* most readily suggested the expression of God's will, yet the terms *revenge* and *vengeance* could be used as well in early modern texts to refer to God's punishments. *Retaliation* recalled the ancient *lex talionis,* a retributive form of justice that attempted to create an equation or fitting balance between crime and punishment (thus, an eye for an eye). *Avenge* and *revenge* as verbal forms both referred to inflicting punishment upon a wrongdoer and vindicating a wronged party, though *avenge* in some cases indicated requital on behalf of another. I tend to use the terms *revenge, avenge,* and *vengeance* interchangeably, as they were used by Shakespeare and his contemporaries, though when necessary I make distinctions or clarify nuances in my use of a concept.

In the pages that follow, I explore the multifaceted character of vengeance, as it is given moral force and compelling dramatic representation in Shakespeare's plays. In the process, I review, refine, and sometimes contest the insights of critics on the ethics of early modern revenge and its attendant passions—anger, resentment, vindictiveness, and hatred. I argue that the fundamental passion motivating revenge is, more often than not, a love of justice. Much criticism has been devoted to showing how Shakespeare calls into question or condemns revenge in both male and female characters. Few critics have wished to marshal arguments for revenge as virtuous or ethically justified, but this is precisely what I do with some of Shakespeare's women and, in doing so, I offer an alternative vision to the negative view of revenge more readily understood and assumed today. By attending to classical resonances in Shakespeare's texts and applying literary analogues to his works, I develop a culturally nuanced ethical perspective on revenge. In some cases, I show how women's vengeance can activate morality, bringing into play an ethic that critiques male acts of revenge and patriarchal systems of governance and law. I show, as well, how women usurp male social roles or incite men to exact revenge.

Just as there is no denying revenge as an aspect of our humanity, so there is no escaping the controversial nature of this subject as it arises in life and literature. This book represents an engagement with difficult ethical questions that matter deeply to all of us. At the heart of this book lies the challenge of how to understand and come to terms with women's passionate, sometimes violent, responses to moral outrages. In the face of injustice and injury, Shakespeare's women choose revenge more readily than they do forgiveness, and there is often just cause for their vengeance. I focus on these bold, outspoken dramatic women, rather than the Desdemonas and

Heros. My study of Shakespeare's women and revenge challenges three prevailing assumptions that have governed Western discourses for centuries: (1) that women barely matter when it comes to the business of men in a man's world; thus, they are not relevant to the story of revenge; (2) that women are to blame for male violence, for both indirectly and directly they lie at the root of men's instinct to avenge themselves; and (3) that if women participate in revenge, they become unnatural and monstrous, descending into the bestial realm rather than ascending into the heroic. Each of these assumptions finds its articulation and counterargument in Shakespeare's plays; such views are not offered uncritically, or without rich mitigating circumstances. This book pays attention to such circumstances and their ethical complexity.

I wish to express gratitude to my seminar students in "Shakespeare and the Theater of Revenge" and "Women and Revenge in Western Literature" at the University of Nebraska-Kearney. Over the years, they have shared my enthusiasm for revenge and motivated me to write the book they wanted to read. Heartfelt thanks, as well, to my friends and colleagues who came for cakes, ale, and lively conversation about revenge in *Twelfth Night* some years ago: Susan Honeyman, William Aviles, John Damon, Randy Robertson, and Beth Robertson. Particular thanks are due to Gene Fendt for his generous and rigorous critiques of my chapters on *King Lear* and *Hamlet,* and to Christine Boeckl for helpful guidance regarding iconography. Others who deserve special mention for their support of my work are Carole Levin, John R. Ford, Robert N. Watson, Kurt Borchard, and Amy Hodge. Closer to home, I wish to thank my husband, Shaun Padgett, and my mother, Nina Tassi, for their warm encouragement of this project from its inception.

I could not have written this book without the generous support of the University of Nebraska-Kearney and the Research Services Council, which granted me a faculty development leave, a well-timed course release, and a grant to cover costs associated with the book. The administrators and faculty I am most indebted to for their encouragement and support are Bill Jurma, Kenya Taylor, Barbara Emrys, Martha Kruse, and Kathryn Benzel. I appreciate the efforts of the university's library staff, especially Alta Kramer, in locating research materials for this book. I am grateful, as well, to Jason Willard for his valuable help with editing and indexing this book.

Warm thanks go to the members of the 2009 Shakespeare Association of America session on *The Merry Wives of Windsor* for their animated discussion of the play, which generated some of my own thoughts on wives and revenge. I am indebted to Pam Brown, who shared her book chapter with me, and Jeanne Addison Roberts, for her appreciative reading of my chapter on *The Merry Wives of Windsor.* I am grateful to Carole Levin for inviting me to give a keynote presentation on Hecuba and Shakespeare's queens (part of Chapter 4) at the Queen Elizabeth Society in March 2010.

An earlier version of chapter 6 was published in *The Upstart Crow: A Shakespeare Journal* 27 (2007/2008): 32–50 (Copyright © Clemson University). The article is reprinted by permission of Clemson University. Special thanks are due to the journal's editor, Elizabeth Rivlin, for her kind support. I am grateful to Arden Shakespeare, an imprint of A&C Black Publishers, for permission to quote a good deal of text from Shakespeare's *The Merchant of Venice,* © John Russell Brown, editor, reprinted by Thomas Nelson and Sons Ltd., 1997.

At times, this book entailed working far from the field of English literature and my specialty in Renaissance drama. I cannot claim the depth of knowledge that specialists in classics, medieval literature, philosophy, and anthropology possess, but I hope that my use of their expertise has helped to yield the nuanced account my subject deserves. To the brilliant scholars whose names and ideas populate this book, I express my great appreciation, for without their inspiration this book would not have been possible. Where there are errors or inadequacies in my use of other disciplines' methods and insights, I claim sole responsibility. This book unfolds as a continuous narrative, but each chapter offers a reading that can stand alone as one possible way to tell the story of women and revenge in Shakespeare. As I have found, this subject is rich beyond any definitive statement.

Women and Revenge
in Shakespeare

Introduction

Tamrya. Revenge, that ever red sitt'st in the eyes
Of injured ladies, till we crown thy brows
With bloody laurel, and receive from thee
Justice for all our honour's injury;
Whose wings none fly that wrath or tyranny
Have ruthless made and bloody, enter here,
Enter, O enter!
         —George Chapman, *The Revenge of Bussy D'Ambois*

Hecuba to Priam. Our sonne is past our helpes. . . .
This bloodie fellow then ordain'd to be their [fates'] meane—
   this wretch
Whose stony liver would to heaven I might devoure, my teeth
My sonnes' Revengers made. Curst Greeke . . . .
         —Homer, *Iliad* (trans. George Chapman)

It is noble to avenge oneself on one's enemies and not to come to terms
with them; for requital is just, and the just is noble; and not to surrender is a sign of courage.
         —Aristotle, *Rhetoric* (trans. W. Rhys Roberts)

BLOOD REVENGE HAS BEEN THE PRACTICE OF PEOPLES IN TRADITIONAL honor-based cultures, from ancient Greece to medieval Iceland to contemporary Montenegro. Revenge is typically perceived in such cultures as the moral and social obligation of men that prize honor above all else. In the public sphere, men visibly gain and lose honor in aggressive confrontations with their social equals and betters. By striking out against enemies through feuds, vendettas, trial by combat, and duels, males communicate a message of zero tolerance for personal affronts and injuries to themselves, their kin, friends, and clan. Through violent retaliation, they uphold a form of justice based on reciprocity (harm for harm, life for life) and reinforce their reputations as honorable, even heroic, men. A failure to act decisively and appropriately in an honor-based culture can have dire

17

consequences—a devastating sense of shame for self and kin, and a loss of public identity.

Western literature offers countless examples of male characters whose passion for revenge emerges when their honor has been affronted. In the *Iliad,* Achilles retreats from the Trojan battlefield when Agamemnon dishonors him by seizing Achilles' war prize, Briseis. When Agamemnon's emissaries entreat him to return to battle, Achilles responds with steely anger:

> Not if his gifts outnumbered the sea sands
> or all the dust grains in the world could Agamémnon
> ever appease me—not till he pays me back
> full measure, pain for pain, dishonor for dishonor.
>
> (9.470–73)[1]

In *Beowulf,* the great Geatish warrior invokes the worldwide custom ("worold-raedenne")[2] of revenge practiced in medieval epics and sagas: Better to avenge a friend's death than grieve too much, he counsels King Hrothgar (lines 1383–89). Such a noble action promises to win warriors fame and glory, the only sure immortality available after death. In Shakespeare's *Hamlet,* the Danish prince encounters his father's ghost, who returns from his grave to stir his son to avenge his murder. Hamlet understands that in fulfilling his obligation to revenge, he cleanses the kingdom of the polluting effects of regicide and fratricide. Revenge narratives such as these convey deeply entrenched cultural norms and expectations of masculine behavior in the face of moral transgressions and perceived injustice. In contemplating these well-known examples, we might be tempted to conclude that stories of revenge are "almost excessively masculine" in their focus and concerns.[3]

Such a conclusion, however, would not be entirely accurate. A broad survey of Western literature reveals countless female characters actively involved in revenge narratives; Tamrya in George Chapman's early-modern revenge tragedy and Hecuba in Homer's ancient Greek epic offer only two such examples. From classical literature onward, female characters articulate claims for revenge, often on rational and moral grounds, expressing passions associated with vengeance—moral outrage and anger, indignation and resentment, vindictiveness and retributive hatred. Like men, women often desire justice for "honour's injury" and articulate the need to move beyond grief into the realm of action, where they can see injustice paid back. We can hear Shakespeare's Queen Margaret, for example, expressing a similar sentiment to Beowulf's: "Oft have I heard that grief softens the mind / And makes it fearful and degenerate; / Think therefore on revenge and cease to weep" (*2 Henry VI,* 4.4.1–3). Female characters in Western literature not only cry out for vengeance, but "do something, and i'th' heat"

(*King Lear,* Folio 1.1.302), exercising their wills, devising plots, and taking action.

When they cannot take revenge in their own person, women incite men to action, reminding them of their ethical obligations to kin and family honor. The trope of female whetting, also known in literature as inciting and goading, proves to be transhistorical and transcultural, appearing in countless Western works of literature. As goaders, female characters exercise a degree of agency and participate vicariously in revenge, expecting their chosen male avengers to take action. Their potent words constitute speech acts that express the purposeful social and moral communications of revenge acts. They represent the voice of elemental justice, speaking not simply for their own integrity, but also for the integrity of their family, tribe, or community. The counterexample of women who cannot revenge, whose prayers, curses, and demands are not answered, reveals how devastating to self, family, and community—and the moral order as reflected in each—a failure or inability to revenge can be. As Harry Keyishian argues, "though revenge may be dangerous and destructive, impotence is worse."[4] "Revengelessness" has its costs;[5] for women, the prospects of unmitigated victimization, loss of integrity and honor, helplessness, despair, and untimely death are frighteningly evident. Yet even in cases of victimization as seemingly clear-cut as Ophelia's in *Hamlet,* a character's impulse toward justice finds some mode of expression. Ophelia, for example, provokes her audience through lament: the guilty feel touched to the quick, and her brother feels moved to seek revenge for the wrongs done to his family.

This book takes women's vengeance seriously. The often marginalized stories of women's revenge constitute a long-standing subversive element in Western literature. To bring to light this less visible tradition, I shift critical attention to *women's* preoccupations with honor and shame, justice and revenge, moral outrage and ethical response. While a complete history of women and revenge in Western literature is well beyond the scope of this study, I can offer a limited examination of the phenomenon through the work of a single dramatist—Shakespeare. In Shakespeare, we find a body of work that offers the subtlety and range necessary for producing a counternarrative to the dominant one of masculine honor, prerogative, and ethics in literature and society. To echo Salman Rushdie, Shakespeare's women have taken over my study of revenge, marching in from the peripheries of the men's stories, demanding to be seen and heard, to have *their* stories articulated in a compelling narrative.

Feminine vengeance has a history in Western literature that has rarely been acknowledged, much less treated, with the nuanced critical praxis it deserves. Such a history must be investigated not only to challenge the partiality of the well-known masculine revenge narrative, but to understand the literature of revenge more fully. Classical female avengers such as

Medea, Procne, and Clytemnestra have a varied textual and artistic after-life; their descendents and their heritage are represented in countless retellings and transmutations of their stories. For the most part, though, critical discourses have vilified female avengers such as these, conceptu-alizing angry women who avenge wrongs as irrational, immoral, and mon-strous. As Alison Findlay argues, the unfavorable views of feminine vengeance reflect "fundamental fears about women, relating to maternal power and to female agency."[6] The very coupling of the concepts of *woman* and *revenge,* much less *mother* or *wife* and *revenge* activates—and upsets—long-standing gender norms of feminine nurturance, domesticity, and subordination that form the basis of Western constructions of femininity. Literature represents not only extraordinarily defiant acts of feminine vengeance, but also a host of ways in which feminine power and agency are awakened through the spirit of revenge. This feminine spirit, connected with ancient deities like the Furies and Nemesis, counters male authority and power by exerting its own power and its own measures for handling injustice.

My concern here is with writing an alternative narrative—provisional, perhaps, but nonetheless potent in its challenge to the prevailing critical wisdom that vengeance is the exclusive province of males in Western lit-erature and culture, and that feminine revenge is aberrant, its function be-ing merely to depict the savagery and moral depravity in vengeance itself, or the essential irrationality and spitefulness in women. I am writing, as well, against a moralistic framing of vengeance that sees vindictiveness and acts of revenge as inherently vicious, unnatural, and antithetical to justice. In doing so, I have marshaled helpful arguments from scholars who argue for the ethical dimension and purposefulness in vengeance and the vindic-tive passions.[7] The cultural and critical work I wish to do here relies upon ethics, ethnographic studies, and literary criticism from scholars who take revenge seriously as a cultural practice and an ethical pattern of action in literature.

I have found that no single critical perspective has proven sufficient to explain the ethics of women and revenge in Shakespeare's plays. To invoke Kenneth Burke's vision of criticism, I wish "to use all that there is to use"[8] and hope that readers will find that differing, yet hopefully complementary, critical methods and assumptions illuminate the texts and the critical issues in fruitful ways. Recent critical studies have offered substantial challenges to the traditional scholarship on and governing assumptions about revenge and have provided an essential foundation for this book. Critics as various in their theoretical stances and methodologies as René Girard, Peter A. French, Jeffrie Murphy, Robert C. Solomon, John Kerrigan, Julian Pitt-Rivers, William Ian Miller, Harry Keyishian, Alison Findlay, Phyllis Rackin, Gwynne Kennedy, Linda Woodbridge, Fiona McHardy, and Linda Anderson have thrown into question long-held academic pieties about revenge, anger, gender, and genre. The present book builds upon these scholars' excellent studies, privileging female rather than male avengers, analyzing the role of gender in vengeance, giving full credence to contradictory impulses underlying acts of feminine vengeance, and highlighting the social, political, and ethical problems that give rise to women's cries for revenge.

As I shall demonstrate, Shakespeare's drama resists a conceptual framework that reduces vengeance simply to a social and moral ill, or to a disease ravaging individuals and societies. Revenge in Shakespeare is not limited to a nightmare of unchecked reciprocal violence threatening to destroy society, a vision René Girard painted vividly in *Violence and the Sacred*. Contrary to Girard's assertion that vendettas and blood feuds mark "the difference between primitive societies and our own,"[9] I argue that the practice of revenge, and the coupling of revenge with justice, is present in the far-from-primitive societies depicted in Shakespeare's plays. Revenge encompasses many kinds of intentions and actions, with differing results in the communities where it is practiced. Shakespeare forces readers and audiences to examine critical truisms and cultural assumptions, particularly those dealing with women's relationship to and participation in revenge.

This book brings the same intense scrutiny and respect to avenging female characters, even those in minor roles, that has been brought to great male protagonists such as Hamlet, Lear, and Titus. Actors do this when they prepare a character for the stage; critics must do this to realize the complex texture of human experience and the network of social meanings found in Shakespeare's plays. Literary theory of late has dismantled the notion of a transcendent, coherent self, a move that exposes the dramatic character as a textual being, or as "a subjected being, an effect of the meanings it seems to possess," as Catherine Belsey phrases it.[10] My approach to female characters recognizes the subjection of the self to signifying practices that precede it by locating such practices in various textual strategies Shakespeare uses to convey meaning and to produce ethical responses in audiences. The resonances and intertextual play of ancient legends and myths represent one such strategy. The use of expressive tropes to define character ethos, as well as polyvalent strains in language and concept, is another significant strategy. My concern with ethics, which I will address shortly, leads to my recognition that Shakespeare constructed character on ethical grounds, such that language displays agency and choice-making as part of the larger design of a dramatic action.

Shakespeare's tragic female characters, however, have been examined by critics not in terms of ethics, but primarily in terms of their victimization, virtuous passivity, and moral monstrosity. Traditional critics tend to uphold a dichotomous view of women: If passive in the face of violence and injury, women are victims and saints; if active, they are tigers, she-wolves, and devils. Contemporary critics and theorists have challenged such a clear-cut division, yet not thoroughly enough in relation to revenge. I contend that the stage image and vocal presence of a vengeful woman, as much or perhaps even more than that of the vengeful male, speaks to a deeply human preoccupation with unpunished crime and unspeakable violations of social norms and moral codes. Feminine cries for vengeance and acts of retaliation point up failures of civic justice and strip bare corruptions in the male-dominated political system. While male avengers like Hieronimo in *The Spanish Tragedy* and Hamlet in Shakespeare's play do this as well, the subject position and constrained social circumstances of women make their plights more poignant and more searching in ethical terms. I will demonstrate how characters such as Cordelia and Lavinia, the former understood often in quasi-hagiographic terms and the latter in terms of an appalling victimization, can be seen, surprisingly, as avengers when understood as protagonists within their own vengeance narratives.

This book's intention is to bring to light the various motives and expressions of feminine vengeance in Shakespeare's plays, and to articulate the ethical character of women's responses to injustice. We shall see how compelling women's concerns with justice become when their honor, virtue, and bodily integrity (or those of a family member or friend) are compromised or harmed. The issues engaged in stories of women's revenge reflect a range of experiences, and the injustice, dishonor, shame, grief, loss of integrity, diminishment in identity, bodily harm, anger, and psychic trauma, all familiar to scholars from the masculine-defined narrative, are in this case colored by cultural expectations regarding women's roles as wives, mothers, daughters, companions, and political leaders. Like men, women may feel the desire to pay back an insult, or they may feel the "terrible obligations of vengeance," to borrow a phrase from René Girard,[11] if there is no judicial settlement for wrongs. They may cry out in frustration against the injustice of men, as does Emilia in *Othello,* when she claims some revenge for women. They may usurp a masculine identity (literally a disguise, as in the case of Portia) to pursue justice in their community or society. When crying out against honor violations, female characters may wish they could be a man, as Beatrice and Paulina do, and thus imaginatively activate the heroism associated with warriors and aristocratic men. They may confer upon themselves the social and ethical right to take public action.

Although they sometimes appear to be relegated to a position of social helplessness, female characters nevertheless must be understood as ethical agents faced with choices: they can suffer shame and anger silently, or they can speak up; they can forgive their assailants, or they can strike back violently; they can retreat from public life, or they can devise a plot to seek their revenge. These are alternatives, each conveying a social meaning, for female characters operating within the social constraints established in patriarchal cultures. Shakespeare's characters negotiate within and sometimes beyond these constraints, in some cases finding a solution to injustice that can be alternately satisfying, moving, and unsettling to audiences.

CROSSING GENRE BOUNDARIES

Vengeance is by no means the sole province of tragedy, nor are revenge-driven plays always a matter of fury, slaughter, terror, and sorrow. Revenge crosses genre borders from the so-called revenge tragedy into the more felicitous worlds of comedy and romance, where we find a plethora of female characters seeking to right wrongs through playful, yet purposeful, acts of vengeance. Shakespeare's comedies and romances have much to do with revenge, challenging us to broaden our investigation into genre in order to find a more comprehensive vision of revenge.[12] Indeed, Shakespeare's comic female characters are pivotal in defining and complicating genre, as well as bringing into focus ethical tensions. Comic characters such as Maria in *Twelfth Night* and the Windsor wives challenge masculine norms by devising ingenious, playful revenges that highlight feminine wit and teach men a lesson. They can do so because comedy offers an hospitable environment for the exercise of feminine agency, creativity, and modes of justice.

Historically, in comic genres we find a rich and varied tradition of feminine revenge, from the ancient Roman comedies to continental novelle and tales of jests. This thought might be rather disconcerting if one tends to conceive of revenge primarily in terms of blood, but as this book will show, revenge comes in many guises, defying cultural norms and gender expectations not simply through unpalatable acts of violence, but also through purposeful scenes of comic plotting and shaming. Comic depictions of revenge can be surprisingly heavy on fantasy, ingenious manipulation, pain, and even violence. The comic mode licenses avengers to go to excess in the name of jesting and poetic justice, to revel in the escalation of violence and humiliation and, further, to suffer little or nothing in the way of repayment or reprisal. What René Girard has claimed for tragedy—"It is the act of reprisal, the repetition of imitative acts of violence, that characterizes tragic plotting"[13]—is equally true for comedy. Witness the merry wives of Windsor in Shakespeare's play of that title: they subject Falstaff not to one, but *three* acts of revenge in an extended drama, each scene of revenge topping the previous one. They move from improvised household theatricals to a masque of public ridicule, inviting the community to join in a shaming ritual—all for a wrong *intended, but not committed.* This is a striking feature of comedy: the wrongdoer is thwarted before any real, lasting damage is done. The act of revenge functions as the blocking device, which if successful manages to forestall further acts of retaliation. Comic revenge can be used effectively as a deterrent, warding off socially unacceptable and morally repugnant behavior. Revenge can teach a lesson, applying physic where necessary.

Yet the comedy of repayment must strike audiences as transgressive itself; it can appear indecorous or excessive in its plotting and execution of destructive and hurtful acts meant to teach a lesson. "Sportful malice" is the fitting oxymoron used in Shakespeare's *Twelfth Night* to describe comic revenge plots. Comedy maintains its generic integrity only because the retaliatory response is merely "sportful," and its malicious effects are muted by the close of the play. The frequent presence of revenge plots in comedy exposes an unexpected truth—the comic genre is *constitutively* violent and vengeful. The questions this truth inspires will need to be examined carefully in the pages that follow: To what degree does comic revenge in Shakespeare act as a balm in restoring communal balance and healing moral defects? Do the virtuous ends of revenge justify its means? Are we, as Shakespeare's audience, guilty coconspirators with comic avengers, enjoying the laughter of cruelty as we enjoy the spectacle of revenge?

Critics have yet to explore fully who Shakespeare's avenging women are, how they express their desire for revenge, how they frame their choices to avenge or to incite vengeance in others, what they accomplish, and whether they affirm negative, positive, or ambivalent views of their gender and of revenge. The larger questions driving this book attempt to uncover the complex relationship between women and revenge in Shakespeare: How does gender matter in the representation of revenge? What difference does genre make in characterizing feminine vengeance? Can female characters perform a curative or regenerative function with their revenges? How do female characters negotiate the frightening, darker energies of revenge—its destructiveness and bloodthirstiness? How do we come to terms critically with the putative *monstrosity* of the female avenger? Can women be perceived as *heroic* in seeking vengeance? How much revenge and what kinds of revenge satisfy the psychic, moral, and social needs of women and their honor? What are the costs of revenge, and how do they compare with the costs of "revengelessness?" What place does feminine lament have in the revenge dynamics of Shakespeare's dramas? How does Shakespeare use the trope of feminine incitement of revenge? And finally, what kind of ethical work can women's revenge do? Because this book pursues the question of revenge's ethics at length, some foundation for that question needs to be set forth here for the chapters that follow.

THE ETHICS OF VENGEANCE

Few of us today regard vengeance as an ethical force, much less a virtue. So, too, it appears was the case with Shakespeare's contemporaries, who received moral and political teachings that exhorted them to leave vengeance to the state, the monarch, and God. Yet Shakespeare's handling of vengeance does not follow standard instruction from his time, for his dramas engage us on ethical grounds to question the nature of justice, and to entertain circumstances in which revenge might be just. We cannot sidestep ethics, particularly when we observe that his female characters' dispositions regarding revenge get at the ethical core of their plays, irrespective of genre. By examining characters' passions, intentions, circumstances, and actions, we can see how Shakespeare establishes the conditions that warrant—or fail to warrant—their moral authority as avengers. In gauging the function and meaning of women's responses to injustice, we can gain an understanding of revenge's potential to do ethical work.

The case for women's revenge as morally warranted must be made on ethical grounds sensitive to cultural norms, but also to agent-based qualities such as virtue and inner strength as they are detected in a character's speech and action. It will be my contention that revenge can be justified and can reflect its relationship with justice when it meets specific conditions, and those conditions, as Peter A. French has established, have to do with *communication, authority, desert,* and *proportionality.* [14] If a character communicates clearly the grounds of her outrage against a moral offense, if she has virtuous intent, if the offender deserves punishment, and if the punishment fits the crime, then her revenge is justified. Each situation imagined by Shakespeare has its complexities, and justification may turn out to be equivocal and a matter of perspective. But in each of the cases of revenge involving women, pressing questions of what constitutes a legitimate response arise. Not all of Shakespeare's female inciters and avengers may be perceived as morally justified, but the situations in which their vengefulness arises, and the moral norms activated and perhaps overrun, need to be carefully examined before value judgments are made.

While Socrates and Plato banished revenge from the realm of justice, regarding it as the return of evil for evil, a tradition of virtue ethics, deriving mainly from the philosophical works of Aristotle and Saint Thomas Aquinas, allows revenge a legitimate place in any serious consideration of justice. Virtue ethics influenced English theologians and their audiences (readers, students, colleagues) far more extensively than has been recognized. David N. Beauregard argues persuasively that Aristotle and Aquinas were "the most formidable authorities on ethics in the Renaissance," and that "Shakespeare relied heavily on these two authorities, and on their work

rests his reputation as a poet of considerable moral substance."[15] Under
certain conditions, some Elizabethans would perceive the justness of Aristotle's assertion in his *Rhetoric* that "[i]t is noble to avenge oneself on one's
enemies and not to come to terms with them; for requital is just, and the
just is noble; and not to surrender is a sign of courage" (1.1367a).[16] The
nobility he speaks of reflects the excellence in character that moves one to
seek justice not only for oneself, but also for others. Aristotle and Aquinas
examine the subjective expression of the agent's passions, weighing them
in relation to virtue and vice. They argue for a balanced or moderate disposition of emotions—Aristotle's golden mean—in one's response to
wrongdoing. A moderate emotional disposition reflects neither deficiency
nor excess. The deficient person exhibits indifference, unresponsiveness to
wrongdoing, and too little anger, while the excessive person displays cruelty, the desire for too much punishment, and incontinent rage. These
philosophers advocate examining the avenging agent's passions and intentions, along with the particular circumstances of the case, in order to assess
whether revenge is a moral action. The passions associated with vengeance
—anger, outrage, resentment, vindictiveness, hatred—may be righteous
and just if held in moderation and if directed against wrongdoing with the
object of correcting faults or injuries.

In literature, as in life, when violations of morality occur (for example,
rape, dismemberment, murder, slander), it is an individual's, group's, or society's moral obligation to counter wrongdoing and punish wrongdoers. If
the appropriate body fails to punish the wrongdoer, if no one rises in defense of justice and the moral order, if no one activates the powers of Nemesis or the Furies, then the characters, as well as readers and audience
members, are made to feel that justice has fled the earth. Justice *belongs* to
the earth, and the agents of justice are human. Such is the sentiment felt
and expressed by many literary avengers, from Hecuba to Titus Andronicus, when they face the violations of family members' bodies and spirits,
and face the moral unbalancing of their world. They are driven to take upon
themselves the obligation to revenge. As Peter A. French argues, the
avenger "empowers morality" when the community's justice system is corrupt, or when such a system is suspended or nonexistent. It is left to the
courageous avenger to seek a suitable kind of revenge that is adapted to the
moral situation of the crime.[17]

Avengers often articulate their commitment to morality and to justice by
speaking in metaphors that express not only how they personally have been
violated, but also how the social and moral structures in their culture have
been violated. They speak of paying back a debt, which touches upon reciprocity as the basis of all relationships. They speak of restoring balance,
which invokes the social good of harmony and the image of Justice with
her balances. They speak of cleansing pollution, which gets at religious un-

cleanness, sin, and bloodguilt. The philosopher Robert C. Solomon points out that metaphors for revenge *"provide the structure of the desire and its accompanying emotions and define the sense of satisfaction."*[18] Like Aristotle and Aquinas, he distinguishes between justified and unjustified revenge, the latter reflecting an individual's desire to do harm under the influence of excessive passion, the former reflecting a "'kernel of rationality' in revenge that requires measure and propriety."[19] Justified revenge is typically not wild, nor is it unduly excessive; it is often the right response, at the right time, to a wrongful action.

Some expressions of vengefulness, however, defy traditional, narrowly defined notions of rationality, yet still possess a sense of justice at their root. Lamentation, funeral dirges, and cursing belong to all cultures in some form or other, and it is women who typically engage in these practices. Their behaviors and raised voices may seem to lack measure and challenge notions of propriety, yet such aggressive activities are fundamental communal expressions of sorrow. When a wrongful death has occurred, when funeral rites are maimed, when there is political corruption, women's lamenting voices become dangerous, for in their insistence upon the rights of the dead there is often an implicit, or sometimes explicit, call to revenge. Through their bodies and voices, mourning women convey an affective ethics, making crimes known publicly and inciting just revenge. When female avengers strike with violence against wrongdoers who commit atrocious crimes, they may be seen to act in the name of justice, albeit a harsh, punitive justice.

Of course, not all expressions of vengefulness are ethically justified. Literature and history both offer examples of vengeance gone awry. Revenge possesses undeniably dangerous elements, which threaten the well-being of the agent, as well as the lives of innocents. While vengeance can be virtuous and rational, just and vindicative, we cannot ignore the darker potentialities in revenge as we find them displayed in Shakespeare's characters and the cultural systems represented in his plays. Obsession, frustration, the excessive desire or appetite for punishment, the eruption of the irrational, the onset of madness: all of these extremes are associated with the "mind of reuenge."[20] Some metaphors for revenge, for example, tap into base human instincts and appetites that affect the mind: it is not uncommon to hear Elizabethan characters express a *hunger* or *thirst* for vengeance. In his Elizabethan translation of Seneca's *Medea,* for example, John Studley exploits such potent metaphors. When Jason asks Medea to spare their second child, after she has murdered the first, Medea rages, "If greedy thyrst of hungry handes that stil for vengeaunce cries, / Myght quenched bee with bloude of one, then aske I none at all, / And yet to staunche my hungry griefe the number is to small" (act 5).[21] In Greek tragedy, we witness the gods inspiring fury and vengefulness in human agents such as Medea and Orestes, the son of Agamemnon who is driven to matricide and then punished with the Furies' torment and madness. In Elizabethan revenge tragedy, we see vengeance recoiling upon the revenger in an act of violence that proves self-wounding or suicidal. With "mad blood stirring" (*Romeo and Juliet*, 3.1.4), revengers can lose touch with rationality and commit excessive acts of violence that are themselves moral violations, leading to further acts of bloodshed, fulfilling the dark assumption many of us have today about revenge's interminable cycles.

The complex structures of drama, the nuances of literary language, and the dynamic flow of stage productions are specially geared toward representing revenge and its passions in a multitude of ways, giving rise to changing attitudes within a single work and conveying a sense of revenge's reflexivity and its duality—its virtuous *and* vicious faces. A complex mimesis, or enactment of revenge, makes possible a "comprehensive and flexible ethics" of reception, as one critic calls it.[22] Shakespeare is particularly apt at showing revenge's Janus face, for in his dramas we see opposing forces in revenge at work in the minds and language of the characters. Revenge has the potential for expressing justice *and* lawlessness, moral restitution *and* savage resolution, properly felt and directed passions *and* the bloodlust of rage and hatred. Revenge can do harm as it attempts to undo harm; revenge demands sacrifice and sometimes self-damage from the avenger, even as it appeases the sacrificed and the damaged. It can rise up with the force of Necessity, as exhibited in ancient Greek tragedy, *and* it can give sway to human depravity. The avenger claims moral justification, yet may repeat offensive acts of violence to punish the criminal. Revenge brings satisfaction and pleasure, yet it may ultimately pain and destroy the avenger. If the avenger is a woman, she steps over the bounds of culturally prescribed gender norms to pursue an action that may be deemed unwomanly. Conversely, a woman's courage or cunning in taking revenge may win her admiration and even praise for her heroism, if not from the other characters in the play, then from the dramatist implicitly, and perhaps audience members as well.

Evidence for the latter view, interestingly enough, can be found in some rather extraordinary stories, real and fictional, found in traditional cultures. Ethnographers offer compelling examples of feminine revenge, though such accounts, like the women themselves, tend to come from the margins of their cultural histories. Like many of his fellow ethnographers, Christopher Boehm characterizes revenge as an all-male cultural practice regulated by norms of masculinity, honor, and redress.[23] Women are mentioned in his study of contemporary Montenegro mainly as functioning outside of the feud—they are typically not targets, nor are they conferred the rights and obligations of revenge. At most, their social role as recorded in his and other ethnographies is to incite male kin to avenge wrongs, thereby main-

taining the social norm of blood feud. Yet Boehm does afford a glimpse of
female revenge and its cultural meaning in his fieldwork. His study of Montenegrin feuding includes brief but tantalizing mentions of heroic poetry
about avenging women and rare real-life instances in which women defy
their culture's expectations:

> [W]hile Montenegrin women were exempt from the warrior's obligations that
> every male faced, and were exempt from blood feud obligations as well, a
> woman did have to supply the men of her household with food and munitions at
> the front; and she was greatly esteemed if she overcame what was considered to
> be her natural weakness and decided to fight as a man. Such rare events are cel-
> ebrated in Montenegrin heroic epic poetry. Furthermore, a woman never was
> obliged to take vengeance for a slain son, brother, or husband; but if she chose
> to do so, she was given more respect than a man who did this out of obligation.[24]

During an interview with a female neighbor, Boehm finds himself unexpectedly listening to a confession involving a revenge fantasy, which
leads to the revelation of a cultural memory. In what seems to be a hypo-
thetical situation, the woman asserts with some passion that she would
avenge the death of her brother. Boehm expresses surprise: "But you are a
woman. I haven't heard that women take vengeance like that." She replies,
"*I* certainly would, by God! And I've heard of one who did it over there in
the White-Paul tribe."[25] She recounts how a wife avenged her husband's
death by killing his murderer. With respect to this case, the woman elaborates, and Boehm paraphrases: "I have been told that modern Montenegrin
courts are unusually hard on killings that are motivated by revenge except
when it is a female who 'takes blood.' In such rare cases, women are so re-
spected for performing this stressful male duty that in several instances
they are said to have been let off with virtually no sentence at all."[26] The
Montenegrin woman recounting this story clearly identifies with women
who take revenge, giving Boehm and his readers a sideways glance into a
culture's lesser known mores.

Such an example—specific, local, and anecdotal as it is—can be helpful
in raising questions about how we approach acts of female revenge in literature. What assumptions are we bringing to literary texts? How are we
understanding the gender norms and ethics informing the texts? Boehm's
example reminds us, first, of the incompleteness of literary historiography
and critical discourses—where can we find editions of the poems he heard
about?—and second, of how cultural attitudes and ethical codes are not always immediately evident. In fact, some attitudes may remain covert or virtually silent until unearthed by chance or systematic digging. The light
sentences in the Montenegrin cases of women's revenge killings and the
admiring storyteller suggest something instructive about buried cultural at-

titudes toward women's revenge—there may be instances in which women receive *more* respect and are conferred *more* honor than men for their revenge ethic. Might such a conclusion offer a clue for how to read some of Shakespeare's women? Gauging the ethics of Shakespeare's vengeful women—how they are perceived within the play's world, how critical traditions have viewed them, and how we might arrive at a nuanced understanding of their circumstances—is the task of this book.

1
Women and Revenge: Some Literary, Iconographic, and Intellectual Foundations

> *Clytemnestra.* No shame, I think, in the death given
> this man. And did he not
> first of all in this house wreak death
> by treachery?
> The flower of this man's love and mine,
> Iphigeneia of the tears
> he dealt with even as he has suffered.
> Let his speech in death's house be not loud.
> With the sword he struck,
> with the sword he paid for his own act.
>   Aeschylus, *Agamemnon* (trans. Lattimore)

WHEN THE ETHICIST PETER A. FRENCH ARGUES THAT "THE LITERARY AND religious story of Western culture is, in large measure, the tale of vengeance,"[1] he does not overstate the case. He charts the course of revenge's "story" from ancient Greek myth to present-day westerns. Of interest here is French's brief foray into gender, which arises when he notices a distinct historical preference for masculine over feminine vengeance. Aeschylus's *Oresteia,* he believes, makes this preference stunningly clear when the younger generation gods, Apollo and Athena, protect Orestes' questionable right to matricide over the ancient Furies' and Clytemnestra's right to kill Agamemnon. The Mycenean king had sacrificed his daughter Iphigenia to the goddess Artemis to pick up the winds that would bring the Greek warriors to the shores of Troy. When he returns from his ten-year campaign at Troy, Clytemnestra slaughters him in his bath. Orestes, their son, is driven then by Apollo to commit matricide. French argues that the outcome of Orestes' trial in *The Eumenides* "clearly endorses male vengeance over female vengeance. Agamemnon killed his daughter, yet Athena will 'set little or no store' by the avenger, Clytemnestra, for two reasons: (1) she is a woman, and (2) to perform the act of revenge she must kill not only a man but her husband, the guardian of their house. Should Iphigenia's killing have gone unrevenged, perhaps because she was a female?"[2] French's question is disquieting. In the end, it would seem that the slaughter of the young princess, Iphigenia, is not granted the moral magnitude of killing a king or a husband. Not only that, but mother love and mourning are suppressed in favor of masculine imperatives—war, conquest, honor. Athena's endorsement of Orestes aligns masculine vengeance with just action, and feminine revenge with primitive unruly passions, thus upholding a patriarchal bias in matters of ancient justice.[3]

Yet we should consider carefully Athena's position in *The Eumenides.* To the suppliant Orestes, she says, "You bring no harm to my city. I respect your rights. / Yet these, too, [the Furies] have their work. We cannot brush them aside, / . . . Whether I let them stay or drive / them off, it is a hard course and will hurt" (lines 475–76, 480–81).[4] She understands the delicate situation before her: to safeguard the rights of all parties, yet to control the damage. She appeases and honors the Furies (also known as the Erinyes), both before and after hearing Orestes' case. Her promises to the Furies—thrones, a sanctuary by the Areopagus, incorporation into the Athenian pantheon, reverence, and the ability to bless—give them an honored habitation and a religious function in Athens; she tempers their vengeance-drive with the peaceful goals of civic life. While the *Oresteia* appears to privilege masculine over feminine principles, Athena's cultural work involves acknowledging the Furies, rather than suppressing or banishing them. They undergo a transformation in the play into the Eumenides (the "Kindly Ones"), but the whole process suggests that, in the guise of a domesticating, placating ritual, Athena has formalized a recognition that Athenian law, that civilization itself, must cope with the vengeance instinct—the law of blood for blood—for it expresses a fundamental instinct for justice. The rages and curses that are a person's figurative Furies are stirred by violations of reciprocity laws honored by the gods themselves.

If we read Western literature with an eye toward feminine vengeance, we shall find the claims of the Erinyes made in a variety of ways. While the cultural worlds depicted in many literary texts seem especially attuned to the claims of masculine vengeance, the assertion of feminine vengeance as an ethical force is undeniably there, sometimes in the periphery of the masculine narrative, and sometimes more centrally in female-dominated narratives. Often, as we see in the clash between the Furies and Apollo in the *Oresteia,* feminine vengeance comes in conflict with male priorities and male modes of vengeance, and can shed light on the unequal treatment of male and female victims.

Evidence of feminine vengeance narratives dates back to the ancient world, where strong imaginative links between the feminine and revenge are made in dramatic texts and in their performances at the City Dionysia

in Greece. Some of the earliest personifications of vengeance are feminine, as are early characterizations of avengers: Gaia, Erinyes, Nemesis,
Ate, Juno, Medea, Hecuba, Clytemnestra, Electra, Phaedra, Circe, Procne,
Philomel, Althaea, and Alcmena are all well-known examples. Major later
figures of revenge include Boudicea, Judith, Kriemheld, Gudrun, Bel-
imperia, Tamora, Margaret, and Evadne. These goddesses, queens, lovers,
and political leaders each have a dark, bloody tale of revenge to tell that
rivals, if not surpasses, any man's tale. The most ancient of feminine histories related to vengeance belongs to the archetypal figures of Gaia, Nemesis, and the Erinyes, who predate Zeus and the Olympian pantheon. The
mother goddess Gaia (Earth) is the oldest of them all, the archetypal avenging wife and female inciter to a male act of vengeance. She embodies the
connection between vengeance and maternal power. When Ouranos (Sky),
Gaia's own offspring and husband, banishes some of their children, sending them back into her womb, she incites her Titan sons to take revenge.
Kronos is the bold son who takes up the scythe Gaia has fashioned for
the father's overthrow, which he accomplishes through an act of castration.
Thus, the powerful mother/wife overcomes the tyrannical father/husband,
and revenge is practiced as the only way "to rectify structurally unequal
situations of tyranny," as Peter A. French puts it.[5] From this primal
vengeance, which robs the archaic male figure of his potency, two feminine forces come into being: from the foam of Ouranos's semen, volup-
tuous love is born in the shape of the beautiful Aphrodite, and from the
drops of his blood, the spirit of vengeance is born in the hideous forms of
the Erinyes.

The Erinyes were initially understood as personifications of curses, anger,
and vengeance. The name "Erinyes" comes from a Greek term meaning "I
hunt up or persecute" and an Arcadian word meaning "I am angry."[6] Re-
siding in Tartarus, the deepest pit in Hades, these ancient female goddesses
rise up from the underworld to hound the guilty. Pitiless, relentless, and
bloodthirsty, the purpose of the Erinyes was nonetheless just—they
avenged crimes against *philia,* the essential bonds established between kin,
friends, and hosts and guests. The moral and cultural transgressions they
punished were of a most serious kind in the ancient Greek world: bloodshed, especially of one's kin, perjury or oath-breaking, disobedience toward parents, disrespect to elders, improper conduct toward suppliants, and
violations of *xenia,* the sacred law of hospitality. In Greek tragedy, particularly Aeschylus's *Oresteia,* the Erinyes express themselves through the
motifs of blood-polluted hands, hunting, and mental frenzy. Ruth Padel argues that the Erinyes embody a "daemonic horror" and the "knowledge that
self can damage other, that this force for damage is unlimited, mad, an aber-
ration in the universe that goes on damaging self and others afterwards
[which] is tragedy's heart."[7] As punitive spirits tracking down the guilty,

they are intimately involved in the anguished experiences that define a tragic self. Yet the Erinyes represent, in social, ethical, and psychological terms, the drive for communal, familial, and individual restitution for crimes, which ultimately enables a process of purification and healing to take place. They seek a form of primitive justice as recognizable, neces- sary, and sometimes terrifying today as it was to the audiences of classical Greek tragedy. Crimes such as Orestes' matricide or Agamemnon's blood sacrifice of his daughter violate sacred and human laws; they *must* be pun- ished. The Erinyes hound, assault, and madden the guilty, applying extreme measures to punish such violators.

In the works of Euripides, Virgil, and later Latin writers, the Erinyes were distilled from an indistinguishable pack into a triad, sometimes named Alecto (Relentless), Megaera (She who bears a grudge), and Tisiphone (Avenger of bloodshed).[8] Early modern English dramatists occasionally used one of these names to represent the Furies and their frightening, puni- tive spirit. In *Gismond of Salerne* (1567–68), a play that merges a Senecan with a Christian ethos, Megaera arises from hell to incite the King to mur- der his daughter's lover. She exclaims, "Furies must aide, when men will cease to know / their Goddes: and Hell shall send revenging paine / to those, whom Shame for sinne can not restraine" (4.1.42–44).[9] Megaera personi- fies the father's rage, which drives him to strangle and disembowel the lover, a harsh punishment for the unchaste.

Another classical goddess that punished mortals was Nemesis, the fig- ure of retribution. She was not concerned particularly with blood crimes, but rather with sins of pride and presumptuousness in humans who over- stepped their bounds with the gods. In emblem books such as Geoffrey Whitney's *A choice of emblemes, and other devices* (Leiden, 1586) and Philippe Galle's *De Deis Gentium Imagines* (Antwerp, 1581), she appears holding a bridle, representative of the control she exerts over the distribu- tion of justice, or Fortune's goods, and the role she plays in reigning in unruly desire. The bridle symbolizes moderation and self-restraint, alle- gorical meanings deemed important to the ethical lives of early modern Europeans. The image in Galle's book includes a measure and a torch, with the accompanying motto: "Trux Nemesis ut iacto cua fulmine flamma. Mortalesq[ue], docet reddere cinq[ue], suum" [Savage is Nemesis when the bolt of flame is cast. She teaches mortals to give back what is due].[10]

Albrecht Dürer's *Nemesis* (*The Great Fortune*) offers one of the most fa- mous engravings of Nemesis, depicting her as a nude, winged female with a bridle and a goblet; in this picture she stands upon a sphere high above the landscape, representing her powerful position. Born of Night and Oceanus, Nemesis in her earliest appearances (Hesiod *Theogony* 223) per- sonified moral reverence for law, fear of moral transgression, and con- science, which associated her closely with shame. In time, she came to be understood as the deity that restored right proportion or equilibrium in human affairs when they had become unbalanced. When Fortuna, goddess of good luck, distributed her goods unequally, those who enjoyed unmerited rewards were punished by Nemesis. Her function as the punisher of the excessively fortunate and the proud characterized Nemesis as an avenger who, like the Furies, hounds the guilty. As Sir Francis Bacon wrote in *The Wisdome of the Ancients* (1619) in his chapter called "Nemesis, *or the Vicissitude of things*," Nemesis is "a Goddesse venerable vnto all, but to bee feared of none but potentates and fortunes fauorites"; her name "doth signifie Reuenge or Retribution"; she has the power to destroy mortals who reach "the pinnacle of prosperity" and felicity.[11]

Yet another ancient goddess concerned herself with vengeance. Ate appears in Greek epic and tragedy bringing destruction, discord, folly, and delusion to humans. She represents a force that invades the minds of avengers, removing reason or self-preservation and bringing with her the spirit of wild destructiveness.[12] Like the Erinyes, she is a feminine goddess that drives men to revenge and madness. Ate is the daughter of Eris, goddess of strife, and Zeus, who hurtled her down to earth after she betrayed him, driving her to tread upon the heads of men. Shakespeare alludes to Ate four times in his plays, retaining her associations with discord, madness, violence, and revenge. In *Much Ado About Nothing,* Benedick compares the fiery Beatrice to "the infernal Ate in good apparel" (2.1.234). "More Ates, more Ates! Stir them on, stir them on!" cries Berowne mockingly to the actor playing Hector during the performance of the Nine Worthies in *Love's Labour's Lost* (5.2.684–85). In *King John,* the French ambassador Châtillon refers to England's "Mother-Queen," Eleanor, as "an Ate stirring him [King John] to blood and strife" (2.1.62–63). In *Julius Caesar,* a wrathful, grieving Antony invokes Ate in his funeral lamentation over Caesar's body, whose very wounds seem to beg for curses and vengeance. Antony prophesies "Blood and destruction," with mothers grown accustomed to their "infants quartered with the hands of war: / All pity choked with custom of fell deeds" (3.1.265, 268–69). Most magnificent of all, he envisions "Caesar's spirit, ranging for revenge, / With Ate by his side come hot from hell," unleashing the "dogs of war" (3.1.270–71, 273).

Literary descendents and counterparts of these vengeance-seeking goddesses can be found in countless classical, medieval, and Renaissance female characters. These women grieve, lament, curse, stir men to anger and revenge and, in some cases, take active revenge themselves. Female characters depicted within honor-based cultures often express "the ethics of vendetta," as Helene P. Foley calls it, through aggressive funerary lamentation, which keeps the cause of the dead alive and incites acts of revenge.[13] Feminine mourning and wrath can lend authority to masculine acts of revenge by insisting upon the moral claims of the dead and of family honor.[14]

Sophocles' *Electra*, for example, rouses the female chorus to lament the death of her father, Agamemnon, and moves Orestes to kill their mother, Clytemnestra. Fury-like, "she tortures Clytemnestra, making her fearful and defensive"; "she drinks her mother's life blood like a Fury," the "Fury who is officially absent from this play."[15] Electra's ethical position gains force particularly when she accuses Clytemnestra of killing Agamemnon for her lover's sake, rather than for her sacrificed daughter, Iphigenia. In Aeschylus's *The Libation Bearers,* Electra insists in her prayer to Zeus before her brother and the female chorus, "There has been wrong done. I ask for right" (line 398), which inspires the chorus to invoke the law or custom (*nomos*) of revenge when blood has been spilled. Together, Electra and the slave women draw Orestes into a long-delayed funeral lamentation, whose theme is violation and just retaliation. Electra emphasizes, as well, in Aeschylus's play how her mother has subjected her to dishonorable treatment, how after her father's death, she was kenneled like a "vicious dog" in a "dark corner," how she was forced to hide "the streaming of [her] grief. / Hear such," she cries out passionately to Orestes, "and carve the letters of it on your heart" (lines 445–50).

The affective power of lamenting female voices can convey devastating reminders of past social and political injustice, moral violation, communal suffering, and personal anguish. Women's words and songs function as speech acts, operating in the theater as counterparts to physical acts of retaliatory violence. In ancient Greek theater, where violence takes place behind the stage's closed doors, it seems conceivable that "the verbal expression of female lament constitutes as powerful an act of violence as the deed of vengeance itself," as Christian M. Billing argues.[16] The ritual performance of grieving can be understood as "one of the most powerfully transgressive acts in Greek tragedy," he continues, and a sign of the political dangers thought to originate in the unfettered female voice.[17] We can see in some ancient tragedy how the ritual of revenge-taking starts with lamenting women as they merge the claims of the dead with the needs of the living. Electra's shared lament with the female chorus in Aeschylus's and Sophocles' plays links memories of transgressive deeds with the incitement of violent punishment. Lamenting female voices, singular or in unison, can be potent and sure in their ability to translate their auditors' grief into wrath, and wrath into vengeance.

A rich tradition in Western literature represents women not only as inciters through lamentation, but as fierce goaders or whetters who drive men to exact revenge and punish crime. Such literary women can appear ruthless and courageous in spirit, animating male-gendered qualities through their bold speech. Indeed, female characters can express eagerness for revenge and align themselves more closely with the spirit of vengeance than men do. The earliest female inciters from classical antiquity can be found

among the gods, as I have shown. The Erinyes, in particular, appear as figures of incitement; they are depicted frequently with goads, or animal
prods, which they brandish in their hands. They deliver figurative blows to
the psyches of their victims, who experience torment, unbridled fury, and
madness. In Aeschylus's *Oresteia,* for example, the Eryines rise from
Hades to "wither their victim 'with pursuit,' drive a murderer from his
mind, and from his place of origin and stability, the place where he should
rule. Their appearance is itself pursuit, a lash or goad."[18] As figures of
tragedy, they "make death matter in living relationships"[19] by acting upon
the resentments of the dead, embodying memory of damage, and inciting
men to inflict further damage.

In ancient Greek drama, Electra appears as the paradigmatic inciter,
translating her lamentation for her dead father, Agamemnon, into passionate appeals for vengeance. She can be seen, as Nicole Loraux argues, as the
"perfect incarnation of . . . living memory [of grief-wrath] that, hardly
metaphorically, is a goad."[20] Furthermore, her words convey the ethical
imperatives of a god and of *nomos.* Apollo has demanded this blood revenge, and Clytemnestra's slaying of king and husband violates *nomos.*

Not only words, but also physical sites, wounded bodies, and memorial
cloths can make up an emotionally charged visual terrain that bespeaks
women's grief, dishonor, and need for retribution. A spatial location, like a
grave site, may be charged with the presence of an unappeased spirit. In the
Oresteia, Agamemnon's grave is the place where his children meet, call to
mind the crimes done to him, and plot revenge. While Agamemnon's body
remains underground, hidden from view, in other revenge narratives the
body can function as a goading sight. In Livy's and Ovid's treatments of
Lucretia's rape by Tarquin, the chaste Roman matron reveals the crime to
her male kin and incites them to avenge her dishonor and their own. She
commits suicide, and her corpse is shown in the Roman Forum. The sight
of her body and knowledge of her defilement incite a revolt against the Tarquins, the ruling family, which results in their exile from Rome and the
founding of a republic. Shakespeare's Lavinia in *Titus Andronicus* recalls
Lucretia; her wounded body appears onstage as the grotesque, living reminder of unspeakable crimes that must be avenged.

The goading woman appears frequently, as well, in Norse, Germanic,
and Icelandic medieval poetry.[21] In sagas, epics, and lays, women's words
can shame and move men to avenge insults to their kin group's honor, particularly when homicide is involved. In the Old Norse legend of Gudrun, a
thrice-married Burgundian princess, we find a formidable example of the
female inciter. In the lay "The Whetting of Gudrun," Gudrun's beloved
daughter, Svanhild, has been murdered by her intended husband, King Iormunrekk. She has been trampled senselessly and brutally by horses as punishment for an imagined infidelity. This "fierce-spirited" mother responds

by whetting her sons "for the fight, / with grim words" (1.3, 3–5).[22] She accuses her boys of lackluster, unmanly behavior and holds up the example of the heroic "temperaments" of her brothers, and the "fierce spirits of the kings of the Huns" (3.4, 5). Her son proclaims, "You have stirred us up to a meeting of swords" (6.2), and they ride to Iormunrekk's court to avenge their sister's death. This incitement scene, known as a *hvot* (from the verb *hvetja*, "to whet"), is indicative of the heroic temperament and rhetorical strength of women in medieval literature.[23] Female whetters preserve family honor and pursue blood revenge, even if it means they must sacrifice their own happiness and the lives of family members. Gudrun's sons know they are doomed, and Gudrun wants nothing more than to die; but they all realize through the psychological acuity and ethical force of her whetting what must be done.

Many women in Scandinavian sagas perform this function of whetting male vengeance, which conveys a sense of a quasi-legal proceeding leading to bloody compensation for slain kin. Carol J. Clover argues that saga women practiced family politics with a degree of emotional and artistic satisfaction in their social role as whetters to vengeance; since saga-age women had no direct legal redress, they received little to no satisfaction and no blood money through judicial resolutions of feuding matters.[24] Their greatest satisfaction lay in blood revenge, a method antithetical to settlement or commutation, yet customary and lawful in many circumstances.

Some scholars have been attuned to potentially misogynist elements in portrayals of female inciters. Judith Jesch regards the medieval female inciter as merely a "literary cliché," and "a useful and colourful myth that accounted for the horrors of violence while removing the blame for it from male shoulders."[25] Jenny Jochens agrees that the general tendency of male saga writers was to scapegoat women and argues that medieval Icelandic storytellers "revived, amplified, and multiplied the ancient figure of the inciting woman in an effort to deflect the blame for men's unreasoning [violent] behavior. Whereas she had appeared as a grand and impressive woman in the distant, mythic setting of [Nordic] poetry, in the familiar Icelandic society she was often vilified and turned into a scapegoat for men's failures in establishing a peaceful society."[26] Some female characters, such as the spiteful, ill-willed Hallgerd in *Njál's Saga*, show vividly the results of what one might understand as a resentful male imagination. Hallgerd instigates revenge acts that appear to be unwarranted and dishonorable. Her jealous provocations at the start of the saga lead to full-blown feuding that takes the lives of her husbands and innumerable men. Yet not all female goaders have a malicious character, nor are the situations they find themselves in identical. Even Hallgerd can be understood to be operating out of a sense of shame and honor, however misguided. Her loveless marriage to

Gunnar and the three slaps to her face that she endures, one from each of her husbands, cause shame and provoke her vengefulness, which results in their deaths. The punishments are out of proportion with the wrongs, but Hallgerd clearly feels shame, which is perhaps the greatest emotional spur to revenge in medieval Scandinavian cultures.

R. George Thomas suggests that saga writers essentially held "a high opinion" of fierce goading women; one saga, for example, states explicitly about such a woman, "She is thought to have been a woman of great spirit."[27] In the Gudrun lays, the poet expresses an attitude of admiration and awe: she is "Gudrun of the line of heroes" ("The Lay of Atli," 29.3); she is daughter of Giuki, king of the Niflungs, father of "heroic children" whose "defiance lives on wherever people hear of it" ("The Greenlandic Poem of Atli," 105.2, 4). She is her brothers' avenger, bringing "death to three great kings, / that bright woman, before she died" ("The Lay of Atli," 43.3–4). Gudrun's temperament is frequently described as fierce. She is formidable, skilled in arms, and kills men. She slays her savage husband, Atli, after feeding him his children, and then burns down his hall.

Strong-willed, vengeance-minded female characters may use bloody tokens and body parts to incite revenge in a quasi-ritualistic fashion. In *Njál's Saga,* Hildigunn feels a keen sense of duty to a slain kinsman and conveys the ethical duty to revenge through symbolic actions. After her husband, Hoskuld, is killed, she turns to her paternal uncle, Flosi, for revenge. Her exhortations are not unjust, nor are they the mere goading of a bloodthirsty woman; they possess "the striking formalism of the ceremonial charge," as William Ian Miller demonstrates.[28] She uses not only verbal appeals and insults, but most provocatively "some real presence of the corpse that could be readily identified as belonging to that corpse."[29] That token is Hoskuld's bloody cloak. When Hildigunn throws the cloak at Flosi, blood clots from the corpse fall all over him as he sits to eat. This ritual obliges Flosi to take up the revenge cause—in using Hoskuld's own blood, the wife and the dead husband make their cause known through the agency of the living. In Carol Clover's analysis of this scene, she shows how the carefully laid structural elements of Hildigunn's goading call Flosi to his duty to avenge the death of his kinsman. She explains, "In a feud situation, women's (and old men's) *words* are the equivalent of men's deeds; it is as incumbent on a woman to urge vengeance as it is incumbent on a man to take it."[30]

The significance of feminine inciting—its social, ethical, and structural functions—is conveyed through ritual elements, rites, and a meaningful arrangement of scenes in the text or on the stage. Goading occurs not simply as nagging and repeated verbal exhortation, but as a ritualized calling to mind of wrongs and obligations, accomplished through lamentation, stylized language, psychologically potent insults, striking gestures, and memorial badges. As we can see in the medieval examples of Hildeburh (the lamenting queen from *Beowulf* whom I discuss in this book's preface), Gudrun, and Hildigunn, feminine literary inciters motivate their chosen avengers by appealing to their culture's ethical codes of honor and duty.

Shakespeare follows his ancient Greek and medieval predecessors in exhibiting a compelling interest in revenge as a complicated ethical imperative (perhaps clashing with other imperatives) and, furthermore, as an aspect of the grieving process. In Shakespeare's dramas, the subterranean presence of lamenting, vengeful choruses, ancient inciters, the Erinyes, Nemesis, and Ate can be detected, not only when they and their attributes are invoked figuratively, but when characters distinctly exhibit their traits or seem to be reviving their angry spirits. The mourning, cursing mothers in *Richard III* offer a powerful example of the ancient spirit of fury and nemesis conveyed through women. The Duchess of York's curse upon her monstrous son, Richard III, is potent, acting upon the spirit world to draw all of his enemies together in a vengeful haunting the night before his fateful battle. Struck by a performance of Shakespeare's *Richard III,* the classicist Nicole Loraux found a Greek echo in the climactic scene with the grieving mothers (4.4), reminding her of how their classical ancestors, the mourning mothers in Attic tragedy, challenged political life as defined by a patriarchal state.[31] Women's fury over violations of relationship bonds, expressed in many of Shakespeare's plays, motivates ethical speech and action: Constance in *King John,* Emilia in *Othello,* Paulina in *The Winter's Tale,* and Beatrice in *Much Ado About Nothing* offer examples of female characters moved to anger and vengefulness by male acts of injustice. They speak with fiery tongues and express a Fury-like drive to hound their male enemies, to make them pay for their transgressions.

Early modern representations of vengeful females often call up the specter of Medea, the most infamous female avenger of them all. Known for slaying her brother to aid her lover Jason, and then killing her children to punish his faithlessness, Medea became the locus classicus of feminine wrath, revenge, and malevolent maternity. For Renaissance interpreters, she also incarnated the spirit of witchcraft. The vengeful Charlotte in George Chapman's *The Revenge of Bussy D'Ambois* (1610), for example, is compared to the sorceress "Medea / With all her herbs, charms, thunders, lightnings"; she "Made not her presence and black haunts more dreadful" (4.2.39–41).[32] In Shakespeare's *2 Henry VI,* Young Clifford's grief-stricken lament for his dead father leads to an excessive desire for revenge that includes slaughtering the infants of his enemy. Such an act leads him to invoke "wild Medea":

> Henceforth I will not have to do with pity.
> Meet I an infant of the house of York,

> Into as many gobbets will I cut it
> As wild Medea young Absyrtus did.
> In cruelty will I seek out my fame.

(5.2.56–60)

Clifford's example invokes the unspeakable, bold act of Medea, who tears her brother limb from limb, and then places his hands and bloody head atop a rock to distract her father from his pursuit of her. This episode is recorded in Ovid's *Tristia* (3.9), yet an even better known scene from the legend of Medea was in Ovid's *Metamorphoses,* where readers found Medea bathing her "wicked knife" in her children's blood, "Not like a mother but a beast bereving them of life" (7.503, 504).[33]

Equally famous during the Renaissance was another legendary mother who kills. Hecuba, queen of Troy, was known not only as the prototypical grieving wife and mother, and Fortune's victim, but also as an avenging mother who kills her son's murderer, the Thracian king, Polymestor.[34] Driven by the extreme passions of maternal love and grief, she joins the captive Trojan women in a wild scene of vengeance: they gouge out Polymestor's eyes and kill his sons. Euripides' ancient Greek play *Hecuba* presents the distraught mother first grieving over the sacrifice of her courageous daughter Polyxena to the angry spirit of Achilles, and then discovering her son Polydorus's mutilated corpse, which inspires her revenge. Ovid, too, recounts both piteous deaths and Hecuba's revenge, while Seneca's play *Troas* focuses on the lamentations of the Trojan women near the end of the war, the sacrifice of Polyxena, and the cruel death of Hecuba's grandson, Astyanax, who was thrown from the walls of Troy by the Greeks. These representations of Hecuba highlight her mother's tears, but many of them are equally concerned with displaying a mother's wrath and madness, for the dishonorable death of her last child is surely the last straw for her. She seizes a wild means of justice. Like Medea, Hecuba is conceptualized as a beast, but here her aged, suffering body *metamorphoses* into a beast, a stony bitch. While Medea is "Not like a mother, but a beast," Hecuba is all mother, her new beastly guise signifying a fiercely protective motherhood rather than an unnatural maternity.

Shakespeare engages such mythological tales of feminine vengeance, tapping into the fierce passions of wronged women. In one of his earliest plays, *Titus Andronicus,* he personifies revenge in a female form. He brings Revenge to the stage as a furious mother promising bloodshed and retribution. The Furies and Hecuba's spirit are awakened in Tamora, the fallen queen of the Goths, who must suffer the brutal sacrifice of her son by her enemy, the Roman general Titus. Conflating the sacrifice of Polyxena and the murder and mutilation of Polydorus, the killing of Tamora's son inspires comparison with Hecuba's legend. Like Hecuba, Tamora is outraged at the injustice of the sacrifice and Titus's failure to observe moral norms (she kneels before him as a suppliant, which he ignores). In time, she helps to orchestrate the ruin of his house.

Shakespeare swerves from the Hecuba legend, however, when he alters the queen's status from that of a captive to that of a newly empowered alien empress of Rome. Furthermore, late in the tragedy, after Tamora has vowed to massacre the Andronici and has sanctioned brutal acts of rape and murder, she appears in a patently theatrical scene, wholly out of character with her Hecuba prototype. She approaches her enemy, Titus, dressed as her bloody ancestor, the "dread Fury" (5.2.82), thus appearing on early modern English stages (through the male actor) as the personified character of Revenge. "I am Revenge, sent from th'infernal kingdom" (5.2.30), she proclaims, locating her dwelling place in the underworld of eternal punishment. She uses the appetitive metaphor of "the gnawing vulture of thy mind" (5.2.31) to appeal to Titus's obsessive need for revenge. At the same time, she exposes how the vengeance instinct becomes a painful, self-devouring force in the mind, giving no rest, no ease, until relief can be gained through "wreakful vengeance" (5.2.32).

Shakespeare's personification of Revenge as a female deity draws upon iconographic and linguistic traditions dating back to classical antiquity, traditions that bear upon the relationship between gender and vengeance. The Latin root of the word *vindicta* is gendered feminine, and Romance languages feminize *revenge* and its related terms: *vengianza* and *vendetta* (Italian), *venganza* (Spanish), *veniaunce* (Old French). A Renaissance tradition of iconographic images and descriptions portrayed revenge as feminine, yet retained suggestions of masculine traits as well. In *Iconologia* (first edition published in Rome, 1603), Cesare Ripa includes the personifications of the Furies and Vendetta. The Furies are described as ugly women with snakes for hair, wearing black dresses with spots of blood. A trumpet blowing flames and black smoke is included in their description. In his second depiction of the Furies, they are red-colored women. Ripa gives two detailed verbal portraits of Vendetta as a militant female wearing armor and a red dress and carrying a dagger. In one portrait, she wears a flaming helmet and looks at a mutilated arm without a hand. A raven with a scorpion in its beak is depicted as well. In the other image, she appears in military dress, with a dagger, and she is biting her forefinger. A lion wounded by an arrow lies beside her.

In a similar fashion, Antonio Tempesta (following a design by Otto van Veen) made a number of etchings of Venganza or Vindicta for a revenge-inspired prose narrative entitled *Historia septem infantium de Lara* (Antwerp, 1612).[35] The figure of Revenge appears in helmet and armor with a dagger in her right hand. She is biting the index finger of her other hand. Breasts, curling long hair, and flowing skirts give a feminine appearance to the form, but the military guise is decidedly masculine. Traditionally, the dagger has been associated with revenge and its secretive operations. Biting the finger, however, presents a suggestive interpretive crux. Figuratively, it may convey the idea of revenge as an involuntary action that is self-wounding. Alternately, it may represent the "biting back" of strong passions. As Kevin Dunn sees it, "repression, revenge, and even the etymologically inevitable remorse" are figured in the gesture.[36] The finger to the mouth may also indicate thought or reflection. Dunn and Frederick Kiefer both associate the gesture with Italian emblems depicting male figures in meditation.[37] A 1556 woodcut entitled *Meditatio vel vltio* (Meditation, or Revenge), for example, portrays a man in a robe standing beside a tree with his index finger at his lips. A significant visual connection is established in this image between thought and revenge, with the word "or" suggesting an ethical dilemma.

Neither Dunn nor Kiefer notes gender differences in these two very dissimilar guises of revenge, but the gendering of the images is revealing. The militant, active figure of Revenge is female, conveying gender ambiguity suggestive of the Renaissance virago, or warlike woman. The quiet, grave, and benign figure contemplating revenge is male. Yet the female figures are biting their fingers, just as the men are. We might speculate that the finger biting symbolism incorporates an aspect of masculine pensiveness into the Renaissance iconography of revenge. Revenge is visualized, then, not only as a virago, but as a contemplative female.

Meditative elements of revenge (weighing of options, delay, ethical questioning, and plotting) appear in literary characters as well. Tamora speaks explicitly of the mind, emphasizing Titus's thoughts about revenge. Tamora's appearance and speech exemplify the dual aspect of revenge found in Renaissance iconographic images. She, too, has a mind attuned to revenge, and she has plotted this meeting with Titus. The actor playing Tamora might have appeared in a fashion similar to Ripa's and Tempesta's depictions. Revenge's costume is described in the text as "this strange and sad habiliment" (5.2.1). *Habiliment* suggests military dress and the aggressive-warrior affect of Revenge, for one early definition for this term was "Personal accoutrements for war; armour, warlike apparel."[38] Tamora's appearance is *strange* in that her guise appears unnatural and threatening, or perhaps foreign and otherworldly, and *sad* indicates her seriousness.

The actor might have appeared in a more gruesome or sensationalized guise if he dressed according to the classical iconography attributed to the Furies. The ballad entered in the Stationers' Register with Shakespeare's *Titus Andronicus* includes a stanza in which Tamora and her sons appear dressed as Furies. Shakespeare's Titus does, after all, refer to the sons as "cursed hellhounds" and their mother as "dread Fury" (5.2.144, 82). In many accounts, the Furies were terrifying to look upon, with blackened bodies or gowns; gorgon-like snakes in hand or hair; bloody, oozing eyes; wings; and torches, goads, and scourges in hand. In Aeschylus's *The Eumenides,* Apollo's priestess describes the Furies as more like gorgons than women, "black and utterly / repulsive" (lines 52–53), with "foul ooze" dripping from their eyes (line 54), and Apollo calls them "lewd creatures" (line 67), "repulsive maidens" (line 68), "loathed alike by men and by the heavenly gods" (line 73). These descriptions suggest strangeness in the form of monstrosity, or the manifestation of the darkest recesses of the mind. The maddening and punitive aspects of revenge led to some dramatic personifications of Revenge as horror-inducing. In Norton and Sackville's *Gorboduc* (1561–62), for example, the stage directions for the dumb show describe the three Furies vividly. Alecto, Megaera, and Tisiphone appear "clad in black garments sprinkled with blood and flames, their bodies girt with snakes, their heads spread with serpents instead of hair, the one bearing in her hand a snake, the other a whip, and the third a burning firebrand, each driving before them a king and a queen which, moved by Furies, unnaturally had slain their own children."[39] This description displays the frightening specter of vengeance, arising in the form of female deities.

The gendered personifications of Revenge as a militant female suggest that deeply rooted in Western mythology is a fear of what lies within the female psyche. Women's fury, grief, scorn, and vengefulness exceed what men would like to define as the civilized bounds of law, reason, and sanity. The ungoverned, dangerous emotional terrain of women's minds seems fertile for breeding revenge. Perceived as a virago, Fury, or tiger, the tragic female avenger on the English Renaissance stage created a disquieting spectacle of threatened or actual violence that defied cultural norms of gendered behavior. Images of violent women exacerbated long-standing cultural anxieties about feminine rage and vindictiveness, and displayed the vulnerability of men to women who trained their furious gazes and weapons upon them. The fierce will and actions of a female avenger appeared more subversive, daring, outrageous, and unbelievable than those of a male because of the historical unorthodoxy of feminine violence in society and women's expected submission to patriarchal authority.

Francis Beaumont and John Fletcher's *The Maid's Tragedy* (first performed in 1610–11) offers one of the most stunning enactments of feminine revenge that undoes cultural norms associated with gender and emphasizes the fearsome will to revenge that can be activated in women. The play evokes audience disbelief and horror, but also pity for its avenging woman. After her brother, Melantius, chastises Evadne for shamefully allowing herself to be seduced and kept by the King, he savagely insists, "Thus far you knew no fear. Come, you shall kill him" (4.1.153).[40] This seems an unusual and cruel punishment for a fallen woman, for in Western literature of all kinds, males do not give a female the task of revenge. If a woman's chastity has been taken, the husband, brother, or father avenges this violation. Female avengers rise up in the *absence* of men, or in extraordinary cases of self-assertion and punitive will. Evadne initially does not think of revenge as a moral or legitimate response to her shameful condition, recognizing that "the gods forbid" such an action against a king (4.1.144). Her brother, however, insists that she must help him to avenge this dishonor to the family name, and he engages her in a quasi-religious ceremony of oath-taking in which the two kneel before each other and the heavens. Evadne then calls upon "all you spirits of abusèd ladies" (4.1.169) to help her perform the deed. When she rises, she sees fully the misery of her condition and wishes to repent, but she can do this only through active penance—and a purification rite reminiscent of ancient Greek tragedy. When the time comes for revenge, she rises in fury, fully owning the role that has been thrust upon her. She visits the King in his bedchamber, and in a grim replay of lovemaking, enacts a bloody rite to "redeem the honour" he "stole" from her (5.1.62). No longer Evadne, or a mere woman, she is the avenging "tiger," a "thing / That knows not pity" for the thief (lines 67, 67–68).

The King insists that Evadne is "too sweet and gentle" to kill him (5.1.74), failing to understand that his corruption has been exposed and that Evadne has imaginatively metamorphosed into the Hyrcanian tiger to overcome her shame. She communicates to him how loathsome he is and stabs him, much to his disbelief, multiple times. To their horror, the Gentlemen of the Bedchamber find the dead body. Their response indicates the same incredulity voiced by the King: "who can believe / A woman could do this?" (5.1.128–29). A mere woman has flagrantly violated Christian and social mores, including most especially the doctrine that upheld the divine right of the king. Melantius had not dared to do such a thing, though he sanctioned the act, and neither had Evadne's husband. For Amintor, Evadne's cuckolded husband, the King, corrupt as he is, is untouchable:

> O, thou hast named a word that wipes away
> All thoughts revengeful; in that sacred name
> "The King" lies a terror. What frail man
> Dares lift his hand against it? Let the gods
> Speak to him when they please; till when, let us
> Suffer and wait.
>
>   (2.1.307–12)

In a startling gender inversion, it is a frail woman who dares to lift her hand. Evadne is rebellious and desperate; she refuses to suffer her shame quietly, choosing instead in the Greek spirit to "wash her stains away" with the King's blood (4.1.282). She does not leave vengeance to God or to her brother, though she is arguably his agent, for he makes it brutally clear to her that his honor (and that of their dead father) has been compromised through her dishonor.

To do this terrible deed, she acknowledges herself a monster; but at the same time, she argues that her lot is pitiable and atones for her sin. In the end, the new king moralizes on the justice of God's punishment of "lustful kings," insisting, "But curs'd is he that is their instrument" (5.3.293, 295). While the "he" referred to here is Melantius, it is Evadne who is the cursed instrument and sacrifice to her brother's honor. Furthermore, when her husband, Amintor, refuses to accept regicide as a rite of purification for Evadne, she kills herself, fulfilling the expected fate of the Renaissance revenger. The dramatist John Ford neatly sums up that fate in *The Broken Heart* (1633): *"Revenge proves its own executioner."*[41]

Like Shakespeare's Tamora, Evadne appears as the force of Revenge—fierce, pitiless, and awe-inspiring. Both dramatic cases emphasize the ambivalence of revenge's promise to restore the self to wholeness and honor, as well as the costs to women who pursue what men have always regarded as their own gender's privilege and duty. When these female characters transgress gender boundaries, taking on a masculine aggressiveness and will to violent retribution, they appear less than human (bestial) and, at the same time, more than human (almost supernatural). They reflect Western culture's projection of revenge's most disturbing, fearsome aspects upon women.

REVENGE, HONOR, AND LAW IN EARLY MODERN ENGLAND

Revenge has been understood by many of its critics largely within Judeo-Christian and psychological frameworks, which construe vengeance as morally reprehensible, fundamentally damaging to self and others, and destructive of social order and patriarchal authority. The modern psychological perspective tends to reflect Karen Horney's psychoanalytic assessment, which casts revenge figuratively as a mental affliction and disease that delays or forestalls a healing process based on acceptance and forgiveness. Horney associates feminine vindictiveness in particular with aggression and masochism.[42] Early modern tracts tend to anticipate Horney's view, while adding a political dimension to their analyses. Francis Bacon asserts in his essay "Of Revenge," "This is certain, that a man that studieth revenge keeps his own wounds green, which otherwise would heal and do well. Public revenges are for the most part fortunate, as that for the death of Caesar, for the death of Pertinax, for the death of Henry the Third of France, and many more. But in private revenges it is not so. Nay, rather, vindictive persons live the life of witches, who, as they are mischievous, so end they infortunate."[43] Bacon characterizes public revenge as "fortunate," which I take to mean he finds them to be justified in political terms. Private revenge, on the other hand, is all about personal "wounds," "mischievousness" and ill fortune; the personality of the private revenger is conceptualized as morally wayward or deformed. Vindictiveness is associated with witches (women mainly) and the supernatural, a view embodied in early modern characterizations such as Shakespeare's Weird Sisters.

The public/private distinction is commonly articulated in early modern English tracts dealing with revenge. Writers condemning private revenge invoke the divine monopoly on vengeance, the political subject's obedience to the Crown, and the essential passivity of Christian virtues. These politically conservative arguments do not address the inadequacies and inequities of the justice system, nor how the populace is to deal with the psychological, emotional, and social costs of trauma sustained through crime, slander, rape, and other dishonoring acts. They attempt to suppress the individual's desire for revenge by orienting victims of crime toward the promises of retribution offered by God, Law, and Crown. To challenge these sources of patriarchal authority through an act of revenge is to commit a second crime and, furthermore, sacrilege and treason. Yet these arguments do not refrain from characterizing the male authorities as avengers themselves, which suggests that the law of the *talion* remained a central principle in English thought and in political and legal practices.

Indeed, English theorists and ministers invoke the threatening specter of God's vengeance for citizens' awe-inspiring regard and contemplation. With fear and hope, church authorities emphasized, those wronged by others should wait for divine shows of justice. The Old Law of an eye for an eye (Exod. 21:24; Lev. 24:20; Deut. 19:21) cannot be practiced by individuals, for vengeance belongs to the Lord (Rom. 12:19). Countless tracts and homilies referred to divine vengeance as a form of ultimate justice, and patience and humility as the appropriate moral responses to wrongs. Yet kings, governors, and other authorized magistrates were called God's "common revengers"; they were the ones legitimized to bring God's judgment and punishment upon offenders.[44] Nicholas Stratford, dean of St. Asaph, neatly sums up the moral, legal, and political position of the time: "So proper is vengeance to God, that it belongs to none besides him, except only those, to whom he hath given special license to execute it; that is, to publicke Magistrates, and Superiors in Authority, who by virtue of their Office, are also Avengers; but what is inflicted by them, is to be accounted no other than the Vengeance of God, because they as God's Ministers are commissioned by him."[45] This explanation shows how the judicial system, with its justified administration of divine will, attempts to "deflect the menace of vengeance"—that is, private revenge—yet it "does not suppress vengeance" altogether. As René Girard argues, "[I]t effectively limits it to a single act of reprisal, enacted by a sovereign authority specializing in this particular function. The decisions of the judiciary are invariably presented as the final word on vengeance."[46]

Yet Elizabethans could not have accepted the judiciary's "final word on vengeance" in all cases. Bacon's "Of Revenge," if read with an eye for subtlety, documents ambivalence more than a solid position against revenge. His essay equivocates between condemnation and defense of revenge. The piece opens with a dramatic conflict staged between revenge and law: "Revenge is a kind of wild justice, which the more man's nature runs to, the more ought law to weed it out. For as for the first wrong, it doth but offend the law, but the revenge of that wrong putteth the law out of office."[47] The language has a figurative appeal and emotional edge to it. The pictures conjured are those of instinct personified and running wild, a garden overcome with weeds, and Revenge giving offense to resentful Law. "Wild justice" is an oxymoron that acknowledges a moral rightness in vengefulness—it is just—but qualifies this sense of justice with an anarchic, uncontrollable element. The essay continues with Bacon giving the moral upper hand to those who can forgive rather than avenge. Yet Bacon could be said to express sympathy for revenge taken in situations in which the law has no claim, for he concedes, "The most tolerable sort of revenge is for those wrongs which there is no law to remedy"; he warns, however, "let a man take heed the revenge be such as there is no law to punish; else a man's enemy is still before hand, and it is two for one," meaning that revenge can result in the law "injuring" the injured again.[48]

Such a situation might involve injury to one's honor, a most valued aspect of private and public identity, which Tudor tracts opposed to revenge tend not to mention. Many early modern English people, no less than their Anglo-Saxon and Roman ancestors, felt that honor violations, from adultery to goading about manhood to daily insults, demanded a strong personal response. As Robert Ashley declares in his late Elizabethan treatise *Of Honour,* honor is a foundation of morality, a statement that echoes the sentiment of his classical source, Aristotle. Honor is both an inner virtue and a public demonstration of such.[49] Communal pressures incite "honorable" men to act to avoid shame. Everyone, except the monarch, was subordinate to someone in this hierarchical, bureaucratic society, which meant that insults to one's honor were possible (and perhaps frequently experienced) across society. Few would not have suffered humiliations that come in the course of paying obeisance to one's superiors. The orthodox position on private revenge did not necessarily square with people's sentiments and experiences, especially when their sense of personal or familial honor had been slighted publicly and the justice system had not or could not restore honor through a satisfactory ruling.

Shakespeare's plays depict cultures in which honor functions as an all-important concept defining self-worth and relationships between self and other. As Julius Ruff points out, "[D]efense of honor was a key concern for all early modern Europeans, aristocrats as well as commoners. Individuals therefore took great personal offense at physical assault, because any attack on an individual represented a lack of respect, and therefore diminished the honor of the victim."[50] In honor-based cultures, as William Ian Miller argues, an emotional economy involving pride, envy, humiliation, shame, revenge, and schadenfreude governs all social interactions.[51] If A dishonors B, he takes from him or her something of value, incurring a debt. The debt *must* be paid back in this system, often with interest; otherwise, the suffering, including feelings of shame and public loss of face, can be tremendously damaging. A usually forfeits (does not beg forgiveness or perform an act of restitution), which requires B to act, to reclaim the debt, usually with violence.

Surprisingly, Bacon's appreciation of revenge's rightness under certain circumstances is not an anomaly in early modern discourses on revenge, for despite the heavy emphasis on patriarchal authorities as ministers of God's vengeance, there were in fact circumstances in which other agents of revenge were morally authorized to take action. In a gloss of Matthew 5:34–48 from his sermon on temporal authority (1523), Martin Luther mentions one such exception: "A Christian should be so disposed that he will suffer every evil and injustice without avenging himself. . . . On behalf of others, however, he may and should seek vengeance, justice, protection, and help. . . . [W]hen [Christians] perform their duties, not with the intention of seeking their own ends but only of helping the law and the governing authority function to coerce the wicked, there is no peril in that."[52] Thus, the charitable Christian might find himself (or herself) in the position to commit an act of revenge "On behalf of others," and to aid authorities in "coerc[ing] the wicked."

Anthonie Marten's translation of Peter Martyr Vermigli's *Common Places* (London, 1583) contains another exception to the private revenge restriction. This text was "an influential source book for Elizabethan preachers," "more important even than Calvin's *Institutes of the Christian Religion*" for the progress of Reformed theology.[53] After arguing that public revenge may be taken by a magistrate, the following passage occurs in Marten's translation:

> But it is not lawfull for priuate men to reuenge, vnlesse it be, according to the prouerbe, To repell violence by violence. This is not prohibited them, when the magistrate cannot helpe them. For somtime the case happeneth so vpon the sudden; as a man cannot straitwaie flie to the helpe of the publike power. Wherefore we may then defend our selues, vsing neuerthelesse great moderation; to

wit, that we onelie indeuour to defend our selues, and them that be committed vnto vs, not wishing with a mind of reuenge to hurt our aduersaries: in such a sort as that action may proceed, not of hatred, but of charitie.[54]

Self-defense and defense of one's charges, as it turns out, comprise yet another important exception to the injunction against private acts of violence. However, Vermigli works hard to disentangle a necessary act of violence from revenge. Such an act must proceed from charity (love), rather than hate or the desire to hurt. He invokes "a mind of reuenge" as that which must be avoided at all costs, which might remind us of the cautionary words Old Hamlet's Ghost gives his son: "Taint not thy mind" (1.5.85).

Yet the circumstance of violence remains a scene unpainted in Vermigli's text, which is hopelessly abstracted from lived experience and real passions. How realistic is it that one would respond to sudden violence without any of the vengeance passions arising: anger, moral outrage, resentment, hatred, a feeling that one's honor has been violated? How can the passion of love *move* one to commit an act of violence? Is not self-defense a retaliatory strike back with the desire to harm so that the aggressor cannot do one further harm? As David N. Beauregard argues, Vermigli's articulation of his position, concerned as he is with moderate passions, intention, and circumstances, borrows silently from the Aristotelian-Thomistic tradition.[55] Without acknowledging Aristotle or Aquinas, Vermigli has made a case for private revenge as a virtuous action. Vermigli qualifies Aristotle and Aquinas, but he seems to be implicitly in their corner when it comes to the pursuit of necessary violence with the proper passion: moral indignation that opposes wrongdoing.

While many Christian humanists and Stoics argued for the virtues of patience and self-restraint, those who followed Aristotle's *Rhetoric* and *Nicomachean Ethics* found anger warranted in cases of injustice. Righteous anger trumped the inappropriate ethical responses of passivity and excessive rage when insult and injury occurred. Christian thinkers could have turned to Aquinas to find perhaps the strongest statement regarding the virtue of vengeance. Aquinas allows that vengeance can be a special virtue, even a form of charity, if it is executed in the right spirit. He attributes "due measure" to lawful vengeance, and sees an act of revenge in the name of God as a principle of exact retaliation.[56] Alternative voices deriving authority and merit from the Aristotelian-Thomist tradition, attuned as well to culturally persistent notions of honor and shame, can be heard in England. While most of these voices are men's, it is possible to hear women's voices, too, especially in the imaginative literature and drama of the early modern period, and they speak with just anger, calling out for vengeance. Each of these terms, *just, anger,* and *vengeance,* are subject to various cultural meanings and connotations, carrying moral weight from various traditions. The contexts of anger and revenge cannot be underestimated in our attempt to understand women's ethics and particularly to make sense of antifeminist accounts of women's anger and vengefulness.

Early modern writers thought of women as more apt than men to possess a mind of revenge, and they (unrealistically) do not tend to see women in a position where self-defense is needed or warranted. Female vengefulness typically crops up in discussions of anger, a passion thought to reflect women's naturally inferior state and moral weakness. Juan Luis Vives writes of women's "feeble and weak nature," in which "anger and the desire to be revenged doth kindle, as it were inflare, continually."[57] As Gwynne Kennedy demonstrates, women's anger was exaggerated or dismissed as trivial by early modern writers, who assumed that male authority and female subordination were natural positions. Women were represented, on the one hand, as possessing a dangerous Clytemnestra-like fury fueled by vengefulness and, on the other, as reflecting harmless, groundless passions.[58] When they are in a position to act upon their anger, women are potentially "dreadfull." As the Jesuit priest Nicholas Caussin writes, "The anger of potent women is above all dreadfull, when they are not with held by considerations of conscience, because they have a certaine appetite of revenge, which exceedeth all may be imagined."[59] John Reynolds's *The Triumphs of Gods Revenge* (1621–35) presents the case of Lauretia, who desires blood revenge for the murder of her lover. Such a desire can only be ungodly and unreasonable: "So as consulting with Choller, not with Reason, with Nature not with Grace, with Satan, not with God, she vowes to be sharpely revenged on him . . . resembling her sexe and selfe, she inhumanely and sacreligiously darts forth an oath."[60] She will trade her tears for her enemy's blood.

These accounts portray feminine vengeance as an appetite that overrules conscience, reason, and grace. In this respect, the moral attack upon women is clear. Indeed, it would seem that Elizabethan legal and homiletic discourses seek to prohibit the expression of feminine anger in order to discourage Christian women from raising voices of moral outrage and actively pursuing justice through whatever means is available to them. Obliquely, what appears to be at stake here in early modern accounts of women and anger is the maintenance of political order and masculine authority within the family, community, and state. Women's anger and vengeance target or sidestep husbands, ministers, and governors, rejecting patriarchal rule in favor of "the rule of primordial feminine law," as Alison Findlay puts it.[61] Early modern men recognized subliminally that women's passions, particularly vengefulness, have the power "to deconstruct male authority, independence, even identity."[62]

As we see in many early modern English plays and in today's anthropological and sociological studies, vengeance often emerges as a natural, deeply felt response to injustice, dishonor, victimization, and helplessness. Lauretia's response to the slaying of her lover in Reynolds's text may have been construed as highly irrational and dangerous, but it is a response intimately bound up with justice. The philosopher Robert C. Solomon, among others, is right when he asserts a radical connection between revenge and justice: "Vengeance may be primitive, but it is still the conceptual core of justice."[63] As the sociologists Pietro Marongiu and Graeme Newman argue, "All acts of vengeance arise from an elementary sense of injustice, a primitive feeling than one has been arbitrarily subjected to a tyrannical power against which one is powerless to act."[64] The fantasies, impulses, and ritual actions of revenge seek to fulfill a longing for justice, which often is not served by the judicial system. In Shakespeare's drama, we often see how men in power fail women in their cause for justice, and in their attempts to maintain honor and self-worth. Under certain conditions, for women, vengeance can be understood as an ethical force rather than a moral ill or social menace. Vengeance can be a moral imperative; it can be psychologically restorative, as well as socially regenerative. Vengeful women seek compensation for a profound sense of shame and dishonor produced by violent crime, moral outrage, and subjection to wrongs, insults, and other humiliations. Revenge can even take on "heroic functions," as Harry Keyishian argues.[65] Certainly in the literature of classical antiquity and the medieval period, the male heroic ideal included revenge as a value, and female characters would occasionally assume the masculine ideal in pursuing revenge.

While early modern European societies witnessed the "judicial revolution," as some critics call it,[66] which gave state law and the Crown a monopoly on judgment and punishment, this is not to say that Elizabethans had lost touch with a deeply rooted sense that justice could prevail through private means as well, and that self-help could be more satisfying than waiting for the state to rule and perhaps to act at some distant point in the future. Julius Ruff points out that in Europe a state justice system "coexisted with another mode of dispute resolution. There persisted everywhere a plethora of customs and practices, quite distinct from those associated with state law, infrajudicial modes of conflict resolution functioning below the level of state justice, with little or no reference to it."[67] These "infrajudicial" customs and practices included forms of earlier self-governance such as blood feud and duels. Even the government could be involved in promoting revenge outside of the legal courts. The Bond of Association, engineered by William Cecil in 1584–85, stands as an extraordinary act of policy-making that put in the hands of a group of men (privy councilors, churchmen, and gentlemen) the right to pursue revenge in special cases where the attempt to harm the Queen was uncovered. The men who signed the bond swore an oath of allegiance to the Queen and agreed to pursue all "means of revenge" upon those who made an attempt, successful or not, upon the life of the Queen. They swore to "never desist . . . to the vttermost extermynacion of them ther counselors and abbettors."[68] Attitudes toward revenge in early modern England clearly depended upon circumstance and context, for arguments could be marshaled to promote or condemn private retaliatory actions.

While the language and dramatic situation of law and the judiciary pervade the literature of Elizabethan England, tales of honor, shame, and revenge were enormously popular fare as well. William Painter's *The Palace of Pleasure* (1566), for example, contains eighteen tales of serious and comic revenge, three of which feature a female avenger. The popularity of revenge tales suggests an artistic response to dissatisfactions with how legal institutions handled injustices, in particular those that dishonored persons and families such that reputations were in the balance. Elizabethan England has been called a "culture of litigation," as large numbers of the population served as litigants, legal practitioners, and witnesses.[69] Though they were forbidden the social roles of juror, lawyer, or judge, Elizabethan women could wage law and certainly did in the thousands in the late sixteenth and seventeenth centuries.[70] Women, however, had greater difficulty than men in bringing a case to court. Significantly overlooked in legal discursive tracts of the period, women were nonetheless as concerned as men were with the law's inadequacies. As victims of crimes and dishonorable actions, and as kin to the injured, women surely suffered emotionally and physically and felt dishonor, moral indignation, humiliation, and shame as keenly as men did. Gwynne Kennedy's study of women's just anger provides extensive evidence from the period that demonstrates this to be the case.[71] Women can be found in the literature of the period inciting men to avenge injustices when the law courts or political authorities could not or would not provide a satisfactory resolution to criminal activity and familial dishonor.

Early modern England may have had a centralized system of governance with ecclesiastical and secular laws in place, but the cultural ethos, values, and imperatives expressed in Shakespeare's plays, whether his characters are located in early modern Windsor, Venice, or Vienna, are reminiscent of older honor/revenge-based cultures found in Mediterranean countries and medieval Britain and Scandinavia. The tensions, problems, and solutions that arise from self-maintenance of individual, family, and clan honor are of compelling interest to Shakespeare, and he conveys that interest, in part, through his female characters.

The next chapter explores how Shakespeare critically engages the traditional literary role of women as inciters to vengeance. From classical antiquity to the early modern period, female characters can be heard demanding revenge from male kin or authorities based on ethical and social grounds.

Honor, kinship identity, and morality were all concerns motivating their arguments. Seen in the context of fierce, goading women from earlier literature, the strong, verbally potent female characters in Shakespeare can be understood as expressive agents, urging a revenge ethic that reflects the priorities of kinship ties and an elemental desire for justice. As Peter A. French argues, our contemporary dismissal of vengeance to "a distant dark corner of moral permissibility has robbed morality of one of its most potent and persuasive elements."[72] The potent and persuasive elements in vengeance were precisely what interested Shakespeare and what he activated in the ethical characters of his boldest females.

2

Valorous Tongues, Lamenting Voices:
The Expressive Ethics of Female Inciters
in Shakespeare's Plays

Lady Capulet: I beg for justice, which thou, Prince, must give.
                                        —Shakespeare, *Romeo and Juliet*

Lady Macbeth: When you durst do it, then you were a man.
                                        —Shakespeare, *Macbeth*

SET IN A MEDITERRANEAN HONOR-BASED CULTURE, *ROMEO AND JULIET*
opens with the eruption of a new conflict in a long-standing feud. While
the male bravado on display—the vulgar wit and gestures—elicit laughter,
the seriousness of feuding is brought to bear in the play. The male citizens
of Verona shed blood in violent skirmishes that seem to reflect the all-male
domain of the feud. Yet it should not elude our attention that women participate in this conflict as well. One prominent female calls out publicly in
the street for justice, by which she means blood revenge executed by the
state. When Lady Capulet's nephew, Tybalt, has been slain by Romeo, she
appeals to the Prince for repayment in kind. As Tybalt's only kin and a female, she follows the cultural norm and feuding code in choosing a male
avenger. The Prince, appropriately named Escalus, is responsible for law and
order, for weighing life against life in the scales of justice. Lady Capulet appeals to him: "Prince, as thou art true, / For blood of ours shed blood of Mon-
tague" (3.1.150–51). Nothing else but the life of Romeo will satisfy her
outrage, and this satisfaction is framed with the rhetoric of justice: "I beg for
justice, which thou, Prince, must give. / Romeo slew Tybalt. Romeo must
not live" (3.1.182–83). The force of her end-stopped rhymes and the imperative "must" reflect Lady Capulet's passionate investment in the *lex talionis*
of feuding cultures. The sense of debt and obligation is clear and the rule of
equivalence—"blood will have blood"—governs the logic of her plea.

Lady Capulet's role as grievant and inciter of revenge establishes her as a voice of elemental justice in the play, reminding the male authority of his ethical responsibilities. She performs this function publicly, which raises communal expectations for retaliatory justice. If the Prince wishes to deter further violent reprisals and execute justice through the state, he *must* act swiftly and decisively. The Prince responds with a moderate and expedient judicial punishment—exile—which was perhaps the oldest method of dealing with murderers. In the literature and cultural practices of many ancient, medieval, and early modern societies, to be exiled from family and community was to lose one's public identity and kinship ties. To his family and to Verona, Romeo will become the "living dead," so in symbolic fashion the Prince recompenses the life lost with a life taken. As Edward Muir explains, in Italian city-states, the principal means a magistrate had for controlling vendettas was to outlaw men: "In outlawing men for crimes of violence the government sought not only to rid itself of public nuisances but also to focus the wrath of the community on guilty scapegoats whose legal death would have a healing effect for the community as a whole."[1]

Yet as one sees in the literature and historical records of classical Greece, Scandinavia, and Renaissance Italian city-states, outlawing as a form of justice can turn out to be ineffectual, for, threatening as the prospect of exile is, the practice allowed vendettas and feuds to persist. The law was difficult to enforce; the outlaw might return home and kill again, as Romeo does.[2] A guilty scapegoat may have suffered a legal death, but the community does not necessarily heal, and a feeling of dishonor may persist in the family of the wronged party. Lady Capulet's feelings of anger and injury attest to this, for she is not satisfied with the sentence and pursues an extralegal revenge for Romeo's crime.

Lady Capulet quickly steps into the role of private avenger when the Prince settles for Romeo's legal death rather than his blood. In a desperate conversation that mingles talk of vengeance and marriage, she reveals to Juliet her plan to have Romeo poisoned in Mantua. Poison is a traditional weapon used by women to take revenge (think, for example, of Medea's poisoned wedding gift), and in Elizabethan literature seems to be associated with Italy. Thomas Nashe famously described Italy as the "Apothecary-shop of poison for all Nations."[3] While a critic such as Eleanor Prosser views Lady Capulet's "perversion of values" as "chilling,"[4] it would seem that her secretive method of obtaining "justice" depends upon an ethic practiced in Verona. In the feud, revenge is a time-honored response to homicide. Lady Capulet believes this response will please not only herself, but her young daughter as well: "And then I hope thou wilt be satisfied" (3.5.92), she exclaims vehemently. Juliet responds with grimly ironic puns: "Indeed I never shall be *satisfied* / With Romeo, till I behold him—*dead*— / Is my poor heart so for a kinsman vex'd" (3.5.93–95, my emphases). This ambiguous response gives voice to two ethical principles simultaneously: the older revenge ethic and an ethic fueled by desire and love. The pivotal position of the word *dead* suggests her secret hope of sexual satisfaction, but it also anticipates a future moment in the tomb scene, when Juliet will behold her Romeo dead. In a startling irony, his suicide weapon is poison attained from a Mantuan apothecary, perhaps the very one Lady Capulet planned to use to attain her revenge.

In the revenge narrative perpetuated in *Romeo and Juliet,* Lady Capulet functions both as the angry voice of justice (or lawful revenge) and as the lawless avenger whose lethal drug is administered in the end by the criminal himself. Romeo's self-sacrifice is matched by Juliet's suicide with the dagger, a weapon also associated with revenge. The feud ceases in Verona in a most sobering and ironic fashion, when the youngest generation of the warring houses turn the weapons of revenge upon themselves.

In the vivid street scenes depicted in *Romeo and Juliet,* male and female characters alike situate themselves in relation to feuding, some objecting and refusing to participate, others drawn into brandishing weapons to prove their manhood, and others inciting violent reprisals. The female inciter can operate indirectly, yet powerfully, in the feud and in the public sphere, calling to mind an ethic of revenge that may be at work explicitly or implicitly in honor-based cultures. The ethic involved cannot be defined inherently as patriarchal, for Lady Capulet's desire for blood revenge counters the pacifist desires of her husband and the Prince.[5] Committed to the feuding principle of exchange, Lady Capulet is willing to pursue revenge herself, which implicitly challenges the Prince's ethics, authority, and political control over the populace.

Lady Capulet's turn to a private means of revenge reflects how dissatisfied she is with the Prince's political handling of her kinsman's slayer. Her anger is personal and political in nature. As Jenny Jochens has argued in another context, the female inciter exists primarily in relation to the larger world of male action. "Providing women direct access to the otherwise exclusively male world of revenge and feud," she observes, "female whetting was basically a political tool."[6] Persuasion, outcry, and lament are crucial expressive and *political* tools for women who choose to assert their valor, courage, and agency when direct action is not possible. While proverbial wisdom had it that "words are women, deeds are men," we shall see that such a simple dichotomy does not clarify the situations of Shakespeare's inciters. Words can be performative speech acts, as John L. Austin some time ago demonstrated.[7] Words can be understood not simply in opposition to actions, but on a continuum with deeds, inspiring and shaping future actions, stating intent, swearing oaths, cursing, bringing harm to others, and so forth. The valorous tongue and lamenting voice of the female inciter recur as literary tropes that represent females as passionately concerned with honor and revenge, just as men are, and perhaps more eager than men for blood settlement of homicide. Female speech acts are not to be taken lightly, as they can activate a potent spirit of vengeance. In some cases, such as the case of Lady Macbeth, the female inciter desires societal goods, such as power and greatness, but in prodding male violence to get what she wants, she defies fundamental ethical codes in her society.

THE SUBMERGED FEMININE VENGEANCE NARRATIVE IN *MACBETH*

In *Macbeth* we encounter Shakespeare's boldest inciter, a valorous female whose call for bloodshed places her in a revenge cycle as both a vicarious avenger and a potential target. The play vividly enacts the dynamics and structure of revenge: Macbeth's criminal act of regicide and tyrannous rule are punished by Macduff's retaliation, a second act of regicide that symbolically undoes the original crime, and exchanges victim and aggressor roles. As Dianne Hunter argues, in this "perfect revenge play," we have a "patriarchal myth" of disrupted father-son succession.[8] Yet in telling this patriarchal tale, the traces of what has been suppressed can be detected. Complementing this myth, one detects a latent revenge play centered on the myth of feminine ascendancy and female heroic mettle. A submerged feminine vengeance tale can be uncovered by attending to classical and historical resonances in feminine speech, gender ambiguity, and the construction of Lady Macbeth's character.

Lady Macbeth's taunting of her husband would seem to define the outer edges of gender difference: "When you durst do it, then you were a man" (1.7.49). Scorn and persuasion are all the woman's; daring action, all the man's. Yet these words, like so many in the play, possess an uncanny potency, as if they were virtual deeds, charms that activate the "future in the instant" (1.5.58). Driving Lady Macbeth's goading is her desire for a heroic identity, for public greatness, which Macbeth's violent action will confer upon her. She has called upon spirits to unsex her, to transfigure her feminine self into a fierce being capable of remorseless violence. She has yielded to the call of Bellona, the ancient Roman goddess of war, and to intimations of warrior violence, homicidal urges, and blood revenge. She would dare to unsex herself and "do it." Opportunity and occasion arise: a weak warrior king has come under her "battlements," and a prophecy has been uttered that her husband will be "King hereafter" (1.5.40, 1.3.50). Her ambition for the throne, for greatness, produces valor and courage that defy medieval and early modern notions of femininity altogether. Through her valorous tongue, which she uses to persuade her husband to commit regicide, Lady Macbeth expresses her agency and will to rule in the marriage and the kingdom. Mac-

beth becomes "Valour's minion" (1.2.19)—that is, Lady Macbeth's minion—in the politicized domestic space of their castle when he dares to kill
the king. Lady Macbeth's insults regarding his masculine prowess drive him
to pervert his sense of honor in order to achieve greatness for them both.

In the end, though, Shakespeare would seem to have made Lady Macbeth
fall short of her potential for greatness as a powerful political agent. When
she descends into madness and suicide, this unfulfilled feminist possibility,
if you will, gives way to a Christian retributive pattern with sin punishing
the sinner in the murky hell of the Macbeth castle. Or as in the ancient Greek
tragedies, blood pollution stains her hands and no purification rite can wash
away her guilt. Yet in his equivocal treatment of female power, Shakespeare
represents a contest with competing ethics, historical accounts, and literary
precedents. Lady Macbeth's character emerges, in part, through radical re-
visionist energies inspired by the Macbeth myth from Scottish legend and
revenge drama from the ancient Greeks and Seneca.

Shakespeare's treatment of Lady Macbeth follows Raphael Holinshed,
his primary historical source for the play, yet he suppresses the ethnological implications in the narrative of the *Chronicles*. In retelling the Macbeth
myth, Shakespeare not only recasts the successful Scottish warrior king
as a villain, but he veers away from the story of feminine revenge—Lady
Macbeth's revenge—at the heart of Celtic Scottish history. Shakespeare
merges the wives of the historical Donwald and Macbeth in his portrayal
of Lady Macbeth. Donwald's wife not only urges murder but shows her
husband the means in their own castle; her motive, like her husband's, involves shame, grief, malice, and revenge, for King Duff had executed Donwald's kinsmen in a spectacle of power shown to the people. Donwald feels
"the reproach which his lineage has sustained," and when he tells his wife
why he is grieving, Holinshed reports, she "bore no less malice in her heart
toward the King for the like cause on her behalf than her husband."[9] This
last phrase strongly suggests the "reproach" to her "lineage," as well. In the
historical account of Macbeth, after his wife hears of the prophecy from the
Weird Sisters, she "lay sore upon [her husband] to attempt the thing, as she
. . . was very ambitious, burning in unquenchable desire to bear the name of
a queen."[10] Holinshed notes Duncan's "small skill in warlike affairs," which
leaves his kingdom vulnerable to rebellion and attack, and he calls Duncan's
reign "feeble and slothful."[11] Holinshed's Macbeth emerges as a powerful
leader, a purveyor of justice who rids the kingdom of a weak ruler.

Shakespeare suppresses other politically and culturally relevant aspects
of the historical record. For Lady Macbeth's historical counterpart, a woman
named Gruoch and descendent of Malcolm I, revenge would have been a
culturally sanctioned motive for a plot to seize the throne. Malcolm II had
slaughtered his way through her family line in order to place his grandson
Duncan I (from a second family branch) on the throne. The historical Lady

Macbeth would have had a legitimate claim to the throne, and when she married her second husband, Macbeth, son of Findlaech, Earl of Moray, he reinstated her line, her rightful succession, through regicide. Shakespeare's Lady Macbeth confesses she would have killed the King had he not looked like her father. His resemblance to her father reminds us of the historical kinship ties Shakespeare buries—Duncan is her kinsman, a cousin, as well as Macbeth's. To kill him is to shed blood of kin, but it is also, again, when considering eleventh-century cultural norms, to assert her rightful ascendency (her claim to the throne was stronger than Macbeth's, which came from a maternal line). As Dianne Hunter points out, "[F]rom the standpoint of the eleventh century, Duncan, not Macbeth, was the usurper; and Macbeth was the vindicator of a true line of succession."[12] Gruoch incites a powerful male warlord to avenge the political wrongs done to her family and, with his aid, she becomes queen.

We should consider, as well, the representation of Scottish women in the *Description of Scotland,* prefixed to Holinshed's *Chronicles.* Muriel Bradbrook was the first scholar to note its relevance to Shakespeare's Lady Macbeth. In the depiction of Scottish women, there lies a paradoxical vision of "tenderness and barbarity, suckling and bloodshed."[13] While these fiercely loyal women breast-feed their own children, carefully nurturing their progeny, they also appear on the battlefield like men of courage, so bloodthirsty they not only "bathed" their swords in the blood of the "first living creature they saw," but "tasted" blood "with their mouths" as well.[14] Bradbrook proposes that here we find the "fundamental character of Lady Macbeth" as revealed in her goading speech to Macbeth. She argues that the "character of Lady Macbeth owes nothing to the Chronicle,"[15] yet the case might be stated more accurately if we allow that Shakespeare interweaves the *Description*'s portrait of feminine nurturance and masculine ferocity with the repeated motif of wife as inciter in the narrative of Donwald and Macbeth from Holinshed's history. In Lady Macbeth, however, Shakespeare reflects gender disturbances of a more troubling kind, for his Scottish female is seen neither nurturing a child nor fighting on the battlefield to protect kin. Rather, like Euripides' Medea, who proclaims to the Corinthian women, "I would rather stand three times / in battle with shield and spear than give birth once" (lines 280–81),[16] she appropriates a masculine warrior rhetoric to describe her mettle as a female in the domestic and political spheres.

Revenge is notably not Lady Macbeth's; and it is her husband who becomes the target of retaliation. The wife and husband are criminals, violators of the bonds held most sacred in their culture, as Shakespeare imagines it. The medieval Scottish cultural economy of shame, honor, and revenge, of political prestige and power, clan protection, and bonding are refracted in the retelling, so that Shakespeare can present a contemporary tale of supernatural intervention and moral depravity, a patriarchal tale of male vengeance and kingdom cleansing, before the court of his own king, James Stuart of Scotland.

Shakespeare's *Macbeth* is indeed a patriarchal revenge tale that derives some of its power from scapegoating and demonizing the feminine in terrifying ways. An atmosphere of terror is figured in the petrifying apotropaic image of the Gorgon, or the Medusa head. When Macduff returns from the murdered Duncan's bedchamber, he can barely speak because he is so filled with horror from the sight; he admonishes the others: "Approach the chamber, and destroy your sight / With a new Gorgon" (2.3.70–71). The strange association of Duncan's corpse with a Gorgon signals us to look deeper into the mythological strata of the play. If Shakespeare rejects women's political claims as they are found in Scottish legend and history, if he valorizes the masculine narrative of male succession, regicide, and revenge, he does so while also exploring aspects of feminine power that are meant to resonate ambivalently and to reflect darkly on male power and succession. The mythic dimension in this play recalls the unsettling ethos and dramatic effects of classical Greek and Senecan tragedy, where aggressive female inciters and avengers often play dominant roles. In Lady Macbeth, we find traces of Medea, Clytemnestra, and Electra, who each in some version of their stories adopt, or parody, a masculine heroic ethos. Like Medea, she seems capable of discarding her gender and killing children; like Clytemnestra, she would kill a king; and like Electra, she pours valor into the ear of her male kin, inciting an act of violence. Shakespeare's subtle use of subtexts from revenge tragedies, along with subterranean elements of Scottish legend, blend suggestively, and perhaps uneasily, with early modern English norms and the overt political agenda at work in *Macbeth*.

The refracted tales of classical feminine vengeance in *Macbeth* repay close attention. As some critics note, Seneca resonates throughout *Macbeth*, reflecting "shared imaginative structures," particularly through Shakespeare's conception of *nefas,* a crime of sacrilege.[17] While in Euripides' and Seneca's plays the killing of the children is a wife's most effective and terrifying revenge against her faithless husband, in Shakespeare's tragedy children are slaughtered as a male tyrant's act of savage revenge against a rebel. Yet Lady Macbeth's imagined infanticide is equally as terrible as the literal slaughtering of innocents. Her infamous words are fierce, betraying a cold fury:

> I have given suck, and know
> How tender 'tis to love the babe that milks me:
> I would, while it was smiling in my face,
> Have pluck'd my nipple from his boneless gums,
> And dash'd the brains out, had I so sworn
> As you have done to this.
>
> (1.7.54–59)

Such an unnatural image of violence prepares the way for a crime against humanity by invoking the malevolent maternal will to kill one's own progeny. Recalling Medea's infanticide, Lady Macbeth's images conceive of violence against one's child as a wife's steely relinquishment of maternity and progeny for the sake of her marital bond. While Medea's infanticide is performed as a blood rite that punishes a faithless husband for his violation of a sacred bond, Lady Macbeth's infanticide is performed as a potent rhetorical act to demonstrate to her husband the gravity of an oath. In Euripides' text, Medea's punishment possesses ethical force and divine sanction (she follows the dictates of her grandfather Helios and invokes Themis, both gods that punish oath-breakers). Medea knows that she wounds herself by this act and will grieve for a long time, but the sacrifice of the innocents seems necessary to her. To kill a child would seem to cause Lady Macbeth pain, as well, as she apparently has had a child at the breast and knows the tenderness of maternal love. Yet she is willing to go to any extreme to restore Macbeth's commitment to the oath he has sworn to her.

The imagined violence done to the innocent babe proves to be the "sticking-place" (1.7.61) in Macbeth's feverish mind. His wife has demonstrated her mettle, and he responds by reanimating the dark bond of criminality they had begun to forge. The thought of infanticide provokes thoughts of illegitimate succession, of regicide, the wife's violation of nature leading to the husband's violation of natural, political, and divine orders. The masculine quality Macbeth admires in his wife is a perversion of valor, a betrayal of feminine nurturance. Yet he responds to such a fantasy with his own, that of an entirely male lineage about whom it could almost be said that there were "none of woman born": "Bring forth men-children only," he commands his fierce wife (4.1.80, 1.7.73).

A further resonance with Medea haunts the construction of femininity in Shakespeare's play. Medea's sorcery and religious devotion from Euripides' and Seneca's versions of her myth are transformed in John Studley's early modern English translation into a rather baleful witchcraft. His vision of Medean witchcraft reflects contemporary European fears of feminine malevolence and demonic practice. As James Stuart asserted in *Daemonology* (1597), witches are typically women (twenty women to every man), for they are morally frail and susceptible to the devil's snares. Furthermore, witches desire only two things: worldly riches and *revenge.* James makes clear that their motive for revenge is malice.[18] Shakespeare devotes an entire scene in the play to the Weird Sisters' vengefulness; when they have been affronted by a sailor's wife, they unleash their malice upon her husband, punishing him with tempests in his bark at sea and demonic sexual possession for his body. They are frightening specters of feminine vengefulness, which subliminally fuse with Lady Macbeth when she calls upon malign spirits and then persuades her husband to kill for worldly acquisition.

Infanticide, wrath, and ambition all figure prominently in the story of Clytemnestra, as well. But her fury for child-murder, a crucial motive in her vengeance, contrasts with Lady Macbeth's emotional and ethical constitution. Yet she might be seen, as the actress Harriet Walter suggests, in light of the bereaved mother, "truly blighted and perhaps vengeful against the world" for her childlessness.[19] While she does not have a direct target to punish, Lady Macbeth may feel that a debt exists; socially, she has been denied the maternal position; politically, she has the status of a thane's wife. If she were to achieve greatness in the political sphere, she could accomplish something substantial for herself and her husband. Focusing on the monarchy channels her procreative function in another direction, rendering Macbeth her "firstling"—the male son she never had—who will commit an act of displaced vengeance against her king/spectral father for her.[20] Clytemnestra's case, however, rests partly on the criminal act (*nefas*) of her husband, Agamemnon, who killed their daughter Iphigenia to appease Artemis before the Greek fleet could wage war on Troy. For ten years, Clytemnestra waits in Argos for the king's return. When he arrives, she exacts her revenge upon him, in part for the blood sacrifice of their child, but also to maintain her position as queen of Argos with her lover Aegisthus. Her kin- and king-slaying is repaid by her son, Orestes, who, sanctioned by Apollo, commits matricide. The Greek cycle featured in Aeschylus's *Oresteia* is compressed into Seneca's *Agamemnon*. Lady Macbeth's resemblance to Seneca's Clytemnestra centers on her dominant persona and the malelike potency of her words, as well as her claims to power and her use of supernatural rites.

Lady Macbeth may recall distantly the figure of Electra in her function as inciter of male violence. Her character seems closest in spirit to Euripides' bloodthirsty Electra, who virtually taunts Orestes into showing the mettle she herself possesses: "prove yourself a man," she insists as he is about to set off to kill Aegisthus while the latter is undertaking a sacrifice (lines 689–90).[21] The religious setting for the murder, coupled with the hospitality Aegisthus offers to Orestes (*xenia*, the Greek law governing guests and hosts), renders the revenge ethically compromised, just as the killing of a divinely sanctioned king and guest is in the Macbeth castle. When Electra fears that Orestes has not killed him, she cries impatiently, "Quick! Let me do the deed!" (line 757). And when Orestes resists killing his mother, she exclaims, "Do not turn coward or lose your manhood" (line 982). Orestes' response, like Macbeth's, is to pursue these "terrible steps" (line 985) toward murder in an altered state of consciousness.

Despite the differences I have noted, Lady Macbeth appears in a familiar light as the traditional female inciter, a literary character drawn from mythological sources and perhaps from the historical behavior of women in warrior cultures such as ancient, prestate Greece and medieval Scotland, where honor and shame defined the emotional constitution and ethical acts, including blood revenge, of men *and* women. When women could not actively kill and avenge wrongs, they provoked their male kin—husbands, sons, brothers, uncles, and nephews—to respond with retaliatory violence. Shakespeare thus subtly calls up classical and medieval representations of feminine vengefulness in *Macbeth*. The ambitious wife desires power and sanctions violence; she possesses warrior-like traits, representing the spirit of Bellona in her marriage. Yet Shakespeare has perverted this daring, transgressive role, for Lady Macbeth does not decry an injustice, as Medea, Clytemnestra, and her historical Scottish counterpart did; rather, she advocates a crime of monumental proportions, a sacrilege, and she encourages shamelessness in her husband, who feels keenly that to prove his manhood and to escape the reproachful gaze of his wife—the cold Medusa stare— he must transgress all recognized cultural bonds and pervert the heroic male ideal.

Through the representation of Lady Macbeth, Shakespeare made visible the potent political and gendered function of the female inciter. While denying her the revenge causes of her historical and literary predecessors and radically compromising her ethical viability, he nonetheless lent her a certain heroic grandeur, recognized by romantic critics such as William Hazlitt and the painter Henry Fuseli. Indeed, we might conclude by recalling Fuseli's remarkable paintings of Lady Macbeth's sleepwalking scene, which offer radical visual interpretations of how gender and heroism are interrelated in the play. Stuart Sillars comments on how *Lady Macbeth Sleepwalking* (1772) "uses the Borghese Gladiator as its basis," which emphasizes in the character an aura of power, yet allows for pathos, as well.[22] Fuseli viewed the Gladiator as "the embodiment of classical tragedy"; thus, his vision of Lady Macbeth in the allusive posture of this grand male figure confers an aura of male heroism upon her.[23] She appears in the painting as a monumental figure of epic strength. Fuseli saw a fallen hero implicit in the text, the character, and the scene, and it was not Macbeth. He chose to locate heroism in the suffering, larger-than-life queen.

An earlier Shakespearean version of the female goader who desires to make her husband the instrumental agent of her greatness can be found in the ambitious Eleanor Cobham, Duchess of Gloucester. In *2 Henry VI*, Eleanor urges her husband, Protectorate of the realm and uncle to the young, effeminate King Henry, to steal the crown. She consults a witch and conjuror to hear prophetic words about her future glory. She has a dream in which she envisions a glorious rise, picturing herself in the seat of majesty at Westminster with King Henry and Queen Margaret kneeling to her. Gloucester's masculine identity rests on honor, loyalty to king and commonwealth, and Christian virtue, all of which his wife's goading seems to threaten. He chastises her for "the canker of ambitious thoughts" (1.2.18), but she asserts, after he departs,

> Were I a man, a duke and next of blood,
> I would remove these tedious stumbling-blocks
> And smooth my way upon their headless necks.
> And, being a woman, I will not be slack
> To play my part in Fortune's pageant—
>
> (1.2.63–67)

Her rhetorical emphasis on gendered roles in "Fortune's pageant" is revealing. Her wordplay with "blocks" and "necks" figures how men violently "smooth" their "way" to make their fortunes. Women in early-modern patriarchal cultures are not dealt the avenger's part, though they may seize it, as do Joan la Pucelle and Queen Margaret in the *Henry VI* tetralogy; rather, they are given the inciter's role. Eleanor, like Lady Macbeth, is ambitious and fierce, sharpening her tongue in an effort to drive her husband to take what she feels should be his. This gendered role complements the masculine roles of warrior, usurper, and avenger; indeed, the female inciter typically chooses the appropriate male to carry out her wishes, which usually involve defending family honor and claiming political blood rights. She is the expressive agent and he the instrumental one in this high-stakes cultural practice, where men and women alike vie for reputation, prestige, and power. *2 Henry VI,* however, charts the fall of the virtuous Humphrey, Duke of Gloucester, who had the interests of the Commonwealth, rather than his own or his wife's, in mind. Eleanor pays for her seditious ambition, her challenge to patriarchal hierarchy, with a form of gendered violence, a shaming ritual staged in the streets of London. She is made to carry a candle and wear a sheet upon which a paper stating her crimes is attached. Her scandal reverts to her husband, staining the man even as he rhetorically clings to his self-perception as "loyal, true and crimeless" (2.4.63). He cannot stave off his enemies, and by the middle of act 3, he has been murdered.

Shakespeare's apparent demonizing of female characters that attempt to involve themselves in the public sphere, however, cannot ultimately distract the audience from what these bold women expose in their monarchs and political systems. Lady Macbeth's and Eleanor's ambitions for power and greatness demonstrate the politically untenable situation of a weak king who cannot inspire fear in enemies and retain the loyalty of his subjects. The early scenes in *Macbeth,* we should remember, register King Duncan's political weakness, for some of his retainers have become traitors and joined with Norway in combat against Scotland. The women's perceptions of a power vacuum and political opportunity are acute. They find themselves in a position to seize the rights of men, or make extraordinary demands upon them.

Shakespeare's female characters exist as meaningful agents in the cultural systems in which they are situated. These sociopolitical systems, while mirroring Elizabethan culture to some extent, tend to operate based on honor, shame, and revenge. Early modern England may not have been a revenge culture in the sense that early Germanic settlements in Britain were, but the reflexive turn to vengeance as a force that regulates shame and honor is pervasive in Shakespeare's plays. Shakespeare's women share a sense with male characters such as Titus and Hamlet that *honor* is a value to be prized above all others. They can, in some cases, exploit a masculine-defined notion of honor, as does Lady Macbeth, only because it is such a definitive cultural value. Yet this is to focus on only one mode of feminine participation in revenge, and there are other modes in evidence. The mental and moral landscapes of revenge yield many passions that are disorienting, as well as clarifying, that unhinge the psyche, or bend it upon a singular goal. This complex inward geography, expressed through speech, gesture, and action, can be perceived in female characters that function in a culture where revenge, justice, honor, moral debt, grief, and shame are all part of the same genetic material. Or perhaps we might state it another way: when Shakespeare seeks to disclose and enact problems of revenge, his female characters carry some of the burden entailed in this kind of moral and artistic enterprise.

The Agency of Feminine Lament and Curses

Curses and lament represent two time-honored feminine vehicles for expressing grief, moral outrage, and a sense of injustice. Shakespeare's dramas offer language and action reminiscent of the powerfully disruptive songs and gestures of ancient Greek lamentation and funerary ritual. Lamenting women bear upon their bodies and in their voices the wretched sufferings of the bereaved, particularly when it is a wrongful death they mourn. In classical literature as in early modern English drama, these women typically do not perform a revenge act themselves, but rather incite others to restore family honor and political rights. Their exposure of failures in earthly justice—patriarchal justice—through lament, curses, and conspicuous grieving functions as a political irritant and a moral challenge to the corrupt powers-that-be. Politically disenfranchised, lamenting women become "queens" of grief, rather than heads of state or authorities in a sanctioned political role, yet their grieving voices and actions are purposeful and express a degree of agency, potency, and political determination. When avenues to institutionally sanctioned justice are closed, they insist on calling to mind unpunished crimes, urging the gods or an avenger to take up the cause of the wronged.

Female characters caught in the political upheavals depicted in the history plays often find themselves calling out for justice, as Lady Capulet does; to command attention, they use vivid rhetorical appeals, lament, and curses. Lady Constance in *King John* and the Duchess of Gloucester in *Richard II* possess intelligence, moral fervor, and a political cause. They are widows, so they find themselves the lone defenders of their family's claim at court. Yet they both, of necessity, must solicit vengeance from a male power, for their agency only goes so far in the public world dominated by men. The Duchess of Gloucester enters the world of *Richard II* briefly to give voice to a dimension of women's experience otherwise ignored and to make intimately known the powerlessness of wronged parties when the revenge target is untouchable. She dominates the play's second scene—her only scene—appearing in a sympathetic light as a mourning widow; her passionate words are meant to spur Gaunt, brother of the murdered Thomas of Woodstock, Duke of Gloucester, to revenge. In his imaginative construction of a royal widow's lament and appeal for vengeful action, Shakespeare rejects Holinshed, who depicted Gaunt and York planning revenge against Richard. In doing so, he strategically replays the conflict from the first scene of the play in another key. The Duke of Mowbray and Duke of Hereford have just appeared before King Richard with a dispute that has touched their honor; the hidden impetus for their conflict, however, derives from their frustrated desire to see justice done for the Duke of Gloucester's murder. They are driven to target each other because the true target of their just revenge is untouchable. Richard II is the guilty party, yet to accuse the king of a crime is treason and a disavowal of the very ties that ensure their honor. As the divinely anointed monarch, Richard represents unquestionable authority and honor that take precedence over any other earthly forms. In theory, all honor in a Christian patriarchal state emanates from God through the king to his subjects. As Julian Pitt-Rivers explains, "The political significance of the sacred is that it arbitrates questions of value, lays the limits to what can be done or maintained without sacrilege and defines the unconditional allegiances of the members of a society. Authority as political power claims always to be a moral authority, and the word therefore enjoys the same duality as honour from the moment that the legitimacy of the use of force is disputed."[24] The Duchess's role as a lamenter and inciter expresses the political subject's helpless rage in the face of an untouchable "moral authority."

The second scene stages an intimate encounter between Gloucester's grieving widow and his brother, Gaunt, refracting political actions through the domestic realm. The Duchess's sole purpose in life lies in avenging her husband's death, and she chooses Gaunt, the closest male kin, to avenge the murder. While he feels the desire "To stir against the butchers" (1.2.3) of his brother's life, Gaunt resists taking such action because "those hands / Which made the fault" (1.2.4–5) are King Richard's, and he must correct it. Leave vengeance to God, he exclaims: "Put we our quarrel to the will of heaven, / Who, when they see the hours ripe on earth, / Will rain hot vengeance on offenders' heads" (1.2.6–8). The Duchess responds to such a seemingly passive, helpless position with taunting words meant to shame him into action: "Finds brotherhood in thee no sharper spur? / Hath love in thy old blood no living fire?" (1.2.9–10). The Duchess may have no bloody token to thrust upon Gaunt, but she can use potent words to appeal to blood and make him see blood, his family's blood, splattered and tainted by this murder. She aspires to be the sharp spur he lacks. She clarifies the ethical light in which she perceives Gaunt's position: a shameful wrong has been done to the royal family and his own brother; such a crime, such a dishonor, must not go unavenged. Gaunt is old, however, as she emphasizes twice. In blood-feud literature and ancient Greek tragedy, the old, having lost their strength and vitality, were generally sidelined when it came to revenge and battle, so she plays upon the symbolism of blood, exclaiming how Gaunt's blood should be on fire to seek his brother's killer.

Her rhetorical questions serve as the opening move in a long, stylized speech, inspired by indignation and an elemental sense of justice. Her figurative language depicts Edward III as the royal tree and his seven sons as branches, but more potently as seven vials of blood, both images leading to figures of violation and violence—the royal son and brother has been "cracked, and all the precious liquor spilt"; "hacked down . . . / By Envy's hand and Murder's bloody axe" (1.2.19, 20–21). Gaunt's duty to avenge this desecration of the royal family is a sacred one. She urges Gaunt's empathetic identification with the corpse: "Ah, Gaunt, his blood was thine! . . . Yet art thou slain in him" (lines 22, 25). Furthermore, since father and son share the same blood (and are one flesh), she argues that a failure to avenge a brother's death is as good as consenting to his father's death. She appeals, as well, directly to Gaunt's individual sense of honor granted by his nobility. To leave his brother's death unavenged is to teach "stern Murder how to butcher thee" (line 32). A nobleman's refusal to protect himself and his kin is cowardice.

This highly charged argument to revenge is met with Gaunt's reassertion of King Richard's guilt and his allegiance to God's deputy:

> God's is the quarrel, for God's substitute,
> His deputy anointed in His sight,
> Hath caused his death, the which *if wrongfully*,
> Let heaven revenge, for I may never lift
> An angry arm against His minister.
>
> (1.2.37–41, my emphasis)

The telling phrase in Gaunt's confession is "if wrongfully," a hedge that suggests Gaunt's political shrewdness. The Duchess sees all too clearly, from her perspective, what looks like Gaunt's fear and weak resolve. It would be a double sacrilege to kill God's earthly agent and usurp God's power in seeking his vengeance. No insult or ethical appeal can resolve the conflict Gaunt feels between the obligation to avenge a brother's death and his duty to the king. Furthermore, King Richard is his blood relative, his nephew, which only complicates matters further for Gaunt. The Duchess responds with resignation, perhaps mixed with contempt: "Where then, alas, may I complain myself?" (line 42). Her shift from naming Gaunt as the defender of family honor, the male kin upon whom she has pinned all of her hopes, to "I" and "myself" indicates with simple clarity that she is alone in her pursuit of justice. Bound by his allegiance to king and God, Gaunt can tell her only to appeal to God, "the widow's champion and defence" (line 43). Richard Levin hears a "parodic rendering of orthodoxy" in this advice, for these lines reflect "the mentality of a docile schoolboy," which would have sounded ludicrous to an Elizabethan audience listening to a great Plantagenet.[25] If Levin's insight is correct, we might conclude that Gaunt has a private agenda, which may include revenge at some future point. Yet how is the Duchess to know Gaunt's intentions, if they remain undisclosed?

The Duchess is a tragic figure whose moment onstage is spent in futility. She invests her last ounce of fury in a curse, which conveys her hope for partial justice through judicial combat. The Duke of Hereford (Henry Bolingbroke) is set to fight the Duke of Mowbray, who, under orders from Richard, killed her husband. She wishes her "husband's wrongs" set "on Hereford's spear, / That it may enter butcher Mowbray's breast!" (1.2.47–48). The Duke of Hereford is the Duchess's kin, her nephew and Gaunt's son. In time, he will defeat Richard II and rise to become Henry IV. The Duchess, however, cannot know of his ultimate victory and her own vindication; thus, she loses heart. At the end of her speech to Gaunt, her grief overwhelms her and she begins to weep. She figures her sorrow and desolation in prophetic lines about her death. Her words constitute a lament, as she imagines herself dwelling in "empty lodgings and unfurnished walls, / Unpeopled offices, untrodden stones. . . . Desolate, desolate, will I hence and die!" (lines 68–69, 73). As Harry Keyishian puts it, with the Duchess's death and old Gaunt's soon after, we witness the "costs of revengelessness."[26]

Such costs are startlingly apparent in the political plight of Lady Constance, as well. Shakespeare's early historical drama *King John* presents a volatile political conflict involving rival claimants to the throne, political betrayal, and maternal power. While King John aggressively asserts his right to the throne, the young Arthur, John's nephew and the stronger claimant, must rely on his mother, Lady Constance, to defend his claim. Her tactic is to appeal to France's power to defend Arthur's right with arms

if necessary. Constance has the political shrewdness and rhetorical authority to incite Philip, King of France, to avenge her cause through bloody battle with England. In the opening dialogue of the play, an embassy asserts
that France backs Arthur's "most lawful claim," threatening "The proud
control of fierce and bloody war, / To enforce these rights so forcibly withheld" (1.1.9, 17–18). King John angrily cuts off the threat, promising to
avenge this political maneuver and defend his right with aggression: "Here
have we war for war, and blood for blood, / Controlment for controlment:
so answer France" (1.1.19–20). In his confrontation with France, King
John boldly proclaims his role as "God's wrathful agent" (2.1.87), justified
in making an enemy bleed.

Constance makes her first appearance onstage just before this hostile
confrontation. She asserts her presence in the political world of *King John*
with strong, effective appeals for political support. When she appears in the
second act, she and Arthur are given a ceremonial welcome from the Duke
of Austria before the wall of Angers. She cautions against unwarranted violence, in the hope that John will abdicate the throne. Immediately, however, she, France, and Austria hear that John is in arms; he arrives onstage
before them just as the ambassador finishes his speech.

A conflict between Queen Eleanor and Constance then arises, for both
are mothers of competing claimants to the English throne, and both have a
degree of power in manipulating the political scene. Constance is driven to
public professions of Arthur's right and accusations against the usurpers;
she attacks Eleanor with ferocious words. King Philip of France is clearly
disturbed by Constance's public attack upon the Queen, for he cries,
"Peace, lady! pause, or be more temperate: / It ill beseems this presence to
cry aim / To these ill-tuned repetitions" (2.1.195–97). Shortly after this
scene, Philip aligns himself with King John, betraying Constance and refusing to give legitimacy to Arthur's right. John seeks to "stop her exclamation" (line 558) by naming Arthur Duke of Britain, which only increases
her passion and grief. Constance's devastation at France's betrayal leads
her to figure herself onstage as an emblem of grief, enthroned as its
monarch. Yet she still has her tongue and her fire, for in the pivotal first
scene of act 3, she cries out, "War! war! no peace! peace is to me a war"
(line 39).

Too often, critics have viewed female characters such as the Duchess of
Gloucester and Constance as essentially powerless, sharing Vittoria's perception from John Webster's *The White Devil* that "woman's poor revenge /
... dwells but in the tongue" (3.2.283).[27] The assumption is that words are
impotent and "prevail not," to echo *The Spanish Tragedy,* in the world of
male-governed principles and actions.[28] Yet this view of the seeming
poverty of vengeful words alters when we consider the potency of words
when they operate as "performatives," to invoke J. L. Austin's concept.[29]

Curses, demands, and oaths are all utterances that perform the action implicit in language. Such speech acts alter reality and the equilibrium of listeners, linguistically enacting, as it were, the speaker's will, emotions, and ethics. Words can be accompanied by meaningful sounds and gestures, too, that produce emotional and physiological effects in listeners. When heard in performance, women's howling and wailing can have a devastating effect; such moving and bloodcurdling sounds can arouse fear and pity and give moral traction to women's position against injustice. The incantatory or spitting out effect of curses can be chilling and viscerally felt by a listener. There is indeed a special power in "a woman's war" waged through "The bitter clamour of . . . eager tongues" (1.1.48, 49), to cite Mowbray in *Richard II,* and such a power is conveyed spectacularly in the theater.

In ancient and medieval cultures, female lamentation was thought to be efficacious; women's wailing could pierce the heavens and call down divine vengeance. As discussed in the previous chapter, ancient Greek mythology imagined the terrifying Furies as a manifestation of curses and the divine answer to them. They embody a primitive drive for justice. The grieving Constance in *King John* may not receive a direct answer to her cries to the heavens for revenge—"Arm, arm, you heavens, against these perjur'd kings!" (3.1.33)—but her excessive, verbalized grief for her son's death defies and threatens those kings and earthly powers by memorializing Arthur, her son, as if he had been king. Placing Constance among the ancient female lament poets who were known as the kingmakers, Katharine Goodland argues that "Constance's impassioned words instill in our imaginations the image of Arthur as a king. Her laments magnify him in our minds and we begin to see this inexperienced and hesitant boy as England's rightful king."[30] Constance's oblique political threat constitutes a form of revenge made possible in the communal space of the theater where an audience becomes subliminally aware of the force exerted by the actor's performance. The affective ethics of revenge is expressed through the actor's vocal and bodily lamentation. Rebukes, curses, wailing, and weeping strike auditors on multiple levels—somatic, psychological, emotional, and moral.

Like Constance, the mourning widows in *Richard III* are often perceived by critics as impotent, even pathetic. The performance history of *Richard III* reflects a long-standing trend in muting the effect of the widows. Their lines are often reduced in number, and the character of Queen Margaret is sometimes cut, as she was long ago in Colley Cibber's revised text. Two well-known film versions of *Richard III,* the first directed by Laurence Olivier (1955) and the second by Richard Loncraine (1995), also dispensed with Margaret. The shared assumption of many directors and critics is that the women's cursing is impotent, repetitive, and paralyzing, a kind of annoying stopgap in the flow of historical action in the play. What can such wailing and cursing *do* in the political arena? The women are perceived as an embarrassment and an annoyance by critics who share the misery and irritation of most of the male characters in this and other dramas that feature clamorous, howling women. This perspective, however, fails to consider the collective symbolic, somatic, and ritual power of cursing, wailing, and lamenting past wrongs, especially as it strikes listeners' ears and eyes in the theater.

Curses were granted supernatural powers in early modern England, as they were in ancient Greece. A parent's curse, for example, was understood as a powerful, damning use of language meant to crush, disown, or even destroy, a child. In drama, parents invoke the Furies and any other destructive force they can think of when they curse their children. King Lear spares his daughters no horror in his curses, which are psychologically and morally shattering in their expressed malice: "Blasts and fogs upon thee!" he rages at Goneril, "Th'untented woundings of a father's curse / Pierce every sense about thee!" (Folio, 1.4.262–64). In productions of *King Lear*, the damaging effects of parental curses can be seen visibly on the actress's face and body. In Richard Eyre's 1998 production (BBC TV), Barbara Flynn's Goneril turns her back to Lear with tears in her eyes as she endures the assault of his curses. Lear strikes where she is most vulnerable: in her womb, and Flynn cringes as if she can feel the curses rendering her barren. He invokes Nature to suspend her purpose by conveying sterility into Goneril's womb. If Goneril must bear a child, he exclaims spitefully, it should be "a thwart disnatured torment to her" (line 245), just as Goneril is to him. These words convey the principle of harm for harm, pain for pain, but performance can show directly how pain can "[p]ierce every sense." Similarly, in Trevor Nunn's 2007 RSC production, Frances Barber's Goneril steels herself against the emotional trauma involved in confronting Lear and withstanding his curse. Yet she nearly cries while he is unleashing his fury, and once he departs, she is wracked with sobs, which she must work fiercely to control.

When the Duchess of York curses her son, Richard III, in the play of that title, he may, in one interpretation of the scene, appear shaken to the core. Certainly his loss of eloquence at this moment is revelatory; he can say only "So" (4.4.183) when the Duchess promises to "never speak to thee again" after her curse (line 182). When she says, "Bloody thou art; bloody will be thy end. / Shame serves thy life and doth thy death attend" (4.4.195–96), he is silenced. At this late point in the play, his fortunes are in decline. A mother's curse can only sharpen his sense that he is lost. The Duchess of York's curses, if granted their full potency, constitute an act of verbal revenge. Under Queen Margaret's and Queen Elizabeth's tutelage, she learns why calamity should "be full of words" (4.4.126)—"though what they will impart / Help nothing else, yet do they ease the heart" (4.4.130–31). The Duchess responds with determination:

If so, then be not tongue-tied; go with me
And in the breath of bitter words let's smother
My damned son, that thy two sweet sons smother'd.

(4.4.132–34)

Her formulation recalls the logic of *lex talionis:* the women's verbal smothering repays Richard's murderous smothering. Margaret and Elizabeth, too, intend their words to do more than curse or lament past wrongs. Elizabeth actually shapes the future by promising her daughter to Henry Tudor and thereby having a satisfying bloodless revenge on Richard III. Her wooing scene with Richard follows the scenes in which Margaret inspires the women's vengeful curses and the Duchess curses her son. Her encounter with Richard may be seen as a tour-de-force performance of revenge as, first, she counters virtually every move he makes in wooing, and, second, she deceives him into believing that she has succumbed to his despicable courtship of her daughter. The realization of Elizabeth's intentions becomes stunningly clear when Stanley informs the audience minutes later through a priestly messenger that "the Queen hath heartily consented / He [Richmond] should espouse Elizabeth her daughter" (4.5.7–8). These lines confirm that Elizabeth's conspiratorial revenge has been borne out in performance.

Some critics view the Duchess of Gloucester, Constance, and other lamenting, cursing females as guilty of "excessive" grief, even "fanaticism."[31] This charge may stem from our modern discomfort with passionate displays of feeling for the dead. Our modern sensibilities have suppressed physical acts of mourning (such as lashing one's face), inconsolable grief, persistent mourning, and urges for revenge. Our sensibilities, however, are not far from those of Shakespeare's contemporaries. Katharine Goodland argues perceptively that the representation of passionate "mourning embodies early modern English culture's ambivalence over mourning widows, theories of vengeance, and the consolations of church dogma."[32] When Richard Levin calls the Duchess of Gloucester "comically inept" in her attempt to draw out the whetting of Gaunt's vengeance, he mistakes the central functions of the grief-stricken goading women, which is to make death matter, to critique the political world of men in an oblique fashion, and to give audiences an emotionally intense experience that is otherwise unavailable in the political arena depicted in these plays.[33] It is important to realize that while the Duchess exits the stage to die pitifully, she has had a moment in the spotlight to give voice to injustice, much as Ophelia does in her devastating mad scene in *Hamlet*. To render her a fanatic in performance or in criticism is to reduce her subversive moral force in the play. She makes Gaunt and the theater's spectators painfully aware of the corrupt ties that bind a tyrant's subjects. In her grief, she vehemently articulates an elemental sense of wrong, which finds an echoing voice in both male and female characters inhabiting Richard II's oppressed realm. While it will be a powerful male, Bolingbroke, who defeats Richard, a helpless female makes clear that there is moral justification for such a daring act.

This gendered dynamic in Shakespeare's drama is evident in his major revenge tragedies, *Hamlet* and *Titus Andronicus*. Seemingly helpless female characters—Ophelia, Gertrude, and Lavinia—convey through various theatrical means the damage done to the state, the family, and women by political corruption and male violence. Their characters can be difficult to get a handle on, as their rhetoric and stage actions form a somewhat obscured narrative. In the cases of Ophelia and Lavinia, disturbing vocal sounds, moans, and lamentation, as well as aggressive, even grotesque, physical movement, mark their performances as disjointed—painful to hear and watch, but nonetheless spellbinding. Through disquieting performances signaled in the texts and borne out on the stage, disenfranchised tragic females make their ethical appeals. The following chapter will focus on the revenge causes of these female characters: how their bodies and voices bear the grief, madness, and trauma of their times, and how they incite powerful males to seek just revenge.

3

Reporting the Women's Causes Aright: Wounded Names and Revenge Narratives in *Hamlet, Titus Andronicus,* and *Much Ado About Nothing*

Aᴛ ᴛʜᴇ ᴇɴᴅ ᴏꜰ *ʜᴀᴍʟᴇᴛ,* ꜱʜᴀᴋᴇꜱᴘᴇᴀʀᴇ'ꜱ ᴍᴏꜱᴛ ꜱᴜʙᴛʟᴇ ᴇɴɢᴀɢᴇᴍᴇɴᴛ with revenge tragedy, Hamlet pleads with Horatio to "report me and my cause aright/ To the unsatisfied," "To tell my story," which he hopes will repair his "wounded name, / Things standing thus unknown" (5.2.323–24, 333, 328–29). He realizes that after death he may be as unappeased as his father was, his reputation an equivocal tale on every tongue, his honor sullied, his actions misconstrued. He anticipates that the Danish kingdom and the peacefully invading Norwegians will want satisfaction—to hear a story that will damn or redeem Hamlet's name. The public's vengefulness will wound his name further, he fears, by making him infamous, rather than heroic. Hamlet dies in fear of history's revenge or, equally as devastating, silence, forgetting, eternal extinction.

When Horatio describes the nature of the Prince's tale, it sounds shockingly lurid, a melodramatic Italianate revenge tale that eludes the complexity of Hamlet's experience:

> So shall you hear
> Of carnal, bloody and unnatural acts,
> Of accidental judgements, casual slaughters,
> Of deaths put on by cunning, and for no cause,
> And in this upshot purposes mistook
> Fallen on th'inventors' heads. All this can I
> Truly deliver.
>
> (5.2.364–70)

Horatio's surprising appeal to motifs from conventional revenge stories rather than unique features of Hamlet's "life" highlights the dominant ethos and sensationalistic appeal of the genre Shakespeare worked so assiduously to deconstruct. Audiences at Shakespeare's play may experience this moment as ironic, and even recoil from Horatio's words, feeling their supreme injustice. Such a speech is designed to give pause. In reflection, we must acknowledge that not even Horatio, Hamlet's confidant, could "Truly deliver" Hamlet's story. The only authentic representation of the character Hamlet lies in our experience of Shakespeare's drama-in-performance and in the text, which itself offers a narrative lying beyond the total grasp of any given director, spectator, or reader.[1]

Horatio's speech represents not so much a failure, then, as it does a reminder of the limited and provisional nature of all narratives, and perhaps of how narrators and listeners cleave to norms and conventions, even unconsciously. Furthermore, his crude attempt to frame Hamlet's cause reminds us implicitly of the other causes in the play that need to be told rightly to the unsatisfied, other wounded names in need of vindication. Among them might be those of Gertrude and Ophelia. A storm of critics have seized upon the task of telling Hamlet's story, and some, too, have attempted to "report" the female characters "aright." I join with these critics in my own attempt to satisfy the women's unappeased souls by telling their obscured stories—or at least providing a satisfying narrative that does more justice to the women than Hamlet's friend does to him.[2] My argument will be, to some extent, a vindication of *Hamlet*'s women as I attend to the broken threads of their narratives. I wish to illustrate how the women deepen our awareness of the central ethical questions of the play, which I take to be: How should the dead be remembered? How do the demands of the dead shape the agency, actions, and being of the living, echoing through them, even as they become the dead? What is the relationship between mourning and revenge? Is revenge self-obliterating, or self-defining? Can revenge be . . . an act of love?

To all appearances, Shakespeare's *Hamlet* is a story of fathers and sons, yet neither fathers nor sons exist without wives, mothers, daughters, and lovers. Hamlet dominates the main plot in the text, in theatrical productions, and in much of the literary criticism on the play, but the female characters prove central to Shakespeare's subtle handling of the ethical tensions at the heart of revenge tragedy. Remove the women, and the play loses some of its depth and ethical potency. Ophelia and Gertrude exist within a corrupt state, where gender constraints give them little defense and few choices in response to harm, threatened violence, and injustice. Before their tragic ends, though, both women will undergo transformations that enable them to promote justice and appeal to others for appeasement. While Ophelia can do so once freed from the socially determined behaviors and restrained speech of a young, rational female, Gertrude will make a choice that takes her life, but enables her son to pursue vengeance as a political necessity and an act of justice. Ophelia and Gertrude participate actively in a culture where honor and shame define the perimeters of selfhood. Both women are reduced to shameful conditions and seek to regain honor for themselves and their beloved kin by inciting revenge.

Ophelia's performance shows us how a sorrowing daughter remembers her father: she runs mad for grief and laments openly before a king and queen who refuse the ethical plenitude of mourning. In her madness and in her grave, she sounds the conscience of the kingdom. If Denmark becomes a figurative grave, the stage literally opens up to become Ophelia's grave. Her body disappears into the same liminal space (the trapdoor) from which the Ghost appears. The two figures—female lamenter and ghost—are deeply connected, I will argue; they both seek appeasement and incite revenge from the living.[3] Gertrude's performance shows us how the remorseful wife, mother, and queen quietly finds a mode of protest in response to the pollution of the kingdom and of her own person. She will love and be silent in the end, but for one act of disobedience that makes all the difference for how the play ends and how her character's function in the drama is to be understood.

Like the Ghost, Gertrude and Ophelia both appear as unappeased grievants. And like the Player Queen, they both will make "*passionate action*" (3.2.128.7) when they are compelled by an inward sense of grief, injustice, or remorse. They bear tragic elements through their bodies and voices, calling in whatever manner they can for rest for their own tormented spirits and those of the men they love. Like a figure from classical Greek tragedy, Ophelia embodies the spirit of damage and moral debt. Her performance is so affecting because she is the sign of sacrificed innocence and disrupted life and death cycles, which must be acknowledged and atoned for in tragedy. Her open, wild grief and passionate actions appall the eyes and ears of the guilty, bringing their awareness to their own spiritual debt and the ways personal and state corruption destroy everything of value. She is the touchstone of truth in the play: she shows us that death brings grief, and grief can be a kind of madness that steals life. Her irrational state of being reflects a fundamental loss of self. Revenge belongs in this wild company: Hamlet knows it and fears it. Thus, he tries to tame grief, wear a mask of madness, and rationalize revenge. Ophelia, in contrast, embodies the dark, eddying recesses of the mind overwhelmed by pain.

Ophelia's significance in *Hamlet* is signaled through polyvalent resonances in her name. Ophelia's name defines not simply her intended (or lost) gender role and social function, but her connection to the ethical and tragic core of the play. One set of meanings clustered in her name suggests her positive womanly and spiritual functions: the Greek *ophéleia* means "use, help, support," "profit," or "succor," and *ophelos* means "advantage."[4] Ophelia's desire to follow the inherent meaning of her name by loving and succoring Hamlet seems cruelly obliterated, first by her father's disapproval, then by Hamlet's repulsion. In a play where designations such as "king," "mother," "father," and "son," are punctured and lose substance, Ophelia loses her name-given ability to give and receive succor. Yet another set of meanings inheres in the rich pun of her name: *opheilema* means debt, spiritual obligation, offense, or sin.[5] Thus, Hamlet says, "The fair Ophelia! Nymph, in thy orisons / Be all my sins remembered" (3.1.88–89), as if her name instinctively calls to mind the Lord's Prayer. In the Greek prayer, the phrase is "forgive us our *opheilema*" and in Old English, following the Latin, "forgive us our *debitum*." The Geneva Bible reads: "And forgiue vs our dettes, as we also forgiue our detters" (Matt. 6:12). Ophelia's name, then, calls to mind debts, sins, offenses needing forgiveness . . . and revenge, for what is revenge, but a canceling of debt. As William Ian Miller argues, historically justice has to do with paying back debts and settling accounts with one's neighbors and with one's god.[6] Hamlet wishes Ophelia to call up his sins, and in doing so to call up his sinful duty to revenge, and to take that debt upon herself, to forgive it; his offenses are great, he knows, and he will burst out with a partial confession to Ophelia in the nunnery scene, which includes identifying himself as "revengeful" (3.1.124). His asking to be remembered echoes his father's ghost's plea. Hamlet's violent railing against Ophelia suggests that he believes she fails him and can provide no spiritual succor. Yet, in a most profound sense, she can be understood to be remembering his spiritual debts and those of the other sinful characters in her person, in her lamentation, and in her death.

If we continue to gaze at her name, as if through a glass darkly, we might find intimations of the serpent (*ophis*),[7] which seems an odd and tenuous connection to make, until we find our clues, which point to how this shard in her name reflects her distant relationship with the Furies. First, we might recall the trope of venomous tongues used by the Player in his tribute to the unfortunate, weeping Hecuba: *"Who this had seen, with tongue in venom steeped, / 'Gainst Fortune's state would treason have pronounced"* (2.2.448–49). Ophelia, too, in her fashion speaks out against Fortune's estate, but the venom in her tongue derives from "the poison of deep grief" (4.5.75). Ophelia's effect on Laertes recalls the Orestean myth, which involves the wrathful justice of the Furies, who are depicted by Aeschylus as dreadful creatures entwined with snakes. We should recall that these ancient feminine goddesses fiercely guard the bonds of reciprocity, or *philia* (once again, we hear Ophelia's name), that maintain the moral health of social relations between kin. They rise up when kin-blood is shed and oaths are broken; they pursue punishment; they "make death matter in living relationships," as Ruth Padel argues, and in this respect they are essential figures of tragedy.[8]

In Ophelia's mad distress, Laertes hears the call to vengeance, as if she were a latter-day Fury, and he responds in grief and anger. Like Electra, the grieving daughter of the slain Agamemnon, Ophelia lives for the day when

"My brother shall know of it" (4.5.70)—namely, the wrong done to their father: "I hope all will be well. We must be patient. But I cannot choose but weep to think they would lay him i'th'cold ground" (4.5.68–70). These lines seem especially ambiguous, pointing in one direction toward Christian virtue and in another toward the classical position of the sisterly inciter. Implicit here may be the hope that Laertes will be the returning son, the avenging Orestes, who will make all well for Ophelia by enacting the revenge that she cannot. Through her grief-stricken consciousness, which brings on madness, Ophelia works upon Laertes' passions, as Electra did with Orestes. She hands him rosemary, insisting, "Pray you, love, remember. And there is pansies: that's for thoughts" (lines 170–71). Her words echo the Ghost's injunction to "remember me" (1.5.91). Remembrance is tied explicitly to thoughts of death and revenge in the play, and Ophelia's call to Laertes to remember her father's wrongful death and burial makes a claim for the second revenge cause in the drama without being explicit, especially about who the target should be.

Far from impotent, then, Ophelia treads the spiritual geography between revenge and forgiveness, spiritual debt and the cancellation of such debt. Through her irrational state, she is constructing an oblique revenge narrative. She performs the role of inciter to vengeance through a kind of broken ritual lamentation. Laertes' response to her lamentation is as fierce as Hamlet's was when he was tormented by the Ghost's tale. He exclaims vehemently, "Hadst thou thy wits and didst persuade revenge / It could not move thus" (4.5.163–64). Although Ophelia does not possess the full intentionality or rational discourse of the Greek dramatists' Electra or express herself with the logical narrative features we hear in the Ghost's tale, her distraught appearance and suggestive language in her final scene give her, at the very least, the *function* of inciter to her father's revenge. And her words, song snatches, and gestures reverberate with some level of knowingness as they strike her audience's consciousness. The effects of her mad scene (4.5) are intended to be devastating and transformative in the watching characters, for in the desolation of an innocent girl the kingdom sees the embodiment of harm's effects, which inspires moral reflection in some, and decisive action in others. Laertes is drawn into conspiracy with Claudius, which leads to the final duel / revenge-taking scene, and Gertrude finds one more grief to add to her store of moral spurs to some action yet unknown.

During the course of the play, Ophelia's honor is cruelly compromised, as is her natural impulse to love. Polonius chastises her for loving Hamlet, insisting that she has failed to conduct herself "As it behoves my daughter and your honour" (1.3.96). He then proceeds to exploit her honor altogether by placing her in a false position so that he can spy on Hamlet. In the nunnery scene, Hamlet bitterly attacks her chastity and maligns her beauty, then continues to pollute her innocence with his provocative wordplay on "country matters" at the play (3.2.110). Once her father has been killed, grief and lack of her brother, or any support, drive her to the far end of despair—into madness and death. Importantly, though, Ophelia's plight triggers the eruption of guilt and shame in Gertrude, Claudius, and Laertes, and perhaps this is what she wishes to effect in others. Ophelia's roles as obedient daughter, loving sister, incapacitated lover, and mad girl place her in a highly sympathetic light. Her character, however, has too frequently been taken by critics simply as an object of pathos and victimization. What has not been sufficiently understood is how Ophelia's responses to grievous injuries to her integrity, from her early distraught account of Hamlet's antic behavior in her closet to her brief soliloquy at the end of the nunnery scene to her disjointed lamentation before the court, give voice—if only briefly—to her sense of injustice and the "pangs of despised love" (3.1.71). Her voice expresses the inward broken condition she endures, and provokes strong feelings of guilt, sorrow, shame, and vengeance in her auditors. Claudius is struck with pity for the girl and feels "battalions" of sorrows mounting in the kingdom (4.5.79). The political threat Laertes represents, which causes Claudius to feel a "superfluous death" (line 96), will only be strengthened by the brother's witnessing of his sister's state.

Ophelia's purpose emerges once she is freed from conventional feminine modesty, obedience, and sanity. Harry Keyishian is surely right when he detects accusation and protest in her songs and passionate speech in 4.5. He attributes a kind of agency to her in this scene, but he ultimately argues that she "lacks the physical and emotional resources to redeem her situation; she simply falls apart, and in her collapse, she demonstrates that though revenge may be dangerous and destructive, impotence is worse."[9] Yet her effect, as Keyishian himself demonstrates, is not that of impotence at all. Every aspect of her performance—her "distracted" appearance, songs, movement, distribution of flowers, punning language, and symbolic appeal—displays ritualistically a potent and poignant laying of blame at the feet of the powerful and, when witnessed by her only living male kin, her brother Laertes, she kindles revenge. Her lamentation, for that is what we should call it, recognizes the "rights of memory" (5.2.373) and, like her Greek forbears, she takes on a traditional feminine role to make the rights of the dead, of memory, felt strongly.

In her liminal state of mourning and madness, Ophelia generates her own fragmented plea for remembering the father and finding justice for his death. Her song snatches, "half sense" speech (4.5.7), "noise" (line 152), and acoustical puns exert their force ethically and politically. Though "Her speech is nothing," as a gentleman reports, "Yet the unshaped use of it doth move / The hearers to collection. They yawn at it / And botch the words up fit to their own thoughts . . ." (4.5.7–10). Like Hamlet's Mousetrap, her performance catches the conscience of her hearers. When Laertes witnesses her "document in madness" (line 172), as he calls it, he finds something "more than matter" (line 168) in her performance. He sees and hears in Ophelia's suffering an outrage that must be answered. Her "document," or lesson, teaches him how profoundly destabilizing and dishonoring the effects of wrongful death and a father's maimed funeral rites are, and how ethically obliged he is to repay such transgressions. For Laertes, the sight of Ophelia is shocking and inspires shame. He cannot bear to see her, and wishes to blind himself, to burn up the sense and function of his eyes: "O heat, dry up my brains, tears seven times salt / Burn out the sense and virtue of mine eye" (4.5.153–55). Almost instantly his thoughts turn to revenge. Ophelia revives in her brother the same kind of rage that kindles Orestes' vengefulness at his father's grave site. The secretive, shameful treatment of their father in death "Cr[ies] to be heard as 'twere from heaven to earth" (4.5.208). Ophelia's cry voices the unheard father's cry from the grave.

What becomes apparent in Ophelia's scene is that her funerary lamentation did not cease at her father's grave site, and with good reason. Her songs convey the pained memory of the funeral and its lack of noble rite and appropriate ostentation:

> He is dead and gone, lady,
> He is dead and gone.
> At his head a grass-green turf,
> At his heels a stone.
>
> (4.5.29–32)

> Larded all with sweet flowers
> Which bewept to the ground did not go
> With true-love showers.
>
> (lines 38–40)

> They bore him bare-faced on the bier
> And in his grave rained many a tear.
>
> (lines 160–61)

As Leslie C. Dunn argues, "the discourse of music has a privileged place" in the play, and it is Ophelia who is most intimately associated with music.[10] The female singer in her sweetness, brokenness, and raw self-exposure becomes a site of resistance—no one can avert their eyes, or stop up their ears in her presence. Her mourning violates the decorum of the court, disturbing all who hear her "broken voice" (2.2.491). Her songs disrupt and resist the authority of the sane and their social pretensions. Claudius and Gertrude try to break in, to contain her or bring her to her senses, but she continues on insistently. The effect of Ophelia's presence—

of the "sweet bells jangled out of time and harsh" (3.1.157)—is more disquieting than that of Hamlet's "antic" presence, because it is unquestionably authentic and not a mask for something else. Her visible and vocal display of trauma, of pain and mental distraction, evokes truth and introspection about the "rotten" state of Denmark. Those watching her find they are capable of being moved, of weeping, of feeling an inward passion that cries out against injustice.

Her performance resonates with that of another dramatic mourning female —the fallen Trojan queen, Hecuba—whose passionate grief is partially enacted by the Player through his vivid recitation.[11] Hamlet has anticipated hearing the Player tell Aeneas's tale to Dido about the fall of Troy. Hamlet starts the recitation himself with "*The rugged Pyrrhus like th' Hyrcanian beast*" (2.2.388), only he has misremembered the simile, inserting the infamous tiger image, perhaps because it matches his sense of Pyrrhus's pitilessness. The Player takes over, speaking in the persona of Aeneas. The Player's description of the raging, remorseless Pyrrhus offers an appallingly brutal double for Hamlet. Such a portrait is derived from epic poetry, which immortalizes the warrior male's honor achieved through battle glory and bloodshed. Hamlet's mind cannot help but recoil from this model; indeed, he is transfixed by Pyrrhus's pause before his furious slaughtering of Priam (there are seven beats of silence in the line that reads "Did nothing"). This hushed moment distills the pause that will come to define Hamlet's ethical being. His imagination, then, rushes toward another image distilled in the vision of a suffering female whose terrible fortune is witnessed by the weeping eyes of the gods themselves: "Say on, come to Hecuba" (2.2.439).

If the frightening specter of the male avenger striking down his victim has been the spectacular focus of the first part of the Trojan narrative, the pathos-inspiring image of the lamenting female shifts the focus to violence's aftermath in the second part:

> *But who—ah woe—had seen the mobled queen. . . .*
> *—Run barefoot up and down, threatening the flames*
> *With bisson rheum . . .*
> *Who this had seen, with tongue in venom steeped,*
> *'Gainst Fortune's state would treason have pronounced.*
> *But if the gods themselves did see her then,*
> *When she saw Pyrrhus make malicious sport*
> *In mincing with his sword her husband limbs,*
> *The instant burst of clamour that she made*
> *(Unless things mortal move them not at all)*
> *Would have made milch the burning eyes of heaven*
> *And passion in the gods.*

(2.2.440, 443–44, 448–56)

This moving rhetorical picture of Hecuba inspires tears and a change in color in the Player's face as he speaks. At a number of removes from Hecuba, he nonetheless can feel pity for her as he observes her in his mind's eye and makes articulate the depth of her grief through his forceful rhetoric.

In ancient poetry and drama and their Renaissance adaptations, Hecuba appears as an aged figure in a state of profound suffering, loss, and even madness. In Ovid's *Metamorphoses,* which Shakespeare clearly echoes here, Hecuba's misfortune moves all those who witness her mad grief. The "ruthe" inspired by Hecuba breaks through enemy lines (Greeks and Trojans alike are moved) and the invisible boundary between the gods and mankind: "her lot / Did move even all the Goddes to ruthe" (Golding's translation, 13.686–87). She is presented by Ovid and later writers as the archetype of human misfortune and suffering. In her study of Euripides' *Hecuba,* Judith Mossman calls Hecuba "the archetype of extreme unhappiness and misfortune from antiquity onwards. . . . [H]er sorrow [has been] used to illumine countless other tragedies."[12] In Jasper Heywood's translation of Seneca's *Troas,* he has Hecuba transform herself into just such an archetype. She laments:

> What ever mans calamatyes ye wayle for myne it is.
> I beare the smart of al their woes, each other feeles but his
> Who ever he, I am the wretch all happes to me at last.
>
> (act 5)

Richard Rainolde's well-known schoolbook *The Foundation of Rhetoric* (1563) includes an oration given by Hecuba after the destruction of Troy that exhibits the rhetorical trope of *ethopoeia,* an expression of the affections and mind of the speaker. The speech emphasizes, and universalizes, the fall of mighty kingdoms and the tragic misfortune of monarchs, then shifts to Hecuba's wounded heart and loss of Hector, and finally gives way to a repetitious rhetoric of pathos: "woe" and "doleful" resound throughout the latter half of the oration.[13]

The Player's tears for Hecuba register strongly upon Hamlet's mind, yet they seem puzzlingly premised on "nothing": "What's Hecuba to him, or he to her, / That he should weep for her?" (2.2.494–95). What would the actor do if he had something of substance, something real, to recite? Hamlet wonders. In a moment of imaginative, mimetic contest, Shakespeare has Hamlet substitute his own story of woe for Hecuba's. In Hamlet's mind, Hecuba's story, as piteous as it is, pales in comparison with his own outrageous, tragic tale. The actor would not simply tear up over Hamlet's tragedy; he would "drown the stage with tears / And cleave the general ear with horrid speech, / Make mad the guilty and appal the free . . ." (lines

497–99). Hamlet responds as audience to his own drama, identifying with the actor's excessive tears, and imagining the audience's horror and madness upon hearing the speech. In Hamlet's deflection of passion and weeping into a theatrical fantasy, the soliloquy obliquely suggests Hamlet's inability to weep freely for his father, for himself, and for Denmark—his inability to *be* Hecuba, or to be fully moved by grief.[14] He feels an anguished detachment from himself, from his own grief, and the fantasy of the weeping actor and moved audience gets at this. The obligation to avenge his father weighs on him as a burden that only further estranges him from any authentic or healing response to death. The cries of Hecuba will resound subliminally in his mind and in the kingdom, but they will burst forth in the voice of Ophelia, for the figure of Hecuba is reanimated later in the tragedy, not through another wife's lament or Hamlet's own, but rather through the sounds and sight of the grieving Ophelia, who appears in the flesh, speaking directly to her earthly witnesses, provoking strong passions and tears. Hamlet will not be witness to this live scene of grief, for he will be physically absent from the kingdom when Ophelia runs mad with grief for *her* dead father.

Ophelia refracts Hecuba's lament through a *daughter's* "burst of clamour," admonishing all those who bear witness to her grief-stricken form and hear her voice to remember the wrongs that have been committed in Denmark. Furthermore, just as Hecuba's speech offers a model for spontaneous grief and an appropriate feeling response—indeed, a just response—to wrongs, Ophelia functions as a model of affective ethics, responding feelingly to injustice and evoking strong responses from others. Grief is wild, unbounded feeling and sound, the ancient tale proclaims. The weeping Hecuba whose tears might almost put out the flames, runs barefoot, and then bursts forth with a terrible cry upon seeing Priam cut to pieces by the hellish, blood-covered Pyrrhus. Those who bear witness to such a scene might with venomous tongues justly cry treason against cruel Fortune and weep for the fallen queen.

Ritual mourning is left to Ophelia, perhaps because only she, "in the archaic recesses of her 'madness,'" and through her intimate contact with the dark, unpredictable forces of myth, can offer the authentic bodily and vocal wildness of a Hecuba.[15] Only she can enter into the liminal state of lamentation, which seems implicitly forbidden and threatening to the Danish kingdom. As Susan Letzler Cole suggests, Ophelia shows us that "mourning is merely madness in the deadened world of *Hamlet*."[16] Mourning, too, seems to be gendered feminine, in keeping with traditional cultural practices and literary conventions of the lament genre. The lament immortalizes women's absolute, inconsolable grief, while at the same time keeping the presence of the dead among the living, conferring remembrance upon them. Lamentation in classical Greece and Protestant England, alike, was perceived as a civic danger, associated with madness or Dionysiac possession, and a threat to the authority and stability of the state. Communion with the dead was perceived as fearsome, potentially unruly, and threatening to the living (especially the guilty ones), and lament could inspire revenge when a wrongful death had taken place. Here is a performative "genre" and social practice that gives women incalculable powers—authority over the dead, a prominent place in funeral rites, and the ability to incite revenge.[17]

Significantly, Ophelia's lamentation invades a political space with indecorous, provocative song. She may be "distract" (mad), but "She is importunate," or persistent, and demanding to be heard (4.5.2). This indecorousness points to the "strange eruption" (1.1.68) in the state and its infection by sin; her madness erupts in Claudius's castle, the site of the state. Thus, her strange eruption before king, queen, and courtiers emblematizes the estrangement of the Danes from honor and justice, and from the ethical treatment of the dead through lament and funeral rites. As a "figure of *song*" and of madness, Ophelia alone carries "the burden of all the unexpressed grief in the play, becoming the real thing" as no other character in the play is free to be.[18] Only in fiction and madness do the bereaved have license to mourn the dead rightly.

While Hecuba's woes provide a touchstone for Hamlet's and Ophelia's grief, the ancient queen's sorrowing image appears as fragmented as her tale, for there is more, far more, to the legend of Hecuba than appears in the Player's recitation, and Shakespeare's audience would know this. During the Renaissance, Hecuba was probably best known for her display of *maternal* sorrow, which readers encountered in translations of Euripides' *Hecuba,* Seneca's *Troas,* and Ovid's *Metamorphoses.* Euripides and Ovid represent Hecuba as an *avenger* who achieves wild justice for the brutal killing of her son before she is transformed into a stony bitch. Her legend suggests that the mother-son bond is the strongest of all bonds in nature; when she sees Polymestor's mutilated corpse in Euripides' play, she exclaims, "This kills me! Oh, what misery! I am alive no more, no more!" (lines 683–84).[19] An avenging spirit rises in her wild song of grief. No such grief cuts down the mother in *Hamlet.* This point is made chillingly evident in the second scene of the play when the bereaved Hamlet faces a seemingly contented mother and queen who commands him to raise his eyes from the dust where his "noble father" lies to the face of his uncle and "friend" Claudius (1.2.71, 69).

Those audience members in Shakespeare's theater who knew the legend of Hecuba would know that the Player's tale breaks off long before she is enslaved and driven to adopt the role of active avenger. They may have recalled that the lines referring to the gods' pity for Hecuba echo Ovid's lines in the *Metamorphoses,* which occur *after* she has taken revenge and become mad. Hamlet indicates he will "have thee speak out the rest of this soon" (2.2.459–60), which suggests he knows where her tale leads and wants to hear it, but in the play's text the rest remains silent. The swerving from Hecuba's vengeance—the rest of her story—is deliberate on Shakespeare's part at this moment in the play, for we are meant to focus on Hamlet's ambivalence about revenge and his fractured experience of grieving. As one of many occluded narratives in the play, Hecuba's story and its barely suppressed *muthos* express their dark, unruly matter on a subterranean level. Hamlet cannot lament as Hecuba does, nor does he consciously contemplate her brutal revenge upon King Polymestor. Hamlet's active grieving has been publicly criticized and suppressed by Claudius and Gertrude, and therefore driven inward, but the case could be put with equal force that his father's ghost has insisted upon a form of remembrance that is external, that imperils Hamlet's very being and distorts the natural grieving process.

The father's ghost directs Hamlet's fate, casting him as the avenging son in accordance with a traditional masculine prototype, but Hamlet languishes in that role, feeling drawn at least as much to the archetypal roles of women in classical revenge narratives. Indeed, rather than taking up the son's duty, as Pyrrhus and Orestes do, he starts to sink into the quicksand of unrelieved secret mourning. He wishes to outdo the Hecuba figure for whom the actor weeps, the Hecuba who inspires the pity of the gods, but in some respects he more closely resembles a famous classical daughter who is cast in an unnatural pause of her own. The Electra figure embodies waiting, enduring, grieving, social displacement, isolation, even madness —here we find a description of Hamlet's condition and his place in Elsinore. His peculiar conflict arises from an irony that plagues his situation: *he* is the avenger he waits for. And Hamlet is the avenger we wait for.

If Hamlet identifies with and inwardly competes with Hecuba's wild grief and shares a fundamental mode of being with Electra, he is not alone in this. The more subtle double, or second self, for Hamlet in this tragedy is Ophelia, the other Electra figure. Adrian Poole states the case well when he observes that Hamlet turns Ophelia "into an image of his own loss."[20] Hamlet's callous words and violent treatment of Ophelia are misdirected attempts at working out his own pain. Ophelia activates Electra's productive roles as libation bearer, dirge singer, and revenge inciter. Indeed, Ophelia's familial situation resembles Electra's as the inciting sister and grieving daughter of a father wrongly slaughtered, a father whose funeral was a shamefully quick, patched-up, hushed-up affair—"No trophy, sword nor hatchment o'er his bones, / No noble rite, nor formal ostentation" (4.5.206–7), as Laertes laments. Like Orestes, this son declares, "His means of death, his obscure funeral . . . Cry to be heard as 'twere from heaven to earth / That I must call't in question" (4.5.205, 208–9). Like Orestes, too, he is not troubled by the cause of the slaughter, the earlier death that occurs before the play—the death that stirred up the whole affair.

Louise Schleiner claims that there was a "strong likelihood" that Latin translations of Aeschylus's *Oresteia* and Euripides' *Orestes* exerted an influence on *Hamlet,* infusing the spirit of Greek drama into his dramatic texts.[21] Her persuasive argument, however, neglects to trace fully the significance of the Ophelia/Electra transposition. In a note, Schleiner points out that both daughters are "father dominated," but that unlike Electra, Ophelia does not show aggression against her father's enemies.[22] This is not altogether the case. Ophelia does indeed confront those she believes have become her father's foes. She gains entrance before the guilt-ridden Queen, despite Gertrude's refusal to see her. Ophelia insists twice that the Queen "mark" her (4.5.28, 35) and her song, which plaintively laments her father's death. We might recall that Hamlet's meeting with the Ghost commences with the word "mark," as well. In Gregory Doran's 2009 RSC *Hamlet,* Ophelia (Mariah Gale) fiercely turns on Gertrude and loudly yelps the word "mark." The unpredictable wildness in the actress's voice echoed the Ghost's barking order to Hamlet earlier in that production when he commanded his son to "mark." Thus, text and performance call attention to a shared function between Ophelia and the Ghost. Old Hamlet's death is conflated subliminally with Polonius's. Ophelia's approach to Gertrude is aggressive, carrying an implicit accusation against her, a royal power by whom Ophelia feels betrayed. Indeed, the sound and the sight of Ophelia call up in Gertrude and in Claudius, as well, the weight of their own "sick soul[s]" troubled with "guilt" (4.5.17, 19).

In Ophelia's "distracted" appearance and words in 4.5, Shakespeare revives the spirits of a classical Greek grieving mother *and* daughter, the maddened Hecuba and grief-tormented Electra. We might even detect in Ophelia the resonance of Cassandra, the mad priestess of Apollo who sees the woes of the world in vivid hallucinations. As Ophelia lamented earlier in response to Hamlet's "transformation," "O woe is me / T'have seen what I have seen, see what I see" (3.1.159–60). The textual and mythological resonances of classical lamenting females echo through the character of Ophelia and magnify Gertrude's refusal to grieve and her seeming indifference to Hamlet's suffering. Gertrude closes her eyes to Cassandra's visions, rejects Hecuba's part, and chooses instead a lustful marriage over grieving widowhood. Ophelia's songs for the Queen force her to see the consequences of her choices, which have been informed by willful blindness, political self-interest, and a strategic memory loss. While Ophelia shows the Queen—and us—the pitiable loss of self in mourning, we see, too, implied losses in the refusal to mourn. Where is the feeling part of Gertrude? Where does her integrity lie? While Hamlet attests to Gertrude's tears for his father, which fell as profusely as Niobe's for her dead children, he, like Ophelia, tries to sound the depths of the Queen's love, calling her to account. Where is that love now? Ophelia's first words in her mad scene are directed at Gertrude, though every character in the play, including the Ghost, might ask such a question, or have such a question thrust upon them: "How should I your true love know / From another one?" (4.5.23–24). Gertrude sheds no tears for young Hamlet, though she is profoundly disquieted when he approaches her in private, giving her an intimate taste of his fury and "madness." Ophelia's words, sung so movingly, must pierce the Queen, for she is fresh from that private scene with her son, deeply stirred, perhaps devastated, by Hamlet's appalling words about Claudius and the murder of her first husband.

When Claudius enters the scene, Ophelia greets him with veiled references to revenge, sin, and penance, which seem to echo Hamlet's antic wit: "Well, good dild you. They say the owl was a baker's daughter. Lord, we know what we are but know not what we may be. God be at your table" (4.5.42–44). "Good dild you" is a corruption of "God yield you" or "God reward you," a common expression of goodwill for those who are just; yet the phrase can be used more pointedly or subversively to express a desire for vengeance against those who are not just, as in "God requite you" or "God repay you."[23] The reference to the owl and the baker's daughter is to a folktale in which Jesus repays the daughter for refusing him an adequate loaf of bread by turning her into an owl.[24] She continues with another expression, which superficially extends goodwill: "God be at your table" (4.5.44). "Table" could be taken as a punning reference to the Ten Commandments, or any other tablet upon which the law is inscribed. It is a subliminal reminder, as well, of the Catholic communion table.[25] "Table" also reaches back to Hamlet's figure for memory and his writing tablet, where he records memory's rights. Figuratively, then, the reference seems to imply Claudius's need to recall his sins, to observe God's laws, and to do penance.

As for her own losses, Ophelia laments the maimed rites of her womanhood—no bride-bed or birthing-bed for her. Like Electra, her lamentation includes libations for her bridal, which finds its grim consummation in burial. Gertrude quietly laments this loss for Ophelia (and Hamlet) as she strews flowers upon the girl's corpse: "I thought thy bride-bed to have decked, sweet maid, / And not have strewed thy grave" (5.1.234–25). The Greek meaning of Electra's name (*a-lektra*) signifies "without a bed"; as Nicole Loraux comments, Electra's "procreative feminine force is diverted to the service of sorrow."[26] So, too, with Ophelia, a young woman whose natural feminine cycles are channeled into sorrowing and loss. She laments the broken condition of her being—of being itself—and the corruption of those she once trusted. For her father and the community, her lament insists on the finality of death: "He never will come again. . . . He is gone, he is gone, / And we cast away moan" (4.5.186, 189–90). The ambivalence of the phrase "cast away" reflects the possibility that her grieving is thrown away, yet equally that we are cast away, that we who are left in this cast-away world are left to grieve the departed. Her final words in the play pursue this relationship among the living, the dead, and the divine: "God a' mercy on his soul. / And of all Christians' souls. God buy you" (lines 191–92). This is her prayer for the Christian souls in Denmark's kingdom— God redeem you—and hearing it, Laertes cries out appalled, "Do you see this, O God?" (the Folio reads "gods"). This moment reaches back to the Player, Hecuba, and the gods: Will God/the gods not be moved to passion, to a passion for justice, in response to such a sight?

Ophelia's function in the drama reveals itself fully when she dies. Unlike the grave site in Aeschylus's *The Libation Bearers,* the grave site in *Hamlet* belongs to a woman and not a dishonored father-king. This seems a significant departure on Shakespeare's part from what was possibly his classical model. Why the mad girl's grave? Why stage the child's interment and not the murdered father's? If "the grave is the birthplace of tragic drama and ghosts are its procreators,"[27] then we come full circle in act 5, into the symbolic heart of tragedy. If the Ghost has risen from Old Hamlet's grave to give birth to tragedy, we find ourselves lowered into the grave with the body of the newly dead as our tragic consciousness and that of the characters intensify. With Ophelia's indecorous mourning at court, she brings the rituals of the grave into the castle. The eerie liminality of the Ghost gives shape to an in-between state of being, and Ophelia embodies the liminal consciousness of the ritual lamenter gone mad. Now dead, the mad girl has brought the court out to the grave. There she lies in the ground, at the very ground of being and truth, at the disquieting heart of the play in that ambivalent space between the living and the dead. Her death, like her mourning song, resonates in the souls of the guilty and the ashamed, the loving and the vengeful. They will all be driven to passionate commitment when confronted with her grave, and their joint commitment will be to revenge.

When Ophelia is placed in the ground, the shock of her death registers first in subdued notes, and then in the passionate outbursts of Laertes and Hamlet. A shocked Hamlet notes the "maimed rites" of the funeral (5.1.208). A shocked Laertes laments three times the dishonoring of the dead with inadequate rites: "What ceremony else?" (lines 212, 214) and "Must there no more be done?" (line 224). A shocked audience onstage and off watches Laertes jump into Ophelia's grave, where he physically inhabits a space with the dead, holding Ophelia once more in his arms. This sight is so provocative it moves Hamlet to reveal himself and jump into Ophelia's grave with Laertes. In their competitive grief and love for the dead girl, they both wish to be "buried quick" (line 268), to stay in the grave with her.

Love and death unite in the grave. It is only at Ophelia's gravesite that Hamlet names himself publicly: "This is I, / Hamlet the Dane" (lines 246–47); and only here that he takes love as his theme, crying out, "I loved Ophelia" (line 258). Finally, he allows the obvious acoustical pun in her name to sink in—"O philia." If *philia* is that profound love one feels for a friend, loving the other as if that friend were another self, to echo Aristotle, then surely now Hamlet finally acknowledges Ophelia as his double, his second self. Surely, he finds the Ophelia within him, meaning he must succor himself, fulfill his debt to his father, and shoulder his own spiritual obligations.

After leaving Ophelia's grave site, we all, onstage and off, feel the weight of death's reality and a sense of the end to come. Having done her share of quiet mourning, Gertrude begins to shift toward the roles of grievant, penitent, and avenger. She clearly has been moved by Ophelia's unnerving public scene of mourning and by the girl's death. Gertrude's crisis in conscience and selfhood comes late, but surely it comes. We must ask, though, what constitutes Gertrude's ethical journey? Of what is she guilty? What are her convictions in the end? We even might ask why the hermeneutic effort here is more tenuous with Gertrude than it is, say, with Hamlet—or with Ophelia, for that matter. She speaks fewer lines than Ophelia, and could be described as keeping her own counsel much of the time. Richard Levin puts her case this way: "Gertrude is the victim of a bad press, not only on the stage and screen and in the critical arena, but also within Shakespeare's text, since she and her libido are constructed for us by the two men who have grievances against her and so must be considered hostile and therefore unreliable witnesses, while she herself is given no opportunity to testify on her own behalf."[28] Levin is perceptive here, though I would challenge his final point. When Gertrude speaks, as Carolyn Heilbrun long ago observed, her words are "concise and pithy," reflecting an ability to see and express reality clearly.[29] While her intentions remain somewhat obscure, as critical debate will attest, Gertrude communicates and acts frankly at times, and her key speeches demand a critical acuity some readers feel she is not worth.

Gertrude, too, has a revenge cause integrally bound with family dishonor and shame. As her narrative makes its shadowy progress, she enters an ethical field whose parameters come into focus only when she acknowledges her shame and feels the weight of her moral and political blindness. Not until the closet scene does Gertrude's character give way to a passionate language that discloses her inner world. At all times, however, as an actor playing Gertrude would argue, we should look for evidence of the Queen's inwardness and moral consciousness informing her presence and the few words she speaks as she responds to Hamlet, Claudius, and Ophelia, especially after the closet scene. Her knowledge that Claudius has betrayed her and her other male kin weighs upon her, altering her fundamental relationships. As G. B. Shand argues, onstage Gertrude's silence can be perceived as not simply "empty or passive but as an active and charged condition of alert receptivity."[30]

In the violated sanctuary of her "closet," a room for privacy, speculation, and devotion, we see and hear a terrified Gertrude driven to remorseful speech as her son harrows her soul. The Ghost had expressed a kind of sorrowing vindictiveness toward his wife: "leave her to heaven" (God's revenge); "thorns that in her bosom lodge" will "prick and sting her" into penitence (1.5.86, 87, 88). But Hamlet cannot leave her to heaven. Hamlet's aggressive provocation unsettles her composure, not only because of what he says, but because of what he has become—before her eyes arises the frightening specter of a violent, murderous, seemingly mad, hallucinating son. This vision of Hamlet gives Gertrude pain. Not only are her outward eyes pained, but her mind's eye is forced to suffer as she gazes inward, seeing herself through Hamlet's blazing, accusative eyes. Hamlet confronts her with his shame and her shamelessness—that is, her indifference to her immoral actions: "O shame, where is thy blush?" She must acknowledge seeing "such black and grieved spots / As will leave there their tinct" (3.4.79, 88–89). She must feel shame now, acutely aware of how she has failed Hamlet and her dead husband, how she has failed to live up to an ethical ideal of wife, mother, and queen. As Ewan Fernie astutely claims, "[S]hame penetrates illusion and is a form of self-discovery. . . . It is a deadly enlightenment, but one that makes way for a new integrity and truthfulness."[31] We could say that Gertrude's experience of shame—the discovery of her shame—"opens a door, pointing the way to spiritual health and realisation of the world beyond egoism."[32]

Hamlet's provocation of his mother begins with his first speech of the play, directed to Gertrude ("Seems, madam . . .") and intensifies with the staging of the Mousetrap. The play-within-the-play arguably functions as a prelude to his private encounter with Gertrude, the term *mouse* linking the two experiences for Gertrude. *Mouse* is a figurative term signifying something weak and insignificant, and it is also an endearment, especially for a woman.[33] The theatrical trap is meant to fill the eyes and ears of this seemingly insignificant, weak queen with scenes that reflect her moral weakness: the loving encounter between king and queen, the queen's protestations of love and repeated insistence that "*None wed the second but who killed the first*" (3.2.174), the poisoning in the garden, her "*passionate action*" (3.2.128.7) upon finding her dead husband, and the wooing and winning of the widowed queen. The private confrontation is meant to bring home to Gertrude how she has lived the worldly ethic articulated by the Player King: "*Most necessary 'tis that we forget / To pay ourselves what to ourselves is debt*" (3.2.186–87). She has forgotten herself and her moral debts. And perhaps in Hamlet's mind, to follow the protestations of the Player Queen, she has as good as killed the King. Her witnessing of the Mousetrap lays the moral groundwork for hearing the horror of her first husband's murder and for understanding her own complicity in Claudius's deceitful reign. When Hamlet meets Gertrude in her closet, he warns her not to let Claudius "call you his mouse" anymore (3.4.181).

As Hamlet destroys the illusions upon which her life with Claudius rests, Gertrude cries out: "These words like daggers enter in my ears" (3.4.93), and "O Hamlet, thou has cleft my heart in twain" (3.4.154). The violence of such images should not be overlooked. Hamlet's words have sliced like a dagger into her ears and through her heart. The Queen feels the pain of his forceful entrance into the privacy of her mind and soul, and she feels the violent severing of the images of her two husband-kings, whom she has treated almost as one continuous body. Gertrude has said little in this scene, but the shock of the scene's revelations has clearly been felt and registers mostly in her silent pain and grief.

Interestingly, in the First Quarto, Gertrude speaks in a more forthright manner, giving clearer evidence that she will join Hamlet in revenge. The Q1 play is less concerned with the ethical conflicts of the Folio; the text follows pagan precepts regarding revenge with less questioning of their rightness. Hamlet characterizes Claudius as a Vulcan figure guilty of murder and rape. Gertrude, then, has been violated and seized. He begs his mother: "assist mee in reuenge, / And in his death your infamy shall die" (G3r). She agrees to "conceale, consent, and doe my best, / What stratagem soe're thou shalt deuise" (G3v). In contrast, the Q2 and F1 texts allow for subtle possibilities in Gertrude for sounding her own conscience and choosing a course of action. She will keep her own counsel and assist Hamlet in his revenge in a most unexpected, yet traditionally feminine, manner.

After witnessing such a harrowing private scene, how can we make sense of the public Gertrude who reports Ophelia's death? Here, Gertrude takes the messenger's part from ancient Greek tragedy to describe a terrible offstage event. Yet Gertrude's speech puzzles many readers, as it does not convey in style or content the catastrophe of death. Her words would seem to lack force and tragic feeling in calling to mind the mad girl's end. I would argue that the key to the speech lies in the mystifying, almost precious aestheticism and in the seemingly indecorous distancing effects of pastoralism. When heard in performance, the style must strike the ear as an abrupt change in harmony, rhythm, and mood: a pretty pastoral elegy has interrupted the furtive, heated plotting of villains. Such a register shift can be gauged in ethical terms, for the speech functions as a just reparation for the evil and cruelty Ophelia has been subjected to.[34] This is Gertrude's tribute—her elegy and epitaph—to Ophelia and her attempt at *poetic* justice in restoring the damaged girl's lost innocence, as Katharine Goodland argues.[35] Here, finally, is something resembling atonement for the girl's ill treatment and death, for the ugly severings between members of the royal household. The idyllic aestheticism of the verse seeks to restore beauty and innocence to the poor girl whose mind became a broken mirror of the violence and pollution in Denmark. Gertrude's speech seems to ask: What can beauty do in the world? What place does beauty have where even lilies are made to fester? If her speech seems woefully out of place, indecorous and precious, it is because that is how beauty appears in the rank garden of Denmark.

The placement of this speech is significant, for Gertrude must interrupt Claudius's hushed words of conspiracy with Laertes in order to report Ophelia's sad death. When the King hears a noise, the Queen enters, but not until after she has had the opportunity, one might argue, to overhear the plan to poison the foil and cup. In performance, the actress may very well signal her entrance noisily to mask her knowledge. In a play that turns on scenes of voyeurism, secrecy, and eavesdropping, it would not be a mere director's fancy to place Gertrude within earshot of the conspirators and to weight her line with ponderous meaning: "One woe doth tread upon another's heel" (4.7.161). In performance, there is opportunity to signal Gertrude's subtle intentionality in this scene. Such an open interpretive process is possible if the actress shows us a Gertrude who is intelligent and wary, and who keeps her own counsel at this point in the play, awaiting an opportunity to expose Claudius. Her epitaph for Ophelia has its poignant emphasis, provoking weeping from Laertes. Laertes' response then inspires fear in Claudius about whether he can control the distraught avenging brother/son and the political consequences of all the woes that have occurred.

Finally, we must turn to Gertrude's death, as we did with Ophelia's, to understand the ethical import of her character. René Girard suggests that Hamlet approaches Gertrude with anger and blame in her closet because he himself is mired in indifference, and would like to work up his mother's passions to the point where she will incite him to revenge.[36] This provocative suggestion follows a premise about revenge (that revenge can *only* be "sick" and destructive) antithetical to my argument, but it is worth considering, especially in relation to the play's final scene, where Gertrude clearly provokes strong feeling and incites violent action from her son. At this late point, she is fully burdened with the knowledge of her sins and those of Claudius. She is determined not simply to be an observer to whatever violence might erupt in the fencing match, but to take an action that will aid and protect her son and, in her mind, Denmark's future. If she knows about the poison, she may have a good idea as she enters this scene of how to strike against Claudius. That Claudius and Laertes choose poison as their murder weapon reflects secrecy and duplicity, and is designed to avoid any legal reparations for Laertes. Laertes then will rely neither on strength nor law to determine Hamlet's end; he becomes Claudius's dupe in his use of guile.

In the public setting at court, Gertrude will find her opportunity not only to atone for her guilt, but also to move Hamlet to take *their* revenge on Claudius, a fully confirmed treasonous murderer in both of their minds. After Claudius has dropped the pearl (which he ironically calls a "union," suggestive of the poisoning of marital union) in the cup and offered Hamlet a drink, which he refuses, she takes the cup and exclaims, "The Queen carouses to thy fortune, Hamlet" (5.2.271). She identifies herself as a royal power in the action she is about to take. She will speak and act as befits a queen. Her invocation of Fortune might remind us of the Player's speech once more, where impassioned witnesses to Hecuba's tragedy would have spoken treason with poisoned tongues against the rule of Fortune. There is tragic awareness in the Queen's line here, as artificially joyous as it must seem to the court. Claudius gives her a direct order: "Gertrude, do not drink" (line 273). She pauses in the space of the five beats left in Claudius's line, and then insists with deliberation, "I will, my lord. I pray you pardon me" (line 274).

In some stage and film productions, this moment registers as a defiant act. Franz Peter Wirth's film (Austria, 1960), for example, focuses the camera on a Gertrude (Wanda Rotha) who watches Claudius drop powder into the cup; she takes the cup from Hamlet's hands not long after, and moves up to the throne where she toasts the King and her son. She drinks in triumph from a cup she knows is poisoned, and clearly expects some repercussions from her death. We might agree with Gene Fendt who argues that "This scene should take our breath away," for "Gertrude opens the door to grace and salvation right at Claudius' side, where no one in the audience would have dared expect it, and where no one in the play—not even Hamlet—can see it."[37] In Wirth's production, Gertrude reflects a moral awareness at this moment that only intensifies as she and Claudius resume their seats. Gertrude's ambiguous silence is displayed momentarily as she looks intensely and knowingly at Claudius. Such a look is full of unspoken intention. She might have Claudius's salvation in mind, or she might be satisfied in the revenge she has just taken. His silence reveals that Claudius loves worldly position and goods more than Gertrude or salvation. When he does nothing and she approaches death, she chooses to reveal him and to incite the vengeance that is justly deserved. She dies in Hamlet's arms. By the time Wirth's Hamlet (Maximilian Schell) comes to his moment of revenge, he has reached cathartic exhaustion. The actor closes his eyes with profound weariness and sadness, and then he scrapes Claudius's body with the poisoned foil; the action is so minimal, the viewer hardly notices it. He then gives Claudius the cup, and tells him to drink; Claudius obeys and drinks of his own will. The actor conveys a resigned acceptance of death from the avenging hands of his murdered brother's son.

Importantly, Gertrude's sacrificial action has given Hamlet immediate justification for killing Claudius. If he has restrained himself all this time from revenge, this public show of treasonous murder—the killing of the Queen—has given him unequivocal cause to answer Claudius's crime with a just revenge. In dying, Gertrude completes the meaning of her sacrifice: she cries out, "O my dear Hamlet, / The drink, the drink—I am poisoned" (lines 294–95). Laertes then is compelled to confess his own treachery and to name Claudius as coconspirator. Laertes makes Gertrude's implicit accusation unequivocal: "the King's to blame" (5.2.305).

What I have attempted here is a possible narrative that uncovers Gertrude's gradual assumption of the role of a reflective, intelligent, sorrowing queen and mother, whose burden of guilt and fear for her son's life gives her a gravitas and ethical fullness she seemed to lack at the start of the play. In fulfilling her tragic role, the end crowns all; in the final moments of her life, she performs an extraordinary act that gives Hamlet motive and cue for killing the King. She incites him to avenge the death of their family at the very moment when she and her son are dying. She has found her way into redemption and loving grief through vengeance. She displays an ethical capacity that does not simply plague her with guilt and shame, but guides her repentance and opens the possibility for her to act in accordance with integrity and justice. In the last scene her choice to drink the poison brings Hamlet face to face with a murderer. With the kingdom's eyes upon him, he must defend his mother's honor—and his own—and avenge the treasonous murders. He must avenge mother, father, and self all in one. As some performances of the character make clear (witness Maximilian Schell), this act of vengeance is not a brute act of violence. It is a complex moral deed, fulfilling the necessities of justice and dramatic action.

In the moment of her death, Gertrude unexpectedly calls to mind the Germanic roots of her name (*ger* means "spear," and *trud* "strength"; thus, "strong spear"), which find fulfillment in her heroic gesture and, in a displaced way, through her son as he moves to kill the criminal-king. Furthermore, at least one seventeenth-century dictionary traces Gertrude's name to Old Saxon, claiming it means "all truth."[38] This etymology may have struck Shakespeare, though it does not appear to have been recorded in a dictionary from his time. A most fitting etymological possibility buried in her name is *geo,* the Anglo-Saxon adverb meaning "formerly" or "once." In death, Gertrude atones; in death, she is vindicated, proving true and loyal once again to her beloved kin. Gertrude's cry reveals the poison, her "envenomed tongue" calling to mind the imagined spectators crying out against Fortune in the wake of Hecuba's sorrow. Poison has insinuated its way into the ears, mouths, tongues, minds, and bodies of the Danes. This truth—"the drink—I am poisoned"—frankly articulates Gertrude's moral condition and partially reveals the insidious network of treachery in the kingdom. Claudius poisoned her when he won her to wife—he trapped his "mouse" before the Mousetrap disclosed that truth—and now she drinks of his poison again, but this time it is of her own volition, so she can expose him. If tragedy is fundamentally about the problems of truth, justice, and judgment, Gertrude taps directly into the heart of tragedy here, attempting to release all three forces. While the Ghost's cries for remembrance and revenge cannot bear fruit immediately in a just conclusion, Gertrude's words and action can inspire a revenge that need not weigh on Hamlet's conscience. The public sacrifice of her life can best be described not as a sign of despair or ignorance, but as tragic heroism. If performance can make such an interpretation legible, Gertrude can be seen to repair her wounded name in a profound act of love, a love that, startlingly enough, calls for just revenge.

But let us not forget Ophelia, for in the end Shakespeare does not. Indeed, Shakespeare remembers Ophelia at the moment of Hamlet's death, signifying how spiritually bound these two grieving children of dead fathers have been. Her ghostly presence is subtle, but present for those with ears to hear and a mind's eye attentive to the nuances underlying iconic scenes in the play. Hamlet's death recalls the scene at Ophelia's grave site, the transitional place for all the characters' journeys into the "undiscovered country" (3.1.78). Here, as in Ophelia's death, is a scene that turns on the anxieties and duties, the anguish and hope, of remembering. Here is memory-work for the audience, as well. Horatio's words spoken to the departing spirit of Hamlet subtly call to mind the girl Laertes swore was a "ministering angel" (5.1.230): "Now cracks a noble heart. Goodnight, sweet Prince, / And flights of angels sing thee to thy rest" (5.2.343–44). We recall as well how Gertrude wished "Sweets to the sweet. Farewell" (5.1.232). For Shakespeare's audience, *sweet* meant free from taint, uncorrupted, and unpolluted.[39] We recall how Laertes insisted upon Ophelia's "unpolluted flesh" at her grave site (5.1.228). Thus, Ophelia and Hamlet are restored to their former sweetness in death. It is not too much of an imaginative stretch, I think, to see in Horatio's figure of ministering angels the spirit of Ophelia, the play's figure of song and the closest Denmark has come to knowing an angel. She is the angel of succor and sin, of love and forgiveness, of revenge and justice. If Hamlet imagines "the rest is silence" (5.2.342), Horatio alludes to how his "rest" might be redeemed with the angelic song of Ophelia. The sweet, mad girl's name is redeemed, too, her story woven into the linguistic, aesthetic, and ethical textures of the play.

Yet as with everything in *Hamlet,* ambivalence and difference have an uncanny way of erupting. The glorious Christian vision of Hamlet ministered to by angelic song is interrupted by the sounds of a "warlike noise," of military assertion (5.2.333). We are treading the earth again, and Fortinbras has come to "embrace [his] fortune" and take his revenge (line 372). Only with the bloody catastrophe of Denmark and with Hamlet's "dying voice" (line 340) is Fortinbras subdued into making a peaceful seizure of the kingdom. He seems a character imported from Saxo Grammaticus's Danish chronicle, where men exert themselves with brute force and seek glory, yet respect those they have killed with funeral rites. The play closes by making us aware that it has all along shared space with Saxo's warriors; with military music and preparations for a battle-hero's burial, that world is made present. Fortinbras has invoked *his* "rights of memory" as justification in taking Denmark (5.2.373), so that the recent tragic history to which we have borne witness suddenly and jarringly reconfigures in our minds as a parallel tale of memory rights. We are made to feel a sublime irony: the kingdom now may resume the work of mourning and may dignify funeral rites with ceremony, but it is an invading prince and the wrong avenger that restores this loss. In their respective journeys into the undiscovered country, Hamlet, Laertes, Ophelia, and Gertrude have each in his or her own way attempted to restore the name of justice to Denmark's kingdom. In the end, however, they become the sacrificial bodies that make possible renewed justice and restored rites in Fortinbras' newly acquired kingdom.

RAPE AND REVENGE:
LAVINIA'S UNSPEAKABLE NARRATIVE

As we have seen in the cases of Ophelia, Gertrude, the Duchess of Gloucester, and Constance, the dramatic function of seemingly helpless, victimized females can be far more significant and far-reaching when we consider the affective and ethical qualities conveyed in their performances. Especially because such women are denied the possibility of retaliating physically for the harm done them or their kin, their grievances, lamentations, and calls for justice are all the more striking. They show us how central women are in activating vengeance, in making vengeance possible by disclosing crime, in justifying revenge, and in moving the able-bodied to take action. Shakespeare's plays show us vulnerable, hurt, angry, and bold women who seek an avenger or an accomplice in revenge, reinforcing the idea that moral outrages against the individual, family, and community must be answered and punished. Female rape victims constitute perhaps the most pitiable cases, as their violation is seen to pollute them as well as their family and to end their normative functions as women in society. Their stories are ruptured by violence. The silenced rape victim, figured most lamentably in Shakespeare's Lavinia, offers the worst case of harm and impotence, for she lacks a tongue to incriminate the violator and incite a just vengeance. She must communicate her story through her body and whatever extraordinary means are available to initiate the ritual of revenge-taking—for revenge is indeed prominent in the minds of rape victims, both in classical and Renaissance tales.

Lavinia, the ravished, mutilated victim of *Titus Andronicus,* offers a powerfully haunting sight onstage. She embodies that which has been irretrievably harmed, that which has been shamed—and that which *must* be appeased. Her speechlessness resonates meaningfully onstage and in the text, for it signifies the unspeakable nature of her violation. Speechlessness also moves her into a range of performance that arises from the traumatized body and shattered self. Spectators must feel not only that they are confronted with the unspeakable, but the unseeable, as well. While Peter Mercer and others look to Titus Andronicus as the emotional center of the play—the "spectacle of his boundless sufferings, the endless nightmare of his wrongs"[40]—we should remember that Lavinia has almost as much stage time as Titus. Her presence embodies the anguished consciousness and defiled honor of the Andronici. Her gaping wounds are the bloodstained mementoes of crime that call the Andronici men to their ethical duty to carry out revenge. Her ruin, more than any other violent wrong Titus suffers, causes profound grief and shame, ultimately leading to his catastrophe. Titus's revenge is a father's revenge; yet his revenge is also Lavinia's revenge. She is not a ghost, like Hamlet's father, nor is she mad, like Ophelia. Unlike these other inciters seeking appeasement, Lavinia can *participate* in the brutal, bloody rite her father undertakes to avenge her rape and mutilation.

Feminist critics have been surprisingly reluctant to acknowledge Lavinia's agency in taking a role in revenge, claiming that she has been forced to submit to a patriarchal script.[41] Deborah Willis, one of the few critics who demurs, reads *Titus Andronicus* in dialogue with contemporary trauma theory, which allows her to demonstrate fruitfully how humiliated, damaged characters like Titus and Lavinia seek a "perverse form of healing" through excessive revenge.[42] Women can be as complicit in revenge's excesses as men are, for in their brutalized states, they turn to revenge for relief and satisfaction, temporary as they may be. The desire to restore honor and repair a shattered self drives trauma survivors to "reenact a traumatic scene with the roles reversed," which is the essence of theatrical revenge.[43] The "reenactment" of Lavinia's trauma places her rapists, Chiron and Demetrius, in the role of victims: they become the powerless, suffering ones. While she cannot wreak violence upon their bodies or insult them, she can be a satisfied spectator to their humiliation and bloody deaths.

Through performance, Lavinia can be shown to aid Titus in a revenge performed as a ghastly form of solace. Present are Caius and Valentine, Andronici kinsmen, and Publius, Marcus's son, as ready participants in this family ritual. While the men bind and gag Chiron and Demetrius, Titus enters the stage *"with a knife, and* LAVINIA *with a basin"* (5.2.165, stage direction). The sight of Lavinia with a basin held between her stumps signals her active role in the family's collective revenge. She is physically incapable of wielding the knife, but she can very well be perceived as psychologically and emotionally thirsty for "guilty blood" (line 183). Titus's first words in this perverse ritual sacrifice are to Lavinia: "Come, come, Lavinia: look, *thy* foes are bound" (5.2.166, my emphasis).[44] Titus calls upon Lavinia to "come, / Receive the blood" (lines 196–97) in language suggestive of ancient ritual sacrifice. Titus's speech acknowledges the meaningful position of Lavinia in relation to her enemies: roles are being reversed ritualistically; victim becomes victimizer. He invites her to watch her violators in torment, and to savor their helplessness as they listen to his "fearful words" (line 168). He affirms his role as *Lavinia's* avenger, first and foremost. Furthermore, he helps to realize Lavinia's curse on Tamora; spoken just before she is violated, this curse finds its initial fulfillment in this scene: "Confusion fall—" (2.2.184). Indeed, confusion, or ruin, has come to the house of Tamora. Lavinia's curse has proven potent, and is ironically answered in Tamora's own words when she is disguised as Revenge: "Revenge is come to join with [Titus] / And work confusion on his enemies" (5.2.7–8).

Titus enacts a form of poetic justice that replicates and repays Lavinia's bloody violation and mutilation. Here the brutal equations of revenge play out as the demands of the genre are met. In gagging the perpetrators and slitting their throats, they are silenced, as Lavinia has been. Their hands are bound, taking away use of their hands. Titus tortures Tamora's sons with future knowledge of how their bodies will be violated—they will be baked into meat pasties (5.2.189) to be consumed by their mother—just as Chiron and Demetrius had brutally revealed to Lavinia what they meant to do to her. Father, daughter, and kin experience schadenfreude, the dark pleasure and psychological satisfaction of revenge, as they watch Lavinia's tormenters suffer before their slaughter.

In a play steeped in classical patterns and prior narratives, Lavinia's character possesses distinct resonances. Revenge stories often reenact familiar structural patterns, and Renaissance revengers tend to be self-conscious about precedents, fitting their urgent needs for revenge into a meaningful pattern. This is eminently true in *Titus Andronicus,* where Shakespeare is at pains to show us that he is retelling ancient tales with a difference, infusing this sense of pattern and deviation into the consciousness of both his characters and his audience. Feminine revenge tales are of particular importance in *Titus,* the most overt of these being the ancient Greek story of Philomel, Procne, and Tereus. Shakespeare deliberately re-animates this tale on a deep structural level.[45] Sometime after the Athenian princess Procne married the Thracian king, Tereus, she longs to see her sister, Philomel. Tereus returns to Athens to retrieve her sister, but upon his journey back to Thrace, he rapes Philomel, cuts out her tongue, and leaves her in a dark wood. Philomel weaves her story in a cloth, which she sends to Procne to read. Struck speechless with grief and anger, Procne fixes her mind upon revenge. During the rites of Bacchus, she finds her way to the woods where Philomel is imprisoned and rescues her. They return to Thrace to take their revenge on the depraved king. Procne kills their son, Itys; the women cook him up in a cauldron; and they feed him to his father. Ovid emphasizes the women's savage joy in the act, and depicts Philomel, stained with blood, flinging the boy's head in the father's face.

The first mention of Philomel in *Titus Andronicus* reflects a grafting of the old story onto a new ruthless revenge cycle. Aaron, a malicious revenger, orchestrates the dismemberment and rape of Lavinia, Titus's beloved only daughter, and the murder of her royal fiancé, Bassianus. These violent actions serve as a perverted sacrifice that reciprocates the "irreligious" sacrifice of Tamora's son, carried out by Titus and his sons to appease their dead. "Philomel must lose her tongue today," Aaron announces to Tamora, and her sons will play not only the part of Tereus, but also murderers who will "wash their hands in . . . blood" (2.2.43, 45). This image of hand-washing suggests Greek rituals of pollution and purification; a virgin is to be sacrificed, but it is a shameful, dire deed, unhallowed in spirit. After the bloody deeds, Marcus finds Lavinia; the sight of her recalls the horrifying story of Philomel and Tereus to him, yet with her hands cut off, he deems the villain a "craftier Tereus" (2.3.41). We recall that like Philomel, Lavinia spoke boldly before she was silenced, reflecting the strong will of a good woman who knows her mind. She defies Tamora and charges her with moral wrongdoing. Her bold, truth-telling tongue inspires the shamed Tamora to set her sons upon Lavinia. Much later in the play, Lavinia reveals her story through the parallel tale in the *Metamorphoses.* Titus exclaims, "This is the tragic tale of Philomel, / And treats of Tereus' treason and his rape" (4.1.47–48). Titus will invoke the story once more as he prepares to enact the final moments of this revenge tale; he appropriates Procne's role to take revenge on Tamora and her sons. As he prepares to slit the sons' throats, he exclaims in rage: "For worse than Philomel you used my daughter, / And worse than Progne I will be revenged" (5.2.194–95). In turning to his model, Titus calculates the justice of the deed he is about to commit, mentally balancing excessive crimes in the scale with an excessive punishment. By having Titus conceive of his revenge as "worse" than Procne's,

Shakespeare emphasizes his competition with ancient myths of revenge, while intensifying his own reenactment of this infamous revenge.

Furthermore, we notice the assigning of revenge to the father rather than the sister, which significantly alters the gendering of alliances and revenge. Is this change in the story destructive to the feminine, as Karen Robertson argues? She claims, "The excision of Progne as agent of vengeance for her sister's rape substitutes the aristocratic male subject for the betrayed wife"; such a change, she says, reflects "a representational norm, the masculine gendering of vengeance in Tudor and Stuart tragedy."[46] In the same spirit as Tudor homilies, Robertson argues, the play repudiates feminine anger. The heroic male assumes the place of the avenger, and rape is understood as a violation of male property, a wounding of the male line, to be punished by the male.[47]

Alternative ways to understand Shakespeare's handling of the deep structure of the Philomel/Procne tale and Lavinia's character are possible, however, and I would like to suggest an interpretation more in keeping with the possibility of a sustained, albeit sometimes inscrutable, feminine agency. First, as I have argued, Lavinia might be perceived in light of the traditional female inciter role. She actively incites vengeance and participates as fully as possible in the family ritual sacrifice of her rapists. Both her body and her text goad male kin to take justice into their own hands (as she has none left). As Robertson notes, "[S]he writes a word that will activate a system of punishment performed by males."[48] That word is *stuprum,* meaning "rape." She *activates* revenge, to emphasize Robertson's own observation, yet I might add that Lavinia, too, is a *performer* in the revenge. She is indeed surrounded by *male* kin as the revenge rite takes place, but she is given a central part to play, one redolent of ancient Greek sacrifice and a symbolic collecting of the rapists' blood to compensate for the loss of her virgin's blood. She may not have hands to wash in her victims' blood, but she has stumps that will help her catch the blood. Titus's enactment of revenge is not just for himself, but for Lavinia, as well, and it is a rite he performs *with* Lavinia on her behalf. His usurpation of the sister's role might be seen not so much as a patriarchal assumption of the rights of revenge, but rather as a sign of the feminization of the male avenger, of revenge as a feminine gendered action, the action of a vulnerable, grieving, disempowered member of the aristocratic community. If Titus's dramatic assumption of Procne's role is a self-conscious reenactment of Ovid's tale, the template is feminine. Shakespeare's construction of his character of the male avenger deliberately follows patterns found in classical feminine revenges: like Procne, Medea, and Hecuba, he witnesses unspeakable violations, weeps and rages, and then justifies savage acts of revenge that involve killing his enemy's children.

The revelation of her violators marks one of the high points in Lavinia's exercise of agency, an agency expressed specifically through literacy. Like her father, Lavinia knows Ovid's tale of Philomel and Procne, for she is "deeper read and better skilled" (4.1.33) than the boy Lucius. This skill serves her well as she turns to the Latin text of Ovid's *Metamorphoses* as the textual vehicle of her revelation. She finds in Philomel's tragedy a master narrative that will "speak" the unspeakable crimes committed against her. Here a tongueless condition signifies, as it does in the Philomel tale, the unspeakable nature of *nefas,* or sacrilegious crime. The Ovidian text, then, is given a special significance here in revealing *nefas* with the authority of classical precedent. Lavinia's case echoes the fundamental connection between silencing and crime made in Ovid's tale: the verb *fari,* meaning "to speak," was related to the word *fas,* meaning "divine law," "what must be done." *Nefas,* "the breaking of divine and moral law" represents the dark undoing of *fas,* and this undoing cannot be spoken. Or it *should not* be spoken: both Ovid's tale and Shakespeare's play represent barbarian males that speak of their crimes, Tereus gloating before Philomel about what he is to do to her, and Chiron and Demetrius joking with Lavinia after they commit their crimes. The men's impious speech is as shocking in both cases as the damage done to the vulnerable female characters.

To reveal *nefas,* Lavinia places herself within a master narrative that can express her agency, which gives Titus the means to translate her woes accurately. She prefaces the revelation with a gesture to the heavens, a sign Marcus interprets as signifying either the number of murderers (two arms for two men), or a plea for revenge; the latter seems more probable. Lavinia then uses her body (mouth and stumps) to inscribe in the sand a text that identifies crime and criminals—*"Stuprum—Chiron—Demetrius"* (4.1.78). Since the artful weaving of Philomel is rendered impossible through mutilation, Shakespeare has us recall Io, another classical rape victim, who due to her metamorphosis into a cow must write her name in the sand to reveal herself to her grieving father (her rape and transformation by Zeus are understood by her father once he identifies her).[49] Once Lavinia articulates her violation through textual precedent and a physically arduous feat of writing, Titus channels his anguish through the Latin text of Seneca's *Hippolytus* (also called *Phaedra*): "Magni dominator poli, / Tam lentus audis scelera, tam lentus vides?" [Ruler of the great heavens, are you so slow to hear crimes, so slow to see?] (lines 671–72).[50] Like *nefas, scelera* refers to heinous crimes, sins against moral law; if the gods are slow to hear and see crime, and therefore punish it, then mortals may turn for moral authority to human precedents for revenge-taking. Ovid and Seneca both offer literary narratives or patterns of *nefas* repaying *nefas.* Marcus, however, turns to Roman history, consciously invoking the right of Lord Junius Brutus to avenge the rape of his chaste daughter, Lucrece. He draws the Andronici together for a quasi-legal vow based on the precedent of Lucrece: "That we will prosecute by good advice / Mortal revenge upon these traitorous Goths, / And see their blood, or die with this reproach" (4.1.92–94). Titus's revenge, however, descends into a darker rite than Lucrece's avengers practiced; by self-consciously fashioning himself in the frenzied feminine role of Procne, the Bacchanalian avenging sister, Titus not only kills his enemy's depraved children, but also feeds them to their mother at a grotesque cannibalistic feast that ends in excessive blood slaughter.

A host of other classical women resonate in the character of Lavinia, as well, suggesting further implications for the treatment of feminine revenge in the play—Hecuba, Cornelia, Virginia, Lucretia, and Lavinia. Her name, to start, derives from that of the ancient queen Lavinia, daughter of Latinus and wife of Aeneas. The city Lavinium, from which the people of Rome derive, is named after her. Virgil mentions Lavinia a number of times in the *Aeneid* in association with the glory of the Trojan line in Italy. In his *History of Rome*, Livy tells more of Lavinia's history, commenting on her force of character, her successful regency, and her son by Aeneas. Lavinia, then, is closely associated with the making of Rome and the Latin assimilation of Greek myths of Troy. As Shakespeare critics have noted, the violations of Lavinia brutally inscribe on her female body the desecration of Rome herself.[51] Her body is a profound symbol that merges ancient with later Rome, rendering it now a "map of woe" (3.2.12)—gashed, bleeding, maimed, silenced, violated by barbarians.

The Andronici associate excessive suffering with the ancient Trojans: Titus invokes Aeneas's anguish at having to "tell the tale twice o'er" of Troy's burning, and Young Lucius sees in Lavinia the figure of Hecuba, the fallen Trojan queen running "mad for sorrow" (4.1.21). The father's and daughter's "Extremity of griefs" (4.1.19) recalls the pattern of a great city's loss and the nobility's unbearable suffering. At the play's conclusion, a Roman lord invokes Aeneas's story of Troy's fall and speaks of "our Troy, our Rome" (5.3.86). As Barbara Mowat argues, "[T]he larger shaping myth is actually that of Hecuba's Revenge, into which the Philomela myth and others are embedded."[52] Mowat's insight is valuable, introducing yet another female avenger into the deep structure of *Titus*. The Hecuba story is particularly resonant, as it represents the grief and rage of a noble parent, like Titus, who endures the destruction of his children and resorts to a savage revenge. Through Ovid and perhaps through Euripides' *Hecuba,* as well, Shakespeare knew Hecuba as the grieving Trojan queen who avenges the brutal murder and mutilation of her son by the Thracian king, Polymestor. Mutilation, grief, revenge: these are essential elements in *Titus Andronicus*. While Titus seems positioned to play the Hecuba figure—he suffers the deaths of many children, falls into madness, and seeks vengeance after his sons have been treacherously killed and his youngest child has been

raped and mutilated—the association between Hecuba and Lavinia, inspired by Young Lucius's observation of Lavinia's distraught behavior,
subtly points to a range of inner experiences in the young female character
that rival Titus's.

Coppélia Kahn argues that Shakespeare suppresses the narrative of
Hecuba's revenge, and thereby "excises a female agency that takes violent
retribution against patriarchy, and retains as the woman's part the effectual
empathic sorrow—witness as opposed to agency—that Titus and the
others ascribe to Lavinia."[53] Yet Lavinia is more than what the other characters ascribe to her. Like Hecuba of Troy, she appears mad with grief, but
her action turns out to be, in reality, the desperate behavior of an avenger:
she is absolutely determined to reveal the identities of her violators and to
repay their crimes with a punishment as terrible as Hecuba's was. Like
Hecuba, she will have a band of avengers gathered around her (Hecuba has
the Trojan captive women aid her in revenge), and she will approve of the
slaughtering of the sons, and the damage done to their vicious parent.

The figure of the chaste Lucrece, as well, lies in the web of classical associations defining the symbolic value of Lavinia's violation, suffering,
and appeal to male kin for revenge. While Virgil's Lavinia is associated
with the founding of Rome, Lucrece functions as a later pivotal figure,
whose rape by Sextus Tarquinius leads to the expulsion of the Tarquins and
the founding of the Roman republic. The political results of avenging Lucrece's rape are highly significant and imply that a similar pattern is taking
shape in *Titus*. The victorious Lucius has made good on his vow to avenge
Lavinia's rape and offers hope of a new order in Rome. Echoing Lucrece's
story from Livy's history and Ovid's *Fasti*, Titus pleads with Lavinia to find
some sign that might reveal her perpetrator:

> Give signs, sweet girl—for here are none but friends—
> What Roman lord it was durst do the deed.
> Or slunk not Saturnine, as Tarquin erst,
> That left the camp to sin in Lucrece's bed?
>
> (4.1.61–64)

Kahn notes that the allusion to Lucrece offers the possibility that Lavinia
will be able to "represent herself, articulate the meaning of sexual violation, and lay the foundation for the revenge that follows."[54] In her estimation, however, Lavinia does not achieve feminine empowerment at all, for
Titus construes her injury as his own. He takes revenge to restore his own
honor that has been lost symbolically through his daughter's defilement.
Her uncle, Marcus, rather than Lavinia herself, initiates the ritual oath-taking that leads Titus to take revenge. Yet Lavinia's part in this scene might
be understood as more active and influential than Kahn allows. Lavinia

cannot speak the demand for revenge in words as does Lucrece when her male family members come to her. Yet, as I am claiming, she functions as the inciter to vengeance in this scene. Marcus must give words to Lavinia's desires, but this does not mean that she has not conveyed her desire for revenge strongly through *signs* in performance. She kneels with her family to vow revenge for the loss of her honor and their honor—and ultimately that of Rome. If one considers Lavinia's pain and shame, it is extraordinary that Shakespeare has the character so actively involved in the revelation of her violators and in the revenge-taking; she is more active, indeed, than Lucrece was. As Jonathan Bate astutely points out, Shakespeare goes beyond his sources even as he follows the patterns they offer, ingeniously grafting sources together and creating new variations and challenges for the characters to face.[55] Without a tongue, without hands, Lavinia is shown as desperate, even mad with the determination to name her violators. The end result could only be appeasement—revenge—for her violation, which, like Lucrece's violation, has broader political implications, inciting men to overthrow a corrupt Rome that fosters *nefas.*

Linda Woodbridge movingly articulates as follows the relationship between the raped female and political overthrow: "In *Titus* and *Lucrece,* rape and mutilation lead to the downfall of a tyrannical government and to Rome's political salvation. Like smashing an atom, smashing these women releases tremendous power. When bodily violence propels them into dangerous margins, when ceasing to be chaste wives they transgress confining boundaries, they release an uncanny power upon the world."[56] Woodbridge looks to *Titus* and Shakespeare's poem *The Rape of Lucrece* as examples of the anthropologist Mary Douglas's theory of the body as a symbol of society. Penetration of bodily margins and the pollution of the body are fearful, dangerous symbols of territorial invasion; as many critics of the play and poem have argued, what is done to these women is done to their cities. Their damaged bodies and their responses to damage—specifically, incitement to revenge—lead to a release from tyranny.

Theatrical performances of Lavinia's character can bear out the interpretation I have sketched by displaying significant signs and sounds of her agency and vengefulness. Performance can make visible an affective aesthetics and ethics of revenge expressed through character. In the Shakespeare Theatre Company's 2007 production of *Titus Andronicus* directed by Gale Edwards at the Lansburgh Theatre in Washington, DC, Colleen Delany offered a vocally provocative and physically active performance of Lavinia, fighting with Chiron and Demetrius as they attacked Bassianus and valiantly trying to prevent the cutting off of Titus's hand. Such a strong, combative characterization contrasted markedly with well-known performances such as Sonia Ritter's (RSC 1987) which presented a Lavinia as broken in spirit as in body. One reviewer noted how Delaney's Lavinia ex-

pressed "absolute glee at the killing of Chiron and Demetrius—even including going to each one as they [sic] knelt bound and caressing their
heads and even kissing one of them. . . . [A]fter the killing . . . she advanced
front and center, outside the closing curtains, and with a spot on her lifted
both her bandaged stumps above her head in a classic gesture of triumph."[57] Her triumph over her barbaric violators is taken seriously in this
production. Just as Ovid's Philomel experiences *gaudia* (*Metamorphoses*
6.660) or "joy" in her mad deed, so this Lavinia rejoices. While it may be
a stretch of the imagination to see Shakespeare's actor triumphing in such
a manner in the public playhouses of London or at court, what this modern
interpretation acknowledges is that Lavinia's wounded name, her violated
honor, and her lost life are compensated for by the only form of justice
available in the chaotic Rome of *Titus Andronicus*—blood revenge. And
that is, as Ovid reveals in his avenging Procne, a *crudelia gaudia* (6.653),
a cruel joy, indeed.

INCITING VENGEANCE IN COMEDY: BEATRICE AS THE FIGURE OF JUST REVENGE

Beatrice: O God, that I were a man! I would eat his heart in the marketplace.
—Shakespeare, *Much Ado About Nothing*

Wounded names, revenge narratives, and the cruel joy of avengers—such
is the genetic material of Shakespeare's revenge tragedies, but this material also belongs to comedy. While the comic genre has much to do with
the joys and trials of love and courtship, it also has to do with moral violation, shame, and dishonor. Vengeful women's voices echo across genre
borders, and comic women, as it turns out, are far from indifferent to
vengeance. In *Much Ado About Nothing*, a play traditionally regarded as
one of Shakespeare's lighter and lesser works, the weightier concerns of
revenge erupt in the comic realm. Just as Othello imports epic values into
the domestic sphere, bringing his warrior honor, shame, and instinct to revenge into his marital life, so characters in *Much Ado* speak and behave in
accordance with the serious principles of honor. Into this seemingly light-
hearted comedy, Shakespeare has introduced the stronger passions of epic
and tragedy. As the play's action unfolds, the female inciter to vengeance
emerges to cry out against injustice and to demand just repayment for a
woman's lost honor.

In the Italian Mediterranean town of Messina, Sicily, the setting of
Shakespeare's *Much Ado*, honor is what men and women live by. For men,
valor, military glory, and good reputation are central values in their culture;
for women, chastity is typically the highest value. When women's chastity

is compromised through slander or sexual infidelity, kinsmen feel their honor threatened as well. Revenge tends to be the instinctive response of men who wish to recover their own wounded honor, yet women, too, may seek revenge in their own name or that of a kinswoman in order to redress a wrong. The justness of such revenge depends on the ethics of the avenger and the circumstances of the wrongdoing. As Linda Anderson astutely points out, Beatrice is the play's "most serious exponent of revenge."[58] Her vengeful spirit rises up in response to the men's dishonoring of women. She meets what Peter A. French calls the authority condition of vengeance, which establishes one's moral authority to act against a wrongdoer in one's community.[59] In *Much Ado About Nothing,* Beatrice takes on the heroic guise of Just Revenge, as she stands in opposition to the destructive force of slander.

The conceptual field of revenge ranges surprisingly far and deep in the comic world of *Much Ado.* The military aristocrats who arrive in Messina at the play's opening have left the battlefield behind to enjoy some peace-time pleasure. They move from the epic sphere of war, bloodshed, and glory to the comedic space of merriment, courtship, and marriage. Yet we discover that the war had been instigated by Don John's malignant spirit of revenge and envy directed toward his brother, Don Pedro, and this spirit enters the peaceful town because Don Pedro has forgiven his brother's faults and allowed him his freedom. No true penance having been done or recompense given, Don John plots to muddy the honor of Claudio and his brother through a cunning revenge: he arranges to have Claudio's intended bride, Hero, seem to be unfaithful to him through her commerce with the soldier Borachio at a window on the night before the wedding. Since the window scene is not performed in the theater, the audience is left with Don John's slanderous words ringing in its ears and his insistence that "it would better fit [Claudio's] honour to change [his] mind" about marrying Hero (3.2.104). The men's fatal "misnoting" leads to Claudio's devastating, wrongful vengeance on Hero, whom he shames at their wedding by accusing her of sexual infidelity. His fragile sense of honor and "fear of shame" lead him to "violent self-assertion."[60]

Thus, masculine vengeance plays out both on the battlefield of men and in the domestic world of women, marriage, and religious rites. Revenge in the domestic sphere, however, proves more devastating to the community and, furthermore, to the integrity of women. If "none of name" (1.1.7) died during battle, someone of name has "died" in Messina, and on sacred ground too. In truth, a double violation has taken place at the chapel—the men's revenge has trampled upon a sacred vow-in-the-making and ruined a woman's life. Hero's loss of name is perceived as a social death with dire consequences; and this inspires the Friar's plan to stage her death in order to make her "live" once more. As S. P. Cerasano indicates, "Slander, popularly thought of as 'the transient murderer,' if not actually the cause of literal death, was thought to lead to public alienation and metaphorical death."[61] The distraught community gathered at the scene of broken nuptials must suffer this truth.

Some critics focus attention on the masculine ethos of *Much Ado About Nothing* and its exploration of male honor, shame, and revenge,[62] but we lose the ethical and emotional balance of the comedy if we fail to give credence to women's experiences in Messina. Feminine honor, shame, and revenge are just as evident in this community. Women's honor is held at a premium in Messina, and when compromised or lost the necessity for revenge arises. Beatrice establishes herself as the defender of women's honor. She is a formidable opponent to any man who wishes to dishonor her or her kinswoman, Hero. Beatrice's identity as an avenging spirit is multivalent, expressing both comic and epic values. Leonato's description of her repartee with Benedick gets at the balance of light and serious elements in her character: "there is a kind of merry war betwixt Signior Benedick and her. They never meet but there's a skirmish of wit between them" (1.1.57–60). These expressive oxymorons—"merry war" and "skirmish of wit"—playfully wed the matter of epic with the spirit of comedy. The tension in these generic values is fundamental to this play, shedding light on the troubled gender relations in Messina and the function of revenge in comedy.

Beatrice's function in the community is signaled initially through her spirited attacks on Benedick. Beatrice is the sublime Lady Disdain and Lady Tongue, a verbal duelist who vanquishes her opponents with little trouble. As a figurative duelist and verbal warrior, she is able to take the offensive position in any skirmish. On a linguistic level, Beatrice and Benedick's witty repartee demonstrates the principle of retaliation. Their witty skirmishes are examples of verbal vengeance, instant and spontaneous forms of payback delivered on the spot.[63] As Benedick complains, she is "possessed with a fury" (1.1.181), a spirited anger that gets stirred up in his presence. The couple's linguistic skirmishes entertain the community and the play's audience, but their encounters bring some of the aggression and violence of the war metaphor into emotional play. In another of Benedick's many complaints about Beatrice's sharp tongue, he exclaims how she hurled "jest upon jest" so that he "stood like a man at a mark, with a whole army shooting at [him]. She speaks poniards, and every word stabs. . . . [Y]ou shall find her the infernal Ate in good apparel" (2.1.224, 225–27, 234). Benedick figures her not only as a Fury, but as Ate, goddess of discord; though beautiful, the classical goddess usually appeared in rags, stirring up powerful forces of havoc and war. Such a comparison renders Benedick the pathetic target of Beatrice's verbal arsenal, implying that comic revenge hurts and has emotional stakes.

Why would Beatrice wish to subject Benedick to her verbal revenge? Why would she wish to hurt him? R. W. Maslen argues that "Beatrice seems determined to teach Benedick, at least, about the damage that can be done with words."[64] Beatrice's pedagogical function with Benedick is of a piece with her vengeful anger over the slandering of Hero later in the drama. The damage done by words lies at the heart of the play: it is slander that can damage the self, both socially and psychologically speaking. The implication in Maslen's statement is that Benedick must be taught a painful truth about language, a truth that Beatrice understands well. Benedick is given to swearing and eating his oaths, and Beatrice is the character most concerned about the consequences of masculine forswearing. When Benedick swears by his sword that he loves Beatrice, she considers his history of oath-breaking and puts the question to him: "Will you not eat your word?" (4.1.277).

That she is the fitting teacher for Benedick is made apparent by the few references to their history together. When Don Pedro observes, "You have lost the heart of Signor Benedick," Beatrice explains, "Indeed, my lord, he lent it me awhile, and I gave him use for it, a double heart for his single one. Marry, once before he won it of me with false dice; therefore your grace may well say I have lost it" (2.1.253–58). The hostile undercurrent in her repartee with Benedick brings the past into the present, a move typical of the avenger, whose memory is long. The meaning of their encounters is reflected in the figurative transfer from the fields of game and emotional debt to that of war and revenge. She has sustained a loss; Benedick's heart was on loan to her, she paid interest for it, giving away twice the value of what he gave. But the economy of love was rotten from the start, based on Benedick's essential withholding of himself. What is worse, he cheats at the game of love. Beatrice's "double heart" may suggest her clever payback in those early days, but the metaphor is equivocal, leaning equally in the direction I have suggested of double interest or return on a loan.

Thus, Benedick is guilty of dishonoring Beatrice with his false oaths, and she uses her wits to repay him. In preparing to play the part of Beatrice, the actress Maggie Steed noticed how Beatrice tends to use the "language of men," sexual bantering and innuendo, to hold her own.[65] It is surprising, then, that Beatrice's quick tongue and bold speech, which seem off-putting to her male peers and many a male critic, do not throw her virtue into question. Don Pedro reflects the community's opinion when he says that "out of all suspicion, she is virtuous" (2.3.157–58). "And she is exceeding wise," Claudio adds (line 159). The community, including Benedick, seems to be in agreement about Beatrice's virtue and wisdom. Furthermore, her language reflects a reservoir of sorrow, which gives her character a seriousness and depth many critics and directors have not been quick to observe. In Barbara Everett's reading of the play, she finds wit *and* sorrow to be contradictions embraced in Beatrice's character; she insightfully argues that Beatrice "is Shakespeare's true heroine, woman as 'wag', the sharp and comical child of sorrow."[66]

Beatrice's social position is of some importance, as well, to understanding the paradoxical expression of her character. When Beatrice responds to Don Pedro's exclamation that she was "born in a merry hour," with the sobering "No, sure, my lord, my mother cried. . . ." (2.1.307–8), we hear a pang of sorrow. What she refers to most likely is her mother's death in childbirth, a sorrowful paradox of life-in-death that marked many early modern women's end. Orphaned, unmarried, and female, Beatrice was taken into the household of Leonato as a dependent living on the kindness of kin, perhaps without an expectation of a dowry. Her intelligence and sharp tongue, however, give the impression of a defiant independence. We might say that she rises above her social condition to claim a freedom of spirit . . . and to maintain her integrity. Her verbal prowess ensures her dignity and keeps unworthy suitors at arm's length. She preempts any second attempt on her virtue from Benedick by rejecting love talk, suitors, and marriage altogether. The ruin of Hero demonstrates precisely what Beatrice, and all smart women, must guard against—the slander and vengeance of men.

In time, the witty comic heroine Beatrice comes to reveal a fierce avenger within—the "merry" drops out of "war" and she crosses the threshold of comedy to enter the domains of tragedy and epic. Her target shifts from Benedick to Claudio. In transcending the comic roles of shrew and romantic wit, Beatrice invites comparison with the epic hero and the female inciter to vengeance. The church scene (4.1) shows us a passionate Beatrice whose desire for vengeance expresses her claim for women's justice. All of the characters' passions are at their highest in this scene, where vengeance is unmasked multiple times. Here Shakespeare imports traditional elements of blood-feud literature, epic, and tragedy into his comedy's ethos. The scene enacts a powerful double climax in which one bond shatters and another is forged unexpectedly. The shocking public slander of Hero is followed by a private scene between the two reluctant lovers, Beatrice and Benedick, who confess their love in one moment, and then swear revenge on Claudio in the next. The language, logic, and passions of revenge are the hallmark of this scene, ushering strong tragic potentialities into the comic world. Benedick's surprised exclamation to Hero's public humiliation, "This looks not like a nuptial" (4.1.67), comically captures the mixing of tones. His response registers the characters' surprise at the deferral of comic resolution. We are now in the space of tragedy, its dark energies threatening the suddenly fragile existence of happiness and social health in Messina.

The emotionally intense church scene unfolds in a three-part structure, each part jolting the audience's moral sensibilities. The emphasis is placed first on a bitter public scene of masculine revenge and feminine shame. The scene then focuses upon the shattered father, Leonato, who experiences intense anger and shame; his expressions of passion are followed by Friar Francis's announcement of his ingenious plot. Finally, the scene shifts to an intimate exchange and pledge of revenge between the lovers Beatrice and Benedick, the only characters/actors left onstage at this point. The first part of the scene represents the fruition of Don John's malicious revenge plot—to compromise the honor of Claudio and Don Pedro, slander Hero, and ruin the marital alliance. Don John can assume the success of such a plot, because he anticipates his male peers' angry response to the infidelity of Hero. They can perceive her moral failing as nothing less than a blight on Claudio's honor and an injury that must be repaid. The church scene puts into motion Claudio's moral revulsion at the "fallen" Hero, and his passionate need to recoup honor, the honor he feels he has lost with her lost virtue.

Once Claudio's slander has damaged Hero seemingly beyond recovery, the scene falls into chaos. Leonato seems convinced at first that Hero's "story" is that of an unchaste woman: "Could she here deny / The story that is printed in her blood?" (lines 121–22). Leonato wishes his daughter to be overcome, quite literally, by shame—to die, that is. The truth is that he is overcome with shame, ready, as Othello was, to tear apart what he loves. Yet there is some margin for doubt here; if she has been dishonored, Leonato claims, he would act upon that wrong:

> If they speak but truth of her,
> These hands shall tear her; if they wrong her honour,
> The proudest of them shall well hear of it.
> Time hath not yet so dried this blood of mine,
> Nor age so eat up my invention . . .
> But they shall find awaked in such a kind
> Both strength of limb and policy of mind,
> Ability in means and choice of friends
> To quit me of them throughly.
>
> (lines 190–94, 197–200)

Leonato works himself up to the fury of the avenger, ready to "quit" himself of his enemies, but his speech is interrupted by the Friar, whose sublimely benign vengeance plot pacifies him and holds out the promise of a bloodless restoration of Hero's "wounded reputation" (line 241). The Friar proposes a "cure" that draws upon Christian and classical myths: Christ's sacrifice on the cross, and Alcestis's sacrifice of her life for her husband.[67] In both cases, the dead are miraculously restored to life and bring life-giving properties to others. They embody the paradox of dying to live. The

Friar emphasizes the Christian values of patience and hope to the disgraced family and community.

Unexpectedly, it is a female character, Beatrice, who continues to seethe with anger at the injustice done her kinswoman. The scene continues to unfold in direct conflict with the values and expectations established by Friar Francis. To Beatrice, his plot must seem like an impossible fantasy, which can do nothing to quell her rage against Claudio. The third part of the church scene, then, gives expression to feminine vengeance born of a passionate instinct for justice. Beatrice is left weeping as characters exit the stage. She may have stayed in this passive feminine state of grief if it were not for the presence of Benedick, who chooses to remain with her rather than follow his companions. Here is a choice that exhibits greater ethical substance than he has formerly exhibited. He approaches Beatrice in kindness and love, and what unfolds in their dialogue is a moving, intimate encounter made possible only in relation to the absoluteness of death. As in tragedy, death is the ground of being and truth. Hero's symbolic death performs a liberating function for Beatrice and Benedick. If they cannot enter into an authentic dialogue at this moment, truth will continue to elude them. In the atmosphere of tragic loss, the antagonistic lovers are able to confess their strong feelings for each other. As Barbara Everett sees it, the couple finally unites in "shared principle"—a heartfelt sympathy for the wronged Hero.[68] Their love blazes forth as they discover in each other a reciprocated feeling of protest against injustice.

Beatrice's passion, however, intensifies; her love for Benedick does nothing to quell a violent desire to enact vengeance—a masculine kind of violence—in retaliation for her slandered cousin's "death." Their dialogue lies far from conventional courtship rhetoric; rather, their words directly engage the charged vocabulary of revenge: *wronged, right, even, man's office, offence, hand, challenge, dear account*. Beatrice sounds the note of vengeance quickly in their exchange. When Benedick gravely states, "Surely I do believe your fair cousin is wronged" (4.1.259–60), she responds with passion, "Ah, how much might the man deserve of me that would right her!" (lines 261–62). Implicit in these words lies a challenge to Benedick's manhood: Will he pick up the gauntlet and take the revenge that will "right" Hero? Will he demonstrate that he *deserves* Beatrice? When Benedick expresses willingness to "show such friendship" (line 263), Beatrice insists there is "A very even way, but no such friend." "May a man do it?" Benedick persists, and Beatrice exclaims hotly, "It is a man's office, but not yours" (lines 264–66). She recognizes an ethical imperative to revenge, but stumbles over the gendered "office" of revenge. What can she do? Her only weapon lies in the valor of her tongue. She "invades the male sphere," as Marilyn L. Williamson puts it,[69] but only through potent words and fantasy. What can Benedick do either, since he is not Hero's kinsman?

As their conversation moves toward vows of love, Beatrice finds a way to give agency to her revenge. When Benedick swears by his sword, Beatrice retorts warily, "Do not swear and eat it" (line 274). Beatrice's metaphor reaches back to the play's first scene, in which she renders an unfavorable portrait of Benedick as a man of hearty appetite with the ladies ("a very valiant trencher-man"), lacking in virtue and courage: "I pray you, how many hath he killed and eaten in these wars? But how many hath he killed? For indeed I promised to eat all of his killing" (1.1.48, 39–42). While Beatrice earlier hurtled the appetite metaphor to wound Benedick's name, now she anticipates how his broken oath might wound her honor. Yet mention of the sword must resonate with Beatrice, for it moves her thoughts toward bloody requital. When Benedick begs Beatrice to give him a task that will prove his worth, she gives him a stunning command: "Kill Claudio" (4.1.288).

The appetite metaphor comes into play further at this point, when Benedick initially refuses the office of revenge. His recoiling from revenge provokes Beatrice to cry out against the "villain" Claudio and implicitly against Benedick's lack of honor: "Is 'a not approved in the height a villain, that hath slandered, scorned, dishonoured my kinswoman? O, that I were a man! What, bear her in hand until they come to take hands, and then with public accusation, uncovered slander, unmitigated rancour? O God, that I were a man! I would eat his heart in the marketplace" (4.1.300–305). Beatrice's passionate speech neatly captures traditional gendered positions taken by men and women in relation to dishonor. Revenge was a "a man's office" (line 266). We might recall, once more, Vittoria's lament in John Webster's *The White Devil* that woman's poor revenge lay in her tongue. Beatrice's lament, however, is far from poor as she urges revenge upon Benedick. Her agency is exercised by playing a role familiar from classical literature and medieval sagas: that of the inciter, the one socially sanctioned to whet the appetite of her chosen avenger to fulfill an obligation to avenge kin-slaying (in Beatrice's case, it is kin-slandering and a symbolic death). This scene functions similarly to that of the *hvot* in saga literature, which I discussed in chapter 1.

Beatrice's bloodthirstiness is conveyed in vivid cannibalistic rhetoric, when she expresses the desire to eat her enemy's heart in the marketplace. The violence driving this image revives the hyperbolic language of epic wrath. We hear an echo of the Trojan queen Hecuba's desire to devour Achilles' liver in the *Iliad:* "I wish I could set teeth / in the middle of his liver and eat it. That would be vengeance / for what he did to my son" (24.212–14), and Achilles' response to his enemy Hector: "I wish only that my spirit and fury would drive me / to hack your meat away and eat it raw for the things that / you have done to me" (22.346–48). The goddess Hera, as well, seems ready to eat her enemies, the Trojans; only then, Zeus says, will her wrath be satisfied (4.31–36).[70] While in the anonymous play *The True Tragedie of Richard the Third* (printed in 1594), King Richard echoes classical predecessors in his taunting wish to eat his enemy Richmond's heart "panting hot with salt" (line 1984),[71] Beatrice's cry is the more surprising, for she is neither villain, warrior, nor tragic queen lamenting a son's death. Yet her passion in response to the outrage of slander and her kinwoman's social death is dignified with epic language. In this moment, the raging spirits of Hecuba, Achilles, and the heroes of epic are revived in Beatrice. She possesses courage and just anger, she aspires to heroic action, and Shakespeare figures her vengeance with a rhetorical excess typical of the epic.

Yet she is aware of her tragic helplessness in the male arena of dueling and blood feud. Of necessity, she must choose an avenger for Hero, and Benedick is the only male available to her. She chooses him, however, only after he has sworn his love, thereby constituting a future kinship bond. Only then does her goading becomes a frank command to "Kill Claudio." We might agree with Linda Anderson in her claim that these two words reflect "the most striking note of vengeance to be sounded in any of Shakespeare's plays."[72] Spoken by a woman who means what she says, "Kill Claudio" is in deadly earnest. That Benedick finally agrees to take up Beatrice's cause signals his shift of alliance from his male peers to the women of Messina and his acknowledgment of the deadly harm men's words can do women. In the name of love and honor, he will treat the avenging of Hero as his own cause. He has suddenly been called to heroic action. The lessons of Beatrice's verbal revenges bear fruit—Benedick is made to care deeply about the deleterious effects of slander on women.

Revenge in Renaissance Messina or early modern London might very well take the form of a duel to the death, and this is what Benedick intends when he says to Claudio: "You are a villain. I jest not. I will make it good how you dare, with what you dare and when you dare. Do me right, or I will protest your cowardice. You have killed a sweet lady, and her death shall fall heavy on you. Let me hear from you" (5.1.143—48). That the women cannot take action themselves is perceived as a loss and a source of suffering. As Beatrice laments, "I cannot be a man with wishing, therefore I will die a woman with grieving" (4.1.320–21). Yet Beatrice's passionate cry for just vengeance and unshakable demand for allegiance and heroic action from Benedick allow her to put her grief to work. She has done some "wishing" through the agency of her imaginative, fiery words of incitement. And Benedick is her man. From her ethical position, she honors Hero and demonstrates how women compensate for their physical impotence. Unnecessary and indecorous as dueling and bloodshed may be in a comedy, *Much Ado* brings us to the brink of such violence with a sense of moral urgency. Beatrice's cries of outrage, her desire to be a man so that she might kill the man who slandered her beloved cousin, are nothing if not reflective of just passions. In keeping with the laws of comedy, however, Benedick does not end up killing Claudio. Because the Watch reveals Don John and Borachio's malicious plot, Claudio's terrible error is uncovered, and he pays for his crime with remorse, guilt, and shame.

While Beatrice, like the other inciters I have examined in these first few chapters, is an avenger in spirit and tongue, other Shakespearean women playfully, maliciously, and justly do a "man's office" by plotting and executing revenges. The finer point, really, is that women often have good cause for inciting or taking revenge, and Shakespeare's dramas display this social truth and ethical imperative in a variety of contexts. *Their* office derives from the need to protect their social identities and honor, and to advocate justice for other women. They display considerable ingenuity, mettle, and spirit, sometimes compromising their femininity, or descending into a disturbingly animalistic ferocity. While Nietzsche claimed, "In revenge and in love, women are more barbaric than men,"[73] Shakespeare displays ambivalence in handling the antifeminist trope of the savage avenging female, or monstrous Other. The male characters figure vindictive females in exaggerated terms only because these women have departed radically from gender norms and conventional morality. Some of his female avengers in the histories and tragedies may appear barbaric, but no more so than the men, and sometimes less so. Tamora's so-called barbarism, for example, is kindled by Titus's barbarism. Her revenges may be malicious, but they are answered by the greatest act of barbarism in Shakespeare's drama, the Thyestean feast cooked by Titus himself. Vengeful characters such as Tamora and Margaret cannot be reduced simply to frightening specters of malignant femininity, or to evil allegorical figures. For their causes to emerge with ethical clarity, for their participation within their honor-based cultures to be understood rightly, they must be seen as social and political players, as defiant women who assert their power over men who have transgressed against them and their kin. This is precisely the light in which I show these characters in the chapter that follows.

4

Hecuba's Legacy:
Wounded Maternity and Vengeance in the
First Tetralogy and *Titus Andronicus*

O female sex, desiring revenge . . . o woman, more fearful than a tigress
of Hyrcania!
> Barthélemy Aneau, *Picta poesis*

More cruel yet than the fate of divine mothers in tragedy is that of mortal women: whether triumphant or heartbroken queens, they are always
wounded in their motherhood. From that moment when mothers obtain
only the horrified sight of the child's corpse to compensate for their
loss, mourning that has already been transformed into wrath becomes
vengeance in deeds. And mothers kill.
> Nicole Loraux, *Mothers in Mourning*

WHILE SOME OF SHAKESPEARE'S FEMALE CHARACTERS APPEAR AS PAS-
sionate inciters to vengeance, as we saw in previous chapters, others take
action as avengers of their own causes. Shakespeare does not suppress the
violent potentialities of feminine vengeance any more than ancient Greek
dramatists did. Like Hecuba, Clytemnestra, Medea, and Procne, his female
characters can do more—far more—than incite men to violent retaliation.
In the histories and tragedies, they lead armies, declare vendettas, and harm
enemies personally. They also play patently theatrical roles, personifying
Revenge and presiding over history as if it were revenge drama. We might
imagine the early-modern male actors playing the parts of Tamora, queen
of the Goths, and Margaret, England's queen, by exploiting the potency and
quasi-masculine aspects of their characterizations. An adult male actor,
rather than some squeaking boy, would be needed to satisfy the requirements of personating such charismatic, mature queens. Indeed, many critics and some of the plays' male characters perceive these unruly females as
usurpers of male traits and prerogatives; thus, performing the female avenger
might involve activating masculine aspects of the actor. At the same time,

these characters are unequivocally female, their gender marked through costume and familial relationships. The dramatic texts make clear that Margaret and Tamora appear as desirable women chosen by male monarchs for marriage and rule. Even more significant, they appear as mothers whose fierce maternal love inspires their strongest passions and actions.[1]

Shakespeare's First Tetralogy (the *Henry VI* plays and *Richard III*) and *Titus Andronicus* complicate audiences' responses to women's active participation in political situations by presenting them in an equivocal light: they are mothers, wives, widows, and lovers, yet they are also bold queens who exhibit traits associated with men in heroic cultures—valor, honor, rage, and vengefulness. Shakespeare's warlike women, Margaret and Tamora in particular, can be understood as possessing an element of the heroic—even if it strikes many as a debased heroism. Or, as some critics argue, perhaps women's usurpation of male traits works as an ethical critique of male heroic values, stripping bare men's pretenses to honor and the ugly realities of war and political machinations.[2] Seen within their sociopolitical circumstances, these female characters evoke complex responses from audiences precisely because they are women made to endure trauma, dishonor, and brutal treatment. They are forced to rise in power and compensate for humiliations through extraordinary means that defy feminine gender norms. They are wounded again and again as women, but most of all as mothers.

Ethical questions regarding the motives, passions, and actions of aggressive women in positions of power are pressing in these plays. When it comes to revenge, such questions are most urgent. For Shakespeare and his contemporaries, avenging women called to mind images of the Hyrcanian tiger, Amazon, and virago, tropes that signify a transformation from a conventionally gendered female into a beast or unnatural creature. Male characters give voice to fear and moral repulsion by verbally metamorphosing female avengers into fantastical creatures, so as to dehumanize them and rob them of any ethical warrant for their rage and violence. Yet it is important to observe how Shakespeare tempers these tropes in his histories and tragedies by invoking complex narratives of woman's revenge derived from classical mythology. In particular, Shakespeare invokes the legend of Hecuba, the fallen Trojan queen and avenging mother, as a political-mythological context in which to read the passions and violence of queens who suffer monumental losses. Women's vengefulness gains ethical justification when female characters are depicted in light of Hecuba as grief-stricken mothers witnessing wartime atrocities and responding actively to unspeakable crimes.

In their wounded maternity, Queen Margaret in the First Tetralogy and Queen Tamora in *Titus Andronicus* part company with other avenging female characters such as Lear's daughters Goneril and Regan. Their *mater-*

nal passions cast Margaret's and Tamora's political and personal ethics in a sympathetic light. Like Hecuba, these Shakespearean queens move audiences specifically in relation to their motherhood. Margaret's defense of her son's political position as England's heir apparent through continued warfare against the Yorkists displays her fierce commitment to her child's claim and to the Lancastrian line. When her son is killed by the York brothers before her eyes, Margaret appears in a most piteous light. The historical record found in Edward Hall's *Chronicle* makes clear Margaret's loyalty to and grief for her son, and Shakespeare's rescripting of Margaret's story gives her an opportunity for Hecubean lamentation. Tamora, the fallen Goth queen, is first viewed onstage in her role as mother of three sons. Her Roman captor, Titus Andronicus, sacrifices her eldest boy to his gods, which drives Tamora to retaliate against the cruel father and his sons. When Margaret and Tamora suffer the slaughtering of their sons, their maternal grief is piercing and terrible to witness in the theater. Their desire for retribution—for the massacre of their enemies—stems from their wounded maternity and, furthermore, from a burning sense of injustice. The lack of any dignified ritual treatment of the princes' corpses through formal lament and burial denies these queens the regenerative possibilities of death rites and shared communal mourning.

As Nicole Loraux writes, "From that moment when mothers obtain only the horrified sight of the child's corpse to compensate for their loss, mourning that has already been transformed into wrath becomes vengeance in deeds. And mothers kill."[3] Herein lies the essential pattern of tragedy articulated through the passions and affective ethics of mothers. Indeed, Shakespeare's engagement with the Hecuba myth in *Titus Andronicus* and the First Tetralogy suggests that maternal bereavement is the supreme expression of loss in tragedy. Vengeance, then, becomes the mother's justified response to an unspeakable crime, or *nefas*.

TROPING THE FEMALE AVENGER:
TIGERS, AMAZONS, AND VIRAGOS

Perhaps the most disquieting cases of feminine revenge are those of avenging mothers. The proverbially ferocious Hyrcanian tiger was linked with savage maternity in some classical and Renaissance texts. In Barthélemy Aneau's emblem book *Picta poesis* (Lyons, 1552), for example, one finds an allusion to the raging tiger in the motto to an illustration of Procne and Medea killing their children: "The rabid Hyrcanian tigress tears herself to pieces, and rends the members of her own flesh. . . . O female sex, desiring revenge . . . o woman, more fearful than a tigress of Hyrcania!"[4] Aneau intensifies the unnaturalness of vengeful women by suggesting that they prey upon their own flesh, like the most savage, pitiless beast known to man. Procne's maternal love for her son, Itys, does not quell her rage against her husband, Tereus, who raped her sister, Philomel. Savage justice prevails: as previously mentioned, she kills the boy, cooks up his flesh, and serves it to his guilty father. Medea's rage against Jason, her faithless husband, drives her to punish him with the killing of their two sons. In John Studley's translation of Seneca's *Medea,* the avenging wife counsels herself to "Exile all foolysh Female feare, and pity from thy mynde" so that she may become tyrannous "as th' untamed Tygers" that "rage and rave unkynde" (act 2).[5] To be like the Hyrcanian tiger is to relinquish feminine qualities, most particularly pity, and to be free to rage even against one's kin (to become "unkynde"): Medea and Procne rend their own flesh to punish their husbands' crimes.

Perhaps the best-known classical example of the tiger trope derives from Virgil's *Aeneid.* In book 4, a raging Dido lashes out at the false Aeneas with an insult as terrible as she can contrive: "nec tibi diua parens generis nec Dardanus auctor, / perfide, sed duris genuit te cautibus horrens /Caucasus Hyrcanaeque admorunt ubera tigres" (4.365–67).[6] Virgil's famous passage is echoed fairly closely in Marlowe's *Dido, Queen of Carthage:*

> Thy mother was no goddess, perjur'd man,
> Nor Dardanus the author of thy stock;
> But thou art sprung from Scythian Caucasus,
> And tigers of Hyrcania gave thee suck.
>
> (5.1.156–59)[7]

The result of inhuman birthing and nurturing can only be unnatural—Aeneas is hard as a rock and pitiless as the tiger that figuratively gave him suck. Another echo of this passage can be heard in the besieged Lavinia's pleas to Tamora's sons in *Titus Andronicus:*

> When did the tiger's young ones teach the dam?
> O, do not learn her wrath: she taught it thee.
> The milk thou suckst from her did turn to marble;
> Even at thy teat thou hadst thy tyranny.
> Yet every mother breeds not sons alike:
> Do thou entreat her show a woman's pity.
>
> (2.2.142–47)

In Lavinia's figuration, Tamora is the wrathful mother-tiger whose milk hardens into marble, yielding obdurate, pitiless sons. She lacks "a woman's pity," or a heart that softens in compassion.

Shakespeare alludes to tigers over forty times in his plays and poetry as a means to convey qualities in human nature that render a person bestial—

pitilessness, wrath, ferocity, and savagery. This trope can work both ways, however, casting a positive or negative light on the human appropriation of tigerlike behavior. In the casting of the trope, gender and context make all the difference. Women are perceived as tigerlike when they are being chastised for morally depraved, unnatural behavior. In *King Lear,* for example, when the Duke of Albany confronts his wife, Goneril, with her harsh treatment of Lear, he calls her and her sister, Regan, "Tigers, not daughters. . . . Most barbarous, most degenerate. . . . for shame / Bemonster not thy feature" (First Quarto, 16.39, 42, 61–62). Albany would like to rip Goneril apart physically, a savage act that would replicate her savagery, but he refrains, for there is little of the tiger in him. Female characters such as Dido, when she was abandoned by Aeneas, or Lavinia, when she was threatened by Tamara's sons, castigate heartless men by claiming their mothers were tigers, and thus the source of their cruelty.

When applied to male warriors, however, the tiger trope works to create a significant analogy or metaphor for battle rage, mettle, and war-justified revenge. When Hamlet thinks of Pyrrhus, the avenging son of Achilles, he misremembers a line from a play, adding in the tiger simile no doubt because he thinks of Pyrrhus's ferocity: "The rugged Pyrrhus, like th' Hyrcanian beast" (2.2.388). When invoked by a leader, the image and action of the Hyrcanian beast can motivate men to attack an enemy with the greatest force imaginable. King Harry's "Once more unto the breach" speech in *Henry V* makes extended use of the tiger analogy in the context of war:

> In peace there's nothing so becomes a man
> As modest stillness and humility;
> But when the blast of war blows in our ears,
> Then imitate the action of the tiger:
> Stiffen the sinews, conjure up the blood,
> Disguise fair nature with hard-favoured rage.
> Then lend the eye a terrible aspect;
> Let it pry through the portage of the head
> Like the brass cannon; let the brow o'erwhelm it
> As fearfully as doth a galled rock
> O'erhang and jutty his confounded base,
> Swilled with the wild and wasteful ocean.
> Now set the teeth and stretch the nostril wide,
> Hold hard the breath and bend up every spirit
> To his full height.
>
> (3.1.3–17)

"Imitate the action of the tiger": such a mimetic act captures the performance of male warriors in a heroic culture. There is a vital metamorphic quality to the imitation that suggests the actor becoming his part: soft sinews stiffen, the blood rises up, the face hardens with rage, the eyes suddenly grow terrible in their gaze, the nostrils stretch wide. The eyes, like brass cannons, become weapons shooting forth on the battlefield. Such a transformation from man into beast wins glory and honor for men at war.

Yet the same trope of metamorphosis when applied to women, even women warriors, is designed to call up strong feelings of disgust, moral repulsion, and horrified awe. Rather than rousing a woman to valor, the tiger analogy is meant to induce shame. Aggressive female characters such as Margaret, Tamora, Goneril, and Regan are perceived as tigers because they exhibit traits that resemble those of the male warrior. They have challenged the "natural" order of things and, in doing so, left themselves open to harsh censure. Their metamorphoses are terrible, as well—both wondrous and deplorable—as "nothing so becomes a [woman] / As modest stillness and humility." There are no cultural sanctions for women disguising their fair natures with "hard-favoured rage."

Yet Shakespeare's females characters are shown to be warranted in taking on a "terrible aspect" and "hard-favoured rage" when they are wronged. Margaret and Tamora, for example, exist within bellicose cultures where revenge is a norm and functions as a political and personal motive that empowers individuals and drives the defeat of enemies. Shakespeare depicts these females as no more bestial than their male counterparts—even if the male characters insist they are—for they follow the same wartime terms of engagement that men pursue, imitating the action of a tiger and using violence to their advantage when opportunities present themselves.

Some critics of the *Henry VI* plays, *Titus Andronicus,* and *King Lear* have appropriated the plays' moralizing rhetoric of bestiality and monstrosity to establish their terms of attack upon female avengers, whom they regard as unnatural in their womanhood and deviant in their moral and political practices.[8] In judging these aggressive, violent females, critics have too easily replicated the negative early-modern views of female rulers found in historical chronicles and political discourses, which preach against the monstrous regiment of women. Early modern texts typically register profound anxieties about women's encroachment upon the male-defined public domain. A woman's involvement in politics and warfare, according to English chroniclers such as Richard Grafton and Edward Hall, could only result in her becoming a "manly woman, vsyng to rule and not to be ruled" who, in defiance of natural order, "pluck[s] the sworde of aucthoritie out of [men's] handes."[9] The manlike woman is reminiscent of the virago of Renaissance legends, a somewhat fantastical figure of equivocal gender—masculine in her war-like valor and strength and feminine in her sexual desire and allure. When critics perceive vengeance-seeking females as viragos, however, they tend to conflate two kinds of appetites—lust and revenge both arise from the incontinent libido. While Margaret, Tamora,

Goneril, and Regan are all adulterous, the ethics of their revenges should not be evaluated as if on a continuum with their sexual mores.[10]

Vengeance in female characters must be understood to arise from specific political and familial situations, and ethics must be examined in relation to the wrongs they have endured. The avenging female is always clear in her motives for attacking an enemy, and she often has multiple causes driving her to use force: to right a wrong, defend her own and her family's honor, to challenge corrupt patriarchal rule, and to avenge the death of a child (usually a male). Furthermore, Shakespeare's images of avenging women in the tragedies and histories force audiences to experience women's grief, resentment, wrath, shame, love, and hate, and to weigh the ethics of their responses to difficult, even harrowing, circumstances. Not only a site of patriarchal conflict and tragedy, Shakespeare's theater of revenge is a liminal space for ruling women to enact their own narratives of revenge. They display fierce resistance in the face of what they perceive to be injustice and potential powerlessness, and they exhibit a will "Not to be overruled," as Goneril asserts in the First Quarto text of *King Lear* (3.16).

Perhaps the most famous stage depiction of an avenging queen on the Elizabethan stage is Shakespeare's Margaret, the late-medieval, foreign-born English queen. She is accused by her enemy, the Duke of York, of having a tiger's heart, for she is pitiless in her treatment of him on the battlefield. We can gauge the fame of this scene by turning to the university playwright Robert Greene's satirical attack on Shakespeare: "[T]here is an vpstart Crow, beautified with our feathers, that with his *Tygers hart wrapt in a Players hyde,* supposes he is as well able to bombast out a blanke verse as the best of you: and beeing an absolute *Iohannes fac totum,* is in his owne conceit the onely Shake-scene in a countrey."[11] Greene exaggerates his case of Shakespeare's intrusion upon the writing profession, rendering the provincial playwright as comically savage and remorseless in his breaking of rank. Significantly, he plays on his reader's recent memory of a stunning scene from the *Henry VI* plays, in which a cruel avenging queen mocks the Duke of York with a paper crown and a cloth stained with his son's blood. In *3 Henry VI,* York assaults Queen Margaret, the "She-wolf of France" (1.4.111), with many bitter words, including those Greene mockingly appropriated: "O, tiger's heart wrapped in a woman's hide" (line 137). He charges Margaret with being "more inhuman, more inexorable, / O, ten times more than tigers of Hyrcania" (lines 154–55). Her woman's face is belied by her "stern, obdurate, flinty, rough, remorseless" qualities of character (line 142). To "Disguise fair nature with hard-favoured rage" (*Henry V,* 3.1.8) most becomes a male warrior, not a female.

This shocking scene has a memorable quality, conveying as it does the brutal revenge of an upstart warrior queen who revels in her unusual position of power. The scene's success depends on Shakespeare's brilliant exploitation of his audience's anxieties regarding gender transgression, while at the same time satisfying their desire for blood revenge. The forceful rhetorical balancing of Margaret's and York's speeches renders her violent retaliation first through a verbal pattern that mimics revenge's pattern of harm for harm, and then through physical violence onstage. One critic argues that the speeches display an "ethical parity of the two sides, and the appallingly wasteful bankruptcy of their policies."[12] This perspective may be tempting to adopt, for at this point in the Wars of the Roses, the violence on both sides has escalated. Furthermore, Margaret's attacks on the Yorkists are not sanctioned by Henry, her husband and the Lancastrian king. Critics such as Juliet Dusinberre perceive that "Margaret's violence in *Henry VI* reflects the pattern of moral inversion—unscrupulousness, infidelity, meaningless vengeance—set in motion by the Civil War."[13] Jean E. Howard and Phyllis Rackin refine this view by observing how "the extraordinary venom directed against Margaret within the play, and the gratuitous cruelty with which Shakespeare invests her character reveal her convenience as a scapegoat for the chaos around her."[14] Indeed, Edward, York's son, blames Margaret for instigating the Wars of the Roses when he says, "Hadst thou been meek, our title still had slept, / And we, in pity of the gentle King, / Had slipped our claim until another age" (*3 Henry VI*, 2.2.160–62). But his words are disingenuous and barely conceal his vitriol against a powerful foreign-born queen to whom he and his kin refuse to give obeisance. While the specter of a French "Amazonian trull" (1.4.114) at England's helm (York's disparaging phrase) seems monstrous to most of the male characters, Margaret has a clear ethical imperative in seeking to protect what a father should have been capable of safeguarding, his son's inheritance of the throne.[15]

Margaret is more politically astute than Henry in recognizing York as their enemy. Margaret goes after the Duke of York and his forces with a militant determinism. She is a figure of terror and fury in her infamous moment on the battlefield, her ferocity comparable to that of any classical epic hero. She may be cruel, but she enters the war zone with a purpose—to fight for her son's claim to the throne, which the fearful Henry bargained away. When York promised Henry a quiet reign if, upon his death, he would give over the crown to him and his Plantagenet heirs, King Henry gives in, eager to end civil war: "I am content. Richard Plantagenet, / Enjoy the kingdom after my decease" (*3 Henry VI*, 1.1.174–75). As Henry himself confesses, he "unnaturally . . . disinherit[s]" his son (line 193), which is the sacrifice he is willing to make to broker a fragile and, as it turns out, false peace. Shortly thereafter, he is betrayed by the Yorkists. If Henry VI is too weak and fearful to fulfill his patriarchal obligations, his wife then is forced to do what she can for the survival of their line. She will do a man's office, if necessary. Margaret's army, with the Queen as its general, takes up the battle for what Henry has fearfully discarded.

QUEEN MARGARET: WARRIOR, MOTHER, AVENGER

In developing the character of Margaret of Anjou in the First Tetralogy, Shakespeare depicts a woman's active participation within historical revenge cycles. A comparison of the early texts of the tetralogy with their later revisions reflects Shakespeare's increased attention to Margaret's potency as a political figure. In his careful consideration of textual alterations, Steven Urkowitz observes that the 1623 Folio histories, unlike the 1594 texts, represent Margaret as a commanding presence; her bold speech and "visual dominance of the stage" are evident.[16] For example, in Margaret's abject position before the French king in a scene in which she sits upon the ground in a despairing posture, the stage action and speech work to support a performance that "arrests and holds our attention even in moments of political weakness."[17] In the course of four plays, from *I Henry VI* through *Richard III,* Margaret dominates countless scenes, charting a journey that moves from youth to old age in images of courtship, amorous alliance, monarchical power, military leadership, wartime brutality, political embassy, motherhood, and widowhood. In contending with Margaret's character, critics and directors too often miss the cues Urkowitz has emphasized in the Folio text, which illustrate the complex characterization of a self-possessed, bold queen and fiercely loving mother. Too often, Margaret is contained within stereotyped categories, such as vindictive virago, adulteress, and madwoman, that diminish the dramatic and ethical potentialities in this rich female character. Careful attention to the First Folio characterization of Margaret as a bold, intelligent queen naturally disposed toward preserving self-worth and as a passionate mother concerned with her son's well-being and inheritance can uncover in her an affective ethics, a canny political awareness, and a psychological astuteness.

Margaret's maternity, often overlooked, downplayed, or maligned by critics, is reflected crucially in language and performance. She perceives herself as protector and guardian of her son, Edward, as well as King Henry, who cannot fathom, much less participate in, the political machinations at court and in his kingdom. Margaret's maternal feeling for her son and her commitment to his claim to the throne motivate her actions, offering a degree of justification for her engagement in battle and the vengeance she wreaks upon York. Furthermore, through resonances with the Hecuba legend, Margaret can be seen by the end of *3 Henry VI* as a queen of woe and loss and, most strikingly, as a bereaved mother.

Perhaps the insights and sensitivities of the modern actress or female director are best suited to the project of transcending the gender stereotypes
and moral censure of Margaret. The actress Penny Downie, who played
Queen Margaret in Adrian Noble's 1988 and 1989 productions of *The Plan-
tagenets* (an adaptation of the First Tetralogy), discovered her character to
be "altogether so original that labels are unhelpful."[18] Her view counters
typical critical perspectives of Margaret as an "unnatural" and "domineering" "archvillainess," or as an adjunct of Joan La Pucelle, the other powerful French female represented in the histories.[19] Downie portrayed what
she called Margaret's "spiritual ageing" in gradual stages. Young Margaret,
a "mixture of naïve and knowing" in her first scene with Suffolk, becomes
a woman with a "political brain" who "grows to genuine statesmanship";
a queen with a sense of honor, especially protective of King Henry; an
amoral warrior capable of primal, animal behavior; a mother and lover provoked to grief; and finally an "ageless figure of moral nemesis . . . purified
by suffering to play this final moral role."[20]

In directing the First Tetralogy for BBC-TV, Jane Howell paid close attention to Margaret's "education in violence," charting the terrific emotional costs for a woman trying to survive in a warrior culture.[21] When
Margaret stabs Richard of York, the actress Julia Foster registered a "look
of shock," which "defined this act as Margaret's first real blooding and
contrasted strongly with the casual attitude of the men around her."[22]
Howell's production highlighted Margaret's Hecuba-like lamentation over
the slaughtered body of her son. She holds out her arms, as the bereaved
Hecuba is depicted doing at the discovery of Polydorus's body in Renaissance illustrations, such as Antonio Tempesta's, of that moment in Ovid's
Metamorphoses.[23] She then weeps and embraces her son's body in a gesture reminiscent of the pietà, the Virgin's lament over her dead son,
Christ.[24] The final image in the tetralogy was Howell's most controversial,
in part because it is not Shakespeare's. At the close of *Richard III*, Margaret
returns to the battlefield once more to upstage King Richard; surrounded
by corpses, Margaret sits cradling his corpse in her arms, like an avenging
Fury appeased at last. The image for Howell "was purely instinctive," she
explains in an interview; "apparently it's a classic image for revenge, a reverse pietà."[25] Equally as instinctive was Howell's echoing of the earlier
pietà—the dead boy Edward in Margaret's arms—which subliminally links
Margaret's revenge with the killing of her son.

Margaret's first appearance in the tetralogy occurs at the end of *1 Henry
VI* when the Earl of Suffolk captures her from a battlefield and woos her
for Henry VI, partly as a covert strategy to win her for himself. This scene
(5.2) is strategically positioned between the capture of Joan La Pucelle and
Joan's curse upon England before she is ushered offstage to be burnt at the
stake. Joan's function as a scourge to the English is taken over by another

foreign female, but this Frenchwoman will ascend the English throne and come into her own as a female monarch and dramatic character in her own right. While she does inflict punishment upon some of the English, she also presides over the royal line as mother to the heir apparent. Her militant actions fuel violence, yet she protects the interests of the Lancastrian bloodline, which she herself has joined through marriage and procreation.

Margaret's first words in *1 Henry VI* boldly declare her name and rank to her English captor, Suffolk: "Margaret my name, and daughter to a king, / The King of Naples—whosoe'er thou art" (5.2.72–73). Suffolk has queried, "Who art thou?" (line 71), after delivering a speech of adoration, which sets the erotic tone of their encounter, and conflates eros with military and political matters. Gazing upon Margaret's beauty, touching her, he speaks lovingly and gently to her, and soon turns away to think how he might have her for his own, yet woo her for the English king. Margaret's speech in this scene is frank and pragmatic as she asks, "What ransom must I pay before I pass? / For I perceive I am thy prisoner" (5.2.94–95). When Suffolk hesitates and then insists he has a secret to reveal, Margaret secretly hopes, "Perhaps I shall be rescued by the French, / And then I need not crave his courtesy" (lines 125–26). In her asides, she plays upon the words "enthralled" and "captivate," calling her secret musings "*quid* for *quo*" when Suffolk desires to hear what she says (line 130). When Suffolk proposes a "bondage happy, to be made a queen," her reply is worthy of a queen, reflecting high-mindedness. She insists that "To be a queen in bondage is more vile / Than is a slave in base servility; / For princes should be free" (lines 133–35).

When Suffolk paints a picture of Margaret as a free queen with the attendant symbols of monarchical power (scepter and crown), he slips by saying, "If thou wilt condescend to be *my*—" (line 141, my emphasis). Margaret sharply interrupts him: "What?" And Suffolk corrects himself: "*His* love" (lines 141, 142, my emphasis). The subtext of Suffolk's self-interested wooing of Margaret, and her detection of it, is clear at this point. Though she may be in a vulnerable position here as a political prisoner caught up in an international conflict, her future uncertain, Margaret appears as a self-possessed princess quick to pursue an advantage when she sees one. She agrees to marry Henry. When she tells Suffolk to convey her "pure unspotted heart, / Never yet taint with love" (lines 203–4), to the English king, Suffolk steals a kiss from her. She lets him have his prize, but reduces its value to no more than that of "peevish tokens" (line 207).

Suffolk has recognized Margaret's virtues, which he reports to Henry in his persuasive courtship speech. Though lacking a dowry (a point of detraction emphasized by her enemies later), Margaret is "fit for none but for a king," Suffolk proclaims:

> Her valiant courage and undaunted spirit
> (More than in women is commonly seen)
> Will answer our hope in issue of a king.
> For Henry, son unto a conqueror,
> Is likely to beget more conquerors,
> If with a lady of so high resolve
> As is fair Margaret he be linked in love.
>
> (5.4.69–76)

Suffolk's praise of Margaret as nearly male in her valor, courage, "undaunted spirit," and "high resolve" wins over Henry, who accepts her as his queen. Suffolk's promise of a strong, courageous queen to beget a conqueror-son frames the marriage within a political context redolent of mythic conquests. Suffolk's final words in the scene, however, cast the royal union in his own private fantasy of conquest. He engages the Troy legend, ominously fashioning himself a Paris to Margaret's Helen. But Margaret is no Helen, and Henry is no Menelaus. Though she does take Suffolk as a lover, Queen Margaret makes good on his rhetoric of praise by becoming a political power, diplomat, general of the Lancastrian troops, and mother of a prince. Later, in *3 Henry VI*, King Henry refers to England as Troy and his supporter the Earl of Warwick as "my Hector, and my Troy's true hope" (4.8.25). Margaret plays Hecuba to Henry's Priam, only she is a warlike Hecuba, prepared to fight for *her* Troy and her Polydorus, the prince. She sheds tears for the siege of her Troy: "for every word I speak," she says to her troops, "Ye see I drink the water of my eye. . . . You fight in justice" (5.4.74–75, 81). Shakespeare's Hecuba figure weeps for her country, but fights for it too.

Margaret gains tremendous power in *2 Henry VI* as King Henry's passivity, effeminacy, and piousness incapacitate him in the face of rebellion and civil war. Her ambition and political acumen make her a suitable, albeit unexpected and controversial, candidate for filling in the power vacuum left by Henry. Her rise to a position of political leadership comes into play as Henry reveals himself incapable of defending their throne and, furthermore, bargains away their son Edward's patrimony.

A crucial turning point for Margaret comes when Henry banishes Suffolk as punishment for his part in killing Humphrey, Duke of Gloucester. Her husband and son are not Margaret's only concerns. Margaret is presented onstage as vulnerable, first when Henry grieves for Gloucester and refuses to respond to her woes and then when Margaret begs Henry to spare Suffolk from exile, which he, in one of his rare moments of decisiveness, refuses to do. In her passionate outburst to Henry in 3.2, she attempts to sway him to show his allegiance to her rather than to Gloucester. She ends

her appeal by invoking an episode from Virgil's *Aeneid* in which Venus
sends Cupid in the image of Ascanius, Aeneas's son, to Dido to inflame her
love. She exclaims that she has "tempted Suffolk's tongue . . ."

> To sit and witch me, as Ascanius did
> When he to madding Dido would unfold
> His father's acts, commenced in burning Troy!
> Am I not witched like her? Or thou not false like him?
>
> (3.2.114, 116–19)

Yet just as Suffolk's earlier association of Margaret with Helen is only partially fulfilled (she does become his lover, yet also a political power), Margaret's self-identification with Dido is a partial truth, for her passion is
kindled and devastation heartfelt with the loss of Suffolk. Henry's distancing from Margaret is marked by his lack of response to such an affecting
(albeit equivocal) evocation of Dido's plight.

In her farewell to Suffolk, Margaret wishes that "threefold vengeance
tend upon thy steps!" (*2 Henry VI*, 3.2.304). When Suffolk indicates he
wishes only to feel the sorrow of leave-taking, Margaret bursts out angrily,
"Fie, coward woman and soft-hearted wretch! / Hast thou not spirit to curse
thine enemies?" (lines 307–8). Vengeance and curses, for Margaret, are
natural responses to suffering and dishonor; thus, she resorts to negative
gender stereotyping in calling Suffolk "coward woman" for his "soft" response to his treatment by Henry and his enemies. Suffolk does not take
the bait, responding instead as a despondent lover, grieving at the immi-
nent departure from his beloved. Margaret soon responds in kind, wetting
his palm with tears and kisses. On his sea journey to France, Suffolk is captured and killed by pirates off the coast of Kent. These pirates may very
well be Yorkists, involved in a conspiracy against Suffolk, and linked to the
Jack Cade / Kent uprising.[26] Their murder of Suffolk is represented as a
vengeance-killing. A gentleman onboard comments,

> O barbarous and bloody spectacle!
> His body will I bear unto the King.
> If he revenge it not, yet will his friends;
> So will the Queen, that living held him dear.
>
> (*2 Henry VI*, 4.1.146–49)

When Margaret appears again onstage in 4.4, she is cradling Suffolk's head
in her arms, grieving and thinking of vengeance.

Communal mourning and honorific burial rites are impossible due to
Suffolk's political (and sexual) transgressions. Thus, Margaret, in pain,
must mourn alone, enlisting only the audience's sympathy with her lament:

Oft have I heard that grief softens the mind
And makes it fearful and degenerate;
Think therefore on revenge and cease to weep.
But who can cease to weep and look on this?
Here may his head lie on my throbbing breast;
But where's the body that I should embrace?
(2 Henry VI, 4.4.1–6)

Margaret's traumatic loss is figured hauntingly through the image of an incomplete or grotesque pietà. With no body to embrace, there is only the head, which becomes, in a peculiarly affecting transformation, a baby at her breast. Margaret's regressive image of the babe at his mother's "throbbing breast" echoes Suffolk's desire, expressed to Margaret in the face of his banishment, to die like a "cradle babe" "with mother's dug between its lips" (3.2.392, 393). The nature of Margaret's grief, thus, takes on the poignancy of a mother's devastating loss. Worse than the death of a lover, Suffolk's death is experienced as profoundly as that of her own child, the body memory of both lover and baby merged in her intense longing and grief.

Mourning invites compassionate identification and pity for the devastated Margaret. When June Watson played Queen Margaret in the English National Theater's 1990 production of the *Henry VI* cycle, she appeared onstage like a somnambulist, cradling the decapitated head of Suffolk, her lover, like a baby close to her breast, whispering to herself as she glided across the stage. In a fusion of the grotesque and the pitiable, this disturbing moment shared between actress and audience highlighted Margaret's maternal feeling and capacity for grief. Articulating Shakespeare's text in such a moving performance can produce aesthetic and emotional effects— awe, horror, pity—and a complex awareness of Margaret's tragic circumstances. In the scene, Margaret's psyche comes into focus, reminding the audience that she has been damaged by loss; that hard as she appears, she can be broken; that she is not simply a figure of unnatural or monstrous femininity or sheer political calculation; that she is a woman who can be pierced, who can suffer. The figurative associations between a lover's loss and maternal grief in this scene humanize Margaret while at the same time anticipating her final devastation as a mother in *3 Henry VI*.

Margaret's mourning rite ceases at the scene's end when she confides in the audience: "My hope is gone, now Suffolk is deceased" (4.4.55). Such a simple acknowledgment—all hope in her has been killed with the death of her lover—proves to be pivotal. Soon, her grief converts to anger, vengefulness, and purposeful action in battle, which will be motivated by mother love for both Suffolk and her son. Margaret grows into her political role as queen, standing in for Henry as general of the Lancastrian troops and the

Crown's power. Her vengeance, far from "meaningless," as Dusinberre called it,[27] is both politically and personally motivated, emanating from the desire to protect her family's monarchical interests and to crush the York- ist rebellion. Her vengeance, like that of the male protagonists, is part of the ethos of a warrior culture in which slaying one's enemies on the battle- field is justified.

The climactic molehill scene (1.4) in which York is captured and killed in *3 Henry VI* seems, in part, to be a delayed response to Suffolk's death. Her maternal treatment of Suffolk's head sets up the emotional equation of revenge: life for life, child for child, head for head. Shakespeare radically revises the chronicle accounts when he brings Margaret to this scene of reckoning, a scene from which the historical Margaret was absent.[28] He has the "ruthless Queen" demand the "hapless father's tears" (line 156) as re- payment for her "mother's tears" shed for Suffolk. Yet somehow, in the bar- rage of provoking questions to which she submits York, one senses that even torturing her enemy fails to bring ultimate satisfaction. She wants to humiliate York and, furthermore, to hear evidence that he feels humiliation as she has felt it. She wants his suffering to pay back the humiliations she has endured as the queen and wife of a passive king impervious to honor's claims, as a hated foreigner "crowned with infamy" (*2 Henry VI*, 3.2.71), and as a grief-stricken lover. Too much psychic remediation rides on this one act of revenge, which ultimately does not reclaim honor for Suffolk or for herself (not in the eyes of most of her peers, in any case), nor does it as- sure Henry and Margaret's place on the throne.

Grim as her vengeance has been, though, the killing of York must be un- derstood within the context of *talionic* law. Her battlefield revenge serves a legitimate dynastic purpose and, ultimately, she can claim that she seeks "to right our gentle-hearted King" (*3 Henry VI*, 1.4.176). That she humili- ates and torments York suggests a lack of proportion in her treatment of an enemy, yet an enemy he is. When Northumberland weeps for York, Mar- garet's fitting, albeit harsh, response captures the sense of just retaliation: "What, weeping-ripe, my Lord Northumberland? / Think but upon the wrong he did us all, / And that will quickly dry thy melting tears" (lines 172–74). Following this declaration, meant to shame Northumberland, Margaret and Clifford stab York. She then calls for him to be decapitated and the head placed on the city of York's gates.

Later in *3 Henry VI*, she visits King Lewis of France, appealing for "just and lawful aid" for her son against the Yorkists (3.3.32). Lewis admires her "dauntless mind" (line 17) and offers to relieve her sorrow over her fallen circumstances. In an affecting performance, she humbles herself before him and invokes the image of her former self as "Great Albion's Queen in former golden days" (line 7). "But now mischance hath trod my title down," she laments, "And with dishonour laid me on the ground" (lines 8–9).

Lewis is moved by Margaret's appeal and, despite Warwick's interference, he agrees to give her support. King Henry had predicted Margaret's effect on the French king, describing her as "a woman to be pitied much: / Her sighs will make a batt'ry in his breast; / Her tears will pierce into a marble heart; / The tiger will be mild whiles she doth mourn" (3.1.36–39). His allusion to the tiger is striking, for audiences recall the vivid words of York earlier in *3 Henry VI:* that Margaret's heart is a "tiger's heart wrapped in a woman's hide" (1.4.137). Henry now conceives of Margaret as a supplicant whose sighs and tears may move the tiger-hearted French king. Or, to emphasize the ambiguity here, Margaret remains the tiger, yet in her mourning, she becomes mild. Henry fears, however, that Warwick's appeals will supersede Margaret's tears. This might have come to pass had Edward not reneged on his promise to marry Lady Bona, daughter of the Duke of Savoy. Warwick feels the shame of the situation and renounces the Yorkists to join with the Lancastrian royal family. He and Margaret agree upon a political marriage of their children, and Warwick vows revenge against Edward. Now the King of France, Margaret, and Warwick are allies, and Margaret sends word with a messenger to the usurper Edward: "Tell him my mourning weeds are laid aside, / And I am ready to put armour on" (3.3.229–30). The militant Margaret rises up—a Hecuba in arms —ready to go to battle again.

The Yorkists' rise to power, however, proves unstoppable. The most pitiable image of Margaret comes at the end of *3 Henry VI* when the York brothers—Edward, Clarence, and Richard—stab her beloved son before her very eyes. Shakespeare would have found the description of the killing of the prince in both Edward Hall's and Raphael Holinshed's accounts, but neither chronicler reports that the mother bore witness to the slaying of her son. Hall remarks on the suddenness and piteousness of the murder, Holinshed on the cruelty of it, and both insist upon the moral design of history. As Holinshed phrases it, the murderers "in their latter days drank of the like cup, by the righteous justice and due punishment of God."[29] The presence of Margaret at her son's death scene in Shakespeare's drama meaningfully suggests that God's justice works to repay maternal suffering and grief.

In Hall's chronicle, Margaret's life back in France is depicted as "more lyke a death then a lyfe." Hall describes the fallen queen as "languishyng and mornying in continuall sorowe, not so much for her selfe and her husbande, whose ages were almost consumed and worne, but for the losse of prince Edward her sonne (whome she and her husband thought to leue, both ouerluer of their progeny, and also of their kyngdome) to whome in this lyfe nothyng coulde be either more displeasant or greuous."[30] Shakespeare elaborates upon the "continuall sorowe" of the mother, giving it not only poignancy but agency. Shakespeare stages a scene of pathos that etches into the audience's consciousness the mother's unforgettable grief. Margaret is pierced mortally by the death of her son. Like Hecuba, she wishes to die. And like Hecuba, Shakespeare's Margaret will rise in vengeance before she dies. In departing from historical accounts such as Edward Hall's, Shakespeare reaches back to ancient Greek tragedy, where he find an ethos and emotional potency suggestive of how Margaret's role as avenging mother might play out. In the Hecuba archetype, he found his model.

In Shakespeare's scene, we see Margaret subjected to the callous violence of her male enemies. She is brutally paid back for the killing of the Duke of York, and what the balancing of scenes betrays is that it is Clifford's murder of York's young son, Rutland, and Margaret's subsequent taunting of the father with the blood of his son that weigh most heavily in the scale of wrongs. The Yorkists' revenge is aimed against her maternity—their father's son for her son. Shakespeare is quite deliberate about making this equation in vengeance—the killing of the innocent sons makes for a devastating sight and a stark commentary on the unsparing, brutal quality of revenge: children's blood is sacrificed in payment for their parents' crimes.

The young prince Edward's death scene is emotionally powerful and morally outrageous, recalling the strong affective responses evoked by Rutland's death earlier. Audience responses to the boy's killing are intensified, however, with the presence of the mother onstage, helpless to defend her child. In shock and disbelief, Margaret cries out, "sweet Ned" is but a "child, / And men ne'er spend their fury on a child" (5.5.51, 56–57). But we know she is wrong, for the audience has witnessed Clifford's killing of the young Rutland, who pleaded so piteously for his life. Clifford's vengeful fury in that scene seemed out of proportion, his slight, youthful target "too mean a subject for [his] wrath" (1.3.19). Indeed, he speaks with the fury of a Senecan revenger:

> Had I brethren here, their lives and thine
> Were not revenge sufficient for me.
> No, if I digged up thy forefathers' graves
> And hung their rotten coffins up in chains,
> It could not slake mine ire nor ease my heart.
> The sight of any of the house of York
> Is as a Fury to torment my soul:
> And till I root out their accursed line
> And leave not one alive, I live in hell.
>
> (1.3.25–33)

For Clifford's wrath and savagery and for her mockery of the father's paternity, Margaret must pay. Her grief is total; her heart is "burst" (5.5.59, 60). The costs of revenge are steep and paid with tears and maternal trauma. She now cradles the body of her son in her arms, subliminally recalling the earlier scene of devastation when she grieved like a mother over the head of Suffolk. She begs, even taunts, the brothers to kill her. They are not men; they are "Butchers and villains! Bloody cannibals!" (line 61). To kill her would complete their butchery of the defenseless. Richard is ready, exclaiming, "Why should she live to fill the world with words?" (line 44). But King Edward hesitates fearfully: "Hold, Richard, hold, for we have done too much" (line 43). Shedding royal blood is not simply a matter of political expedience and gives Edward pause at this moment and a guilty conscience in time. He leaves her to be ransomed and sent back to France. Richard's question, however, proves apt, for it predicts the ethically significant function Shakespeare grants Margaret as the once powerful queen and grieving, wrathful mother in the final play of the First Tetralogy.

Shakespeare's Margaret survives with a vengeance. "England's bloody scourge," as the Duke of York calls her (2 *Henry VI*, 5.1.118), makes a spectacular comeback in *Richard III*, as if to impress upon the kingdom and the theater audience the prophetic truth of York's title for her and the answer to Richard's canny question. In an early scene, the audience hears Margaret fill the court with sharp, piercing curses that unnerve her listeners. Her final words in *3 Henry VI* had been to curse Edward, Clarence, and Richard: "So come to you and yours as to this Prince!" (5.5.82). She reappears in *Richard III* not as a weapon-wielding avenger, but as an onstage spectator and mistress of retaliatory justice—Revenge, or Nemesis—desirous of seeing her curses fulfilled. Margaret's line "Here in these confines slily have I lurk'd" (4.4.3) suggests that she may be onstage for much of the drama, functioning as its presiding spirit much the way Revenge does in Thomas Kyd's *The Spanish Tragedy*. In her dramatic function, she forges invisible threads of complicity between herself and the audience.

As one critic argues, "Margaret acquires the legitimacy of the Greek Furies, insisting on retribution in future generations."[31] In Greek tragedy, the Furies relentlessly pursue those who shed kin's blood and violate laws of hospitality, friendship, and filial relations. The Wars of the Roses were predicated on violent competition among kin, and kin-slaying ran rampant. Shakespeare emphasizes the horror and absurdity of the wars in the famous allegorical scene in *3 Henry VI* when Henry witnesses a father's terrible discovery that he has slain his son, and a son finds that he has slain his own father. Both a father and a son have killed their own kin indiscriminately, yet accidentally, and Shakespeare has them both imagine how the mother and wife in each case will rage and shed tears, and "ne'er be satisfied" (2.5.104, 106). Revenge in such cases cannot redress wrongs, heal psychic wounds, or provide satisfaction; bloody retaliation would signify meeting one senseless atrocity with another. A greater form of retribution is needed to "satisfy" grieving families and to cleanse the kingdom. Margaret represents the necessity for such large-scale retribution to heal the multitude of wrongs that plague the kingdom.

According to the historical record, Margaret could not have been present at King Edward's court.[32] The Folio dialogue hints at this when in *Richard III* Richard asks, "Wert thou not banishèd on pain of death?" and Margaret replies, "I was, but I do find more pain in banishment / Than death can yield me here by my abode" (1.3.167–69). In giving Margaret the stage once more, Shakespeare alters history for a compelling dramatic and moral purpose. She has materialized at court to give voice to her hunger for revenge, which figures the urgent hunger of all those victimized by the wars and by Richard: "Bear with me," she says to Queen Elizabeth and the Duchess of York, "I am hungry for revenge, / And now I cloy me with beholding it" (4.4.61–62). At this point in the tetralogy, Margaret has lost everything—husband, son, lover, army, throne—but she has yet to lose a reason to live. While she cannot regain any of these losses in material terms, she can gain a measure of satisfaction by gorging herself figuratively, filling her eyes with "the waning of mine enemies" (4.4.4).

While Richard III, "hell's black intelligencer" (4.4.71), appears to the audience and critics alike as the focal point of the drama, Margaret's position as privileged spectator at a "direful pageant" (4.4.85) is akin to the audience's position. Her theater metaphors connect historical drama with life; indeed, she speaks to the satisfaction of *our* appetite for revenge in the theater. We, like the Elizabethan audience, expect retributive justice to rule the day, and Margaret lends fuel to that expectation. Margaret's opening speech in 4.4 invites us to feel, as she does, the satisfaction of history transformed into a theater of direful revenge. We, like Margaret, have watched with grim satisfaction as her enemies begin their decline:

> So now prosperity begins to mellow
> And drop into the rotten mouth of death.
> Here in these confines slily have I lurk'd
> To watch the waning of mine enemies.
> A dire induction am I witness to,
> And will to France, hoping the consequence
> Will prove as bitter, black, and tragical.
>
> (4.4.1–7)

Margaret's potent curses not only set the tone for the "dire induction" to this play of "English woes"; they seem peculiarly attuned to the predatory spirit of revenge that devours political agents and innocent babes alike. When she hears Queen Elizabeth call upon the souls of her children to hear her lamentations, Margaret replies in an aside, as if instructing the ghostly babes, "Hover about her; say that right for right / Hath dimm'd your infant morn to aged night" (4.4.15–16).

Margaret's language invokes the principle of *lex talionis*—"Plantagenet doth quit Plantagenet: / Edward, for Edward, pays a dying debt" (4.4.20–

21). Her speech thrills auditors with the dreadful tallying of revenge's balance sheets:

> Thy Edward he is dead, that kill'd my Edward;
> Thy other Edward dead, to quit my Edward;
> Young York, he is but boot, because both they
> Match'd not the high perfection of my loss.
> Thy Clarence he is dead, that stabb'd my Edward;
> And the beholders of this frantic play,
> Th'adulterate Hastings, Rivers, Vaughan, Grey,
> Untimely smother'd in their dusky graves.
>
> (4.4.63–70)

"Richard yet lives," she exclaims, praying that God might "Cancel his bond of life . . . / That I may live and say 'The dog is dead'" (lines 71, 77–78). Revenge upon Richard would constitute divine retribution: *that* would satisfy Margaret's hunger, for her revenge, then, would be in keeping with the natural and divine order of things.

Margaret has been a political agent herself, the Lancastrian general that led troops against the Yorkist uprising, an avenger that has shed blood, and an ambassador to King Lewis of France. She recognizes her fate; like that of the English nobles, like that of Queen Hecuba, she is Fortune's victim: "One heav'd a-high, to be hurl'd down below" (4.4.86). In *Richard III* Margaret may be displaced from history's arena, but her political significance is undiminished. She is in an enviable position as the untouchable "living ghost of Lancaster, the walking dead, memorializing the long, cruel, treacherous bloody conflict of the years of civil strife and pitiless butchery," as A. P. Rossiter envisions her.[33] In the fulfillment of Margaret's prophetic curses, we see her functioning as scourge, Nemesis, and Fury, presiding over the incantatory cursing, political intrigue, and bloodshed of revenge theater. She reminds her enemies and the theater's audience that historical drama structures human actions and passions around the principle of retribution. Yet her force in the theater is conveyed through a vividly realized bodily and vocal presence, more than the "nominal flesh and blood" Rossiter and other critics might grant her.[34] She is the physical embodiment of Revenge, and that is precisely what we see once again on Shakespeare's stage in the characterization of the fierce Goth queen, Tamora.

QUEEN TAMORA: "I AM REVENGE"

In *Titus Andronicus,* Shakespeare's revenge tragedy in the Senecan vein, revenge is figured once again as a hunger that *must* be satisfied, a hunger that rages and gnaws upon its victim's mind. The play serves up far more unsavory fare than the history plays: avengers carve up their prey; a woman is raped and mutilated; and a cannibalistic feast features a mother eating her sons. Shakespeare brutally calculates the costs of violence on (and in) the bodies of his characters, which become maps of woe, almost too pitiful, too horrific, to look upon. Virtually every character in the play is degraded or violated in some terrible manner, and consequently driven to satisfy the "gnawing vulture" (5.2.31) of the mind with revenge. *Titus Andronicus* subordinates the larger concerns of the history play to the tragic motives of a vendetta between a single noble family in Rome, the Andronici, and the newly empowered foreign queen, Tamora.

Shakespeare represents Tamora as a charismatic, cruel queen, awe-inspiring in her maternal fury and will to revenge. Making nine appearances onstage and speaking over 250 lines (in the quartos as well as the First Folio), Tamora is a dominant presence in the play. She is a fierce, compelling female who can easily rule Rome's new emperor, Saturninus; at the same time, she proves to be an almost elemental force bent on crushing the Andronici. Emanating strength of will, sexual vitality, and passion, actresses such as Jessica Lange and Estelle Kohler have demonstrated not only how commanding the Goth queen is, but also how sympathetic her revenge cause is—at least initially.[35] As a fallen queen and captive female, Tamora appears in a vulnerable light at the opening of *Titus Andronicus*. Tamora's maternity is emphasized at the start, for she is flanked by her three sons. The scene that unfolds reminds an audience of the cruel fate of women in war, "always wounded in their motherhood," as Nicole Loraux observes.[36] In her maternity, Tamora is most vulnerable, for not only as a queen, but also as a mother, she kneels before her captor to plead movingly for her son's life.

When her eldest son, Alarbus, is sacrificed by Titus to appease the souls of his dead sons (blood for blood), Tamora gives voice momentarily to supplication, which fails, and then to the captive woman's traditional lament. Her grief converts quickly to a black, maternal wrath and vengefulness. The desire to repay Titus for his cruelty consumes her, just as it did her ancient prototype, Hecuba. Once she unexpectedly gains a position of power in Rome, having made an amorous conquest of Saturninus, Tamora unleashes the furious energy of a wronged mother's ire upon a predominantly masculine Rome. As her paramour Aaron says admiringly of the Queen, "Upon her wit doth earthly honour wait, / And virtue stoops and trembles at her frown" (1.1.509–10). Tamora's function in the play is greater than the personal or political, as Aaron's praise hints. She belongs to the subterranean ground of the play where primordial forces gather strength. She is the "dread Fury" (5.2.82) brought to Rome by Titus himself, ironically, to make the warrior pay for a life steeped in blood. As the actor Brian Cox puts it, Titus "will be forced to pay the price for the self-brutalization of his own nature. . . . The play is going to make him pay,"[37] and it is Tamora who exacts the exorbitant fee. She and her men (Aaron and her surviving sons) function as scourges in this tragedy of revenge. Like the militant image of Revenge in Cesare Ripa's *Iconologia* (1677) or the classical representation of Nemesis, and like Margaret in *Richard III,* Revenge in *Titus Andronicus* is personified as feminine.

Typical of revenge tragedy, *honor* is the bass note sounded heavily at the beginning of the play. There is no mistaking that Rome defines itself as an honor culture. Men's honor is displayed here most spectacularly through military prowess, political power, and funeral rites, all exhibited in the first act. Honor is integrally bound with masculine *virtus,* a term derived from the Roman god Virtus, who exemplified bravery and military prowess. In the city of Rome, however, honor quickly becomes imperiled and proves less easy to protect and demonstrate than on the battlefield. Tamora, too, comes from an honor-based warrior culture; her people, a tribe of Teutons, perhaps from Gothland, a province in southern Sweden, are no more barbarian in behavior than the Romans, though of course they are named and perceived as "barbarians," like all of Rome's enemies. Indeed, three times in the first act, Tamora's honor is invoked: Titus refers to her honor when she is to be transferred to Saturninus as his prisoner (1.1.262), and she refers twice to "mine honour" (1.1.441, 471) once she is elevated to the status of empress. While Titus acknowledges that Tamora has honor, which warrants respectful treatment from Rome's emperor, Tamora's own assertion of her honor is bound up with private revenge. When she publicly brokers a peace upon her honor between Saturninus and the Andronici, she secretly plans to recoup the honor she has lost at the hands of the same family by pursuing her own vengeance. State vengeance will not satisfy her need to see her enemies punished; they must be *massacred,* hewed and lopped like her sacrificed son. Given all of the losses she has sustained, Tamora's jealously guarded honor cannot be easily restored.

We can start gauging Tamora's losses by considering Titus's ten-year campaign against her people, and the royal Goth family's presence as captives in Rome. Their capture after a siege reminiscent of the ten-year Trojan war and Caesar's Gallic campaign suggests steep losses and degradation for Tamora and the Goths. Like the Trojan queen, Hecuba, she has been enslaved; she and her captured sons are "honour's spoils" (1.1.39), and she will lose all of her children, and her own life, before the play ends. The staging of Titus's entrance calls for a public spectacle of shame for the Goths, which serves to heighten Titus's honor. Swiftly upon the heels of Titus's first speech, he and his sons prepare a funeral rite to honor their dead kin and "appease" the "groaning shadows that are gone" (1.1.129). "Religiously they ask a sacrifice" (1.1.127), Titus asserts, and within moments, there is hewing and hacking of the eldest Goth prince offstage. Onstage, the moving spectacle of Tamora's grief is on display as she, the royal prince's mother, suffers the knowledge of what is being done to her beloved son.

Deborah Willis emphasizes the social and psychic meanings underlying this situation: A "hostile audience of foreigners" bears witness to "the offense to [Tamora's] honor."[38] For Tamora, this situation is deeply humiliating; Titus has brought her to her knees, rejected her supplication, and publicly lorded his power over her.

The "sacrificial revenge" against Tamora and her son, as Ronald Broude rightly calls it,[39] reveals Titus's warrior ethos and pagan piety (he has been surnamed Pius by the Romans). In her speech, Tamora challenges the very grounds of Titus's piety. She defends mercy as the highest good, the quality that draws humanity nearest the gods. She appeals to him to recognize her son's pious service to his own country. Unmoved, Titus rejects the rights of the suppliant, which she has implicitly invoked, and responds with an implacable determination to fulfill what he perceives to be religious duty. When Tamora calls Titus's sacrifice of her son an act of "cruel, irreligious piety" (1.1.133), we hear in the oxymoron a subliminal reminder of the ancient ambivalence in the sacred. The word *sacrifice,* which Titus and Lucius use to characterize the religious nature of their act, derives from the Latin word *sacrificium* (to make sacred), but the concept of *sacer* refers at once to the holy and to the accursed.[40] When the Andronici "feed the sacrificing fire" (1.1.147) with the limbs of the Goth prince, the holy and the foul meet.

Reminiscent of ancient Greek and Roman tragedy, the staging of human sacrifice plays a pivotal role in triggering the revenge cycles in the play. The spilling of blood, even when done in the spirit of Roman piety, bodes ill. Tamora's words remind the audience of the ancient doctrine of pollution when she cautions Titus to refrain from *staining* "thy tomb with blood" (1.1.119). There is criticism and a veiled warning in her words. We might recall Pliny the Elder, who claims in his *Natural History* that ancient Romans had ceased engaging in human sacrifice by the first century BCE.[41] Shakespeare establishes Titus's brand of Roman piety as archaic and problematic. His original audience would have savored the irony in hearing the "barbarian" queen charge the great Roman general with "irreligious piety." Roman piety seems a reflexive drive, motivated by fear of dreadful repercussions from the *manes,* the spirits of the dead, if they are not given blood offerings.[42] These spirits demand a funerary sacrifice as repayment for their deaths, and perhaps for their current "vulnerable and shamed state" before honorable burial.[43] Lucius calls for "the proudest prisoner of the Goths,"

> That we may hew his limbs and on a pile
> *Ad manes fratrum* sacrifice his flesh
> Before this earthly prison of their bones,
> That so the shadows be not unappeased,
> Nor we disturbed with prodigies on earth.

$$(1.1.99-104)$$

A terrible irony reverberates through the final line; in the Andronici's effort to forestall unnatural disturbances from the spirit world, they manage to stir up a spirit and prodigy of another kind—the bloodthirstiness of the victim's mother, who swears a vendetta and makes good on her implicit threat and bloody oath. In the classical world, when blood is spilled on the earth, the Furies awaken and rise up from the underworld. Tamora's function in the play, and in Rome, thus, takes shape with the shedding of her son's blood. She will rise up in fury.

Tamora's character belongs to an ancient line of female avengers originating with the Furies. Allusions to Revenge and the Furies, Hecuba, Semiramis, Tomyris, and Diana comprise a mythological substructure in *Titus,* which characterizes Tamora at various moments as pitiless avenger, grieving mother, proud, cruel queen, amorous lover, and huntress. These allusive images and narrative threads offer depth and emotional resonance to the character. The Goth queen pursues her enemies, the Andronici clan, with the terrifying, merciless drive of those ancient goddesses that hounded murderers, oath-breakers, and kin-slayers. Like the punitive gods of ancient Greek literature, she is bent on destroying Titus's house.[44] Titus in fact *has* slain kin, his son Mutius, in a shockingly rash act; thus, Tamora's function as Revenge incorporates the Furies' traditional role in relation to impious or socially transgressive violence. But it goes deeper than this. When she disguises herself as Revenge, Titus calls her "dread Fury" (5.2.82), recognizing the mask and Tamora as one entity. She appears before Titus and the theater's audience as the visible embodiment of not only her own bloody cause, but also the violent retributive energy at the core of the play's world.

Early in the drama, Tamora's revenge narrative is linked explicitly with that of the legendary Trojan queen. Barbara Mowat, as I mentioned earlier, has recognized Hecuba's Revenge as a shaping myth that operates structurally "at a very deep level" in Shakespeare's play.[45] As a fallen, captive queen and fierce avenging mother, Tamora resembles Hecuba, who avenges the brutal slaughter and mutilation of her son, Polydorus, by Polymestor, a Thracian tyrant. Hecuba's revenge is partly motivated, too, by the sacrifice of her daughter Polyxena to the spirit of Achilles, who made known to the Greek warriors his demands from beyond the grave. For early modern writers and audiences, Hecuba is a symbol of the tragic effects of Fortune's reversal, or *de casibus* tragedy. With the turn of her wheel, the goddess Fortuna can ruin the greatest of queens. More particularly, though, Hecuba's circumstances as a female suggest the unbearable sufferings and misfortunes felt by women during war. She suffers loss upon loss, witnessing the burning of Troy, her homeland, and the deaths of her husband, King Priam, and children. She then is captured and enslaved by Odysseus following the ruin of Troy.

In the first scene of *Titus Andronicus,* Demetrius appeals to the gods that assisted Hecuba to favor his mother, the queen of the Goths:

> The self-same gods that armed the queen of Troy
> With opportunity of sharp revenge
> Upon the Thracian tyrant in his tent
> May favour Tamora, the queen of Goths
> (When Goths were Goths and Tamora was queen),
> To quit the bloody wrongs upon her foes.
>
> (1.1.139–44)

The allusive charge of Hecuba's name sends the audience's thoughts back to the legend of Troy and to the bereaved mother's plight. The invocation of Hecuba's tragedy at this early moment in the play evokes the audience's sympathies. Like Hecuba, Tamora feels compelled, justly, to "quit" the bloody wrongs done to her and her son.

In the *Metamorphoses,* Shakespeare's most immediate source, Ovid retells the tale of Hecuba's revenge with even greater descriptive vividness than Euripides, his ancient Greek source. In his translation of Ovid, Golding feelingly captures the scene in which Hecuba first gazes upon the wounds of her dead son's body and then pursues revenge:

> Shee looked on the face of him that lay before her killd.
> Sumtymes his woundes, (his woundes I say) shee specially behilld.
> And therwithall shee armd her selfe and furnisht her with ire:
> Wherethrough as soone as that her hart was fully set on fyre,
> As though shee still had beene a Queene, to vengeance shee her bent
> Enforcing all her witts to fynd some kynd of ponnishment.
> And as a Lyon robbed of her whelpes becommeth wood . . .
> Purseweth him though out of syght: even so Queene Hecubee. . . .
>
> (13.650–56, 658)

The Ovidian scene of maternal grief is pitiable, and the mother's metamorphic wrath, awe-inspiring. Shakespeare's Hecuba figure, Tamora, bears witness to the horrifying sight of the Andronici burning her son's entrails. She, too, feels the spirit of vengeance overcome her as the intimate connection between mother and son is severed. The memory of her son is now overlaid with a traumatic, unspeakable image, which sears Tamora's heart.

With the killing of her eldest son, Tamora swears not simply to kill Titus or to dispatch his son as repayment for her son's slaughter, but to "massacre" the house of the Andronici. Her desire reflects the Senecan principle from *Thyestes:* "scelera non ulcisceris, / nisi vincis" (lines 195–96) [Great crimes you don't avenge, unless you outdo them].[46] She employs her male kin— sons, lover, and husband—to strip her enemies of their honor in public and to destroy their house. Her revenge overflows the measure, reflecting the legacy of Hecuba. Her satisfactions multiply as she pursues wild justice, targeting each of Titus's children as Hecuba sought out Polymestor's sons. Her revenge is *sharp,* a word that connotes both appetite and pitilessness. Since no pity was shown to the mother, the mother will become pitiless. The excessiveness in her vendetta would seem to render her potential heroism debased, yet we might recall the avenging warriors of the *Iliad* and *Aeneid* who were brutal and merciless in cutting down their enemies.

Like Hecuba and Shakespeare's other fierce avengers, Tamora is associated with animals, the tiger in particular. While Hecuba is transformed into a dog in Ovid's account and her lot mourned by Trojans, enemy Greeks, and gods alike, in Euripides' play her canine transformation is predicted for some future moment. The drama's focus in its final moments lies in handling the question of what constitutes a fitting revenge. After accomplishing her revenge, killing Polymestor's children and gouging out his eyes, Hecuba asserts herself before Agamemnon, her earthly judge, and the Thracian tyrant, who exclaims, "What humiliation! It seems I shall be defeated by a woman, a slave, and lose my case to one who is an inferior" (lines 1252–53). She responds, "And is this not just, given the crime you have perpetrated?" (line 1254). When he wails for his lost children and eyes, she says contemptuously, "You feel pain at this? Ha! Do you think I feel no pain over my sons?" (line 1256). She has achieved justice and made him feel what she has felt, fulfilling the empathic function of vengeance.

The treatment of her enemy's daughter, Lavinia, represents the first brutal realization of Tamora's vendetta and a swerving from the more sympathetic aspects of the Hecuba myth. Shakespeare reimagines the more brutal elements of that tale in Tamora's encounter with Lavinia in the woods (2.3), where amorous intrigue, hunting, and rape become darkly entwined. Ironically, Lavinia will take on some of Hecuba's sympathetic qualities as Tamora expresses the avenging mother's rage and pitilessness. Just as Euripides' Hecuba appealed to the wily Greek Odysseus for mercy, to save her daughter's life, and then to take her life instead, so Lavinia supplicates Tamora, appealing for mercy, asking her to take her life, rather than let Tamora's sons take her chastity. Unmoved, Tamora replays Odysseus's role, showing no pity and allowing the force of Necessity—revenge as necessity —to seal her fate.

More immediately, Tamora reenacts Titus's initial role in relation to her earlier suppliant's role. When Lavinia insists that Tamora should spare her life because Titus saved Tamora's life, she misses the point. Tamora's memory of Alarbus's death is raw, and she desires nothing more than fueling her vendetta with an exchange of child for child. Grief, rage, and pitilessness rise up as she proclaims fiercely to Lavinia and to her sons,

> Hadst thou in person ne'er offended me,
> Even for his sake am I pitiless.
> Remember, boys, I poured forth tears in vain
> To save your brother from the sacrifice,
> But fierce Andronicus would not relent.
> Therefore away with her and use her as you will:
> The worse to her, the better loved of me.
>
> (2.2.161–67)

Lavinia, too, has humiliated Tamora by interrupting her amorous liaison with Aaron and accusing her of adultery. Tamora is incensed and ready to kill Titus's daughter herself: "Give me the poniard. You shall know, my boys, / Your mother's hand shall right your mother's wrong" (lines 120–21). She imagines her boys as audience to an act of just retaliation. She reasserts the maternal claim here, only to restrain herself with the thought that her sons can desecrate Lavinia's body as repayment for the desecration of Alarbus's body—the rape will be both the brothers' and the mother's revenge. Deborah Willis notes how the rape of Lavinia becomes a "family enterprise" through which Tamora reconstitutes her own and her postwar family's honor.[47] She wants Lavinia dead as soon as her sons have finished with her; that they mutilate her instead counters Tamora's will, an excess that Tamora herself is not guilty of.

Tamora does not stop at the desecration of one child, but targets Titus's two sons, as well. Aaron's maliciously playful spirit of vengeance suits Tamora's cause: he is eager to "back thy quarrels, whatsoe'er they be" (2.2.54). While Tamora imagines their encounter in the woods in the spirit of Dido and Aeneas's amorous pastime when a storm surprises their hunting party (*Aeneid,* book 4), Aaron insists, "Vengeance is in my heart, death in my hand, / Blood and revenge are hammering in my head" (lines 38–39). He relates part of his plot to undo Titus's children, and Tamora approves, saying, "Ah, my sweet Moor, sweeter to me than life!" (line 51). Shortly thereafter, Saturninus, Tamora, and the royal hunting party come upon Martius and Quintus, two of Titus's sons, trapped in a pit with the corpse of Bassianus. It turns out that Aaron has written an incriminating letter, which he gave to Tamora, who now reads it to Saturninus. The letter casts the sons in the worst light, for it reveals (falsely) that they hired a huntsman to kill Bassianus. Saturninus immediately has them arrested and then imprisoned. Later, with another trick, Aaron convinces Titus to cut off his hand to give to Saturninus as payment for his sons' lives. Aaron must know that they are to be executed; thus, as a cruel jest, he sends back Titus's hand along with the boys' heads. "Thy grief their sports," laments the Messenger bearing the heads and hand (3.1.239). Tamora's revenge has more than repaid the debt incurred by Titus's sacrifice of her son; in pursuing revenge excessively, she has departed from the realm of justice and entered the arena of sport.

In response to the rape and mutilation of his daughter and to the unjust killing of his sons, Titus must *do* something. He retaliates with equal, if not greater, sharpness by literalizing appetitive and cannibalistic metaphors that attend the dramatic history of revenge. Titus grows into Hecuba's role; anguished over his brutalized child, he lays claim to the emotional and ethical imperatives for revenge.[48] He weeps the tears of Hecuba as he laments the degradation of Lavinia's body. Lavinia is associated again with Hecuba when young Lucius, frightened by her frenzied appearance, invokes "Hecuba of Troy" who "Ran mad for sorrow" (4.1.20–21). Titus identifies his own grief with that of Aeneas, who suffers over burnt Troy (3.2.27–28) and, at the end of the play, a Roman Lord attests to the Andronici's appropriation of Trojan sufferings. He appeals to Marcus to tell the Romans "who hath brought the fatal engine in / That gives our Troy, our Rome, the civil wound" (5.3.85–86). Titus's mounting passions, great as Hecuba's and Aeneas's, become the emotional center of the play. As his griefs accumulate, the audience becomes absorbed in his revenge cause and loses the sympathy for Tamora it had had earlier in the play.

Yet Titus moves to the extreme edges of revenge, where the drive for payback loses touch with justice. He moves beyond Hecuba to another prototype of female revenge: Procne. His mad appetite for revenge drives his imagination, as he decides to follow Procne's precedent. He transforms himself into a cook that feeds his own hunger by feeding Tamora the flesh of her children. He replays one of the most perversely satisfying and disturbing revenges from classical antiquity, that of the Athenian noblewomen Procne and Philomel who serve the Thracian tyrant, Tereus, a feast composed of his son's body. After Tereus raped Philomel and cut out her tongue, Procne, her sister and his wronged wife, fiercely desires revenge; she convinces her sister to join with her in making the feast. Rape, the severed tongue, and the breaking of oaths are repaid through the fatal feast, which pollutes the savage Tereus. In *Titus* the gender reversal at the feast creates perhaps an even greater horror—an unspeakable crime (*nefas*) and stage image of a *mother* consuming her young.

Viewers and critics tend to find the ethics of revenge in *Titus Andronicus* deplorable, reserving their harshest judgment for Tamora. Yet the drama's textual interplay with classical models and allusions suggests complex resonances informing the characterization of Tamora and her function in revenge tragedy. At least one critic has argued that she should be perceived as heroic, even though her character does not reflect the inward, tragic awareness of her male counterpart, Titus.[49] Her nascent heroism might be seen in light of Hecuba, but it could be understood, as well, in relation to militant heroic women from antiquity. Tamora's name associates her with Tomyris, widowed ruler of the Massagetae during the sixth century BC.[50] In an attempt to annex Tomyris's kingdom, the founder of the Persian empire, Cyrus the Great, made a pretense of proposing marriage. When Tomyris refused, Cyrus became warlike, entered her country, and tricked her army with a great banquet of food and spirits; with the army asleep in their intoxicated state, the queen's son, the army's general, was captured by Cyrus. Tomyris sent word to "Bloodthirsty Cyrus" to return her son and depart from her country, threatening to give him his fill of blood if he refused.[51] Cyrus disregarded her threat; meanwhile, her son committed suicide in shame. Tomyris avenged his death by waging a fierce war against Cyrus. After the battle's end, which claimed the lives of most of the Persian army, she shamed the Persian tyrant's body by dipping his head in a skin full of human blood, proclaiming, "'Though I live and conquer thee, thou hast undone me, overcoming my son with guile; but even as I threatened, so will I do, and give thee thy fill of blood'."[52] As James Hall notes, "[T]he episode came to be regarded as a symbolic act of justice, and paintings of it were commissioned to hang in courts of law."[53] Tomyris was one of the classical females often included in the French medieval cult of the Nine Worthies, individuals known for their heroic contributions to civilization.

Another powerful female warrior ranked among the Nine Worthies was Semiramis, a legendary Assyrian queen who conquered much of Asia. She was born of a goddess and reputed to be lustful. In his *Inferno* Dante placed Semiramis in the second circle of hell with the lustful. Aaron praises Tamora, his erotic conquest, as a powerful, destructive, feminine force: "this queen, / This goddess, this Semiramis, this nymph, / This siren that will charm Rome's Saturnine / And see his shipwreck and his commonweal's" (1.1.520–23). Lavinia calls Tamora "Semiramis," yet asserts that only "Tamora" is a fitting name, perhaps hearing the acoustic puns *amor* and *Moor,* which emphasize the Queen's erotic impulses and her focus on a racially different love object. Aaron is a slave, as well. To couple and breed with Aaron displays Tamora's transgressive crossings of a number of social boundaries maintained in Rome, and perhaps among the Goths as well. Yet like Tomyris, Semiramis is a political force, a bellicose queen capable of ruling well and vanquishing enemies.

In terms of theatrical models, Shakespeare would have reimagined possibilities for feminine revenge in light of Thomas Kyd's *The Spanish Tragedy.* The play opens with the entrance of Revenge and the ghost of the slain warrior Don Andrea. Andrea's opening speech tells of his love for Bel-imperia, his death, and his visit to the underworld. When he arrives before Pluto and Persephone, the queen of the underworld takes charge of his fate; she determines his revenge. She whispers instructions in Revenge's ear, and then Revenge takes Andrea through the gates of horn, which symbolize prophetic dreams. Revenge and Andrea become onstage spectators at the Spanish court, watching events transpire as in a revenge tragedy. In time, they witness Bel-imperia become Andrea's avenger by stabbing his killer, Balthazar, while performing in a play before the court. Revenge delivers the play's final chilling lines: "This hand shall hale them down to deepest hell, / Where none but Furies, bugs, and tortures dwell / . . . . For here, though death hath end their misery, / I'll there begin their endless tragedy" (4.5.27–28, 47–48).

Modern critics and directors assume Kyd's Revenge to be a male figure,[54] but this may very well be a false assumption, as I argued in chapter 1. Nemesis, the classical goddess of retribution, is clearly female, and so, too, are the Furies. In the play, for example, Horatio casts "wrathful Nemesis" as a feminine force bringing about Don Andrea's death: "She, she herself, disguised in armour's mask, / (As Pallas was before proud Pergamus), / Brought in a fresh supply of halberdiers . . ." (1.4.16, 19–21). Tamora's astonishing appearance before Titus in the guise of Revenge (5.1) recalls Kyd's dramatic personification. In *Titus Andronicus,* however, Shakespeare has woven Revenge's part into the play's action and delayed the personification until a late moment in the drama.

Tamora's personification of Revenge functions on multiple levels in the drama. Some aspects of the scene return us to the Hecuba myth. While the Ovidian Hecuba "armd her selfe and furnisht her with ire" (Golding's translation, 13.652), Tamora literalizes the metaphor of arming, dressing herself in warlike "habiliment," ready not only to trick, but to conquer Titus with a "determined jest" (5.2.1, 139). Hecuba, too, tricked her enemy, Polymestor, by promising him gold if he met her in her tent. Shakespeare's Hecuba figure takes deceit to the level of art, conceiving herself as a sort of revenge dramatist, playing the part of Revenge herself. She plans to "temper" Andronicus with her "art" and "devices" (4.4.108, 111). When Tamora declares her part to Titus, her words disclose the character's function as the presiding spirit of the play:

> I am Revenge, sent from th'infernal kingdom
> To ease the gnawing vulture of thy mind
> By working wreakful vengeance on thy foes.
>
> (5.2.30–32)

Tamora's visual presence and potent iconographic language reach back to ancient images of the Furies. Her figure of the gnawing vulture represents the pained mental state of the avenger, who is often driven mad by the Furies. The figure captures the ambiguous character of revenge, which gnaws like a hunger, yet promises to ease hunger.

The terrible cycle of torment and relief experienced by the avenger recalls the Promethean myth. For his sins of fashioning man out of clay and bringing fire to humanity, Prometheus is punished by Jupiter: Chained to a rock in the Caucasus, he is visited by an eagle that devours his liver. The liver regenerates itself overnight, so that the eagle can return each day to continue his torment. Yet another classical myth is suggested here with the vulture reference—that of the giant Tityus (also Tityos, Tityon), whose name resembles Titus's. In the *Aeneid* (6.595–600) and *Metamorphoses* (4.457–8), Tityus appears in Tartarus, the deepest pit of the underworld. In both texts, the Furies are the gatekeepers to Tartarus. After they are described, the horrible sight of Tityus comes into view: his body is stretched out while a great vulture feasts upon his chest; he is given no relief, for his liver regenerates itself. The liver, as James Hall notes, is the "seat of emotions" for antique writers; thus Renaissance humanists regarded Tityus's story as an allegory of passion's enslavement of the body.[55] Wrath was perhaps the dominant passion associated with the liver, and thus the connection between the gnawing vulture and revenge is brought to light through this myth. Tityus's crime, however, recalls Tamora's sons' rape of Lavinia, for Tityus is punished for attempted rape. And thus the subtext prepares for the scene that follows Tamora's performance, in which Titus relieves the gnawing vulture of his mind by punishing Demetrius and Chiron for rape.

On the level of dramatic action, Tamora's performance is far from the triumph she imagined. Unknown to her, Titus sees through her disguise and plots a savage jest in return for her brutal treatment of his children. He tricks her into leaving her sons with him. He performs a chilling blood rite on stage, redolent of religious sacrifice, recalling the unseen sacrifice of Tamora's eldest son. He then bakes the boys in a pie and serves them for their mother's supper. Titus masters the revenge game, playing the final jest on Tamora. He plays the woman's part (first Hecuba, then Procne) in having his revenge, and he does it ironically to avenge himself on the play's female avenger. Here we have a grim jest indeed. In the end, Tamora's "sharp" revenge is returned by the "knife's sharp point" (5.3.62) when Titus kills her at the cannibalistic feast.

The final words of the play are devoted to the treatment of the avenging mother's body, which returns us to the play's preoccupation with desecrated bodies, maimed funeral rites, and the devouring passion of revenge:

> As for that ravenous tiger, Tamora,
> No funeral rite, nor man in mourning weed,
> No mournful bell shall ring her burial,
> But throw her forth to beasts and birds to prey:
> Her life was beastly and devoid of pity,
> And being dead, let birds on her take pity.
>
> (5.3.194–99)

The final emphasis on the word *pity* is damning and carries a strong retributive thrust—no pity for the pitiless. Rather than mother or queen, in the end Tamora is "that ravenous tiger," an embodiment of cultural prejudices against angry, vengeful women. The savageries of revenge accumulate in images of the monstrous maternal body—a body that devours its own, a body that metamorphoses into a beast, a body that vultures gnaw upon. Tamora is made to function as Rome's scapegoat; she is made to pay not only for her own transgressions, but those of Rome too.

What gets lost in the rapid enactment of revenges and punishments at the play's end is the early image of maternal grief and the ethical motivation for the mother's vendetta against her enemy. This is a loss indeed, for Shakespeare initially gave moral authority to Tamora's passion for revenge. *Titus Andronicus* ends with a deliberate staging of failed sympathy for the mother—a move that should give us pause. Indeed, what Shakespeare's artistic reworking of the Hecuba myth accomplishes is a graphic display of the dangers bereaved mothers pose to the state. Tamora's tears, black wrath, and audacious avenging spirit, worthy of her ancient predecessors, command attention. She embodies the Furies' justice, which opposes a mother's vengeance to a father's. Because the story of Rome is that of fathers, and of male conquest, achievement, and valor, women's place in the city and empire can be only a subordinate and marginal one. Tamora is the interloping, furious feminine force that Rome wishes to suppress. For a time, that force brings Rome to its knees.

The next chapter will examine *King Lear,* a revenge-driven tragedy that takes up some of the concerns expressed in *Titus Adronicus.* While Lear's eldest daughters pursue a pitiless revenge upon their father-king, stripping him of home and dignity, the youngest daughter, Cordelia, pursues revenge in the anointed king's name and, by metaphysical extension, in the name of the gods. Shakespeare depicts Goneril and Regan as lacking the essential conditions that render vengeance just: the moral authority to punish, and a proportionate fit between sin and punishment. Their pursuit of vengeance fails to activate a morality based on justice. Like Margaret and Tamora, they embody an elemental force of retribution at work in the political and domestic spheres. Like Titus, Lear becomes a suffering victim of a mechanism that his own sins have triggered, and his eldest daughters are intimately involved in that "mechanism," punishing him in a most cruel, vindictive fashion. Lear's own flesh ministers what Albany calls the "cup of . . . deservings" (Folio, 5.3.279). Cordelia, too, pursues revenge, but her vengeance stands apart from that of Margaret, Tamora, Goneril, and Regan, for she is selfless and works to counter the bitter, destructive revenges desired and enacted by her sisters against their father and the father against his daughters. In the end, Cordelia gives Lear a "cup," as well, to follow Albany's metaphor, but it is a "cordial" that is better than he deserves.

5

"Revenging Home":
Cordelia and the Virtue of Vengeance

Two vices are opposed to vengeance: one by way of excess, namely, the sin of cruelty or brutality, which exceeds the measure in punishing: while the other is a vice by way of deficiency and consists in being remiss in punishing, wherefore it is written (Prov. xiii. 24): *He that spareth the rod hateth his son.* But the virtue of vengeance consists in observing the due measure of vengeance with regard to all the circumstances.
— Thomas Aquinas, *Summa Theologica,* "Of Vengeance"

In circumstances in which no community system for the administration of appropriate penalties exists or in which such a system is corrupt, the virtuous avenger is the last best hope of morality.
— Peter A. French, *The Virtues of Vengeance*

THE VAST SCHOLARSHIP ON *KING LEAR* HAS TOUCHED UPON THE CONCEPT of revenge from time to time, yet few critics have delved into how the play examines the question of revenge's legitimacy or ethical capacity. In truth, *King Lear* is a profoundly disquieting revenge play, its structure of injury, suffering, and punishment enacting the reflexive nature of revenge.[1] The play enacts the dynamics of revenge by showing us the eruption of vindictive and vindicative passions in characters, and how those passions not only extend to retaliatory actions in the world, but also function inwardly as operations of the mind and heart. The deeply affecting quality of the play lies in its unremitting obedience in structural, moral, and psychological terms to revenge's reflexivity, while at the same time offering a sublime countervision of revenge as a virtuous action that seeks to undo harm and transcend reflexivity altogether. Such a beneficent vision of revenge—a daughter's revenge for her father—defies the conventional expectations we harbor regarding ethics, gender, and tragedy.

Western attitudes toward revenge, as I argued earlier, have been largely negative, casting the passions and actions of revenge as morally reprehensible and psychologically aberrant. Such an understanding may seem to

148

shed light on the viciousness at work in the characters of Regan, Goneril, Cornwall, and Edmond. The *virtue* of vengeance would seem an elusive, even counterintuitive, concept. Yet such a notion derives from the philosophical tradition of Aristotelian-Thomistic virtue ethics, which would have been known to Shakespeare and his contemporaries through any number of translations, commentaries, and textual permutations produced during the Renaissance period on the Continent and in England. David N. Beauregard has argued persuasively for the preeminence of Aristotle's *Nicomachean Ethics* and Thomas Aquinas's *Summa Theologica* in Renaissance thought and literature.[2] Of particular relevance, Elizabethan sermons and political tracts forwarded arguments that supported the legitimate vengeance of properly motivated, divinely appointed earthly ministers. Such arguments may very well have followed Aquinas who, in his *Summa,* conceives of a lawful avenger as one that acts upon the fervor of love or *caritas,* rather than rage, self-interest, or malicious pleasure, and one that intends the removal of injury, rather than the infliction of harm. Such an avenger seeks punishment only to restore the "equality of justice' when wrongs have unbalanced the scales of justice.[3] The emphasis for Aquinas lies in "the mind of the avenger,"[4] just as it does for the Ghost in Shakespeare's *Hamlet,* who warns his avenging son to "Taint not thy mind' (1.5.85). Indeed, Shakespeare positions Cordelia in the same role as Hamlet—the avenging child—only she, unlike her masculine predecessor, perceives her cause, from the start, to be unproblematic in its justice. She is guilty of neither excess nor deficiency, as Hamlet is in moments of bloodthirstiness and dispiritedness during his prolonged engagement with the question of revenge. Cordelia, thus, is an avenger capable of exhibiting "due measure" in enacting the "special virtue of vengeance."[5] This she does by forcefully resisting her sisters' corrupt exercise of power and applying physic both to her abject king and corrupt kingdom.

Shakespeare's examination of the ethics of revenge is nothing if not thorough in *King Lear.* Different notions of revenge inform characters' passionate responses to the terrible and tumultuous actions that occur in the play. As they stake their claims in an inscrutable cosmos and volatile political climate, most of the characters express a natural disposition to revenge. Lear, Goneril, Regan, Cornwall, and Edmond pursue revenge as the returning of harm for *perceived* harm. The vindictive passions they express—anger, resentment, and malice—exhibit an incontinence and brutality in their desire for revenge or in their revenge-taking. As Aristotle points out in his *Nicomachean Ethics,* "[A]nger by reason of the warmth and hastiness of its nature, though it hears, does not hear an order, and springs to take revenge. For reason or imagination informs us that we have been insulted or slighted, and anger, reasoning as it were that anything like this must be fought against, boils up straightway" (1149a).[6]

For other characters, however, the desire for revenge is deeply bound up with an innate sense of justice, order, and hierarchy, and grounded in a metaphysical and moral worldview. Kent, Albany, and Gloucester, for example, articulate a belief in divine vengeance as cosmic justice, investing hope in heavenly "justicers" (4.2.47) and "wingèd vengeance" (3.7.64).[7] Such rhetoric brings into focus the play's central questions regarding the colossal injustices in humankind and the moral legitimacy of revenge. If divine vengeance is never direct and often a long time in coming, how are human acts of revenge to be weighed in relation to it? When is the divine imperative to revenge a legitimate human imperative? The play, however, forces us to ask, as well, whether the gods themselves might be cruel revengers, as Gloucester comes to believe when he says in a moment of bitterness, "As flies to wanton boys are we to th' gods / They kill us for their sport" (4.1.37–38). In its most positive social function, human revenge cannot answer for the gods, but it can operate *as if* the gods were just and cared about unjust human suffering, *as if* virtuous repayment of wrongs mattered in the cosmic scheme of things. Vengeance can work to restore justice and promote ethical, loving bonds of both personal and political kinds. Cordelia enacts the virtue of vengeance, as articulated by Aquinas. In doing so, she fulfills the expectations that lie deeply rooted in Gloucester's hope, shared by Kent and Albany, that "These injuries the King now bears will be revenged home" (3.3.10–11).

The interconnectedness between revenge and home lies at the core of *King Lear,* with the external manifestations of repudiation, revenge, atonement, and integration signifying the wrenching internal processes at work. Some of the play's avenging characters fall headlong into homelessness, wretchedness, grief, and exile. In their state of homelessness, they are driven *home* in the adverbial sense—"to the very heart or root of a matter; into close and effective contact" with reality and one's self "so as to touch, reach or affect intimately."[8] The further the dispossessed travel from a place of kinship and nurturance, the greater their capacity to "see . . . feelingly," as the blind Gloucester phrases it (4.5.141). Characters stripped of their native land, homestead, affection, and kinship ties struggle to find some temporary metaphysical and physical sense of home and, at the same time, live for the promise of justice, of *revenging home.* Gloucester speaks not only for the homeless, wronged Lear, but for all those "unaccommodated" persons (3.4.95–96) that inhabit the threatened, fragile world of *King Lear* when he insists the King's injuries will be revenged home. Lear echoes this sentiment pathetically when his desire for revenge—punishment for his tormenting daughters—overcomes his shameful weeping: "I will punish home. / No, I will weep no more" (3.4.16–17). Weeping incapacitates Lear; punitive measures are what he desires. The terrible irony haunts him that his daughters find the capacity to "punish home," while he himself has been rendered helpless due to his folly. In Lear, the reflexive nature of revenge is exhibited—their punitive treatment of him mirrors Lear's own drive to punish home.

For Lear, "burning shame" (Q, 17.47), wrath, and pride lie at the root of his vengefulness. From these passions springs his desperate desire to save face, to legitimize himself in the public eye and before his daughters. He not only deluges his court and daughters with vindictive words, but wrongfully exercises his power to take swift revenge upon Cordelia and Kent. Cornwall repeats this abuse of power in his treatment of Gloucester, insisting, "our power / Shall do a curtsy to our wrath, which men / May blame but not control" (3.7.24–26). In his pursuit of "traitorous" Gloucester, the fiery Cornwall speaks of the "revenges we are bound to take" (3.7.6), which leads him to pluck out the Earl's eyes. He, like Lear, cannot stem the tidal wrath that overcomes him, nor can he prevent the reflexive actions of revenge that ensue. For his excessive punishment of Gloucester, Cornwall is paid back immediately by a morally outraged servant, who gives him a fatal wound in order to stop him from hurting Gloucester further. Revenge's mechanism springs instantly again as Regan kills the servant for his bold deed. In time Regan will be repaid for her cruelty and passion for Edmond with poison administered by the jealous Goneril.

This lack of measure distinguishes the unjust revengers, exposing vicious passions and an appetite for cruelty. Vengeful rhetoric and action take on a dark, appetitive quality when they emanate from these characters' private resentments and perceived injustices. Goneril, Regan, Edmond, and Cornwall function like Lear as injurious home-wreckers and unjust revengers. They gain rather than lose in the material geography of home, in native lands, powers, and properties; they are driven to become fiercely protective of those gains and are reduced to savage expressions of self-preservation and aggressiveness. Goneril and Regan lack all measure in their desire to "revenge home," to reduce what was once home, embodied in father and king, to shame, powerlessness, and nothingness. As revengers, they may act from a history of psychological hurt and humiliation, but they are guilty of the sins of cruelty and brutality, to invoke Aquinas. They show up revenge's dark capacity to satisfy resentments through excessive punishment. And such a revenge is vicious at its core, representing harms that must be removed by a virtuous avenger.

Motivating the rhetoric and action of rightful revenge is the sense of loss characters suffer—of home, status, justice, integrity, honor—and the desire to recoup losses totally. Gloucester and Kent hope passionately for external agents of vengeance (the heavens, God, foreign armies) to punish wrongdoers. They hope for a restitution not only of political order, but of psychic and moral integrity as well, thus restoring order to all aspects of home—king, subjects, domicile, country, and world. The adverbial use of *home* in the phrase *revenging home* signifies a revenge taken directly, thoroughly, and unsparingly. This is Gloucester's meaning when he articulates a moral certainty that through revenge, all can be restored to the King. His strong desire for an avenging power and his suggestive coupling of "injury," "revenge," and "home" presume the legitimacy of Cordelia as the punitive force that will avenge and restore home. In Cordelia lies the promise of a sanctified avenger. Mysteriously, Cordelia finds herself bound with Lear at the base of the coiled spring of revenge in the play. In her presence and in response to her measured words in the play's opening abdication scene, Lear sets in motion the reflexive dynamic of revenge. Because he lacks the very virtues his daughter expresses (measure, just vengeance), Lear rashly calls up the Furies and, once unleashed, their destructiveness and pitilessness turn back upon the King, devouring what honor, authority, and power he once possessed.

Revenging home, thus, suggests an essential metaphor for the enactment of familial, political, and ethical (or unethical) actions, which tear asunder or seek to repair the world of Lear. The metaphor expresses the fundamental structure of the drama and the internal drives that motivate its characters. Both malicious and restorative impulses drive the expression of revenge, which can be seen in the clashing ways and differing moral degrees in which Lear's daughters *revenge home:* while Goneril and Regan engage in destructive personal and political revenges enabled by their newly gained political power, Cordelia grows into the role of public avenger, leading an army against her sisters with the intent to "bring home" her king and father in a heroic restoration of kingdom, paternity, sanity, and justice. Lear's daughters actively participate in and help generate the tensions underlying the retributive patterns of the play. The horror of this revenge tragedy lies in the harsh truth it forces upon its audience: with the King's abdication of power and his abuse of the "form of justice" (3.7.24), the destructive force of vengeance is allowed to shatter home. The only counterforce great enough to reconstitute "home," in the fullness of its meaning, lies surprisingly in vengeance itself, but it is the special virtue of vengeance, to invoke Aquinas once more, that must be enacted. The virtuous avenger, as it turns out, must sacrifice everything—her commitment must be total—in order to bring all unjust, unmeasured revenges to an end.

Literary critics typically fail to see Goneril and Regan as dogged female revengers, partly because Lear, if any character, articulates most vehemently the Senecan rhetoric of *furor* and vengefulness. Yet Lear's revenges are integrally bound up with his daughters' revenges. The King's unmeasured fury gives rise to rash actions and wrathful curses that leave him vulnerable to his elder daughters' abuse. Lear enables their revenges against him by irrationally empowering them and then depending upon their bounty and goodwill. With steely vindictiveness, they turn upon their father and king, sending him into a geographic and metaphysical homelessness meant to kill him. Their malicious desire to revenge themselves upon Lear manifests in a death sentence: as Gloucester miserably reports to Kent, "His daughters seek his death" (3.4.146).

Critics tend, as well, to miss Cordelia's significance as a female avenger. Cordelia has been perceived, especially by those who follow the 1608 Quarto, as a redemptive figure and sainted martyr, a politically naive and abject figure. Alternately, some critics and directors have emphasized negative qualities in Cordelia—pride, stubbornness, coldness, and insensitivity —perhaps to humanize her and level the moral playing field a bit. My contention is that the Cordelia we find in the 1623 Folio is a strong-willed female avenger and military leader, who rises to this public position in response to political and familial crisis. The Folio's text gives the clearest indication that Cordelia has the rectitude of soul required for just reflection and action; she is the assertive moral agent who follows through with her claim that "what I well intend, / I'll do't before I speak" (1.1.223–24).[9]

Shakespeare, however, allows conflicting expectations to arise about how revenge might function in tragedy and, furthermore, how women participate in retaliatory patterns within familial and political contexts. As a play strongly invested in the revenge dynamic, *King Lear* presents a suffering protagonist who desires vengeance, but unlike the avengers of plays that clearly fulfill the genre's conventions (e.g., *Hamlet, Titus Andronicus, The Spanish Tragedy, The Revenger's Tragedy*), he cannot find cathartic relief through retaliatory acts of violence, much less potent speech acts. Indeed, the play dramatizes the pathetic helplessness of the once great king. Only Cordelia, and surprisingly Cordelia, steps into the role of avenger, taking bold public action in his name. Cordelia functions in a traditionally masculine-defined role as heroic avenger, the son Lear would have wanted, battling forces of destruction in her country.[10] Cordelia might be perceived in light of the heroic Talbot, from Shakespeare's First Tetralogy, honor-bound in war to avenge the death of Salisbury with a zealous massacre of Frenchmen. Yet gender and other generic impulses create an effect altogether different from that of avenging male warriors such as Talbot. The generic drives of comedy and romance—to remedy all losses and to effect transformations in self, other, and community—are frankly expressed in Cordelia's motivation to avenge her wronged father.[11] Following classical and medieval philosophy, Cordelia seeks justice as the form of psychic unity.

Cordelia, however, should not be perceived as a static character; arguably, she grows into her role as a political person, queen, and avenger as she faces her father's crisis, his overwhelming need, and her own estrangement from home. Her journey involves struggle and growth, much of which she undergoes privately in a state of exile. She feels no instinct to act upon the cause Lear gives her for retaliation—"No cause, no cause," she insists when her broken father expects revenge (4.6.68). During the time lapse and at a distance from home, she has found within herself the capacity, or *measure,* not only to feel heart's sorrow and just anger when appropriate, but also to know how to act appropriately upon such passions. Fulfilling the ethical demands articulated by Aristotle and Aquinas, Cordelia is guided by a love of justice and a strong feeling of moral indignation when she takes revenge. Her actions, silence, and speech, far from being self-effacing, as some critics might deem them, are self-defining, and her identity as royal daughter, queen, and moral agent is given expression first in her resistance to her father's unjust demand to flatter him publicly, then in her war against her sisters, and finally in her function as sacrifice.

Cordelia appears only five times in the play, and only in the explosive first scene and later momentous scenes in acts 4 and 5. At the end of the play, two of her appearances are silent and emblematic: in 5.2 she and Lear appear with soldiers crossing the stage "*with drum and colours*" (s.d.), and in the final moments of the play, she is shown as a corpse in her howling father's arms: "*Enter LEAR with CORDELIA in his arms*" (5.3.s.d.). These two images, appearing close in time, form a diptych of triumph and defeat, hope and despair, just vengeance and subverted justice. Although her absent presence can be felt throughout the play, the material fact remains that she is often *absent* from the stage, removed to France, gathering forces for her return to Britain. We might regard this absence as a subtle counterpart to the conventional time lapse in revenge tragedies between injury and retaliation. In Cordelia's case, rather than artfully contriving against her father's life, or the lives of her sisters, she prepares herself militarily to retaliate against Regan, Goneril, and their husbands. She will launch a just war, returning to her father's kingdom as a loving royal daughter and military leader, both aspects of her identity reflected in the stage images from 4.6 and 5.2.

Let us turn to the beginning of *King Lear* to see how Lear's unsparing, wrathful words and actions against his one virtuous daughter, Cordelia, give rise to the play's central action—the enactment of revenging home. Cordelia's and Kent's speeches function as perceived offenses that dishonor their king in a profoundly shameful way. Lear's response, to banish his loving daughter and his servant, recoils upon him in time as he discovers that this action was self-exiling. The error in Lear's unmeasured response is monumental. The rest of the play unfolds under the shadow of revenge's unremitting law of reflexivity, which shocks audience expectations about what might constitute a fitting repayment for Lear's first vengeful actions. While some kind of harsh counterresponse would seem logical and psychologically warranted from Cordelia and Kent, neither of these characters retaliates against Lear, which is not to say that they do not both become avengers. They do, but they seek vengeance in the name of justice against the King's true enemies, all of whom are present in the royal chambers to witness Lear's appalling vindictiveness. By the end of the first scene, Lear has left himself vulnerable to the secret vengefulness of his other, ambitious daughters; even worse, as king and father he has committed a grave injustice, an act of vicious revenge, that proves to be his own undoing, causing psychological disintegration as he faces the nature and consequences of that action and his own powerlessness to make whole what he has severed.

What has Cordelia's part been in this most extraordinary scene of paternal and royal revenge? In the crisis of the moment, Cordelia defines herself as a bold royal daughter outfacing injustice in a measured way. A love of justice characterizes Cordelia from the start and prepares her to step into the commanding role of queen, but how she is to become a heroic avenger in the course of time is yet hidden. The first scene establishes her sisters as vindictive, competitive, and ambitious, as they anxiously welcome newfound power and begin to define themselves as revenging daughters, uniting forces in the heat of the moment. Their actions as civil warriors and jealous siblings in fierce competition with each other are barely intimated, yet the groundwork has been laid.

When Lear commands Cordelia to speak so that she might "draw / A third more opulent than your sisters" (1.1.83–84), her response is frank and spare. She "speaks home," in the colloquial sense of that phrase: "Nothing, my lord" (line 85). "Nothing" sounds like Cordelia's acknowledgment of failure, yet it is, in actuality, an assertion of will. The word, with its opaque, vertiginous depths, seems poised to yield some truth, but at this point in the scene it is unclear what it means. Cordelia continues with a measured protest, asserting her relationship to Lear on just terms: "Unhappy that I am, I cannot heave / My heart into my mouth. I love your majesty / According to my bond, no more nor less" (lines 89–91). Cordelia's language here carries intimations of justice and legally binding obligation. The image of Lady Justice with her scales, or balances, seems to be invoked in the notion of a bond and the precise diction of "no more nor less." More or less would be "unbalanced"—in excess or deficient—and therefore unjust and truly calling for a rebalancing restitution. Cordelia's assertion of the pressing claims of a familial bond implies that obligations must be met on both daughter's and father's parts; her words, cold as they sound to Lear, are appropriately even and measured, asserting her fulfillment of a naturally binding obligation. Lear's command to hear his daughters proclaim their love for him in public has violated the letter and spirit of that bond by making public what should be private, performative what should be authentic, compulsory what should be free. In her distressing situation, Cordelia sees Lear's violation clearly.

Her speech is a model of restraint and equipoise, which can be seen particularly in the two rhetorically balanced lines in which she proclaims Lear's natural, just position as father: "You have begot me, bred me, loved me. / I return those duties back as are right fit— / Obey you, love you, and most honour you" (lines 94–96). She emphasizes her sisters' disingenuous, immoderate words in her sly division of "all" into two halves:

> Why have my sisters husbands if they say
> They love you all? Haply when I shall wed
> That lord whose hand must take my plight shall carry
> Half my love with him, half my care and duty.
> Sure, I shall never marry like my sisters.
>
> (lines 97–101)

Frankness, moral outrage, balancing the "halves" of affection, "right fit": the rhetorical aesthetics of her speech reflects the powerful aesthetics and iconography of justice, as well as the symmetry that lends revenge its reflexive dynamic. Her measured speech reflects a love of justice that transcends obedience to a father's unjust demands. As William R. Elton emphasizes, Cordelia respects "due proportion," while Goneril and Regan "move within a universe of confused proportions in which the only unit of measurement is quantitative, and the main value word, 'more.'"[12] Lear, too, operates in this universe of confused proportions.

Lear takes Cordelia's response as a provocation, responding rashly to her rightful resistance to a father-king who not only demands "all," but wishes to retain the authority to determine who loves him most. He has asked not whether the daughters love him, but rather, "Which of you shall *we say* doth love us most" (1.1.49, my emphasis). Lear exercises his authority most inappropriately here, revealing perhaps a craven desire to satisfy himself with superficial shows of love that prop up his public identity. Furthermore, Lear's determined desire "to set [his] rest / On [Cordelia's] kind nursery" (1.1.121–22) betrays the motive and unconscious risk underlying his abdication and love test. His choice of words recalls the gambling card game of primero, in which stakes, agreed upon *from the start,* are kept in reserve, but once lost, the game ends.[13] Lear has staked all on Cordelia, desiring her to be unjust in a way that pleases him; this test of Cordelia's obedience is to lead, ultimately he believes, to his taking up his final abode with her. With the *absoluteness* of his intentions (yet another meaning implicit in "setting down one's rest"), Cordelia's future seems imperiled. She would be consigned to the roles of care-giving daughter and foster mother indefinitely, despite the marriage that is apparently to be brokered in this scene. And furthermore, she would be required to sacrifice her innate sense of justice. The notion of *nursery* is closely tied to that of home, embodying as it does a sense of nurturance, child care, protection, and safety, all of which lie at the heart of home. Lear's wish to have his last home in Cordelia's "nursery" suggests not only an infantile desire for a return to maternal care, to the womb, as psychoanalytic critics might have it, and therefore a usurpation of Cordelia's life, but also a desire to retain Cordelia's "kindness" all for himself, and to reassure himself of the stability and protectiveness of home. When Lear banishes Cordelia, then, he banishes his nursery, and all that it promised in terms of future welfare, kinship bond, and psychic safety.

Another meaning of *nursery* bears relevance here, as well; the term was commonly used in early modern texts to refer to a place or school for fostering a quality, attribute, or skill.[14] We are led by Lear's use of this word to question what he might have wished, most likely unconsciously, to foster in himself under the care of Cordelia. What does Lear have to learn from Cordelia? If the mystery of Cordelia's meaning for Lear is wrapped up partly in her name—a name he conferred upon her—then it is the heart (*cor, cordis, cœur*) and "core" meaning of his being that Lear is unschooled in. The Greek *delos* means "revealed," rendering Cordelia's name as "revealed heart." Lear's hidden desire, then, is to go "home"—to go "to the very heart or root" of his existence, where justice should lie. Yet, to do this, Lear unfeelingly and unjustly tramples on his daughter, unaware of her as anything but an agent for his needs and demands. Though she initially asserts measured boundaries between self and father, she will, in time, minister to him totally, fulfilling another meaning of her name found in the Latin *cordialis*, which associates her with the medicinal cordial that invigorates and restores the heart. When Cordelia is reunited later with her traumatized father, she prays for cures from the gods: "restoration hang / Thy medicine on my lips, and let this kiss / Repair those violent harms that my two sisters / Have in thy reverence made" (4.6.23–26). Here she fulfills Aquinas's notion of justice as medicinal, but she need not minister the punishment that was to physic the offender and the state, for Lear has suffered in the extreme. Finally, it can be observed that Cordelia exhibits, as well, the courage called to mind by the phrase *cœur de leon,* which her name seems to invoke.[15]

The price Cordelia pays for her resistance to Lear's injustice is notoriously steep. By attempting to honor the just measure of things, the natural bond of father and daughter, royal subject and ruler, she succeeds in humiliating her father and king in public. In doing so, she unintentionally acts upon her name by revealing Lear's heart, but in a most painful and terrifying way. For her refusal to declare publicly a love beyond all bounds for her father, Lear recoils upon her with a wrath that knows no bounds, thus reflexively returning measure for measure. With curses, he repudiates his flesh, severing kinship ties, confessing and then revoking his love for Cordelia. He wants to hurt the creature he has loved most in this world because she has injured his pride, authority, and secret belief, or fantasy, that she loved him above all, including justice. His revenge is to deny her "paternal care, / Propinquity, and property of blood" (1.1.111–12), a triple estrangement to match the carefully balanced threefold bond she asserted. He assaults her very identity as a royal daughter and, in reducing her to "a stranger to my heart and me" (line 113), he speaks unknowingly of his own self-estrangement.

The horrifying images of the "barbarous Scythian" (line 114) and a cannibalistic parent feeding on his young "To gorge his appetite" (line 116), remind us of the unnatural excesses of Seneca's *Thyestes,* known to Shakespeare and his contemporaries through Jasper Heywood's translation. Yet one need not hear the Senecan subtext here to see the spontaneous, terrifying revelation of something unnatural at the heart of Lear's relationships with his daughters. The fantasy of devouring his offspring returns them to his body, ceasing generation, punishing them, and sparing himself further hurt. Such a fantasy enacts the reflexivity of revenge in a profoundly disquieting way. Lear's mind and passions undergo a horrifying transformation in the grip of vindictiveness.

Lear's response to his daughters reflects an emotional and moral extreme beyond the measure of the ancient *lex talionis* and Aquinas's principle of lawful vengeance. For their public rebelliousness, their exercise of power over their weakened father, and their dishonoring and shaming of him, all of Lear's daughters must pay dearly. Cordelia's suffering comes immediately in physical and psychic estrangement. Goneril and Regan suffer verbal retaliation in the form of Lear's curses and are threatened with unknown, inchoate "terrors of the earth" (2.2.448). Not long after the opening scene, Lear swears vicious revenges upon the elder daughters. His wrathful cursing of Goneril is shocking, as it is yet another paternal curse upon a child, no small thing in Shakespeare's time, and therefore potent in its malice. Lear first calls upon the goddess Nature to rob Goneril of fertility, of "A babe to honour her" (1.4.243). He then utters a curse that expresses a more fitting revenge focused on the pain caused to parents by ungrateful children. Lear's revenge fantasy conjures a mirror image of his tormented self in Goneril, whose "brow of youth" (line 246) is to be stamped with wrinkles, tears carving paths down her cheeks, all care and kindness turned to "laughter and contempt" (line 249) by a thankless child. He wishes literally that his curse could wound and pierce her body. He wants her to suffer as he has, to feel "How sharper than a serpent's tooth it is / To have a thankless child" (1.4.251–52).

Regan is subjected to hearing Lear swear vengeance on Goneril before
he includes her in his curse:

> She hath abated me of half my train,
> Looked black upon me, struck me with her tongue
> Most serpent-like upon the very heart.
> All the stored vengeances of heaven fall
> On her ingrateful top! Strike her young bones,
> You taking airs, with lameness!
>
> (2.2.324–29)

The curse, once again, focuses on Goneril's body, striking it with an ail-
ment akin to Lear's physical weakness. When Lear learns of Regan's conspiracy with Goneril, he appeals to the gods to "Touch [him] with noble
anger" (line 442) and then utters his final curse upon both daughters, whom
he calls "unnatural hags" (2.2.444):

> I will have such revenges on you both
> That all the world shall—I will do such things—
> What they are, yet I know not; but they shall be
> The terrors of the earth. You think I'll weep.
> No, I'll not weep. I have full cause of weeping,
> *Storm and tempest*
> But this heart shall break into a hundred thousand flaws
> Or ere I'll weep.
>
> (2.2.445–51)

As Gordon Braden observes, Lear's frightening words "induc[e] a sense of
the abyss opening behind so many powerful words"; they recall Atreus's
furious rhetoric as he seeks a fitting revenge in Seneca's *Thyestes*.[16] While
Atreus quickly imagines a gory precedent for his revenge in Procne's cannibalistic banquet, Lear, blinded by shame, cannot see what "terrors" are
in store for his daughters, what he will do to them, given the opportunity.
Clearly his appetite for revenge is excessive, as the dark subterranean images of the Senecan tale betray, and his rage knows no bounds, as it seems
to be conveyed through the tempest in the acoustical atmosphere of the theater. What he *can* envision is his own heart virtually shattering with the
pressure of shame and revengelessness.

The opening scene, with its few clues regarding the nature of the father's
relationship with his daughters, asks us to consider the conditions that have
produced such strong, vindictive women as Goneril and Regan, and such
an unexpected shaming of the King as we witness from Cordelia. Cordelia's
history with Lear seems reflected in his line, "I loved her most" (1.1.121),
and Goneril's complaint, "He always loved our sister most" (1.1.285–86).
Cordelia's treatment of her father in the moment of crisis comes as a heart-

felt response from an entitled child who has her integrity; she feels betrayed by the humiliating public spectacle Lear stages. While Cordelia would rather "Love and be silent," her father demands, "Speak" (lines 60, 84). When she does speak, her words seem to mock Lear's authority and his intentions. The elder daughters appear in a contrasting light, less loved and loving, less entitled, and more willing to speak in order to reap benefit. Their treatment of their father following this scene suggests a reservoir of malice, resentment, and fear that could be explained only by years of neglect, even victimization, for they seize upon their father's weakness as an opportunity to wreak their vengeance upon him. Their hostility seems to derive from jealousy of their sister, parental tyranny, and powerlessness within the political system governed by their father. Their hunger for power and revenge seems to be the end result of years of compliance and enforced speech, of having been subjected to the rule of a rash, willful father and king, and marriages of their father's choice. They refer early in the play to Lear's "long-engrafted condition" (1.1.292), his impetuousness, and they do so with some trepidation, fearing that their future treatment will be even worse than their past treatment. When they strike back at Lear, it would seem that his own faults come hurtling back at him through the agency of his daughters, flesh and blood repaying flesh and blood.

In the first scene, after Goneril and Regan have duly flattered Lear, they watch from the sidelines as their father plays out what may very well be their own fantasy of revenge against their sister. In one of Shakespeare's sources, *The True Chronicle Historie of King Leir and his three daughters* (1605), the sisters treat the public love test as "fit occasion offred us, / To be reveng'd upon [Cordella]. / Nay our revenge we will inflict upon her, / Shall be accounted piety in us" (1.2.169–72).[17] Such an interlocking of justice and piety would seem to echo Aquinas, yet here we have a debasing of the notion of just vengeance. The sisters connive against Cordella for perceived injustices, bargaining on gaining the husbands they want, while realizing that Cordella will protest against the Irish king whom Leir has chosen for her. They thrill to the revenge plot, with Ragan claiming, "Not all the world could lay a better plot, / I long till it be put in practice" (1.2.196–97). In *King Leir,* Ragan and Gonorill share the conventional stage role of villain-revenger, laying a wicked plot to hurt their sister.

Shakespeare's scene is far more subtle; the sisters do not overtly conspire against their sister, and only later do they reveal their vindictiveness in stark confrontations with their father. Shakespeare's first scene in *King Lear* concludes with a private exchange between Goneril and Regan that indicates their desire to join forces against their father; they agree they "must do something, and i'th' heat" (1.1.302). The satisfaction they receive from their father's treatment of Cordelia can be inferred, though it is only equivocally represented in the text. Cordelia has been removed from the scene; therefore, she is no longer a threat to their ambitions. Lear has done all the work for them in enacting *their* revenge against their sister; furthermore, the ground is now laid for *Cordelia* to forge an alliance between piety and revenge when she finds fit occasion. Her marriage to the King of France, who will make a just and kind husband, demonstrates the beginning of such a union.

Like many stage revengers, Goneril and Regan feel their father *owes* them for wrongs he has committed against them; indeed, they feel he is remiss in making such a late payment on this personal debt with his division of the kingdom. When Lear exclaims in outraged hurt, "I gave you all," Regan gives a chilling reply, "And in good time you gave it" (2.2.415–16). Her words open an emotional vista into an inner world teeming with resentment, unfulfilled desire, and vengeful fantasies. As Lear attempts to make his nursery in Goneril's hall, she complains of her father's "wrongs"and proceeds to humiliate him:

> By day and night he wrongs me. Every hour
> He flashes into one gross crime or other
> That sets us all at odds. I'll not endure it.
>
> (1.3.3–5)

The daughters' words and actions now demonstrate the reflexive nature of revenge at work. Once the enactment is underway, they find fit occasion to "revenge home," taking a pitiless and complete revenge. In behaving so, they appear as exiles from justice, if we consider justice to be the truest home and intention of vengeance.

Goneril and Regan's relinquishing of all filial care, propinquity, and property of blood replays Lear's rejection of Cordelia. They mimetically reproduce Lear's sins, showing up the mirroring or reflexive dynamic in revenge. They send him into a state of homelessness, a stranger to their hearths and hearts. They go one step further by plotting their father's death; yet, even that desire has been anticipated by Lear's furious wish to annihilate his ingrate daughters. In the Quarto, Albany calls Goneril and Regan "Tigers, not daughters," "Most barbarous, most degenerate" (scene 16.39, 42), echoing the language and associations conjured in Lear's disowning of Cordelia. As René Girard points out, the daughters desire what they inevitably destroy— royal authority. "The beauty of this process," he continues, "is its perfect symmetry, and its saving grace its perfect justice; it turns the two monsters into the divinely impartial avengers of their own crimes."[18]

The Folio, however, notably drops Albany's lines, as well as much of his attack on Goneril in 4.2. With fewer vitriolic lines from Albany, the Folio's scene more sharply brings into focus the question of revenge's legitimacy in the political arena. Goneril complains to Edmond that Albany refuses to

"feel wrongs / Which tie him to an answer" (4.2.13–14). Albany has failed
to respond to the arrival of the French troops or Gloucester's "treachery"
(4.2.6) with heated vengeance; rather, he feels the wrong that Goneril has
done and withdraws as both husband and general of their troops. Angered,
Goneril gives Edmond charge of the troops and swears, "I must change
names at home, and give the distaff / Into my husband's hands" (4.2.17–
18). She attacks what she perceives to be Albany's lack of masculine honor.
She will fight for her right, her rule, her honor, her law even if she has to
appear in the field as a man. Her fierceness is awe-inspiring, yet terrible to
witness, just as Tamora's and Margaret's ferocity is in their respective
plays. The unwarranted cruelty in her actions, however, sacrifices whatever
ethical right her cause might have had.

     Albany's response to Gloucester's misfortune reinforces this sense of
Goneril's unmeasured desire and action. When Albany hears of the servant
that killed Cornwall after he plucked out Gloucester's first eye, he asserts,
"This shows you are above, / You justicers, that these our nether crimes /
So speedily can venge" (4.2.46–48). Vengeance in the hands of the servant
becomes legitimate when seen as an act emanating from the "justicers"
above. Yet he must bear hearing that Gloucester lost the other eye, too. And
Edmond's part in the cruelty shown his father is stunningly vicious—he
"quit the house on purpose that their punishment / Might have the freer
course" (4.2.61–62). Such shocking revelations of violence done to the
Earl move Albany to swear *he* will "revenge [Gloucester's] eyes" (4.2.64).
What he encounters here is the excess in revenge, which Aquinas holds to
be in opposition to rightful vengeance; it is "the sin of cruelty or brutality,
which exceeds the measure in punishing."[19]

     If we shift our perspective to the cosmic, moral order invoked by Albany
and others in Lear's world, Goneril and Regan might be understood, as Girard sees them, as agents of wrathful divine vengeance or unrelenting cosmic justice. They are more than this and less. Their actions turn back upon
themselves, while at the same time punishing Lear for his treatment of
Cordelia and a lifetime of callous disregard, not only for them, but also for
the poor, homeless creatures in his kingdom. Lear himself takes this view
in a painful moment in which he envisions his own flesh revenging home:
"Judicious punishment: 'twas this flesh begot / Those pelican daughters"
(3.4.69–70). Legend had it that the mother pelican wounded her own breast
to feed her young. The motif became associated with Christ's sacrifice on
the cross and could be seen as an attribute of personified charity. As James
Hall indicates, in relation to charity, the pelican was "said to be 'in her
piety.' To the Romans, *pietas* signified devotion to one's parents."[20] In his
distraught state in the hovel, Lear feels the enormity of his daughters' ingratitude, their lack of *pietas* for him, and he self-pityingly thinks of his
own sacrificial position. Bittersweet paradoxes play out for the fallen, des-

olate king when he finds himself his own daughters' victim. Only through punishment and suffering can Lear truly atone for wrongdoing. Only in a state of homelessness and lovelessness can he feel the same abjectness as those he harmed. Only in casting away his heart and his most beloved daughter can they be brought home to him. Only in enacting his revenge upon Cordelia can he create the opportunity for this daughter to respond with a most undeserved, spontaneous response, a rare action that lies in virtue *and* vengeance, justice and love.

Cordelia's role as avenger is the enactment of moral necessity, contrasting significantly with the roles her sisters enact. As a justice-seeking avenger in an early modern revenge-driven drama, she is anomalous in a number of respects, which can be summed up by reference to her gender and virtue. She represents a highly unusual instance of a daughter avenging harms done to her father, which alters the conventional dramatic history of masculine revengers, many of them sons, like Hamlet, who are bound by duty to restore familial honor, slay enemies, and remove usurpers from the throne. As Barbara C. Millard notes, Cordelia has rejected the traditional gender role of "self-obliterating" daughter/mother for the "heroic militant role reserved for the son/father."[21] Cordelia's revenge indeed plays out in the masculine world of battle when her French forces take up arms against her sisters' armies headed by Edmond. Her *tragic* heroism might be defined, as Millard sees it, in "Cordelia's struggle to attain her identity while poised between political necessity in a patriarchal world and her own moral wisdom" and in "her simultaneous movement toward retribution and atonement."[22] Not only is Cordelia attempting political retribution, to gain back an anointed king's right for Lear, but by 4.6 she is clearly attempting to reconstitute her father's shattered self, giving an answer to Lear's lament, "Who is it that can tell me who I am?" (1.4.195). In doing so, she atones for her sisters' malicious treatment of Lear. Her virtuous revenge exerts a powerful counterforce in a world governed by greed, ambition, envy, and wrath, all unleashed by Lear's own "ungoverned rage" (4.3.19). The goal of Cordelia's revenge is not simply to fulfill "the terrible obligations of revenge,"[23] but to end all such grim obligations by restoring justice to the state.

As an avenger, Cordelia parts company with her feminine predecessors in Shakespeare's histories and tragedies. Her essential motive—love of father within the bounds of justice—distinguishes her from avenging queens such as Tamora and Margaret, for, unlike them, Cordelia acts unequivocally as the "heart" of justice, exhibiting no savagery or desire for a personal vendetta. Like Tamora and Margaret, though, Cordelia is a royal power to contend with, an actor on the political front. Cordelia's use of force, however, is neither brutal nor bloodthirsty. Cordelia does not act directly in her own interest. As Aquinas emphasizes, vengeance is virtuous when the avenger's intent is not to harm, but to remove the harm done both in society and in the soul of the harmer. She offers a doubly paradoxical image of a measured female avenger, a fusion of the two feminine icono-graphical figures of Justice and Revenge that transcends classical and Ren-aissance prototypes. She is an anti-Senecan avenger, offering an antidote to wrathful revenge, so terrifyingly embodied in Lear. The 1608 Quarto in-cludes a scene in which Cordelia's patience and sorrow are reported by a gentleman; he stresses that she is moved by Lear's plight, but *"Not* to a rage" (17.17, my emphasis). At the same time, she is a warrior queen bent on defeating enemies, and the omission of this scene from the Folio places the emphasis on Cordelia's reunion and political alliance with Lear. She cannot do anything in Lear's world if she simply functions as a symbol, or a dramatic character defined largely by patience and grief. The Quarto scene would seem to dissolve Cordelia's agency in her tears, though it con-veys an essential point about Cordelia's lack of Senecan rage.

Following conventional Elizabethan doctrine, some avengers in early modern drama assert their public role as God's ministers, declaring, as Shakespeare's Henry V does in the play bearing his name, "War is his [the king's] vengeance" (4.1.158). In *King Lear,* Cordelia does not declare her-self God's avenger or scourge, but her virtue-inspired words and heroic po-litical action enact the divine sanction of measure for measure. In "seeking to give / Losses their remedies" (2.2.154–55), she is rightly understood by the virtuous characters (Gloucester, Kent, Albany) as actively delivering a divine response, if ever there is one in the play. These enigmatic lines are Kent's, whose reverence for authority—of royalty, of the gods—is re-flected in his unwavering faith in King Lear as rightful king and rightful "home" of divine justice, even when Lear, with his flawed humanity, has not merited his position. Kent speaks these lines from the stocks, where he has been placed for his vengeful words and actions taken against Oswald in defense of the King.

Early modern audiences, schooled in sermons and scripture, would have followed Aquinas's basic tenet about revenge: that it gains its greatest moral palatability and virtuous force when some assurance of divine sanc-tion seems evident. Revenge is stripped today in the Western world of any transcendent dimension and set in opposition to state justice, but it was not regarded as inherently morally wrong by Shakespeare's contemporaries, despite what critics such as Eleanor Prosser and Fredson Bowers argue.[24] If authorized ministers took public revenge in keeping with God's law, their actions were lawful and not evil. Virtuous characters like Kent believe that the vicious wrongs done to the fallen Lear and blinded Gloucester will be avenged by the gods; yet, at the same time, characters realize they must trust human agents—if not the gods, then men and women must act for the good. If regarded from the pious perspective offered by Gloucester, Kent, and Albany, Cordelia is a most virtuous instrument of vengeance, seeking to affirm positive values in a morally disoriented world. Cordelia alone in *King Lear* fulfills Thomas Aquinas's requirements for the lawful or virtuous avenger: her rank and position as queen are appropriate to public revenge, and her intention is directed toward the good and against sinners, even in the first scene. As she prepares to meet the British troops, she affirms, "O dear father, / It is thy business that I go about. . . . No blown ambition doth our arms incite, / But love, dear love, and our aged father's right" (4.3.23–24, 27–28).

Early modern theologians would agree with Aquinas that Cordelia "does not usurp what belongs to God, but makes use of the power granted [her] by God. For it is written (Rom. Xiii.4) of the earthly prince that *he is God's minister, an avenger to execute wrath upon him that doeth evil.*"[25] The Tudor Reformer and church authority Thomas Cranmer confirmed this view in his sermons, calling "kings and governors" "common revengers" ordained by God.[26] In a gloss of Matthew 5:34–48 from his sermon on temporal authority, Martin Luther asserted this view as well, distinguishing as the English Reformers did between forbidden private revenge and sanctioned public vengeance: "A Christian should be so disposed that he will suffer every evil and injustice without avenging himself. . . . On behalf of others, however, he may and should seek vengeance, justice, protection, and help. . . . [W]hen [Christians] perform their duties, not with the intention of seeking their own ends but only of helping the law and the governing authority function to coerce the wicked, there is no peril in that."[27] Cordelia seeks vengeance on behalf of her father, whose "business" requires both bloody action and spiritual remedy. The French invasion of Britain is a political action intended to restore law, order, and a moral "governing authority" in the kingdom.

The brutality and violence of war are inescapable, yet Shakespeare's reduction of the battle scenes to emblematic moments and reports diverts the audience's attention from physical to spiritual and psychic violence, the severing of familial bonds, and the anguished homelessness of some of the characters. Neither the 1608 Quarto nor 1623 Folio depicts Cordelia engaged in any act of violence. She could very well be armed as she crosses the stage with her army, but her hands are never bloodied and she never expresses bloodthirstiness; thus, the audience cannot help but view her as a sanctified avenger motivated by love of justice. Shakespeare represents Cordelia as paradoxically transcending the violence and terror of revenge in the very act of pursuing vengeance. She certainly shows the avenger's moral indignation, fierceness, and courage when she says to her father, "Shall we not see these daughters and these sisters?" (5.3.7), anticipating a confrontation with her father's enemies, to which he responds, unable to face them, "No, no, no, no" (5.3.8).

Tragically, however, Cordelia's rightful vengeance offers only a momentary remedy for Lear's traumatized sense of self and the devastated homeland in the play. The French invasion raises hopes that are all too quickly crushed. In an immediate sense, it is a failed revenge, a revenge that provokes swift repayment with Cordelia's life. The "promised end" (5.3.237) hoped for by the suffering, dispossessed characters and emotionally involved audience is brutally denied. While we expect the death of conventional revengers, we do not expect such an unconventional avenger as Cordelia to follow the pattern. Indeed, most readers and spectators do not perceive, at least on a conscious level, the vengeance dynamic structuring the play and motivating Cordelia's actions. When we see her dead body carried onto the stage, we can feel only the horror, the waste. The play's concluding scenes seem shrouded in terrible ironies, about which Cordelia can do nothing: the reality that Lear does not want his kingdom back; that his political abdication and refusal to acknowledge Cordelia's love have destroyed home beyond recovery in the political realm, and the body of state is now thoroughly "gored" (5.3.295) by the actions of his daughters' vicious revenge; that while Lear wished to go happily home with Cordelia to prison, their time together is fleeting, and the restoration of "home" provisional at best. Even life together in prison is denied them. In the end, her avenging actions are fought in the *name* of justice and honor; what she helps achieve is the exorcism of the unjust and, politically, the restitution of justice. Her death, then, is her sacrifice to higher ideals and the payment exacted by the cosmos for exorcising the wild fury of revenge from Lear's kingdom.

Cordelia's exchange with Kent upon her return to England clarifies her purpose in Lear's world. As she recognizes the good in him, she exclaims, "O thou good Kent, how shall I live and work / To match thy goodness? My life will be too short, / And every measure fail me" (4.6.1–3). She wisely predicts her failure, yet she affirms the virtues she and Kent fight for in the world. Kent's response echoes Cordelia's rhetoric of measure from the first scene and underscores acknowledgment of virtue as a reward in itself: "To be acknowledged, madam, is o'erpaid. / All my reports go with the modest truth, / Nor more, nor clipped, but so" (4.6.4–6). At least in Cordelia's and Kent's acknowledgment of good—in our acknowledgment of Cordelia's *measure* in all senses of the word (capacity, balance, proportion, attempt at good, restraint)—there is a hope, a meaning, expressed in the darkness of tragedy. As Stanley Cavell rightly sees it, "Cordelia's death means that *every* falsehood, every refusal of acknowledgement, will be tracked down. In the realm of the spirit, Kierkegaard says, there is absolute justice."[28]

Cordelia belongs to the world of *King Lear,* a world governed by honor, shame, and revenge. While she does not create the conditions in which revenge becomes a necessity, she enacts the moral imperative to revenge home when necessary. For Cordelia, a failure to act appropriately would be a violation of the moral order and of her own integrity; she would be guilty of "a vice by way of deficiency," as Aquinas phrases it.[29] *King Lear* imagines a world so naturalized, so accustomed to revenge that characters instinctually call upon the heavens for revenge, curse those they perceive have wronged them, and follow the primal instinct of revenge, the urge to strike back. Lear can no more control his vengefulness than Cornwall or his cruel daughters can. The lack of measure or recognition of desert that accompanies their revenges is shown to have a destructive, devouring quality, which is figured in the cannibalistic parent and the pelican daughters. The excessiveness of the two daughters' ingratitude is played out through the extremity of their revenges.

Given the pervasive presence of revenge in *King Lear,* perhaps we might conclude by acknowledging once more the complex interaction of destructive and constructive elements in revenge and its rightful basis in justice. It is something of a paradox that revengeful actions can both tear down and build up, and that they have a disturbingly reflexive quality. For Lear's failures as parent and king, his daughters Goneril and Regan fail him in his time of need. Yet, no matter how psychologically penetrating our understanding of the elder sisters, how shamed we feel they must have been by their father, we understand that Goneril and Regan ultimately pursue a destructive, self-interested revenge that tears down others so that they may gain mastery over their own destinies. That their target is their father and king, that they wish to destroy him and others, that they gain a perverse pleasure in their revenges, makes their case morally appalling.

As Confucius said long ago, Before you embark on a journey of revenge, dig two graves. Tragically, the aphorism applies as well to Cordelia, though the public revenge she pursues in her war against her sisters might rightly be called virtuous. Her goals are nothing short of the transformation and healing of her father and kingdom. She is a morally legitimate avenger in that she does not set out with the intent to harm her sisters; rather, she is resisting evil in Lear's world. After France sees her weeping, he pities her cause and allows her to send troops into her father's kingdom. She targets her sisters through legal means in a just war. Shakespeare represents this action in an almost abstract fashion, as if it were a bloodless attack, so that our focus stays fixed on the darkest kinds of physical and psychic cruelty. In the end, Cordelia does not have to harm her sisters. Their vindictiveness consumes them: Goneril poisons Regan, and then commits suicide. When their bodies are shown onstage, Albany seems to echo the moment in the *Inferno* when Dante learns not to pity: "judgment of the heavens, that makes us tremble, / Touches us not with pity" (5.3.205–6). Neither Cordelia nor Lear bears witness to their deaths—no sense of malicious satisfaction taints them in the end. The notion of trembling before the "judgment of heaven" suggests that Albany and Shakespeare's audience see feelingly the terrible aptness of revenge—for the pitiless, dishonorable daughters come deaths not worth our pity. The vengeance is harsh, yet just.

With her rightly measured revenge, Cordelia seeks to restore her kinship with her father, demonstrate her loyalty to her king, and save the heart of Britain itself. Although her enactment of revenge ends with multiple graves, her vengeance has been heroic, a final noble act to cease the downward spiral of revenge. Though she does not live to see it, the kingdom is momentarily restored to Lear; furthermore, she has set things right in the kingdom, anticipating a new, just rule. Albany, by default, becomes the "absolute power" in Britain, and speaks for her, conferring power back to Lear:

> You lords and noble friends, know our intent.
> What comfort to this great decay may come
> Shall be applied; for us, we will resign
> During the life of this old majesty
> To him our absolute power; you to your rights,
> With boot and such addition as your honours
> Have more than merited. All friends shall taste
> The wages of their virtue, and all foes
> The cup of their deservings.
>
> (5.3.271–79)

The emphasis on rights, desert, and punishment are reinforced here at the end of the play. After his harrowing and cure, though, Lear does not want his kingship; he appears not to hear Albany's words, as his heart is shattering once more with the death of Cordelia. His final stab against injustice, the vengeance killing of Edmond's officer who hanged Cordelia, may seem to show an appropriately directed anger, as Harry Keyishian emphasizes, but such an action is pointless. This revenge restores nothing for Lear, except perhaps a momentary resurgence of his heroic, warrior self.[30] What he desires now is lost forever. Yet the sacrifice of Cordelia seems to be a debt paid in deeper symbolic, even religious, terms, as René Girard might see it.[31]

Lear, too, must die, and so it is Edgar who remains to prove himself Cordelia's worthy counterpart as Britain's new king. Like Cordelia, he has loved, avenged, and cured his father by striking back at a guilty sibling, and now he carries the "weight of this sad time" (5.3.298). Homeless, fatherless, and kingless, he must, if he can, apply balm to the wounded, bloodied body of Lear's former kingdom. Most of the characters have revenged *home* in both senses of the word—they have fought for and against kin thoroughly and unsparingly, and the personal and political losses have been catastrophic. Edmond's excess of revenge as a means to overcome homelessness and lack of degree, and Goneril and Regan's vicious attack on home show up the volatile energies of envy, desire, and power-hungriness at the heart of the family and the political system in *King Lear*. If, in the words of one critic, "Shakespeare removes providential sureties and leaves his characters alone to destroy each other or to create a positive ethic out of their own need,"[32] at least that positive ethic has been a force to contend with in Lear's Britain. While the surviving characters persist in their belief in an otherworldly justice, what has been at work in the play is a worldly, yet spiritual, ethic of measure, justice, and virtue, embodied most tragically in Cordelia, whose life was too short, and whose every measure seemed to fail her. To Goneril's anarchic self-assertion before her husband, "the laws are mine, not thine. / Who can arraign me for't?" (5.3.148–49), Cordelia answers with greater personal courage and political force than any of the resisting members of Lear's kingdom. She recognizes a higher law and moral order that must be obeyed. Her purpose in the terrible, moving revenge play that is *King Lear* is to counter the destructive chaos of personal revenge with a just public vengeance. That the world continues to fall apart around her is a function of that world and not the failure of human virtue itself. That her sacrifice eventually might have a reconstituting effect on the kingdom is its last best hope.

In the chapters that follow, we will change the key, turning from jangled, harsh bells of tragic revenge to the light, varied music of comic vengeance. In the realm of comedy, revenge has a surprisingly multivalent presence and purpose. Like tragedy, comedy allows for revenge's dual potentiality for virtuous and vicious expressions of the will. Shakespeare crosses generic boundaries to explore the ethical dimension of women's vengeance in the domestic sphere, where matters of chastity, honor, security, oaths, and marriage are of pressing concern. Women's vengeful responses to moral outrages against themselves and others turn out to align with the ethical purposes of comedy itself. The next chapter looks deeply into the question of genre in *Twelfth Night*, exposing at the roots of comedy the generative seed of vengeance.

6

Twelfth Night, or What Maria Wills

Fabian.   . . . Maria writ
The letter, at Sir Toby's great importance,
In recompense whereof he hath married her.
How with a sportful malice it was follow'd
May rather pluck on laughter than revenge,
If that the injuries be justly weigh'd
That have on both sides pass'd.
—Shakespeare, *Twelfth Night*

FOR SOME TIME, THEATER PRODUCTIONS AND LITERARY CRITICISM OF Shakespeare's *Twelfth Night* have acknowledged the disquieting nature of the revenge plot carried out against Malvolio; yet the degree to which directors and critics allow revenge to unbalance romantic comedy varies significantly, as do perceptions of how the dynamics of revenge operate in this comedy. These interpretive differences arguably arise from Shakespeare's use of multivalent figures for revenge, which create tonal ambiguity and destabilize generic boundaries. Complexities in tone and genre are directly related to the avenger's character and function in the play. Critics have generally overlooked the role of Maria, Olivia's lady-in-waiting, as the lead avenger. Unassuming as she is, Maria takes the part of Nemesis, goddess of retribution, whose righteous indignation and resentment against pride and undue disturbances of Fortune and Justice drive her "to give what is due" (the Greek root of *nemesis*). The avenging Maria stands as a figure for comedy's contradictory impulses; her vengeance generates *and* undermines comedy from behind the scenes, eliciting both uproarious laughter and moral disquietude. Her journey's end, like Viola's and Olivia's, is comedic, but her function as Nemesis complicates the play's generic purposes. Her ingenious plot fuels communal resentment and retribution, revealing not only that comedy is hospitable to revenge, but, most surprisingly and rarely observed by critics, that vengeance, with its attendant passions and pleasures, cruelties and humiliations, is *constitutive* of the genre.

Twelfth Night raises troubling questions about revenge as a means for individual and communal retribution; at the same time, questions about generic integrity come into focus. To what extent does comedy license revenge? What conditions give rise to the transformation of revenge fantasy into reality? Can revenge be constructive or therapeutic, or does it simply encourage further injury? Does revenge teach a lesson? How much revenge is enough? Such questions betray how awkwardly *Twelfth Night*'s revenge plot fits into traditional saturnalian views of comedic design espoused by critics such as C. L. Barber and Northrop Frye.[1] Critics who defend the poetic justice of Malvolio's treatment are, according to Ralph Berry, "bent on repressing instincts which, outside the theatre of *Twelfth Night,* they would surely admit."[2] We need only examine the figurative language used to characterize the revengers' plot and the play's final moments of awkward reconciliation to detect textual complexities and contradictions that cannot be glossed over or laughed away. Malvolio's exit line and Fabian's peacemaking speech offer ready examples. In comedy's world, we somehow need to make sense of the harsh, discordant notes of the persecuted steward's cry, "I'll be reveng'd on the whole pack of you!" (5.1.377). This threat, with its intimations of tragic fury, the bearbaiting ring, and bloodthirsty dogs, demands to be taken seriously. Alternately, if the Folio's question mark at the end of this line were to be used by an actor, we might feel a sense of pathos and remorse upon the shamed steward's exit.

Fabian's speech, quoted in part above, seems intended to provide clarification and justification for the avengers, while at the same time preserving the wonder of the play's final scene. But his words succeed only in leaving us with a nagging sense that attempts at reconciliation have been too hasty, and that harmonious resolution is a far more fragile business than the characters —or we comedy lovers—admit. Words such as *recompense* and *sportful malice* sit uncomfortably with *married* and *justly weigh'd.* We wish to reconcile them, to say with Feste, "that's all one" (5.1.406), especially since the play itself seems to demand such graciousness or moral deafness from us.[3] We observe Malvolio's failure to gain insight, yet we feel some justification in his cry for vengeance, both of which point up comedy's vulnerability to tragic forces, to the spinning whirligig of time and revenge. The play's end offers wonders indeed, but they do not let us forget the shadowy undercurrents of vengeance, which "Taint the condition of this present hour" (5.1.356). For the audience, if not for the play's characters, there is a lingering sense that some darker purpose of comedy has been at work.

John Kerrigan observes, "Such plays as *Much Ado About Nothing* and *Twelfth Night* are strongly driven by vengeance—as Malvolio discovers to his cost—and it would be interesting to work out why it should be revenge plots which so often carry tragic materials into comedy."[4] This line of thought lies beyond the purview of Kerrigan's book, but we might take it up here and start by observing how the "shifting, tonal complexity"[5] Kerrigan finds in revenge tragedy has suggestive implications for *Twelfth*

Night's wildly shifting tones. Maria's revenge plot is Shakespeare's invention, so his stretching of generic norms might be understood as a deliberate move to complicate genre—indeed, to invoke the anticomic genre of revenge tragedy. Yet why in *Twelfth Night* do the explicitly comic dynamics of revenge darken so radically and give way to malicious laughter, psychological violence, and shame? In *Much Ado About Nothing,* the tragic potentialities of revenge are roundly defeated by the Friar's felicitous death trick in which Hero dies to live, and the comic Watch's revelation of the truth. In *Twelfth Night,* "sportful malice" results in the victim's utter humiliation and the community's awkwardness in the play's final moments when harmony should reign. Kerrigan's view helps to clarify things: "Repeatedly, vengeance generates, from out of its dramaturgic potential, a strain of awkward comedy which raises laughter, and kills it."[6] The dynamics of revenge spontaneously provoke oddly conflicting responses, which seem inappropriate to the festive dimension of the genre. Once revenge's energies are unleashed they are difficult to contain or to reconcile with comedy's lighter generic purposes. Attempts at a harmonious resolution to the revenge plot at the end of *Twelfth Night* cannot defuse vengeance, which has taken shape and rooted itself within the comic world. In the play's final movement, the revengers' revels may be over, their appetite for sport having sickened and died, but another victim with a cause for revenge now compels attention. Perhaps because we laughed so heartily at the letter trick in *Twelfth Night* we find ourselves drawn almost unawares into the trajectory of revenge, which eventually plunges us into pained silence and guilt when we witness its aftermath. At certain moments, *Twelfth Night*'s comic premises seem to have come embarrassingly unseamed to expose a rather savage tragicomedy at work.

By imagining a tonally complex comic variant of revenge tragedy, *Twelfth Night* clearly stretches generic expectations to include moral responses we might prefer to deny. The norms governing blood revenge have been inverted "for the love of mockery" (2.5.18), yet comic revenge proves to be just as aggressive and disruptive as its tragic counterpart. We sense the shadow structure and dynamics of tragic revenge underlying the comedy. Like Hamlet's Denmark, Illyria is an aristocratic, honor-based society whose inhabitants instinctually seek to preserve their reputations. Insults to one's honor destabilize both self-identity and position in society. Malvolio represents the greatest threat to the reputation and position of Olivia's householders. While Malvolio's "crimes" are minor compared to regicide, rape, or murder, typical motives for revenge in tragedy, he nonetheless has committed wrongs over time, which others resent and perceive as unjust. The audience witnesses firsthand his humiliation of Feste, Sir Toby, Sir Andrew, and Maria. His verbal abuse of Feste early in the play establishes his character's ill will and seems representative of a host of insults for which he is guilty. Malvolio asserts his will to control Olivia's household and, even worse, her favor, which he does by representing her household revelers in the worst light. Maria's revenge is directly provoked by Malvolio's threat to bring her out of favor with Olivia. This threat is coupled importantly with Malvolio's overweening self-regard and desire for social advancement through marriage to the countess Olivia. Thus, comic revenge responds not only to perceived past and present wrongs, but also to traits and desires that seem absurdly funny, inappropriate, and vicious. Just as Nemesis punished the proud and redistributed Fortune's goods according to a person's desert, Maria responds to Malvolio's presumptuous, injurious character by giving him his due.

Maria is something of a cipher; she operates behind the scenes mostly, coming out of the shadows only in her pivotal scene (2.3), where she boldly inverts social norms through the invention of a revenge plot. As an avenger, Maria appropriates a conventionally male-gendered social and theatrical role and, in doing so, experiences the pleasures and dangers that attend revenge plots—the exhilaration of artistic invention, secret conspiracy, self-empowerment, and power over others, on the one hand; escalation of the intrigue, loss of control, unchecked malice, and the possibility of suffering retaliation, on the other hand. Her ingenuity leads to creative *and* destructive ends, activating both comic *and* tragic energies. By taking up the pen rather than the sword or dagger, she creates the infamous "obscure epistles of love" (2.3.155–56), a stage property and script in one, which puts into play a fantastical revenge comedy. She manages her own coterie theater, inspiring scenes of farce and violence, which veer dangerously between physic and cruelty.

Critics' and directors' responses to Maria's part in the gulling of Malvolio range between light and dark poles of comic experience and reflect the degree to which they desire—or do not desire—*Twelfth Night* to be a joyous, festive comedy.[7] The Royal Shakespeare Company's productions of the play in the 1980s demonstrate how the pendulum swings back and forth in directorial emphasis. In his 1987 Royal Shakespeare Company production at Stratford-upon-Avon, the director Bill Alexander staged Maria's plot as "very vicious, very vindictive," while John Caird in his earlier RSC production (1983) had emphasized her wit and resourcefulness in making the "festival side of this play work out."[8] These examples from performance history reflect opposing views of an ambiguous character, as well as antithetical understandings of comedy's potentialities. The popular traditional view of Maria as unequivocally good and benign seems naïve, yet the opposite, more recent view demonizes Maria as morally depraved and far worse than the ill-willed Malvolio. Neither extreme plumbs the depth of this character, or considers the play's delicate balance of dark and light energies.

While the proliferation of critical and directorial perspectives on Maria stems from cultural and theoretical preoccupations, without a doubt, the text itself overflows with critically suggestive figurative terms used to describe Maria's character and her plot. Our very attempt to contain Maria runs counter to the dramatist's will to have her function in a multitude of ways in the comedy. She is a "most excellent devil of wit" (2.5.206–7), displaying her mischievous ingenuity for the pleasure of onstage and offstage audiences. She is a satirist who successfully eviscerates a deserving opponent; a moral physician who applies medicine to the sick; the lead dog in the pack that baits the bear; a "noble gull-catcher" (2.5.187) who traps her gull; and Lady Fortune (or The Fortunate Unhappy) who brings ruin upon the fool who trusts that "all is fortune" (2.5.23). She is a plot-maker and intriguer, as well, which gives her the privileged seat of power in bringing catastrophe to an unwitting enemy and a "providential" escape for herself and Sir Toby. Above all, she is an avenger and figure of Nemesis punishing, or giving what is due to, a prideful enemy. Maria's identity multiplies as rapidly as perspectives in a glass, and by the play's end she vanishes, evading responsibility and punishment, absorbed into the romantic ends of comedy through a surreptitious, offstage marriage.

Thus, *Twelfth Night*'s figurative language offers contradictory signals to playgoers and readers about how to view Maria's will. Her intrigue is conceived, born, extended, and exposed in the wake of numerous tropes, including revenge, recompense, improbable fiction, physic, sport royal, dream, infection, device, practice, gulling, baiting, knavery, punishment, penance, pastime, jest, and whirligig of time. These figures, like "a very opal" (2.4.75), color the audience's theatrical and reading experiences with a shifting palette of meaning. On one end of the spectrum, we might anticipate the therapeutic or curative functions of a plot associated with physic and penance. On the other end, we are given a plethora of metaphors involving violence and illicit forms of play, such as bearbaiting and gullcatching. Of the darker figures, however, it is revenge that suggests the greatest degree of moral ambiguity and emotional upheaval, challenging the very premises and generic boundaries of comedy as a social revel.

Maria's identification of her "device" as revenge reflects comedy's (and Shakespeare's) dependence on sometimes painful and destructive means to achieve restorative actions. After being humiliated (yet again, we presume) by Malvolio, Maria sizes up her enemy's vulnerabilities and considers a fitting revenge: "The devil a Puritan that he is, or anything constantly, but a time-pleaser, an affectioned ass, that cons state without book, and utters it by great swarths: the best persuaded of himself, so crammed (as he thinks) with excellencies, that it is his grounds of faith that all that look on him love him: and on that vice in him will my revenge find notable cause to work" (2.3.146–53).

Maria's portrait of Malvolio has a satiric quality to it, but more importantly it savors of resentment, indignation, and retaliatory fantasy. Her penetrating analysis of the "affectioned ass" resembles Iago's canny portraits of Othello, Cassio, and Roderigo; both revengers have the wit to size up their opponents' weaknesses.[9] Like Iago's, Maria's cause is personal and "notable," rather than noble. Naming her theatrical project as "*my* revenge" (my emphasis) personalizes the enterprise, highlighting her initiative and agency. At the same time, her revenge becomes the community's revenge, pursued "in the name of jesting" (2.5.20), and, in that sense, takes shape as saturnalian play. By the time Maria sends her fellow revengers off to bed, they have begun to relish the fantasy of an upcoming "Sport royal"; she tells them to "dream on the event" (2.3.172, 176). Revenge fantasy is about to invade daylight.

Maria's self-willed role as comic Nemesis enables her not only to punish Malvolio's pride and "pluck on laughter" (5.1.365), at least temporarily, but also to pursue a covert courtship. The play's alternate title, *What You Will,* suggests that the will to shape an identity, as fantastical as it might be, governs Illyria and stands as a guarantee (liberating or troubling) against essential selfhood and class immobility. Maria's forged letter promises in jest what the characters wish to believe in earnest: "thou art made, if thou desir'st to be so" (2.5.154–55). Not only does *Twelfth Night* conjure "a world in which one's social estate is a matter of desire or will rather than birth or title,"[10] it does so in decidedly theatrical terms, positing *personation* as the model of identity. Characters devise personae for themselves, as well as shape roles for others through imaginative constructions. Maria's self-determined witty persona allows her to function with an unusual degree of agency in Olivia's household and, ultimately, to make a match of her own choice. Her motives for masterminding the revenge plot against Malvolio seem to have to do, in part, with Sir Toby Belch. If Malvolio's transgression lies partly in his wish to cross class lines through marriage—to become *Count* Malvolio—so, too, does Maria's. Ironically, she seeks to punish Malvolio for a desire she secretly harbors. Revenge advances her suit, which is to become *Lady* Maria. Thus, we might say that Olivia's "gentle" servants, Maria and Malvolio, pursue twinned plots of social ambition, which lead to a pair of plots (one carried out, the other threatened) centered on revenge.

If we examine Maria's class aspiration from the perspective of genre, we see how, like twin threads binding one design, a submerged romantic plot is directly related to the revenge plot. The trope of recompense unites the disturbingly twinned goals of revenge and marriage in the play. Some critics have felt that the "play is not interested in the precise nature of the relationship between Maria and Toby," because they do not belong to the "leisure" class.[11] While it is true that their "romance" is not given the surface-interest value of Orsino, Viola, and Olivia's love triangle, there are underground currents of importance here that reflect on the other couples and the purpose of comedy. Sir Toby *is* of the leisure class, and Maria's destined marriage with him renders their relationship a kind of murky, albeit playful courtship. Their conspiracy to humiliate Malvolio energizes the would-be lovers and solidifies their alliance. Over the body of the scapegoat, the lovers seal their bond.

Maria's identity and relationship to other characters can be understood within the tangled, fluid network of signs that indicate social aspiration, status, and hierarchy. As the third female "heroine" in the play, Maria's character comes into focus partly through her similarities to Viola and aspirations regarding Olivia and Sir Toby. She and Viola, for example, are twinned as "gentle" servants waiting upon superiors who languish in self-absorbed fantasies of impossible love. Like Viola, Maria has a rather ambiguous position in an aristocratic household, and her history, too, is a "blank." Her status as a gentlewoman, however, is unassailable.[12] Countess Olivia functions as Maria's patron, bestowing favor upon her. Maria is a social dependent, a courtier and waiting-woman to her aristocratic superior. Although we do not hear Maria speak directly of the matter, it is implied that she depends significantly upon her alliance with Olivia, for this position represents her livelihood and maintains her public identity. We can infer that she is a gentleman's daughter in need of a place in the social network. To fall out of the Countess's favor would court social punishment—rejection and the shame of social placelessness. Her bantering with Feste when he returns from unlicensed leave reflects her understanding of the consequences of disfavor. Maria's figurative example of such a fate—a hanging—is served up in a joking manner, but a palpable threat lurks just beneath the mirthful veneer of such a prospect.

For Maria, we might conclude, revenge is partly an act of self-preservation. Her plot against Malvolio aligns her advantageously with Sir Toby, first and foremost, which leads to a more secure place in Olivia's household and a social status far superior to Malvolio's.[13] While Maria appears to serve two masters, Olivia and Sir Toby, in truth she serves no one but herself. Maria's revenge plot against Malvolio skillfully directs Sir Toby and the others to a fruitful recognition of her wit and, more importantly, her worth. Because Maria's wit has been spent, in part, for the sake of his honor (Malvolio has sought to dishonor Toby), Sir Toby thinks in terms of recompense. Certainly he owes something to Maria, but why does he think of *marriage* as the best recompense for the brilliant favor she does for him? "I could marry this wench for this device," he exclaims, "And ask no other dowry with her but such another jest" (2.5.182, 184–85). Sir Toby's offer is both fanciful and awe-inspiring. Audiences must feel a degree of surprise when they hear later in one brief line that Sir Toby has made good on such an incredible promise. It is Fabian who tells us, using a precise economic metaphor: "In recompense whereof he hath married her" (5.1.363). Shakespeare, in effect, makes good on comedy's promise here: a woman's witty revenge pays off with interest in a world where jests and revels function as acceptable social currency.

Romantic desire for "Sweet Sir Toby" (2.3.132) may very well be the loftier inspiration for Maria's jest, yet she seems shrewder than this. Maria not only wishes to please and impress Sir Toby; more importantly, she wishes to master him through an inversion of the social and gender order. In his admiration for her, Sir Toby places himself in a position of mock subordination, which hints at what is to come: "Wilt thou set thy foot o' my neck? . . . Shall I play my freedom at tray-trip, and become thy bond-slave?" (2.5.188, 190–91). Sir Toby is Maria's ideal spectator, one infinitely capable of appreciating a jest. He understands, as well, that payment must be made for his pleasures. Indeed, he himself has been a jest-maker, though if Olivia tells true, the jests were "many fruitless pranks," which he "botch'd up" (4.1.54, 55). His duel plot involving Sir Andrew and Cesario/ Viola is a case in point. He botches it in the end and wins a bloody coxcomb. Maria's vengeful plot, with Sir Toby's added device of the "dark room," proves far more successful and exceptionally fertile than any plot Sir Toby initiates on his own. He has recognized Maria's superiority in using her wit and her device to help humiliate and thwart his enemy. Maria kills off the disturbing specter of *Count* Malvolio, mocking the steward's pathetic fantasy of taking revenge on "my *kinsman* Toby" (my emphasis, 2.5.55).

Malvolio's social status and position in the household are perhaps less ambiguous and more colorfully marked by willful fantasies of self-fashioning and punishment than Maria's; in this respect, he is both Maria's distorted twin and inevitable target. What is his value in the household in relation to Maria's value? Is he a gentleman? Olivia declares that she would not have Malvolio "miscarry for the half of my dowry" (3.4.62–63). Is she exaggerating? Perhaps not, considering that a steward was the chief manager of domestic order in the early-modern aristocratic household. Olivia depends upon Malvolio to reflect and enforce her will in the household. Yet Shakespeare seems to have deliberately toyed with his audience by withholding the answer to the question of gentility until late in the play. It is only when Malvolio is imprisoned and told he is mad that he desperately calls for light, ink, and paper, proclaiming, "as I am a gentleman, I will live to be thankful to thee for't" (4.2.85–86). He is called *gentleman* twice in the final scene of the play. This term, like *steward* and *chambermaid,* is more fluid than it might seem in a play in which characters' aspirations and self-perceptions fluctuate according to their wills. Sir Toby's provoking question, "Art any more than a steward?" (2.3.113–14), is rhetorical, with an implied assertion of his own rank (he is a knight and a blood relation of the countess Olivia). In Sir Toby's estimation, Malvolio is no more than a functionary. He might be a gentleman by birth, or perhaps a social upstart who "*achieve[s] greatness*" (2.5.145), but he is distinctly lacking in gentle manners and a proper respect for place and duty, which are faults that render him a threat to an aristocrat such as Sir Toby. Others name Malvolio a gentleman only at the play's end, where again there is the suggestion that he is something less than a gentleman in his behavior and attitude. Olivia's "poor gentleman" (5.1.278) sounds pitying, or perhaps patronizing. In her naming his gentility, though, there may be a suggestion of his dishonor; Malvolio had appealed to "the modesty of honour" (5.1.334) when he had begged Olivia to explain why she had tormented him. With the exposure of the letter trick, however, Olivia's "poor gentleman" shades all too easily into "poor fool" (5.1.368).

On a social level, Maria's revenge can be seen as a retaliatory measure or skirmish in class warfare and household politics. She makes a bold move to protect her own privileges, as well as Sir Toby's, against the encroachment of an upwardly mobile member of the lower gentry or underclass. The competition for favor is fierce—all's fair in love and service—perhaps because it is a limited commodity in the household. Maria has assessed her situation, and, when it comes time to choose, she aligns her fate with Olivia's blood relative, Sir Toby Belch. In the pivotal reveling scene (2.3), his call, "A stoup of wine, Maria!" (2.3.119), may be heard as the challenge, and her insult to Malvolio, "Go shake your ears" (2.3.124), as her decision in favor of Sir Toby.[14] Her revenge on Malvolio displaces him as the household's chief officer and authority. She subverts his position by asserting her own authority and standing in for the steward.[15] She ably manipulates and rearranges the domestic hierarchy, subordinating the householders, all men, to her will.

Maria plays out a secret fantasy not only to master Malvolio and Sir Toby, but to master her mistress, Olivia, as well, through an act of impersonation. Her handwriting, which is "very like" her lady's (2.3.160), stands in for a noblewoman's hand. Her forgery of the love letter is an act of social and individual usurpation, which exploits her lady's fantasy of wooing beneath her station.[16] The lack of "distinction of our hands" (2.3.161–62) that Maria perceives expresses her desire for social distinctions to be erased as easily. Maria not only "feelingly personate[s]" Malvolio in the epistles of love (2.3.159); she also transgresses multiple boundaries of selfhood, decorum, and class by feelingly personating Olivia. The tropes attending this device echo Olivia's interview with Cesario (1.5), which also turned on the figures of identity and writing—conning, personation, usurpation, veil.

Maria's letter-writing inspiration reveals how her will expresses itself through the multivalent hand metaphor.[17] The ubiquitous figure of the hand (appearing along with its variants thirty-four times in the play) becomes most significant as Maria employs her "sweet Roman hand" (3.4.28–29), her italic handwriting, to take revenge *and* secure her husband's hand, as it were. *Hand* suggests agency, authority, literacy, skill, and a pledge of one's faith, all of which come into play in the course of Maria's plotting. Furthermore, there is a fitting linguistic and symbolic equivalence of hand for hand established in the scene of revenge-plotting, which subtly invokes the biblical law of an eye for an eye ("life for life, eie for eie, tothe for tothe, hand for hand" [Deut. 19:21]). When Malvolio threatens Maria with the oath "by this hand," she imagines a fitting repayment by her hand:

> *Mal.* Mistress Mary, if you prized my lady's favour at anything more than contempt, you would not give means for this uncivil rule; she shall know of it, by this hand.
>
> (2.3.120–23)

> *Maria.* I will drop in his way some obscure epistles of love, wherein by the colour of his beard, the shape of his leg, the manner of his gait, the expressure of his eye, forehead, and complexion, he shall find himself most feelingly personated. I can write very like my lady your niece; on a forgotten matter we can hardly make distinction of our hands.
>
> (2.3.155–62)

Malvolio's threat to report Maria's insubordination to her superior "by this hand" carries multiple connotations of authority, punishment, and literacy. The phrase betrays his will to be superior, and perhaps conveys a sense of his literacy as a point of pride and status. Later in the "dark room," Malvolio will depend upon his hand to save him. Yet it is Maria's superior literacy that rules the day. As Karen Robertson argues, Maria inverts gender norms through her "avenging female hand," and exposes Malvolio as a "bad reader who has dangerously simple notions of gender."[18] What will become abundantly clear in the letter-reading scene, furthermore, is Malvolio's *illiteracy* regarding himself, which is cause for both a great deal of laughter and perhaps a bit of pity.[19]

On emotional and psychological levels, the performance of the letter-reading scene may provoke pity, as we watch the spectacle of a man's fall due to his sin of self-love. But the dominant feeling has to be sheer pleasure at watching an insufferable man get his due, at witnessing a comic Nemesis at work. Only at the edge of our consciousness might there arise a slight reservation, something that erupts full blown later in the play when we are finally confronted with a disheveled, humiliated Malvolio. When he pathetically insists to Olivia before her household, "Madam, you have done me wrong, / Notorious wrong. . . . Pray you, peruse that letter. / You must not now deny it is your hand" (5.1.327–30), the vengeful joke has taken air and tainted. Maria's revenging hand is unmasked in these final moments as evidence that she and her conspirators have done "Notorious wrong."

The linguistic play with *lex talionis,* so satisfyingly exemplified in the hand-for-hand trope, occurs elsewhere in the play, making good on revenge's aggressive character, as well as carrying the past into the present. Revenge thrives on recompense, equivalence, and remembrance. At the play's conclusion, we hear his words recoiling upon Malvolio in the fullness of time. Malvolio had sworn during the letter-reading scene that he would "baffle Sir Toby" (2.5.162), only to hear Olivia unwittingly give voice to the repayment for his vindictive intention with her pitying acknowledgment, "Alas, poor fool, how have they baffled thee!" (5.1.368). Both uses of *baffle* refer to a victim being subjected to public disgrace, but Olivia's use invokes the French *beffler,* which means not only to deceive, mock, gull, or confound, but to do so with fair words.[20] One thinks immediately of Maria's fair letter. At the play's end, Feste throws back at Malvolio his taunting words, which have been etched painfully in the Fool's memory: "But do you remember, 'Madam, why laugh you at such a barren rascal, and you smile not, he's gagged'? And thus the whirligig of time brings in his revenges" (5.1.373–76). The law of *lex talionis* operates powerfully for Feste and the other avengers, as it does for Malvolio, who strikes back verbally and immediately with his infamous, "I'll be reveng'd on the whole pack of you!" (5.1.377). In the play's world and ours, public shaming demands a response; if Feste is right, it is in the nature of time itself to repay such insults. So, too, does it appear to be in the nature of comedy to accommodate Nemesis and her implacable will.

Is it possible, then, to argue that Maria and her coconspirators take on social and moral obligations—comedy's obligations—to respond to "ill will" (the meaning of Malvolio's name) in their community? To address this question, let us look again at the various tropes for the plot, which are held in maddening tension with one another. By examining the polar extremes, the popular Elizabethan pastime of bearbaiting and the medicinal metaphor of physic, we can see just how morally ambiguous and volatile revenge is in *Twelfth Night.* Bearbaiting, like theatrical revenge, implicates spectators, whetting their appetite for violence and spectacle. This trope introduces notions of victimization, mob violence, and theatrical blood sport into the aristocratic world of Illyria. When Sir Toby recruits Fabian to the revenge cause, we learn that Fabian has staged an illicit round of actual bearbaiting on Olivia's grounds. The very space in which Maria and her coconspirators initiate a theater of revenge has accommodated a sport of another kind or, shall we say, a disturbingly similar kind. As Ralph Berry sees it, the "dark room" scene *is* "theatre as blood sport."[21] Fabian's complaint against Malvolio is that the steward "brought me out o' favour with my lady, about a bear-baiting here" (2.5.6–8). Viewing the revengers' treatment of Malvolio in light of Fabian's sport makes their revenge look like an act of vindictive repetition. Sir Toby's response to Fabian is, after all, to imagine reprisal in kind with the figurative transformation of Malvolio into a bear: "To anger him we'll have the bear again, and we will fool him black and blue" (2.5.9–10). Maria too exults in delightful malice with the language of bearbaiting: "I have dogged him like his murderer" (3.2.73–74). Malvolio's cry for revenge against the "pack" employs the trope one final time, revealing that Malvolio has in truth experienced his torment as a baiting and his persecutors as savage. At least one director, Bill Alexander, has exploited the potentialities of the bearbaiting trope by having Malvolio chained to a stake onstage.[22]

The trope of physic suggests an entirely different range of emotions and intentions driving Maria's jest. When Maria uses this medicinal metaphor, "I know my physic will work with him" (2.3.172–73), she gestures toward a potentially positive, even virtuous, dimension of revenge. While the adage "to give someone a taste of his own medicine" may underlie Maria's use of the term *physic,* it is equally possible she entertains a vision of a healthy outcome to the retributive spectacle of shaming. Of all the tropes we have examined, physic comes the closest to asserting a socially productive, curative function to revenge. *Physic* could mean "mental, moral, or spiritual remedy," "medicine," and "the healing art."[23] In this sense, Maria takes upon herself the role of a moral physician who will cure the vice (overweening self-love) in her patient, Malvolio. Early in the play, Olivia diagnoses Malvolio's disease and points up what he lacks: "O, you are sick of self-love, Malvolio, and taste with a distempered appetite. To be generous, guiltless, and of free disposition, is to take those things for bird-bolts that you deem cannon-bullets" (1.5.89–93). In summoning up a medical figure of speech, Maria implies that she can provide a healthful diet of laughter, for, as another adage goes, "laughter is the best medicine," and the ability to laugh at one's self is a great restorative. A "distempered appetite" reflects medical terminology, as well, signaling an unhealthy imbalance in the humors. Purging the body of its excesses is analogous to the cathartic purgation of comedy. Thus, we might see Maria in a similar light to Viola and Feste, who, as John R. Ford claims, "minister to their patients through wit, song, or mockery designed to allow these characters both to empathize with another and to laugh at themselves."[24]

But does Maria in fact cure or rehabilitate the offending patient? Can her revenge be regarded as constructive? Not surprisingly, critics have answered these questions in different ways. Those who emphasize generic integrity are more likely to view Malvolio as cured, or purged of his sin, or even to see a cure as beside the point.[25] Yet, the questions raised by vengeance's presence in comedy are not so easily laid to rest. After being abused so abominably, Malvolio has not necessarily ceased loving himself in excess; he has learned that he is not loved by all, and that festive play and drunken revelry are just as destructive and dangerous as he judged them to be. Duke Orsino may "entreat him to a peace" (5.1.379), attempting to invite Malvolio into the comedy's circle, but Malvolio will have none of it. Seen in its most positive light, the ethics of Maria's revenge might be regarded through the helpful moral frame Peter A. French offers us: "[T]he avenger shoulders the moral duty of empowering what is morally right. No character transformation on the part of the offender is required for that to be successfully accomplished. The act of vengeance is an expression of the effect of morality in and for itself. Morality has been mocked by the offender, but, through the avenger's agency, morality will yet have a very significant effect on the offender's life. It may well end it."[26] Or life as the offender knows it. Malvolio has enjoyed a high status in Olivia's household and the respect, dignity, and honor such a status confers. But he has mocked morality in his abuse of his authority, and Maria's revenge has empowered a process of moral recompense.

Maria's talent as physician is less equivocal and more socially productive in her skillful redirection of Sir Toby's energies from drink and carousing to therapeutic vengeance-taking and, finally, marriage. If Malvolio is Sir Toby's adversary, Maria does Sir Toby a service by organizing scenes in which he can watch Malvolio suffer and undo his credit with Olivia. He is distracted by the jest—indeed he is surfeited on the jest—to the point of sobriety. Eventually he proclaims, "I would we were well rid of this knavery. If he may be conveniently delivered, I would he were" (4.2.69–71). The all-engrossing, emotionally exhausting theatrical project of revenge has opened the door for marriage as the cure for Sir Toby's humor imbalances and "ill will," for he, like Malvolio, dishes out insults, lacks self-restraint, and evades self-knowledge. Maria's revenge, ironically, works to redress these imbalances.

The metaphor of physic calls to mind the therapeutic or cathartic function of theater itself. In *Twelfth Night*, revenge not only makes for satisfying theater; it *is* theatrical in its very conception and structure. Stage vengeance naturally thrives on intrigue and comes into its own, as it were, by realizing its dramaturgic potential: revenge must be plotted, opportunity found, roles cast, properties found, the stage set, and so forth. In exploiting the dramaturgic potential of revenge, Shakespeare not only reminds us that *Twelfth Night* is an "improbable fiction" "played upon a stage" (3.4.129, 128), but also that revenge is a cathartic experience structured to provoke emotions of both pleasurable and painful kinds. Like Maria's onstage troupe, we gain satisfaction from witnessing poetic justice at work, but at the same time we cannot help but catch glimpses of ourselves as voyeurs and predators, indulging individual and communal feelings of schadenfreude. When she gives her own fantasies and Malvolio's an air of

reality with the letter, fantasy begins to invade his waking life. Yet Malvolio was already acting upon—indeed, *performing*—his fantasies, if only to
his shadow and eavesdroppers. It takes only the ingenuity of the witty
Maria to take such a performance to a new, rather frighteningly comic level
of "reality," that of a household revenge comedy.

As Maria's exuberant imagination bodies forth a plot, script, and local
habitation for revenge, the comedy-loving audience thrills to the jest. There
is first the "box-tree" or letter-reading scene in which the conspirators secretly watch, laugh, and comment on Malvolio's (mis)reading of the forged
letter. Maria's letter becomes Malvolio's unwitting script; with each word
he utters, he becomes further lost in the role she has "feelingly personated"
for him (2.3.159). She has cued his costume, facial expression, and speech,
reflecting her uncanny ability to read his heart's secret desire, "To be Count
Malvolio" (2.5.35), with all this implies about identity, social mobility, the
will to power, and violated decorum.[27] Her onstage spectators are positioned in the "box-tree," from where they view the laughable spectacle.
Later, when the letter bears fruit in a full-blown performance, Maria is present, secretly playing Mistress of the Revels, witnessing the cross-gartered
Malvolio in yellow stockings approach Olivia. She invites Olivia to witness the spectacle of a madman: "He's coming, madam, but in very strange
manner. He is sure possessed, madam. . . . he does nothing but smile . . .
for sure the man is tainted in's wits" (3.4.8–9, 11, 13). With the success of
the letter and Malvolio's ridiculous performance before Olivia, the revels
begin to darken. Maria and her troupe have laid the groundwork for their
next scene in the "dark room."

The scene of dissembling before the "dark room" (4.2) is a disturbing
comic exercise in the escalation of vengeance and the surfeit of appetite.
At this point, many readers and theatergoers may feel revenge has become
a parody of justice, exhibiting little more than gratuitous psychological violence. The revengers move from staging the public entertainment of the
yellow-gartered fool pressing his love suit before an astonished Olivia to a
private theater in which the victim is bound in the dark and told repeatedly
that he is mad. This second scene of vengeance takes shape with Maria's
insistence; her role resembles more that of a Fury than that of Nemesis, as
she and the others "pursue him now" (3.4.132). Riding on the heels of
Maria's triumphant letter plot, Sir Toby proclaims, "Come, we'll have him
in a dark room and bound" (3.4.136–37). Their goal in taking revenge shifts
from ridicule to something more reprehensible—to drive a man to madness, as the Furies often did. Or to look upon the scene in a different light,
the revengers will attempt to exorcise the mad spirit of pride and ambition
that possesses the steward. Still very much in charge, Maria sees to the details of the "production," but, as with the first scene, she mostly stays
"backstage." She directs Feste, her player, in his part and costume: "Nay,

I prithee put on this gown, and this beard; make him believe thou art Sir Topas the curate; do it quickly. I'll call Sir Toby the whilst" (4.2.1–3). Sir Toby, however, soon recognizes that they have gone too far with the "dark room"; he fears repercussions from Olivia and wishes to be "well rid of this knavery" (4.2.69–70).

In the end, the comic device of revenge "overfulfills" its function.[28] Too much comedy leads to tragicomedy. What initially appeared to be a communal act of cathartic play becomes a theater of cruelty in which Maria and her coconspirators each try to get a piece of Malvolio. As in Anton Artaud's radical concept of cruelty, the revengers reflect an aggressive determination to fulfill the details and ends of their project. In a number of respects, Maria's revenge mimics destructive patterns in tragic vengeance; she loses sight of the social and moral benefits of her project to apply physic to the sick man and manages in the end only to produce a darker mimetic response in Malvolio. In the play's most chilling line, we are promised, all of us, further retaliation: "I'll be reveng'd on the whole pack of you!" (5.1.377). Yet Maria's words, spoken with satisfaction at the thought of driving Malvolio mad—"The house will be the quieter" (3.4.135)—are equally as chilling, and strangely ironic, in that Malvolio was the advocate of quiet and Sir Toby, of caterwauling. Malvolio is far from quiet at the drama's end, however, when his voice sounds the deadly tragic spirit of revenge, giving full expression to malice with no trace of the sporting spirit of his persecutors. Malvolio's treatment sparks elements of tragedy within the comic world; his revenge, in its fury, promises to usher in some serious action far more appalling than what he has just experienced.

While Malvolio's voice cannot be quieted, attempts to defuse his malice must be made. The laws of comedy demand it, for the aggressive force of vengeance threatens to unbalance the comic dispensation of Olivia's household and *Twelfth Night*'s world. Not surprisingly Olivia gives the counterresponse to revenge in offering Malvolio the means to reconciliation and reintegration into society. She holds out the olive branch, as her name would lead us to expect, calling for an end to the feud. She attempts to redirect Malvolio's malice and redress his injured honor with the promise of truth, justice, and legal reparations. She assures him that in time he will play plaintiff and judge in a household court of law. "Institutional" justice, not personal or communal revenge, is her way, and she will allow the victim to preside over the hearings. Importantly, she acknowledges that harm was done to Malvolio and that the nature of the harm warrants justice. This is far more than Malvolio gets from his persecutors, and the lack of remorse or acknowledgment of injury from them proves problematic.

Once the disheveled Malvolio makes an appearance in the final scene, Fabian, naturally, wishes to see an end to the affair immediately: "let no quarrel, nor no brawl to come, / Taint the condition of this present hour"

(5.1.355–56). He freely confesses and embellishes his part in the device, takes responsibility, and names Sir Toby and Maria as collaborators, though he reduces Maria's role considerably (perhaps to protect her). He implies that their device was motivated by just resentment "Upon some stubborn and uncourteous parts / We had conceiv'd against him" (5.1.360–61), but pleads equity regarding the injuries: "If that the injuries be justly weigh'd / That have on both sides pass'd (5.1.366–67). The implied image of Justice's balances, weighing wrongs on both sides, sounds promising for the restoration of harmony and a joyous conclusion. Indeed, the highest claim revenge or Nemesis might make is that it brings things back to even, restoring a lost equilibrium. In one balance, the householders' injuries are suspended; in the other balance, Malvolio's sufferings have accumulated.

Clearly, the rub lies in the very phrase "justly weigh'd." From whose perspective are the weights determined? How should the two elements of Fabian's troubling oxymoron "sportful malice" affect the balance in which Malvolio's humiliating sufferings rest? Attempts to assuage Malvolio's anger may seem painfully inadequate because of what many, including Olivia and some of the play's audience, perceive to be a clear imbalance in the scales of injuries. The lack of proportionality is rather stunning; upon reflection readers and audience members may realize that tragical mirth is born from this very imbalance. In the common economic trope of revenge, the avengers have incurred a debt. They have exceeded repayment of Malvolio's wrongs. The perpetrator has become the victim, and he now feels he is owed a further piece of his former victims' pride. He will become perpetrator once more, and thus the whirligig will keep spinning. In the Illyrian community, Malvolio's pride, self-preservation, and self-worth depend upon it. Through revenge, he will hope to recover a lost sense of worth. Forgiveness and the acknowledgment of the legitimacy of pain could dismantle the explosive mechanism of revenge, but Fabian does not ask for forgiveness, nor does Feste. One can assume that Maria and Sir Toby, both absent from the scene, lack remorse, enjoying instead a sense of satisfaction. Malvolio, even if he were inclined to forgive, has not been dignified with this possibility. While the punishment has suited the crime, the excessiveness is troubling. To follow Aquinas, we might say, "by way of excess" there arises the "sin of cruelty or brutality, which exceeds the measure in punishing."[29]

Our laughter dies not only with the knowledge of how deeply humiliating, even traumatic, Malvolio's experience has been, but with the recognition that the tormentors have reaped benefits at his expense. The interpersonal dynamics of Maria's revenge plot reveal a larger truth about the play's world and its inhabitants: the play's emotional and social economies are driven by debt and recompense.[30] One form of recompense (revenge) is integrally related to another (marriage). Through revenge theater, Maria and her coconspirators have pursued their own comic ends. For Maria, the revenge plot has been her investment in the domestic comedy of marriage, or so we might imagine, if Sir Toby can accept love as the cure for drunkenness and self-loathing ("I hate a drunken rogue," 5.1.199). In the end, Maria rests on her laurels, having witnessed the triumph of her wit and orchestrated a secret courtship. Malvolio's threat of revenge and Olivia's anger are lost on the revenge artist and her admirer as they enjoy an offstage union. The marriage of Sir Toby and Maria guarantees their part in the social regeneration of the Illyrian community. While some members of the larger community may feel pity for Malvolio, they will shore up together, some as happy couples focused on their own comic ends. The intrusion of revenge's dark business upon their happiness may be fleeting at best. For the audience, however, comic closure seems far more provisional, as Feste's song suggests: "Present mirth hath present laughter: / What's to come is still unsure" (2.3.49–50).

Present mirth has already given way to a hesitation about our (and the lovers') responses to comedy's excesses. Malvolio has been humiliated and exposed before the community (and himself) as "the most notorious geck and gull / That e'er invention play'd on" (5.1.342–43). The "invention" of the householders has brought to light Malvolio's character flaws and fantasies, forcing him to view himself through their eyes. As the humiliated steward, he is truly a pitiable sight. One might argue that there is an element of shame in his experience, as well, though the shame does not seem to bear moral fruit in the end. The psychoanalyst Léon Wurmser describes the experience of shame as fundamentally dehumanizing: "The loss of love in shame can be described as a radical decrease of respect for the subject as a person with his own dignity; it is a disregard for his having a self in its own right with its own prestige. . . . The thrust of this aggression is to *dehumanize*."[31] This process of dehumanization in comedy threatens to render the "subject" a mere object of ridicule, a comic butt. Far from being a crowned lover, far from being loved by anyone, Malvolio is reduced to the role of a "*madly-used*" fool (5.1.310). Yet the darker notes of tragedy may be found in the text and struck in performance, for in humiliating Malvolio, Maria and her fellow antagonists establish the psychological conditions for vengeance. When it does not produce remorse and moral self-recognition, shame motivates the wounded self to retaliate; if Malvolio is to save face and live with himself once again in the eyes of his community, he must reassert his self-worth, his honor. Historically, revenge has been a popular means, though certainly not the only means, by which individuals recoup honor. At the end of the play, we might say that Malvolio has been shamed, but he does not feel ashamed for his faults. He is bewildered, confused, and outraged, but not ashamed of himself. Before the householders made sport with him, he had felt a sense of his place and his honor in the household. Now he feels only the desire to avenge the wrongs done to him.

The play presses upon its audience the question of whether there are moral differences between Malvolio's and Maria's vengefulness. Surely, these characters mean different things when they use the word *revenge*—or do they? Intangible wrongs, such as slights to one's honor, breaches in class deference, verbal insults, and so forth, committed in the private arena of domestic households, as they are in *Twelfth Night,* evade legal punishment; thus, the play entertains the fantasy of a private theater of revenge in which jesting, aggressive prosecutors bait and punish the insufferable Malvolio. As Francis Bacon asserted in his essay "Of Revenge," "The most tolerable sort of revenge is for those wrongs which there is no law to remedy."[32] In keeping with this view, the Elizabethan law student John Manningham recorded in his diary an appreciation of the revenge plot as "good practice," ignoring altogether the question of morality or the potential for tragedy.[33] His sympathies were unequivocally with the revelers and their dream of lawless revenge.

Couched in figures of aristocratic sport and physic, Maria and her troupe's treatment of Malvolio attempts to pass as a socially acceptable comic inversion of revenge tragedy, meant to entertain and "pluck on laughter" (5.1.365). No blood is spilled and no one dies, after all; the overarching laws of comedy, while having been stretched like a chevril glove, are still intact. Vengeance, psychological torment, physical deprivation, and public humiliation have been mobilized to teach the prideful steward a lesson (even if he has learned nothing productive). Malvolio has been a fitting target for Nemesis. Feste gives revenge a sporting air when he figures it as the product of Time's spinning top: "thus the whirligig of time brings in his revenges" (5.1.375–76). Yet this figure, like so many in the play, suggests a troubling indefiniteness—in picturing the whirligig, we see the rapid blur of the spinning top and sense the possible loss of control. As the whirligig keeps whirling, it promises to bring in not a single revenge, but revenge upon revenge. Yet this is to abstract or mystify what is, in the end, a product of individual and social will. As Bacon cautioned in *De Dignitate et Augmentis Scientiarum,* "He that did the first wrong made a beginning to mischief; he that returned it made no end."[34]

The provisional, tragicomic closure of *Twelfth Night* points to the problematic status of the comic genre and its rather indiscriminate celebration of ludic pleasures—taken too far, they produce a surfeit of aggression, a distempered appetite unchecked by morality, law, or authority. The representative of festivity and holiday foolery, Feste, speaks to comedy's darker truth: "pleasure will be paid, one time or another" (2.4.70–71). The excesses of revenge point up the excesses of comedy. Shakespeare unmasks comedy's dependence on such volatile constitutive forces as revenge, which appeal on the one hand to a fundamental desire for justice (or poetic justice) and on the other to darker desires for pranks, tricks, and gulling of a victim. What becomes clear through Maria's twin plots of punishment and courtship is that revenge's motives and means, like comedy's, are never pure.

In the chapter that follows, we shall see another example of revenge pursued through theatrical sport, but in the case of *The Merry Wives of Windsor* Shakespeare brings to the fore a pressing moral and social concern for wives—their need to vindicate their honor once it has been assailed. This may sound like a pure motive, and to some extent it is, but an inevitable ethical question arises, and the Windsor wives themselves pose it: "May we, with the warrant of womanhood and the witness of a good conscience, pursue him [Falstaff, their revenge target] with any further revenge?" (4.2.195–97). The following pages explore the rich ethical situation of wives who take upon themselves the defense of their own honor by pursuing revenge not once, but three times, on a would-be seducer.

7

Feminine Vindication and the Social Drama of Revenge in *The Merry Wives of Windsor*

[F]or women, revenge is an art form; fine, delicate precision engineering, largely beyond male capabilities.
— Kate Saunders, *Revenge*

Mistress Page: We'll leave a proof, by that which we will do,
Wives may be merry and yet honest too.
— Shakespeare, *The Merry Wives of Windsor*

MORE THOROUGHLY THAN ANY OTHER SHAKESPEARE COMEDY, *THE MERRY Wives of Windsor* enacts the root relationship among *vindictive, vindicative,* and *vindication,* showing how aptly suited drama is for the ethical purposes of feminine revenge. The Latin *vindicare* means "to avenge," and *vindicatio* means the "action of claiming, defending, punishing." *Vindication* conveys meanings that, taken together, conflate revenge with emancipation, defense against censure, and justification by proof.[1] In this domestic comedy, the women of Windsor seek playful forms of revenge to justify their moral worth, defend their honor, and strike back against wrongdoing. The play seems ingeniously constructed as Shakespeare's and the wives' dramatic *proof:* by directing their vindictive passions and vindicative self-assertion into plots that display feminine ingenuity and social mastery, the female characters do cultural and ethical work to emancipate women from a harmful stereotype. All of the merrymaking that accompanies comedy is directed toward our laughing away the deplorable cultural assumption that merry wives are dishonest, particularly in their lack of chastity.

Margaret Page and Alice Ford prove their moral worth and superior wit through the orchestration of a revenge drama that follows a pattern similar to the "social drama" described by the anthropologist Victor Turner. The phases of a social drama, according to Turner, are the *breach, crisis, redressive procedures,* and *reintegration.*[2] The *breach* occurs when a societal norm governing social relations is transgressed. A rule "ordinarily held to

189

be binding, and which is itself a symbol of the maintenance of some major relationship between persons, statuses, or subgroups," is broken.[3] The breach in Windsor is committed by the visiting knight Falstaff when he tries to seduce Mistresses Page and Ford, two upstanding wives in the community. The *crisis* involves people taking sides in the conflict expressed over the breach. Crises can be contagious, calling up antagonisms, unconscious desires, and anxieties in community members. Violence may erupt. This phase possesses "liminal" characteristics, as it occurs "between more or less stable or harmonic phases of the social process."[4] The crisis for the wives, whose virtue has been assailed, is taken up by all of Windsor; thus, the entire community is aligned against Falstaff. Strong passions arise, particularly regarding women's honesty. The *redressive* phase involves conflict resolution and in some cases the performance of public ritual. There is a degree of reflexivity and self-scrutiny in this phase, and a "liminal space . . . is often created."[5] The ritual process may require an "act of sacrifice, in which the tensions and animosities of the disturbed community are discharged."[6] The revenge scenes enacted by the wives and the community perform the redressive aspect of the social drama. In place of legal reparations, there is an imaginative, symbolic inversion of the breach and a meting out of punishment.

The wives imaginatively transform domestic and natural spaces in Windsor into liminal spaces for social drama. Shakespeare's theater becomes the wives' comic revenge theater, so that a theater-within-the-theater effect is created. The quality of liminality, of in-betweenness, suggests itself here, and takes on a particularly fluid quality as the wives' scenes anamorphically shift between Italian commedia dell'arte and English bourgeois life, contrived scenario and "real life" activity, the festival spirit of fantasy and the everyday domestic. The wives have only so much control over these shifts, for the flux of real life enters their rough theater, presenting a degree of unpredictability in the outcome. When Falstaff crosses Mistress Ford's threshold (from Latin, *limen*), he unwittingly submits his fantasy to the superior imaginative powers of the mistress of the household. In the spirit of commedia dell'arte, Mistress Ford plays Franceschina to Falstaff's Pantaloon, or the Lover to his braggart Captain.[7] The women's use of domestic materials to stage a social drama of Falstaff's humiliation is fitting payback for the seducer that imperils domestic harmony. In his efforts to escape the Ford household, he must first submit himself to the buck-basket, allowing himself to be transformed into a "buck" stifled in dirty linens. He then submits to a shameful disguise, allowing Mistress Page to dress him as the fat woman of Brentford. These two playful punishments staged in Mistress Ford's home ritualistically defuse the lusty knight's potency. His sexual fantasy is thwarted by the stronger imagination of the women and their cunning redeployment of their own domestic goods for the purposes of didactic punishment. For the women, these commedia exercises in the rough theater of revenge are about vindication—their defense, proof, and punishment all in one. In a "merry" spirit, they use what they have at their disposal in their known world to assert their ethical defense.

In Windsor Forest, too, we find ourselves in the liminal, with the significant addition of the "wild," a place on the margins of civilization. The women extend their field of revenge to the woods, contriving a fitting guise for Falstaff—Herne the Hunter, or a half-male, half-beast horned figure—then subjecting him to humiliation. The disguised children (fairies) pinch and burn him, exorcising the spirit of lust from his body and the community. The community is exorcising its animosities by making a symbolic sacrifice out of the "hunter." This scene leads into the final phase of Windsor's social drama.

In the final phase, at its best, a *reintegration* of parties occurs. The social drama is "*satiated,* so to speak," and restoration of peace ensues.[8] The Windsor community experiences the satiation of their appetite for revenge, and virtually all parties involved are soothed. With Mistress Page's suggestion that they have a good laugh over this sport (the social drama) "o'er by a country fire, / Sir John and all" (5.5.236–37) the final phase promises to involve integrating (and perhaps harmonizing) their experiences through storytelling. Here we have the suggestion that members of the community will weave tales to "explain that event, extol it, ethicize it, excuse it, repudiate it, name it as a significant marker of collective life-experience, as a model for future behavior."[9]

In Shakespeare's comedy, some of this narrative commentary has occurred already in the unfolding of the social drama itself. In particular, the characters "ethicize" their social roles and experiences at different phases of the drama. The purpose of the wives' social drama is made clear: they do not intend to "reintegrate" Falstaff into the community, as he was never integrated in the first place, but rather to reintegrate *themselves* into the social fabric of Windsor in a more prestigious, ethically justified position. Their ultimate end is to vindicate themselves—and all "merry wives"—once and for all. The young Anne Page, too, vindicates herself by grafting her marriage plot onto the final scene of the wives' revenge; in the end, she achieves the status of "merry wife," a social category that has been renovated and celebrated by the enactment of a meaningful social drama.

The female characters possess the ultimate comedic resource, a quick wit, which gives them the capacity to avert victimization and to deflect shame onto their morally indecorous suitors. They have a sense of their own integrity and the imaginative resources to place themselves in a position of mastery over those who wish to master them. Anne Barton, among others, sees the wives as *heroines*, emphasizing their self-awareness and loyalty to their husbands.[10] These admirable qualities are apparent in the married women, but I wish to locate their heroism more specifically in their authoring of revenge plots as a mode of vindication for women and, furthermore, in their acceptance of risks that attend their theatrical proof of virtue. They take the liberties afforded female characters in the comic genre, but they also risk slander and exposure at inopportune moments during the phases of the social drama.

The wives' use of drama promises vindication, as well as laughter, but such an ambiguous entrance into liminality, as Turner might see it, is fraught with potential danger. The very mode by which the women defend and prove their honesty involves secrecy, conspiracy, duplicity, and, furthermore, a bold flirtation with the scandals of adultery and theater.[11] This paradox brings to light the disquieting problem of how difficult it is for women to prove their honesty once it has been assailed. In the material world, a woman's "honour is an essence that's not seen," to echo Iago's tantalizing statement to Othello (4.1.16). This destabilizing "truth" inspires the drama of jealousy and revenge in the masculine imagination. "Proof" of feminine virtue seems to require extraordinary means to instill belief. Some measures resemble those used in a law court—rhetorical facility, logic, defense provided by reliable witnesses—but the wives' more inventive measures are drawn from the resources of comedy, *novelle* intrigues, and domestic life.

In *performing* their proof, the wives are alone with the theater's audience in understanding the nature and intent of the first two revenge scenes. Only we are in on the joke, and the entrance of the husbands, Caius, and Evans adds an "extra joke" as these men inadvertently get caught up in the act.[12] Blind to the improvised social drama in which they are "performing," the men will need the "joke" explained to them. In the end, the weight of the proof rests largely on the narrative the wives weave about the true intent of their revenge scenarios. They must convince their husbands that their mirth has produced a proof of chastity; they must make them laugh rather than yield to suspicion, jealousy, and anger. As Pamela Allen Brown's study of the moral community of female neighbors emphasizes, "To an unusual degree *Merry Wives* trades on the paradox that a supreme commodity, female chastity, is not empirically demonstrable and that truth is generally a consensual affair, a matter of narrative credibility and rhetorical prowess."[13]

In their united front against Falstaff, the women gain safety in numbers. A woman acting alone would be at great risk in the moral community and in her marriage. Alice and Margaret's affection for each other and their shared revenge suggest that their bond is the strongest one in their community, perhaps stronger and more stable than marital bonds. When they receive the seduction letters, they share them with each other and experience a double outrage. They both think of revenge and agree to plot together. Mistress Page heatedly asserts, "Let's be revenged on him. Let's appoint him a meeting, give him a show of comfort in his suit, and lead him on with a fine-baited delay, till he hath pawned his horses to mine host of the Garter" (2.1.83–86). Mistress Ford agrees, but with a note of anxiety, betraying higher stakes for her in the women's attempt at revenge: "Nay, I will consent to act any villainy against him, that may not sully the chariness of our honesty. O, that my husband saw this letter! It would give eternal food to his jealousy" (2.1.87–90). "Villainy," "sully the chariness of our honesty," and "food to his jealousy" indicate a number of dangers that might mar their intrigue. That their actions might be perceived as dishonest and villainous—actions against morality or law—is something to be feared, for if they get caught in the act (and the "act" is not understood as playacting, or a legitimate redressive phase in a social drama), they will surely pay a steep price. This is undeniably a risk they take. And finally, the threat of violence that results from masculine jealousy is fearful to Mistress Ford, who has undoubtedly felt its effects before. Ford closely monitors their household and his wife's behavior. Despite the attendant dangers, however, they will "make merry over" Falstaff, meaning they will ridicule him, because his insult to their virtue is sharp and their desire to teach a lesson and vindicate themselves is strong.

If *The Merry Wives* were a revenge tragedy, we might witness the husbands challenging Falstaff to a set of duels, with the women remaining in the background. Or worse, we might hear that the seducer has robbed the women of their chastity, or the women might choose to engage in adultery, or the husbands, like Othello, might be duped into believing that their wives lack chastity. This final tragic possibility is explored, but mostly to comic effect, through Master Ford's paranoia about his wife. In a tragedy, the husbands would feel pressure to avenge such wrongs through murder. And the wives, if adulterous or thought to be so, might lose their lives. Comedy alters the essential features of the tragic revenge plot: here the male aggressor is unsuccessful—it is the attempt and not the deed that wounds their honor—and the female targets strike back to teach a lesson. Their lesson is aimed not only at Falstaff, but also at the play's audience, and the key terms undergoing renovation in their didactic revenge are *merry* and *honest*. The cultural stereotype they take aim at insists that *merry* women indulge in pleasures, and not all of those pleasures are of the innocent kind; that they invite wantonness by their open laughter and conviviality; and that "levity of spirits, in a woman, implies a corresponding levity of morals," as Anne Parten phrases it.[14]

Mistress Page's response to Falstaff's letter hints at this as she reflects on her behavior and conversation in the knight's company. She concludes, I "was then frugal of my mirth" (2.1.22–23); yet her words sound a defensive note, as Falstaff has dared to assay her despite her own perceived modesty. Because of the cultural stigma attached to feminine merriness, the necessity for the wives' self-defense and vindication arises: "We'll leave a proof, by that which we will do, / Wives may be merry and yet honest too. / We do not act that often jest and laugh" (4.2.99–101). The wives will not act upon Falstaff's lewd invitation, but they will "do" in the dramatic sense of playact to make their proof that merry wives are honest. Their revenge comedy, like Hamlet's staging of *The Murder of Gonzago,* is intended as a proof to catch the conscience of spectators, but in this case it is to challenge those who think poorly of merry wives.

The wives insist upon making the proof themselves without consulting their husbands, parson, or community authorities. They turn to their husbands and the community only after they have had their fill of revenge on Falstaff and driven out his wantonness to their own satisfaction. Such satisfaction comes with ministering their own form of vengeance *personally* —they devise the scenes, manage them, playact their roles, and enjoy the position of audience as the spectacle unfolds, taking on a life of its own. Their "heroic" effort is exemplary, and the experience of revenge, for themselves and ultimately the Windsor community, is cathartic. Their scenes humiliate their would-be seducer by trapping him in the very part he *desires* to play, which is a supreme irony and a fitting revenge. They exploit his desire and colonize his role, rescripting the drama of seduction, lost virtue, and thievery as feminine revenge comedy.

Yet Falstaff is not their only target, for by the time they devise the second revenge scene, Mistress Ford's husband has presented himself as another male who threatens feminine integrity and honor. If Falstaff is the polluted body sunk far in moral laxity, the oily whale beached at Windsor, Master Ford is the polluted mind overtaken by dark sexual "figures" (4.2.205), the excessively jealous husband lurking within Windsor. He presents a more challenging and dangerous target for the wives. He unwittingly enters their "theater of revenge" in search of Falstaff. They subject the jealous Master Ford to the laughter of his peers and bring him to the abject position of a penitent "heretic" who shamefully admits that he lost faith in his good wife's honor.

The retaliatory principle that energizes the wives' social drama, their drama of virtue assailed and honor maintained, can be found driving many of the characters in their community. Male honor, however, tends to be defended with arms and violence, even in comedy. Witness Caius and Slender's intended duel, and Shallow's nostalgia for the sword, which could settle his grievance with Falstaff with a swift slicing of metal—"Ha, o' my life, if I were young again, the sword should end it" (1.1.36–37). The anthropologists Julian Pitt-Rivers and Jacob Black-Michaud identify male honor as "belong[ing] to those who can both morally and physically command it. . . . Successful defence of honour by force of arms safeguards the

prestige of the defender."[15] Shakespeare illustrates women's honor as belonging to those who can both morally and *imaginatively* command it.
Through the force of playacting, jest, and wit—and the ability to turn men's
fantasies against them—comic women have the tools to safeguard their
own honor. Ultimately, we see in *The Merry Wives* that women's ability to
control the "plot"—the story of their honor, the avenging of moral insults,
the choice of a marriage partner—confers prestige on them. Shakespeare
dignifies his female characters with the function of plot-makers, attentive
to structural and ethical elements as well as the essential cathartic experience of drama.

"GOOD PLOTS THEY ARE LAID"

Far from the artistic embarrassment modern critics often claim it to be, *The
Merry Wives of Windsor* is an exuberant celebration of what dramatists do
best—lay plots—and Shakespeare's best example lies in the ingenious
plotting of his avenging female characters. We find a liberal banquet of intrigues and potential plots at work in the comedy, imaginatively engaging
aspects of social anxiety, tension, and fantasy in the community of Windsor. *The Merry Wives* calls attention to the fertility of revenge plots in particular, one plot begetting another to the point where the play, like an Italian
Renaissance comedy, "becomes a network of 'supposes.'"[16] The comedy
brilliantly reveals revenge's capacity for repetition and escalation in the enactment of the wives' plot—their social drama, to invoke Victor Turner
once more—which is the essential unifying action of the play. Rather than
storytelling and narrative, the play seems fixated on *plotting:* how actions
are motivated or generated and how they are sustained and completed. In
particular, feminine plotting is highlighted as the source of male anxiety
and admiration. Master Ford represents vividly men's fears about women's
plotting. "Good plots they are laid" (3.2.34–35), he fumes suspiciously
about his wife; "Then she plots, then she ruminates, then she devises"
(2.2.289–90). Master Page takes a more liberal approach, wishing to see
his wife's "plot go forward," and asks with piqued interest, "What is your
plot?" (4.4.12, 44). Master Fenton, Anne Page's favored suitor, refers to
Mistress Page's "plot" (4.6.31), for surely she has one, to trick her husband
out of his desired match for their daughter. Clearly, feminine wit exerts its
authority through the inspired and secret devising of plots to be played out
by social actors, some of whom assist with the scenes, some of whom unwittingly play parts. Most of the male characters cannot sustain their imagined parts as lovers, duelists, plotters, and cuckolded husbands. Conversely,
the wives and Anne Page successfully manage their chosen roles and cast
their imaginative nets wide to serve them to the end. Men prove to be failed

plotters and poor actors; women prove to be superior dramatists and social actors.

Shakespeare's wives find their counterparts in the clever wives who out-wit their husbands or lovers in Roman comedy, Renaissance Italian popular comedy, commedia dell'arte, fabliaux, and novelle.[17] Shakespeare's emphasis on women's marital chastity and the wives' triumph, however, marks a departure from many of his possible sources, where wives are often adulterous and punished. He retains a significance in threes and a tripartite structure to the scenario, which can be found in commedia dell'arte scenarios and some novelle. Falstaff's insult to feminine honor motivates not one act of vengeance, but three, with each new act representing an intensification of his punishment and arguably the wives' pleasure. After staging two scenes of revenge, the wives realize that their jest must come to an end eventually, so they reveal themselves as "ministers" of revenge to their husbands. In revealing themselves, they not only display the justice of their actions, but they also inspire a larger-scale action to complete their revenge comedy. When the husbands agree that "the poor unvirtuous fat knight shall be . . . further afflicted" (4.2.206–7), they invite the community to participate in one final revenge to bring a "period to the jest" (4.2.210–11). This final scene brings revenge to a different level of theater and signification: the stage becomes the site of potentially wild energy channeled into a purgation ritual of burning, pinching, and chanting. As comedy, *The Merry Wives* must involve the community, and as revenge comedy, the community must be involved in the final cathartic cycle of retaliation, unmasking, forgiveness, and reintegration.

The driving force shaping the play's comic plots is revenge, a hostile passion more conventionally associated with bloodshed and masculine honor than laughter, practical jokes, merry wives, and bourgeois citizens. Yet revenge is clearly this comedy's obsession and modus operandi, a point underdeveloped in most critical studies of the play.[18] From the play's first line with Justice Shallow's complaint against Falstaff to Dr. Caius's threat to "raise all Windsor" (5.5.205–6) at the play's end, vengeance is the keynote. It is the passion motivating no fewer than seven attempts at plotting in the play; and it is the aggressive energy that culminates in a public shaming and purgation ritual at the play's conclusion. During the course of the play, most of the Windsor inhabitants, whether native or stranger, swear revenge and involve themselves in at least one revenge plot. Even the young lovers, Anne Page and Fenton, participate in the communal revenge masque, though they are far more concerned with their own elopement plot, which evolves along conventional lines as the younger generation's defiance of their parents. Their plot, however, is a kind of revenge as well, for Anne's ingenious plot, which she reveals to Fenton in a letter, counters the parents' plots to marry her off to their chosen suitors. When we consider the intricate plotting of revenges with their differing motives in *The Merry Wives,* the drama takes on the complexion of an extended investigation into the passions and motives of revenge and, furthermore, an exuberant exploration in the comedy of feminine vengeance.

While most of these revenge plots are abandoned or yield nothing in the end, the wives' retaliation against Falstaff for his attempted seductions dominates the play and succeeds in preventing the corruption of the women, the cuckolding of their men, and the theft of their gold. Shakespeare grants his feminine characters self-determination and artistic virtuosity in their dramaturgic roles as plotters of revenge comedy. Furthermore, in the gender dispensation of the play, masculine revenge appears futile or destructive, while feminine revenge is socially and ethically productive, self-defining, and relatively harmless. Indeed, avenging females are central to bringing about a renewed sense of faith in marriage (the husband's faith in his wife's fidelity, in particular) and in shared communal values in Windsor. We might say that the wives' revenge actions become the ground upon which the community reaffirms itself. When Falstaff enters the community, he carelessly abuses Windsorian hospitality and tramples upon many a citizen's sense of honor. With such a bold, disruptive force asserting itself in Windsor, the community feels obliged to take action. A failure to respond would lead to losing face, a sense of shame felt among all of those Windsorians exploited by Falstaff. Thus, revenge erupts into the comedy, defining the nature and contours of its dramatic action. Falstaff becomes Windsor's scapegoat, as many critics have argued, but a comically willing one at that, punished to excess for both the crimes he committed and those he intended.

In the text—and, most delightfully, onstage—one cannot miss how Falstaff's girth and physicality figure the very quality of excess. Because he lusts after the Windsor wives, sexual excess becomes associated with him, and he comes to function as a site of sexual pollution. The community bands together to punish his lustful body, even after the wives have "scared out" the "spirit of wantonness" in him (4.2.198–99, 198). While the women's bodies remain intact, chaste, inviolate—and their minds pure and bent on punishing wickedness—the fat knight's body oozes and leaks, and then is subjected to soiling, pinching, and burning. Bodily fluid and food metaphors convey the wives' perception of him as polluted: "Flemish drunkard," "guts . . . made of puddings," "tuns of oil in his belly," "greasy" (2.1.19, 26, 57, 97). The mixing of the greasy knight and soiled linens in the buck-basket represents a fitting comic revenge; stewing in his own juices, as it were, Falstaff must be made to feel what it means to sink in filth. Yet Falstaff's "dissolute disease" is so progressed that he "will scarce obey this medicine" (3.3.176–77), declares Mistress Page, ready to increase the dosage. Such figures turn the audience's imagination from the realm of law to health, or the psychic and moral health of individuals and social bodies. Sexual impurity violates Windsor's essential values; the polluted body of Falstaff figures that violation to excess and must undergo some kind of purification ritual—multiple rituals, in fact—if he is to be chastened, instructed, and cured rather than simply expelled from the community. The wives' plot can be understood as fundamentally ethical and cathartic in aim.

As in *Twelfth Night,* the female avenger is a moralizing physician; she must fit the medicine to the patient's disease. After the first revenge scene, which ends in disgrace for Falstaff, Mistress Page proclaims, "we will yet have more tricks with Falstaff" (3.3.175–76). "Trick" is yet another metaphor for their action, this one emphasizing the playfulness of their device. Falstaff's disease, lust, is moral in nature and ludicrous to behold, since it is clear that he is a *senex amator* (an old man in love). The shaming of the old lecher in the dirty linen basket is sublimely appropriate, yet not enough to cure him. To purge the sin, they must effect a transformation in character. As W. L. Godshalk demonstrates, Falstaff undergoes a "purgative course," losing "first his dignity, then his masculinity, and finally his humanity."[19] The wives' figurative language gestures to matters greater than theme or mere device; both plot and medicinal metaphors reflect the larger goals and ethical action of the comedy. Their metaphors fuse drama, jest, morality, and medicine. As Ruth Nevo notes, "The medical analogy between the progress of a comedy and the progress of a disease toward amelioration" persisted from the classical tradition through the sixteenth century.[20] Shakespeare's employment of this analogy reflects comedy's ends.

The wives make clear that Falstaff's crime against them lies outside the reach of the law; therefore, they must consult their own consciences regarding their authority to punish his socially impermissible behavior. Just as skimmington rituals in English towns tolerated aggressive women humiliating and punishing men, so revenge comedy allows "merry" women a degree of social sanction in dealing with men who compromise their integrity.[21] While victims of the skimmington tended to be cuckolds and browbeaten husbands, the victims in the wives' shaming rituals, the adulterous suitor and the jealous husband, exhibit inappropriate sexual appetite and fantasy. These men are fundamentally dishonorable, both in their own lack of integrity and in their assumption that the wives have no honor. The "putting down of men" (2.1.24), or the willful subordination of men by women becomes necessary when their behavior poses a threat to women's chastity, reputation, and social status. When Mistress Page receives the appalling seduction letter from Falstaff, she exclaims, "Why, I'll exhibit a bill in the parliament for the putting down of men" (2.1.23–24). No sooner has she uttered these words than she realizes how preposterous they sound, and how impossible it would be to pursue her case in court. She immediately follows with the assertion: "How shall I be revenged on him? For revenged I will be, as sure as his guts are made of puddings" (lines 25–26). Both ethical necessity and revulsion drive her words, and in sounding the word *revenged* twice, there arises an intimation of the kind of plot that will satisfy her ethical requirements.

The play entertains the question of ethics and law from the start with threatened litigation and a lively mock trial. The opening scene impresses upon the audience how near Falstaff is, already, to wearing out his welcome in Windsor. Falstaff enters the stage a marked man, guilty of minor transgressions. Although he is able to evade legal punishment with a show of wit, the strong sense of wrong and vengefulness expressed by Justice Shallow and Slender unleashes an undercurrent of justified hostility into the play's world. Shallow's opening declaration is initially a heated call for justice, which gives way to a lament that he is too old to pursue his secret fantasy, to avenge the wrong privately with a duel. He calls for a Privy Council hearing to try Falstaff; barring that, a local mock trial will have to suffice. Shallow's sense of wrong involves not only property violations, but class antipathy, as well, for his first words smart from the wound to his name: "If he were twenty Sir John Falstaffs, he shall not abuse Robert Shallow esquire" (1.1.2–3). As an esquire, Shallow is a gentleman bearing an "old coat" of arms (line 15), as he and his kinsman Slender are at pains to establish. In his public statement of complaint before Master Page, who stands in as "judge," Shallow verbally hurls Falstaff's title at him, insinuating that he has disgraced himself and dishonored a near social equal: "Knight, you have beaten my men, killed my deer and broke open my lodge" (1.1.104–5).

Sir Hugh Evans and Master Page serve as conciliatory characters, both offering peaceful resolutions to potentially violent situations. The first words of the play, "Sir Hugh, persuade me not" (1.1.1), indicate that Evans has been attempting to assuage Shallow's anger. As a parson, Evans should represent a virtuous force mitigating violence and hostility. He suggests that friends arbitrate the matter between Shallow and Falstaff, and that Shallow shift his energies to a "device" more socially productive than these "pribbles and prabbles" (his Welsh conflating of brabbles, or brawls, and quibbles, 1.1.50): the marriage of Slender to Anne Page and her seven hundred pounds. Anne's "goot gifts," as Evans comically puts it (1.1.59–60), are indeed distracting. The mock trial quickly runs its course, and the mercenary courtship plot takes precedence over the revenge plot, reflecting Shallow's limited ("shallow") imagination. Law is then set aside as an inadequate means to secure justice or social order. The poacher remains on the loose, free to poach upon other "grounds."

Other potential revenge plots arise and evaporate as quickly. Falstaff's discarded men feel resentment toward their leader and, with the "humours of revenge" (1.3.86), Nim swears to pursue Falstaff with both wit and steel. They take revenge by revealing Falstaff's mercenary seduction plot to the husbands. This betrayal leads to Ford's revenge plot, which is carried out to a greater extent than some of the others. His plot joins ironically with Falstaff's and the wives' plots, creating an intricate comic layering of revenge devices. But in the end, the wives' revenge stands alone as the most sustained form of plotting onstage.

Let us briefly examine the letter scene (2.1), which sparks the women's plotting. The scene opens with Mistress Page alone onstage reading a letter. She first exclaims in disbelief, "What, have I scaped love-letters in the holiday-time of my beauty, and am I now a subject for them?" (lines 1–3). She then reads the outlandish letter to the theater audience, entertaining us with the ridiculous specter it raises of the aging gallant and the outraged matron. Indeed, as an improbable "subject" of a love letter, the good wife Page immediately translates her role out of the romantic, illicit lover Falstaff intended into the determined female avenger. The actor playing Mistress Page has the opportunity to savor the letter with the audience and give us a taste of her outrage. There is a degree of moral circumspection thrown in as she scans her conscience and finds that she is guiltless in her behavior; she has said nothing to encourage the old knight's advances and been "frugal" of her "mirth" (2.1.22, 23) in his company. She casts Falstaff in the role of comic villain, an aging "Flemish drunkard" (2.1.19) that proves the world wicked. Her thoughts quickly turn to revenge, for such an affront to her chastity, to her very identity as a good Windsor wife, cannot escape punishment. Mistress Page's vow to avenge herself on Falstaff—"revenged I will be, as sure as his guts are made of puddings" (2.1.25–26)—suggests with a comic flourish her determination, as well as a sense that there is no more appropriate action to take than revenge in a case like this one. If women cannot, realistically speaking, "exhibit a bill in the parliament for the putting down of men" (2.1.23–24), they can do the next best thing by taking matters in their own hands. A private offense requires private means to redress it.

Mistress Ford then enters with her letter from Falstaff, and the comedy escalates. The women's speech makes it apparent that they have every intention of sharing letters and "counsel" with each other (line 36). Mistress Ford first pretends to have been flattered by Falstaff's advances: "O, woman, if it were not for one trifling respect, I could come to such honour!" and "If I would but go to hell for an eternal moment or so, I could be knighted" (2.1.38–39, 42–43). She playfully parodies Falstaff's view and that of the ambitious citizen wife who for social advancement might be willing to sacrifice "one trifling" thing and spend an "eternal moment" in hell (lines 38, 42–43). Such mockery makes light of the high moral stakes for women who trade one kind of honor for another—namely, chastity for social distinction. That Mistress Ford can easily mock such a temptation, however, is to her credit. When they hold the letters up together for comparison, Mistress Ford is outraged: "What doth he think of us?" (line 74). Mistress Page once again "wrangle[s]" with her "honesty," questioning whether Falstaff could "know some strain" in her that she herself is unaware of (lines 76, 78). The women engage in a bit of bawdy repartee on "boarding," which leads directly to Mistress Page's second vow of revenge. Only now there will be conspiracy, two against one: "Let's be revenged on him" and "Let's consult together against this greasy knight" (lines 83, 96–97).

The scenes preceding this one give us a sense that the wives belong to a community, but the more subtly implied community to which they belong is the moral community of women, "the local arbiters of competing narratives about chaste and unchaste behavior."[22] Their response to an insult to their chastity will be handled by themselves, rather than brought to the judgment of men. Mistress Page and Mistress Ford take control of their narrative, and find they can do so most effectively and pleasurably through social drama.

In larger terms, the wives are defenders of the social order against thievery—the robbing of wives' virtue, husbands' honor, and families' coffers. Falstaff's intended transgressions render him a sexual menace, as Jeanne Addison Roberts observes.[23] While the mercenary motive underlies his seduction plot, to the married couples Falstaff represents "uncontrolled sex,"[24] which cuckolds men and ruins wives. He underestimates both the women, who are not easily preyed upon, and the men, who quickly close ranks against an outsider. The wives take charge of rechanneling Falstaff's sexual drive and seduction plot. They achieve this goal by exploiting another kind of energy, the energy of drama. The wives' skillful dramaturgic redirection of Falstaff's plot creates a pleasurable sense of doubleness in intrigue: it allows Falstaff to act out his sexual fantasy and the wives to gratify their own desire to thwart him. A simple rejection would cut short these pleasures and prevent the women from achieving sublime mastery over a male predator. The intricacy in comic plotting (Falstaff's plot overlaid by the wives' counterplot) is further complicated by Ford's plot to undo his wife, which leads to his unexpected intrusion into the already layered scene unfolding in his own house. The spectacle of the men's folly creates a double catharsis—for the wives and for the theater audience—which is repeated with amazing success three times. This pattern of plotting becomes not simply an extensive diversion from the rather tepid romantic plot involving Anne Page and Fenton, but the very pattern of the play's action, defining the comedy's joint aesthetic and ethical purpose.

Let us examine in some detail the language and structure of the two "scenes" of revenge that unfold in Mistress Ford's household. Act 3, scene 3, starts with a flurry of activity, as Mistress Ford calls in her servants. They

202 WOMEN AND REVENGE IN SHAKESPEARE

arrive carrying a huge buck-basket, which they set down on the "stage."
Already we get the sense of how domestic material will be at the service
of theater; here is a stage prop that awaits its purpose in the scene. The servants are instructed to "be ready here hard by in the brew-house" (3.3.9),
awaiting their mistress's call to take up and remove the basket at a moment's notice. Falstaff's page-boy Robin appears to announce that his master is ready at the back door. Acting as a go-between and stage hand, the
boy has been sworn to secrecy, and now, in effect, announces the arrival of
the lead actor.

As the wives prepare for Falstaff's entrance, they use language drawn
from the theater—*cue, act, hiss*—revealing a self-conscious pleasure in the
dramaturgic nature of revenge.[25] As Mistress Ford prepares to deliver her
part alone "onstage," the women exchange excited preperformance words:

> *Mistress Page:* I'll go hide me.
> *Mistress Ford:* Do so. . . . Mistress Page, remember you your cue.
> *Mistress Page:* I warrant thee: if I do not act it, hiss me.
>
> (3.3.31–34)

They anticipate the pleasure in taking charge of Falstaff's plot, making it
their own by turning it into a jest at his expense and a proof of their fidelity
and chastity. In the very moment before Falstaff crosses the threshold (from
tiring house to platform, street to house interior), the actor playing Mistress
Ford speaks directly to the theater's audience, expressing the intention of
the scene: "We'll use this unwholesome humidity, this gross watery pum-
pion; we'll teach him to know turtles from jays" (3.3.35–37). While the tur-
tledove was a recognized emblem of faithfulness, the jay suggested moral
laxity. Falstaff is the morally lax one here, his corpulent, oozing body inspiring her metaphors of unwholesomeness.

Once Falstaff unwittingly enters the liminal space of revenge drama, the
wives enact a discreet production, a household revel in which they act their
parts and position the male "actor" in his foolish part. Mistress Ford plays
the inamorata to Falstaff's braggart lover, allowing him to woo her for a
time before Robin interrupts them with news that Mistress Page is at the
back door. She gives him the illusion that his plot goes forward, and that
he is now in the typical situation of the lover who must hide so as not to be
discovered. The audience receives a tantalizing glimpse of the humiliation
in store for Falstaff as their eyes move back and forth from his great body
to the great buck-basket. Here is a comic image of the buffoonish Captain
from commedia dell'arte, startled out of his swagger, searching helplessly
for his exit. In Mistress Page's breathless conversation with Mistress Ford,
she emphasizes the *shame* of the adulterous situation in the house and, in
a deliberately suspenseful, ambiguous dialogue, she conveys the message

that Master Ford and "half Windsor at his heels" (line 105) are on their way to the house. The uncertainty of whether this is true or not carries some of the scene, increasing the comic effect of Falstaff's submission to a humiliating escape in the buck-basket.

While they may be able to establish the basic elements and roles of a commedia dell'arte scenario, the wives cannot control precisely how the scene will play out or even who might enter the scene. When the husbands and others burst in on the scene, Mistress Ford and Mistress Page unexpectedly find themselves spectators to "improvisational material" they had not anticipated, but the relinquishing of some of the control to the new "actors" on the "stage" plays out better than they could have anticipated. The pleasure is all theirs, the pain all Falstaff's . . . and the paranoia all Ford's. Ford displays hysterical certainty that his "sport" will yield a "fox" (lines 155, 150). After much ado about "buck," he sends the men on a wild errand searching every nook and cranny in the household. In the midst of this frenetic search for the cuckold-maker, the wives "merrily" devise a second plot, this one including the jealous husband.

We might pause to recall a story and image well known to Shakespeare's contemporaries that might have been suggested by the sight of Falstaff in the buck-basket: that of the Latin poet Virgil's shameful suspension in a basket under the window of the Roman emperor's daughter. In sixteenth-century England, this story and its variants proved popular. [26] According to legend, the poet Virgil fell in love with the emperor's daughter. She took offense at this and comically avenged this affront by giving him false hope—promising to raise him to her window in a basket for an assignation, but then leaving him dangling halfway up to her window. The Dutch engraver Lucas van Leyden rendered this scene in two series of woodcuts and a number of engravings. His visual interpretation of the tale emphasizes how the ridiculous figure of Virgil becomes the talk of Rome. The public onlookers are in the foreground, and the figure in the basket is rendered small and pathetic. The lesson of the tale and the image is clear: even a great, wise poet such as Virgil can be rendered an object of ridicule by a witty woman. Similarly, even the famous wit Falstaff, imported from the popular *Henry IV* plays, can be rendered an object of ridicule by women.

Importantly, the conclusion of the scene marks the women's first moment of vindication before the community. Page, Evans, and Caius chastise the frantic Ford, insisting that he is distempered and suffers from a bad conscience. "Fie, fie, Master Ford, are you not ashamed? What spirit, what devil, suggests this imagination?" exclaims Master Page (lines 199–200). Both Evans and Caius insist that Mistress Ford is honest, and Ford is pressured into asking pardon from his wife and Mistress Page. The women, then, are left to delight in the "double excellency" of their plot, with Mistress Ford exclaiming, "I know not which pleases me better, that my husband is deceived, or Sir John" (lines 162, 163–64). In their mirth, they feel vindicated, but they know they have not achieved the full satisfaction that revenge promises. It is apparent to the women that their target has not been truly cured or reformed. Furthermore, they have another target in their range. Mistress Ford confesses, "I think my husband hath some special suspicion of Falstaff's being here, for I never saw him so gross in his jealousy till now" (lines 172–74).

In response, Mistress Page skillfully begins to improvise another scenario in which the Jealous Husband becomes a direct target in their revenge and further motivation for plotting: "I will lay a plot to try that, and we will yet have more tricks with Falstaff. His dissolute disease will scarce obey this medicine" (lines 175–77). The scenes in the Ford household reflect "imaginative configurations overlapping" as Falstaff, Ford, and the wives each play out their fantasies.[27] While Falstaff and Ford both find themselves trapped when the material conditions of the scene fail to correspond with their own imaginary fields, the wives enjoy both the unfolding and extension of their imaginative field. Mistress Ford relishes the chance to "punish" her husband for his "fantastical humours," as Sir Hugh Evans calls them (line 156), and desires to "give" Falstaff "another hope, to betray him to another punishment" (lines 180–81).

Shakespeare's construction of the second revenge scene (4.2) dispenses with the "setting of the stage" and opens directly with a wooing scene between Falstaff and Mistress Ford. This intimate moment is interrupted almost immediately by Mistress Page with the news that the husbands are on their way to the Ford house. The wives and Falstaff scramble to find an exit plan for Falstaff, yet all the while the wives are toying with Falstaff. When Mistress Page hits upon the idea of a disguise, her brilliant plotting shows that the wives will control the comic scenario once again. The ambiguity of whether the disguise was planned or thought up in the imaginative unfolding of the scene is part of its appeal. They have Falstaff groveling before them, submitting to yet another humiliating device. They dismiss him from the "stage," sending him upstairs to put on his feminine costume.

The women gather their forces before Master Ford and the other men arrive. Ford is truly on his way home and in a rage about the basket. Multiple plots are about to converge in the charged space of the Ford household. With the wives' setup of Falstaff, however, they control the most significant variable in the unstable unfolding of the scene, and their knowledge of Ford's character gives them some assurances as well. They anticipate with relish the beating Falstaff is sure to get at the hands of the irrational Ford. Indeed, Mistress Page wishes for divine intervention to "guide him to thy husband's cudgel" (lines 84–85). Regarding her husband's distress over the laundry basket, Mistress Ford proclaims, "We'll try that" (line 89), and devises a second scenario based on their previous performance with the buck-basket.

While Mistress Ford attends to a second buck-basket jest, the actor playing Mistress Page turns to the audience to clarify again their intention. His/her words are uttered in the liminal space shared by audience and actor:

> We'll leave a proof, by that which we will do,
> Wives may be merry and yet honest too.
> We do not act that often jest and laugh;
> 'Tis old but true: "Still swine eats all the draff."

(lines 99–102)

Their "doing" or "acting" is to be distinguished radically from the adulteress's, figured in the filthy image of the "still swine" who surreptitiously "eats all the draff." The wives' action is a "proof," like the old adage, that counters ungenerous cultural interpretations of the actions of merry wives. There is no *essential* virtue in "stillness," quiet, and passivity, Mistress Page implies in her declaration.

When the men burst upon the stage once more, Ford plays into the wives' jest by exposing himself as a fool and a lunatic. He is met by the servants with the buck-basket on their shoulders. Ford believes that this will be a spectacle of shame for his wife and vindication for himself. He insists that Mistress Ford come to watch his mad search through the basket, exclaiming, "Now shall the devil be shamed" (lines 113–14). When no knight is found in the basket, Mistress Ford can gloat: "Are you not ashamed?" (line 130). Ford must conclude, "Well, he's not here I seek for," and Page responds, "No, nor nowhere else but in your brain" (lines 149–50). "Brain" reverberates ironically, for not moments after this, we witness the materialization of the fantasy in Ford's brain as the old woman of Brent/Brainford. Here is the very man he seeks, but all Ford can see is a detestable witch whom he beats mercilessly. Figuratively, the wives have orchestrated the brain beating that Ford needs through the agency of the physical beating out of lust that Falstaff needs. The doubleness of this fit exhibits the wives' ingenuity in plotting, and Shakespeare's brilliant handling of the convergence of multiple plots in this scene. With the mad exit of Ford and the others, the wives are left to reflect on the accomplishments of their social drama and to contemplate how to make a "period to the jest" (lines 210–11).

MAKING A PERIOD TO THE JEST:
THE LIMITS OF REVENGE

In the domestic space of the household, the women have practiced an ethics of social theater that has paid dividends in laughter, pleasure, and moral instruction. They have shared the role of judge to Falstaff's crime and sentenced him to a series of playful humiliations—his lovemaking interrupted, his exposure threatened, his exits unceremoniously handled, his body beaten—and all the while, the women have been laughing at the sight of the groveling knight as he pays for his base desires. But as the wise fool Feste chimes darkly in *Twelfth Night,* "pleasure will be paid, one time or another" (2.4.70–71). Will the wives pay for their pleasure? Have the wives overindulged in their revenge? The time for calling to mind the ethics of their situation arrives. They pause in a moment of reflection after their second successful scene of humiliation to contemplate questions of moral legitimacy and excessiveness in revenge. Is there a limit to how far revenge can be taken, before it loses its virtue and becomes something more unsavory, even cruel? Their moment of contemplation is the fulcrum upon which the revenge comedy rests. Mistress Ford's question seems to confront us directly, while the play hangs in the balance: "What think you? May we, with the warrant of womanhood and the witness of a good conscience, pursue him with any further revenge?" (4.2.195–97). The rhetoric here ties this question directly to gender, law, and morality. Their need to protect their womanhood (and everything that means in their culture) has provided the "warrant" for their actions, and their consciences have borne witness to the virtue of their actions. But perhaps they have reached the end of what their culture's notions of womanhood and conscience permit.

Is more revenge necessary for the wives' vindication, which is the essential action of their revenge comedy and Shakespeare's play? When the wives agree to tell their husbands about their revenge, are they seeking the cloak of male approval in order to justify more merriment with Falstaff beyond what the vindication of their virtue calls for? To answer such questions, let us see what emerges as Shakespeare keeps the wives' plot unfolding. In sharing the fruits of their revenge with their husbands, the women are moving beyond themselves and a private theater of revenge to public acknowledgment for themselves and public shame for Falstaff. Mistress Ford gleefully proclaims, "I'll warrant they'll have him publicly shamed, and methinks there would be no period to the jest should he not be publicly shamed" (lines 209–11). The very repetition of the phrase "publicly shamed" reflects the expansion of their imaginative field from private to public space, and an extension of their fantasy into communal fantasies. The scene concludes with Mistress Page's exuberant invitation: "Come, to the forge with it, then shape it: I would not have things cool" (lines 212–13). The proverbial "Strike while the iron is hot" serves the wives' turn imaginatively: they exit the scene determined to forge another revenge plot, and they seem sure that their husbands will approve of their actions and warrant further revenge. In the end, they decide to stretch revenge's limits, come what may. They will pleasure themselves further, but also extend satisfaction to their husbands who, just as they suspect, do not turn down an offer to pay back Falstaff for his attempts on their wives' honor. Their moment of reflection, then, yields a virtual confession, for they desire more revenge—they still have an appetite, even though they seem to have accomplished what they set out to do.

Most significantly, though, in disclosing their revenge plot to their husbands, the wives begin their efforts at public vindication. Act 4, scene 4, opens just after they have disclosed to their husbands and Parson Evans the nature and results of their plots, placing their virtue, worth, and good sense on display. The first line is given to Evans, the play's only religious authority, who exclaims with admiration: "'Tis one of the best discretions of a 'oman as ever I did look upon" (4.4.1–2). Given his religious profession, the Parson's voice carries moral weight; he can see no harm in what the wives have done. Mistress Ford then enjoys the supreme satisfaction of hearing her wayward husband yet again ask for her pardon before the others, and this time he sounds like he means it:

> Pardon me, wife. Henceforth do what thou wilt:
> I rather will suspect the sun with cold
> Than thee with wantonness. Now doth thy honour stand,
> In him that was of late an heretic,
> As firm as faith.

> (lines 6–10)

This dramatic moment emphasizes how dependent marital harmony is on *faith*. If honor is an intangible virtue, easily assailable by seduction letters and slander, then in Windsor men and women must guard their honor with vigilance. Mistress Ford's case reflects the need for women's self-monitoring and defense, as their husbands may prove "heretics" in marital faith, as did Master Ford.

The wives' approach, from the start, has involved a mixture of amusement, indignation, and hostility. Before they take revenge, Mistress Ford establishes the extremes to which she is willing to take things: "I will consent to act any villainy against him, that may not sully the chariness of our honesty" (2.1.87–89). Her language betrays a tension between self-protection and public aggression. She is aware of the high stakes involved in acting, as well as the imperative to act: a woman's reputation must be guarded against slander, yet she must risk suspicion and disbelief if she makes public an account of how her virtue has been assailed. Mistress Ford's "consent" indicates agency and choice; her will counters Falstaff's. The term "villainy" rests awkwardly in her declaration. Is she unconsciously revealing the malice of her intent to revenge? Does it reflect her impression of the male predator as villain, and her usurpation of that role in turning the tables on him? During their second staged scene, an escalation in aggression (even a note of malice) can be detected in Mistress Page's "Hang him, dishonest varlet! We cannot misuse him enough" (4.2.97–98). The quality of pitilessness in revenge, usually associated with the Hyrcanian tiger in tragic female avengers, as we saw in chapter 4, is here implied. They may call him "poor" "afflicted" knight, but their tone is mocking and ironic.

As the circle widens from private theater to public communal spectacle, the revenge motive indeed becomes more aggressive. We see that once again, as in *Twelfth Night* and *Much Ado About Nothing*, Shakespeare experiments with comic vengeance as a wellspring not only for laughter, but for darker impulses as well. Revenge proves surprisingly well suited to the production of comic plots, yet merriment can go awry when the festive spirit of revenge intensifies. The impulse to cruelty may go unchecked, and the victim may learn nothing from his punishment. The victim may strike back. One might find one's self contemplating Nietzsche's words, taken from a different context: "Without cruelty there is no festival: thus the longest and most ancient part of human history teaches—and in punishment there is so much that is *festive!*"[28]

Indeed, the pleasurable festivity of revenge is a quality that marks many of the novelle from the Continental tradition. As Geoffrey Bullough and Leo Salingar have demonstrated, the Italian novelle exerted a deep influence on Shakespeare's dramaturgy.[29] Many of those medieval and Renaissance tales of intrigue, love, and deception involve the harsh revenges of male and female characters—women are seen most often ridiculing and duping unwanted suitors or husbands, and men take cruel revenges, sometimes against women, in the name of honor.[30] Take, for example, Giovanni Francesco Straparola's tale of Filenio Sisterno (*Le Piacevole Notti* 2.2), which Shakespeare could have read in various sources.[31] In this novella we find some parallels with the merry wives' situation. An outsider, a student from Crete, attempts to seduce three married women of Bologna. They turn out to be friends, and when they share their stories, they resolve to have some fun with him and take their revenge—ladies, too, the narrator interjects, may play tricks.[32] But these tricks prove to be cruel, bringing shame and near death to the student. They each feign sexual interest and invite the student, Filenio, into their houses, all the while intending to punish him. When Emerentiana's husband interrupts their amorous interlude, she hides the nearly naked Filenio under her bed, where she has prepared the ground with thorns. With every move he makes during the night, he is pierced by thorns, until his whole body is covered with blood. When Filenio visits Panthemia, she has him undress, then sends him into a closet to hide, where he falls through the floor into a warehouse, nearly breaking all his bones. Upon Sinforosia's invitation, he joins her in her room, where she drugs him and, with the help of a strong maid, carries him to the street and leaves him there sleeping. Upon waking, he finds himself in miserable health and barely recovers in the course of time.

These female avengers go too far with their jests, the third one being nearly fatal. Filenio becomes incensed and plots his revenge on them. He feigns amorousness toward them, rents beautiful lodgings, and invites them to a feast. There he subjects them to a cruel scene of humiliation. He has them strip off their clothes as they quake in terror and tears, and then he drives them into bed together, where they are covered only by a sheet. He locks the door, and then invites their husbands to come in for an amusing peepshow. He allows the men to see only parts of the women's bodies, so they do not recognize them, but then he shows them their wives' clothes, which causes suspicion. After dishonoring them, Filenio returns the wives to their homes, where they find themselves in a vulnerable situation with their husbands, and subjected to shame every time they meet Filenio in the street.

Comparison between this novella and *The Merry Wives* is instructive regarding the issues of excessiveness and cruelty. While the premise of this tale is similar to that of *The Merry Wives*—the chaste wives take their revenge on the adulterous suitor—the ethical structuring of the tale differs in important ways. Unlike this Italian tale, Shakespeare's married women dish out rather tame punishments and then exhibit the wisdom of disclosing their actions to their husbands. Revenge plays out favorably for the women, and they end up earning respect, rather than shame, for their ingenuity. Unlike Filenio, Falstaff cannot retaliate, for the Windsor wives have been smarter than the Bolognese wives in allowing others to inflict pain, and drawing their men and the community together as participants in one final, grand jest.

In *The Merry Wives of Windsor,* the third revenge scene brings a satisfying period to the jest, but not without suggesting that revenge has a kind of wild energy, once it takes hold in the community. As revenge escalates, so too does pain, humiliation . . . and cruelty. The mixed tone of *The Merry Wives* arises from the doubleness of revenge—its tendency toward obsession and violence, on the one hand, and virtue and just vindication, on the other. Revenge can be closely allied with a sense of justice. There can be a moral imperative to revenge or a virtue in vengeance, as we have seen in some of Shakespeare's female characters. When an immoral action takes place, a response must communicate that this action is wrong and is not tolerated by an individual or a community. Revenge can be the justified palliative when the wrong falls outside the province of law. Revenge, too, can be violent, cruel, antisocial, and destructive, which explains the "certain quality of brutality" some critics detect in revenge comedies.[33]

If brutality and cruelty rear their heads anywhere in *The Merry Wives,* it would have to be in the figure of the jealous husband, Ford. Self-deluded and paranoid, this vengeful husband elicits laughter in the theater, for, like Falstaff, he goes to excess in his role. We are able to laugh, however, only because we are complacent in our knowledge that he is a fool who will be thwarted, shamed, and mocked. Not so funny is the vindictiveness he exhibits toward his wife, which is as destructive to his psyche as it is to his wife's honor and their marital harmony. His desire to vindicate himself serves as the darkly unjust counterpart to the wives' need to vindicate themselves. Some modern performances have focused on the disturbing implications underlying the play's amusing surface by emphasizing Ford's hysteria. Ben Kingsley's performance of Ford in the 1979 RSC and BBC productions, for example, brought out the lunatic quality of jealousy, revealing a family resemblance between this comic character and other tragically deluded Shakespearean husbands such as Othello and Leontes. Ford's psychological distress and revenge plot comically anticipate these later representations of the blinding fury of masculine jealousy. Seen in this light, Ford introduces into the comic world a frightening specter—he is funny, but terrifyingly so. His paranoid imagination perceives that "Good plots they are laid" (3.2.34–35); ironically, good plots *have* been laid, but he mistakes the nature, intent, and outcome of these plots. He fantasizes about a public scene of violence in which he shames the offenders. The scene involves torturing his wife while "all my neighbors shall cry aim [i.e., applaud]" (line 40). This powerfully imagined shaming ritual will find its release elsewhere in the somewhat excessive abuse of Falstaff in Windsor Forest. If Ford fears himself to be an Actaeon (a mythological figure associated with the horns of cuckoldry in the Renaissance), then a substitute or scapegoat Actaeon (Falstaff) is needed to play out his aggression. The counterforces of reconciliation and good cheer, represented in the attitudes of Master Page and the Host, defuse the aggression of vengeance to some extent, but only after the community unites in indulging their drive for vengeance.

Ford's linguistic *jouissance* is hard to miss: the spilling over, eruptive quality of his asides barely conceals his pleasure. His "performance" in his own household when he relentlessly seeks out his own cuckolder embodies this perverse drive. One detects in him a savage compulsion, a need for self-exposure, which includes the exposure of his wife's imagined sin, as well. Like a fanatical reformer, he seeks to expose vice and humiliate the fallen. He engages in a strange fantasy of a double cascade of shame and vindication in his own cuckoldry. The "figures" that need to be "scrape[d]" out of his "brains" (4.2.205, 204, 205) are virtually pornographic: images of his adulterous wife and Falstaff, the licensed cuckolder, mingle with his self-generated image of a horned husband. The fantasy leads to a secretive revenge drama of his own making in which he perversely takes a disguise as Master Brooke to pay Falstaff to cuckold him.

If Ford realizes the darkest potentialities of revenge, the merry wives would seem to be at the other end of the spectrum, activating revenge's sportful levity. Yet some critics and directors have disagreed with this assessment, seeing in the figures of the wives the spirit of cruelty. The former RSC director Bill Alexander insists there is "a strong element of cruelty in the play"; it is a "play of quite unnecessary revenge," he maintains, suggesting that the wives might simply have written back a letter, saying, "'We're deeply offended, please don't come round here again'"; instead they punish Falstaff without warrant.[34] "Unnecessary revenge" sums up Alexander's view, implicitly giving a negative answer to the fundamental question of revenge's ethical intent. Ralph Berry is unsparing in his disregard for the play, which he sees as a "brutal farce" and a mechanically written "by-product of Shakespeare's career" that "does not appear to contribute organically to Shakespeare's development."[35] Berry's perception is that the play cannot justify itself, reflecting as it does nothing more than base farce and the worst of human aggressions.

If these views hold true, if the wives' characters are tainted by sadistic intentions and unwarranted revenge, if they are merely the dancing puppets of farce, the play's effect is superficial, and the social commentary on women and gender relations becomes dire—or trivial. If revenge taints the united ethical and aesthetic functions of the action, then the play is despicable and the humor brittle. In their extreme reaction to elements in the play, Alexander, Berry, and others have overemphasized the play's farcical energies, failing to engage with other potentialities in the text. A balanced vision such as Jeanne Addison Roberts offers is more in keeping with the play's ethos: she argues that *The Merry Wives* is a complex drama with cathartic effects that belong squarely in the realm of comedy; the play's world "is not the random world of farce," she rightly insists. "If farce is absurd and ruled by whim, one is forced to conclude that the eighteenth century was right: *The Merry Wives* is not farce but comedy."[36] The play can be wildly funny and farcical at moments in performance, but *The Merry Wives* has serious concerns underlying it, as does another "lighter" comedy, *Much Ado About Nothing,* which has often been dismissed as farce, as well. In these comedies, Shakespeare brings to light pressing social and moral issues for women: their need to protect their honor at all costs, the vulnerability of their reputations to slander, the destructiveness of masculine jealousy, and their need for resources in deflecting (and ideally outwitting) male antagonists. Furthermore, as I have been arguing, the wives enact their own vindication, which is warranted due to their dishonorable treatment by Falstaff. As philosopher Trudy Govier writes, "A victim of wrongdoing will be vindicated if it is shown that she did nothing to deserve her ill-treatment or dishonor, if it is asserted or reasserted that she is a worthy human being who merited better, and that in the conflict between her and the wrongdoing, she was right. To vindicate oneself is to show that one was right all along. . . ."[37]

As witty avengers rightfully defending their chastity, the Windsor wives gain the audience's sympathy. Most productions will bear out the truth of this statement. Male and female spectators alike understand the stakes for women when their virtue is assailed, and recognize the aesthetic fittingness in their playful handling of a response. Falstaff does not need to be successful in ruining them to deserve their revenge and, because of his failure, he wins some sympathy for himself, too. Clearly, then, Ford's baseless suspicions and vicious revenge fantasies contrast strongly with the wives' "merry" and morally justified revenge on Falstaff. Again, the wives win sympathy in their baiting of Ford. Indeed, their desire to protect their honor (and by extension, the honor of their husbands) strongly suggests a virtue in their vengeance and an ethical motivation shaping the play's action.

When revenge becomes the mutual goal of the community in this play, *The Merry Wives* fulfills its end as revenge *comedy*. Falstaff becomes not only the wives' humiliated suitor, but also Windsor's target. Mistress Ford justifies this final scene by invoking the necessity of closure: "methinks there would be no period to the jest should he not be publicly shamed" (4.2.210–11). Mistress Page agrees, relishing the continued pursuit of their art: "Come, to the forge with it, then shape it: I would not have things cool" (lines 212–13). The heat of the plot is compared to that of the forge. Both arts involve the necessity of shape—the form must have its beginning, middle, and end. Here is the dimension of necessity that the director Bill Alexander rejected, or failed to see as compelling, when he suggested that the wives might have sent a rejection letter to Falstaff. Yet here is where we see Shakespeare's awareness of artistry reflected: in his fusing of the shape of revenge with the shape of the plot, ethics and aesthetics are united.

The final scene must be considered in terms of revenge's achievement as a formal plot element as well as an ethical motive. As John Kerrigan states, the "tragic shaping of *The Merry Wives* is impeccable."[38] Falstaff's punishment is "shrewdly adjusted to the demands of retribution. As he is tweaked and pricked with pins, Falstaff is like the victim of a revenge masque."[39] The festive effects of this final trick are essential to its meaning; there is a kind of fullness and voluptuousness—and yes, some cruelty, as Nietzsche, Alexander, and Berry would have it—to this final movement in the drama. The excesses figured in Falstaff are met with the excesses of festivity and merriment in the revenge masque in the woods. His punishment is not severe, and certainly not deadly, which is fitting, given that he does not actually ruin the women, or their husbands' reputations. Yet he did steal deer, he did intend to possess his female dears, and he did intend to cuckold some of the Windsor husbands. For these crimes and ill intentions, a moral debt has been incurred; the tripartite revenge action makes Falstaff pay with interest.

The logic of revenge and the demands of the revenge plot, then, dictate that Falstaff must continue to play the role of sexual predator turned prey, and he must now go public, so that his transgressions—all of them—can be ritually exposed and punished before the community. In symbolic terms, certainly, he is made Windsor's scapegoat, but not with the base effect of unleashing sadism in Windsor and on the play's audience, as Ralph Berry would have it.[40] He stands in not only for the cuckolded husband, but for all men who would reduce themselves to thievery and to preying upon women in a most dishonorable fashion. It is his shameful entrance into the Windsorian community that catalyzes the energies of revenge, for he is an interloping figure of thievery and "lust in action," to echo sonnet 129. The proliferation of body metaphors betrays how the Windsorians see in the Falstaffian body "a waste of shame," to finish that same sonnet's line. The use of the Garter motto, *Honi soit qui mal y pense* [Shame to him who thinks evil of it], emphasizes how thoughts of evil bring shame; Falstaff's appetites and thoughts manifest themselves in his vast waist and braggart behavior.

Finally, Falstaff's enforced transformation into Herne the Hunter, a legendary gamekeeper who haunts the forest after having hanged himself from a sacred oak, can be read in ethical terms as a fitting punishment. While the buck-basket experience reflected his soiled honor and base morality, the feminine costume and beating robbed him of masculine potency; finally, he is costumed once more, and this time with a buck's head, which makes him into a ridiculous, conflated figure of the cuckolded male and the "Sir Actaeon" Ford feared he was (2.1.106). Years ago, John Steadman interpreted Falstaff's transformation in light of the Actaeon myth and Renaissance illustrations of Actaeon as a stag, made familiar in Whitney's depiction in *A choice of emblemes*.[41] While Steadman focuses on how Falstaff evokes the Actaeon figure, we might turn to the shaping role of Diana in the fate of Actaeon to complete the mythological allusion here. In the Ovidian account, Actaeon has dared to view Diana secretly as she bathes. Through his voyeurism, she becomes an erotic object. This violation of her privacy and integrity causes her to feel outrage and spite, and to take vengeance by transforming him into a beast. Furthermore, she drives his hounds to hunt him down and tear him to pieces. The wives share the role of Diana, incensed that they have been viewed in an illicit manner and their chastity tried. In their final revenge on Falstaff, they replay Diana's revenge, though in a comparatively benign version of the Ovidian tale. Falstaff's body is subjected to some rough treatment from the children of Windsor, but he remains physically intact to the end.

Another supreme moment of vindication arrives for the wives once the fairies have sung their song to exorcise "sinful fantasy" and "lust and luxury" (5.5.93, 94), and have finished pinching and burning Falstaff. Mistress Page insists that the jest has come to an end, and says, "Now, good Sir John, how like you Windsor wives?" (5.5.106). In her triumph, she directs her husband to view Falstaff's horns: "Do not these fair yokes / Become the forest better than the town?" (lines 107–8). Mistress Ford engages in mockery and wordplay as she lets him down: "Sir John, we have had ill luck, we could never meet. I will never take you for my love again, but I will always count you my deer" (lines 116–18). Falstaff works hard to save face in this scene, groping for vestiges of wit and turning upon the non-native English speakers. When he laments being mocked by Evans, "one that makes fritters of English" (line 142), Mistress Page turns his attention back to herself and Mistress Ford, and to the moral issue of concern to them. She insists, "Why, Sir John, do you think, though we would have thrust virtue out of our hearts by the head and shoulders, and have given ourselves without scruple to hell, that ever the devil could have made you our delight?" (lines 145–49).

Even at this low moment, however, Falstaff seems to lack the authentic shame intended to result from a shaming ritual. Perhaps what we see reflected here is that a man without honor cannot feel shame. After sustaining the verbal blows of the wives, husbands, and Evans, which catalogue his sins and their revulsion of his "Old, cold, withered and . . . intolerable entrails" (line 152), Falstaff merely sighs in resignation: "Well, I am your theme: you have the start of me. I am dejected, I am not able to answer the Welsh flannel, ignorance itself is a plummet o'er me. Use me as you will" (5.5.159–62). This speech hardly reflects a broken or shamed man; rather, Falstaff exhibits characteristic wit and acknowledges simply that he has been had. The accusations of the community are correct, if severe, and he is willing to take the punishment they have dished out. Such is the life of a knight whose integrity can be found in his gut and whose honor is but a "word." The Falstaff in *The Merry Wives* is the logical extension of the Falstaff who uttered the famous "catechism" in *I Henry IV:* "What is honour? A word. What is in that word 'honour'? What is that 'honour'? Air. A trim reckoning. Who hath it? He that died o'Wednesday. Doth he feel it? No. Doth he hear it? No. 'Tis insensible then? Yea, to the dead. But will it not live with the living? No. Why? Detraction will not suffer it. Therefore I'll none of it. Honour is a mere scutcheon. And so ends my catechism" (5.1.133–40). Bound to the realm of the senses, Falstaff rejects the abstract, interior quality of honor, refusing to grant it signifying power. In his estimation, honor is not a worthy cause for death, nor does honor have the power to withstand slander. So what is its value?

The ethical ground of the comedy, however, upholds a virtue in honor, and a virtue in vengeance that would repay acts of dishonor. The wives' revenge action gives energy, substance, and social value to their ethics, and shows their audience, offstage and on, how a "merry" proof of honor can give entertainment as well as catharsis. For the women in *The Merry Wives of Windsor*, honor is an essential virtue to be guarded and actively defended. To their husbands and other Windsorians, honor is an essential public good.

Falstaff's dejected spirits begin to lift, however, when he learns that he has not been the only butt of jokes in Windsor. Indeed, Page extends a conciliatory word to him almost immediately following his speech: "Yet be cheerful, knight: thou shalt eat a posset tonight at my house, where I will desire thee to laugh at my wife that now laughs at thee. Tell her Master Slender hath married her daughter" (5.5.168–71). To make amends for his wife's revenge jest, Master Page will give Falstaff the privilege of dropping a bombshell on Mistress Page and having the last laugh with him. This scene does not come to pass, however, as the men's pleasurable revenge fantasy is muddied with the entrance of a flustered Slender. The Pages have been tricked, too, it turns out, and Falstaff now can feel a degree of satisfaction in watching their failure to hit their target: "I am glad, though you have ta'en a special stand to strike at me, that your arrow hath glanced" (5.5.228–29). Page's targets are his own wife and daughter, who elude his arrow and deftly shoot a number of their own. Now, however, Mistress Page must submit to another female avenger, her own daughter. The period to Anne Page's jest lies in holy matrimony and a vindication of women who choose their own husbands, which bring us squarely into the realm of romantic comedy.

"WHO HATH GOT THE RIGHT ANNE?": THE DAUGHTER'S REVENGE

To conclude, I would like to turn our attention to a plot that remains submerged, or in the margins, for much of the drama. Virtually silent and seemingly passive, Anne Page turns out to be a subtle, witty avenger who can outplot the best of them; in a coup de théâtre, she dupes her parents and unwanted suitors, Caius and Slender. While many of the play's scenes focus on the plotting of her suitors, providing some suggestive paralleling with Falstaff's "courtship" of the wives, only a few brief scenes feature Anne onstage. Yet what she says is important—and what she writes is revelatory. In 3.4, she has a brief romantic interlude with Fenton in which she makes clear that she has chosen him as her favored suitor. "Gentle Master Fenton, / Yet seek my father's love, still seek it, sir" (lines 18–19), she strongly urges him, but then she makes known that she has a plan B, a plot to unite them despite her parents' objections: "If opportunity and humblest suit / Cannot attain it, why then—hark you hither—" (lines 20–21). At this point onstage, the two characters speak privately together, so Anne's plot is withheld from the audience. We are made to feel, however, that she is the "minister" of their destiny; sensing that Fenton will not be successful in his suit, she must use her ingenuity to satisfy her own will, and to ensure that she is not treated like household goods transferred to the buyer of her parents' choice.

Like the wives, she is loath to be subjected to a male suitor, much less a husband and sexual partner, who is repulsive. "I had rather be set quick i' th' earth, / And bowled to death with turnips" (3.4.85–86), she exclaims in one of the play's strangest witticisms. She must use what skills she has to outwit her parents and suitors; such skills will involve deceit, trickery, and a flagrant disregard for any kind of social authority. For Anne, the ultimate authority is her own integrity, which only she can preserve. Integrity is an aspect of honor and virtue, and all three bond together to make up the social (and private) identity of a female. So we might say that it is a point of honor for Anne to resist her foolish suitors, who are unworthy of her. She will run the risk of parental rejection and retaliation, but she is determined to pursue her will—"So far forth as herself might be her chooser" (4.6.11)— and achieve what amounts to a constructive revenge and justice for herself.

Her plot is partially unveiled in the letter she sends to Fenton. While an indirect form of communication onstage, the letter nonetheless establishes Anne's literacy and a connection between writing and plotting. In her ability to write, the "right" Anne is able to disclose herself, and claim her "right" to choose a husband, or so the wordplay cleverly suggests. While the merry wives engaged in improvisational scenes reminiscent of a commedia dell'arte scenario, Anne establishes a written narrative, a revenge narrative, to direct Fenton in how to win her and how their plot shall triumph over her parents' plots. In 4.6 as Fenton begins to relate the contents of Anne's letter to the Host, her character obliquely takes definition:

> I have a letter from her
> Of such contents as you will wonder at,
> The mirth whereof so larded with my matter
> That neither singly can be manifested
> Without the show of both, wherein fat Falstaff
> Hath a great scene; the image of the jest
> I'll show you here at large. . . .
>
> (lines 12–18)

Anne's letter provides "the image of the jest," which suggests visually provocative language that verbally paints "a great scene." Her language inspires Fenton's culinary metaphor "larded" and the puns on Falstaff's size. The opposition of "mirth" and "matter" proves unstable as she recounts the two plots and their interdependence. Fenton does not read the letter directly —he seems to be "showing" the Host where she enlarges on the mirthful matter of her plot against her parents—but the presence of the letter and its author remains. Anne has devised a revenge plot, and the letter serves as the narrative basis from which she and Fenton will act their parts.

In the end, all's well that ends well: this can be said for Anne and Fenton, and for the married couples whose unions are reforged through the revenge jests and a beneficial social drama. The Pages remain unshaken by the news of Anne's deception, resisting the urge to turn upon each other or upon their daughter. Ford's question "Who hath got the right Anne" (5.5.207) is curiously apt, coming at the end of a play of disguises, devices, and deceptions. Clearly no one has the "right Anne" except the man she chooses. Her agency and will determine who "gets" her; and even Fenton must be schooled in wooing and winning, as well as knowing the "right Anne." Every character imagines that he or she knows Anne Page, Mistress Quickly making the greatest assumption of them all: "Never a woman in Windsor knows more of Anne's mind than I do" (1.4.118–19). But they are all cozened in the end when she emerges as a triumphant "merry wife." To set things right, she asks pardon from her parents, which enables them to forgive her and "muse no further" (5.5.233). Fenton's speech emphasizes the shameful nature of "forced marriage" (line 224), and chastises her parents for implicitly wishing "A thousand irreligious cursed hours" on their daughter (line 223). He redeems her deceit and disobedience by claiming, "Th'offence is holy that she hath committed, / And this deceit loses the name of craft, / Of disobedience, and unduteous title" (lines 219–21). She acted to avoid the "irreligious" hours of arranged marriage. By using religious discourse in his defense, Fenton lends authority to marriages based on affection and a woman's choice. His phrase "no proportion held in love" (line 216) signals the underlying ethics of revenge at work. Anne's revenge plot is justified as a spiritual rebalancing of the disproportion in love represented in her parents' matches, which were based on mercenary arrangements. Disproportion in love can only result in unhappiness, misunderstanding, and worse. Where, after all, does the feminine desire for revenge through cuckoldry come from? What are the root causes of masculine jealousy? What would prompt a man to disguise himself and hire another man to sleep with his wife, if not disproportion in love?

The "right Anne" also reminds us that two boys were disguised as Anne (translated into male "Pages," to follow the linguistic punning so rampant in this play) and "married" off to Caius and Slender. The Merry Wives suggests, in the end, the provisional nature of identity and the cultural work achieved by women through play and performance. The idea of "sport" and merriment asserts itself as the Pages let go of their anger and irritation, suggesting that everyone should "laugh this sport o'er by a country fire, / Sir John and all" (5.5.236–37). Plots, tricks, devices, sport—all humiliations suffered should dissolve in laughter around a country fire. As in other Shakespeare comedies, we are left wondering whether all members of the community can be satisfied in such a manner. The humiliated Doctor Caius, for one, seems unlikely to be pacified. When he swears, "By gar, I am cozened. . . . I'll raise all Windsor" (5.5.203, 205–6), the audience may laugh, but like Malvolio in *Twelfth Night,* Caius exhibits disturbing passions associated with revenge—rage and resentment. In his humiliation, the instinct to revenge kicks up. His words are a call to arms; he is reaching for his sword. He has been tricked into marrying a boy rather than the prized Anne Page. Like Falstaff and Slender, he has failed to win his erotic object, but his temperament is more disagreeable than that of the others, so he is less inclined to let go of his rage. He has been shamed by the community and perceives that he has been made an ass and the object of derision. If there is one character unwilling to accept his condition of shame and foolishness, it is Caius; arguably, his burning resentment lingers at the close of the play.

Yet, importantly, Caius has not won our sympathy, and we recognize his character as only one small figure in a larger design. His discordant note registers, but it is only a single note sounded in a dramatic symphony. The women, above all, have had our sympathy, and the greater satisfaction in the comedy arises from witnessing the successful ministering of feminine revenge as a complete and just action. The grafting of Anne Page's revenge onto the wives' action emphasizes doubly the audience's pleasure in participating in a social drama whose end is the vindication of women. Indeed, Lord Byron's famous line from *Don Juan* about women and revenge fits well with the Windsor wives: "Sweet is Revenge—especially to women."[42]

All delight and sweetness in revenge must die, however, as we turn to the dark comedy that is the subject of our next chapter. *The Merchant of Venice* presents us with a notoriously difficult and painful play, in no small part due to the way in which Shakespeare unmasks vengeance as a passion lying at the root of all social exchange in the play. Positioned to thwart Shylock's bloodthirsty revenge, Portia proves herself capable of revenge as well. It appears that Portia's character stakes her identity and destiny on being able to outrevenge the revenger. In redirecting the energies of revenge in the courtroom and bringing them to a bloodless resolution, Portia exercises a game in payback with Shylock, Bassanio, and Antonio, a game that proves to be essential in maintaining her advantage in marriage and in her newly gained social network. Weighing Shylock's vengeful claims and actions against Portia's becomes the ethical burden of the audience and the chapter that follows.

8

The Quality of Revenge:
Debt, Reciprocity, and Portia's "Vantage"
in *The Merchant of Venice*

Antonio. [We] stand indebted over and above
In love and service to you evermore.
—Shakespeare, *The Merchant of Venice*

Portia. . . . my vantage to exclaim on you. . . .
—Shakespeare, *The Merchant of Venice*

IN RENÉ GIRARD'S VIEW, "THE DYNAMICS OF THE THEATER ARE THE DY-
namics of human conflict, the reciprocity of retribution and revenge; the
more intense the process, the more symmetry you tend to have, the more
everything tends to become the same on both sides of the antagonism."[1]
Revenge-driven plays, more than other kinds of drama, arguably strip bare
the reciprocal nature of conflicts in human relationships. Few comedies
demonstrate Girard's insight as subtly and disturbingly as *The Merchant of
Venice,* where revenge enters into relationships between lovers as readily
as it does between enemies. Shylock's famous speech justifying revenge
between enemies ("Hath not a Jew eyes?") aims at the principles of reciprocity and symmetry:

> [Antonio] hath disgrac'd me, and hind'red me half a million, laugh'd at my
> losses, mock'd at my gains, scorned my nation, thwarted my bargains, cooled
> my friends, heated mine enemies,—and what's his reason? I am a Jew. Hath not
> a Jew eyes? hath not a Jew hands, organs, dimensions, senses, affections, pas-
> sions? . . . if you wrong us shall we not revenge?—if we are like you in the rest,
> we will resemble you in that. If a Jew wrong a Christian, what is his humility?
> revenge! If a Christian wrong a Jew, what should his sufferance be by Christian
> example?—why revenge! The villainy you teach me I will execute, and it shall
> go hard but I will better the instruction.

> (3.1.48–54, 60–66)

In Shylock's view, revenge is the only means available to him to requite wrongs that have caused him to lose face and fortune, that have fundamentally degraded him. He figures himself as the wounded pupil that not only imitates *but surpasses* the powerful teacher's instruction, turning his learning upon his master to teach *him* a lesson.

Shylock's speech, particularly in its enumeration of body parts (eyes, hands, organs), equivocates on the Old Testament's *lex talionis* (Exod. 21:23–27; Lev. 24:20). The principle underlying the ancient logic of *lex talionis* ("eye for eye," and so forth) asserts the justice of bringing things back to equal through a reciprocal exchange. Yet equivalences can be difficult to weigh and, furthermore, they can be morally suspect, as we see in this play. The equation of a pound of flesh (essentially, a life) with three thousand ducats, the agreed-upon terms in Shylock and Antonio's bond, seems laughable at first, and then outrageous. So, too, does Shylock's desire to see the terms of the bond fulfilled in court where he intends to carve the pound of flesh from Antonio's body before an audience of Venetians. Shylock has sought more than a strict eye-for-eye reciprocity: he feels that nothing short of Antonio's life will repay the steep losses he has sustained —those of his daughter, his ducats, and his reputation. Even in revenge the moneylender Shylock practices usury, demanding more of Antonio than Antonio has taken from him.[2]

Presumably the *"extreame crueltie of* Shylocke" drew crowds to the Elizabethan playhouses, as the 1600 quarto's title page implies: *The most excellent Historie of the 'Merchant of Venice'. With the extreame crueltie of* Shylocke *the Iewe towards the sayd Merchant, in cutting a iust pound of his flesh: and the obtaining of* Portia *by the choyse of three chests.* From its earliest days in performance, Shylock has threatened to overshadow the play, which was listed revealingly in 1598 in the Stationers' Register as "a book of the Marchaunt of Venyce or otherwise called the Iewe of Venyce." Shylock's revenge is surely one of the most gripping and controversial plots in Shakespeare's comedies, absorbing the attention of most of the play's critics.

Portia's participation in the revenge dynamics of the play has received comparatively little attention. Yet her role is crucial to any interpretation of the play, not because she counters the principle of revenge, but rather because she practices a more skilled and multidimensional game of revenge than Shylock can imagine. Like Shylock, Portia is a creditor that can demand more return on a loan or a gift than the debtor bargained for, and she, too, has a pedagogic bent.[3] Shakespeare's more discreet use of revenge in Portia's hands allows for a fuller examination of the ethics of revenge than we get if our focus is trained exclusively on Shylock. While the "quality of mercy" (4.1.180) is directly invoked by Portia, the more problematic quality under examination in the play is that of revenge. What is the "quality of revenge"? Can there be an excellence or virtue in revenge, as one meaning of *quality* assumes?[4] Do revenge and justice belong to the same sphere, as virtue ethicists allow? Or is revenge in this play the passion and action of a true villain . . . and villainess? What does vengeance bring into the open that has been suppressed in the exchanges between men, and between men and women? Who is owed what and how much repayment will suffice?

I will argue that through the interactions of Portia's character with the vengeance-seeking Jew and the venturing Venetians, Shakespeare reveals multivalent qualities in revenge: its various styles, its capacity to exceed or contain its own limits in helping the avenger to attain a goal, and its function as a measure or standard through which values and behaviors can be illuminated.[5] To gauge the "quality of revenge" in *The Merchant,* I will explore the economic metaphors that govern social exchanges, the multivalent meanings suggested by Portia's name, and the mythological underpinnings of her character that lend it a quasi-heroic dimension.

Portia lies at the center of this comedy of revenge and both of its bond plots—the friendship/flesh bond and the romance/ring bond. In each of the plots, she works out problems of reciprocity and debt for herself and the men of Venice. She uses revenge as a pedagogic tool in both the public and private spheres, negotiating a balance between destructive and constructive ends. Indeed, one might say that Portia pursues and masters revenge, bettering the instruction of all the male characters. She robs Shylock of his day in court and renders her new husband, Bassanio, and his "bosom lover" (3.4.17), Antonio, in her debt: it is to Portia ultimately that these Venetian men "stand indebted over and above / In love and service . . . evermore" (4.1.409–10). As Marilyn L. Williamson has pointed out, Portia is Shakespeare's "most formidable" comic heroine, "intelligent, witty, and capable of dealing with complex legal and, apparently, mercantile questions." She "proves a match" for the men and stands "in control of the action in the Venetian court and in the return to Belmont."[6]

In her disguise as Balthazar, Portia steps into debtor's court to interpret the law and free Antonio. In doing this, she meets Shylock's demands for justice with a reciprocating and interest-bearing justice: "Thou shalt have justice *more* than thou desir'st" (4.1.312, my emphasis). Portia makes an appeal to the ethical ideal of mercy, which would have granted Shylock the moral upper hand in his vengeance-driven suit. Yet he rejects mercy, for he wants "law" and strict justice. Portia then proceeds to execute a form of hard justice that might rightly be called vengeance. Her actions and language call to mind Shylock's earlier revenge speech, reflecting the same drive to teach a lesson and overtax the principle of symmetry.

In her role as wife, Portia avenges the broken faith shown by Bassanio when he gives away her ring. Portia's gift of the ring to Bassanio marks their union as a sacred bond, but one that comes with risks and conditions.

She "give[s] and hazard[s] all [s]he hath" in marriage (2.7.9), but with the ring come new hazards for him. If it is lost or given away, she rather ominously insists, "Let it presage the ruin of your love, / And be my vantage to exclaim on you" (3.2.173–74). While Antonio's and Shylock's lives lie in Portia's balance at the Venetian court, Bassanio's life is at stake in Belmont, for Portia's conversion of her money, estate, and love to him are now what sustain him. When he forfeits the sole term of their bond—he gives the ring to Balthazar as repayment for saving his dear friend's life—Portia gains the advantage in their marriage. It is an advantage gained, sadly, through diminished trust, and Portia must follow through on her threat to "exclaim on" Bassanio. She makes Bassanio believe for a few painful, but crucial, moments that he has been cuckolded, that she has slept with Balthazar, the new keeper of the ring. In his momentary shame and in the belief that his new marriage is in ruins, Portia makes Bassanio feel the same disappointment and humiliation, the pain of broken faith and misplaced trust, that she feels. In the symmetry of passions lies the pedagogic force and hope of revenge—that empathy and perhaps a bit of fear have been aroused. When she discloses her "device" to him, she releases him from the shame of cuckoldry, but she has her young husband at her advantage. He has felt the sting of betrayal and knows experientially what it is to be betrayed. Their joyful union and the satisfaction to be gained through hearing Portia's tale at the comedy's end does not necessarily imply a total forgiveness of moral debt. Portia may forgive Bassanio's failure to keep the ring, and she may credit him again with her trust, but Bassanio's moral failure—and, we must add, his economic dependence on Portia—leave him in the vulnerable position of lifelong debt to a resourceful, clever wife.

LOVING UPON ADVANTAGE

Much significance can be found in Portia's insistence on a "vantage to exclaim on" Bassanio (3.2.174). When she puts her ring upon his finger, she makes clear the terms of their bond: she retains the right to chastise him for breach of contract, as it were, and he must guard the ring with his life, for all of his debts and his newfound love seem crowded within this little gold circle. The linguistic and acoustical relationship between the words *vantage* and *advantage* are telling, especially in the echo of Shylock's phrase for usury or interest, lending or borrowing "Upon advantage" (1.3.65). The *Oxford English Dictionary* defines *vantage* as "Advantage, benefit, profit, gain"; "An additional amount or sum"; "Advantage or superiority in a contest; position or opportunity likely to give superiority"; "opportunity, a chance."[7] Midway through the play, Portia is already making good on her *vantage,* transforming her newly gained position as wife into an advantageous one. In both bond plots, she establishes her superiority through wit, which gives her the resources she needs to protect her financial and emotional interests, and turn opportunities into gains. As Natasha Korda argues, Portia is canny about how to establish credit and how to lend "Upon advantage" in the immaterial sense.[8] In negotiating and respecting strict conditions in bonds, Portia establishes her *vantage* and thereby defines her character's function in the play.

The term *vantage* also suggests a viewing place from which a perspective forms. In the Renaissance art of perspective, a vantage point is the viewer's fixed position from which a rational construction of vision is made possible. Portia's assertion of her vantage offers a wise feminine viewing point from which the audience can put into perspective the exchanges of men—their bonds, business dealings, affections, and revenges. Portia's vantage lies at the ground of the comedy, for not only does her perspective give ethical shape to the action of the play, but her awareness of the limitations and the contingencies of any given vantage point infuses the comic world with pathos. In act 5, Portia's meditation on "the greater glory" that "dim[s] the less," on the "substitute" that empties itself next to the real thing, and on how "Nothing is good . . . without respect" assumes her awareness of a higher reality where the economic business of matter and spirit does not mire love in the "muddy vesture" of debt and revenge (5.1.93, 93, 94, 99, 64). Such a prospect, imagined from the eye of God, it would seem, unsettles all human vision. Portia recognizes the limitations of the human vantage point, of her vantage point, for nothing is "good"—trustworthy, creditworthy—in Venice and Belmont but in relation to its circumstances.

Portia's wisdom grants her an advantage of a spiritual kind, which does much to establish her credit with her male peers, and with the play's audience. She is the play's only successful creditor, a character rich enough in money and love to secure her advantage, to take on the debt of others, to redeem lives, and to benefit from, but not exploit, the debts others owe her. The central characters, Shylock, Antonio, and Bassanio, recognize that she has them on the hip, to echo the wrestling metaphor used by Shylock and Gratiano, and derived scripturally from Jacob's wrestling with the angel. She is, surprisingly, the most skillful player in the mercantile world, and her skills are particularly attuned to using the *talionic* principle to achieve a just end in law and in marriage. She metes out a strict justice for Shylock's unyielding justice; and, as for Bassiano, his forfeit of her ring is repaid by her playful forfeiture of her chastity: "pardon me Bassanio, / For by this ring the doctor lay with me" (5.1.258–59). As William Ian Miller notes, "Nowhere does Portia ever reject the idea of talionic equivalence. She insists on it to a T."[9] Her understanding of *talionic* equivalence informs her attitude toward law and her strategies for gaining advantage. Portia is a formidable match to all male parties, both in the public arena of the Venetian court and the private sphere of her Belmont estate. Neither Shylock nor Antonio, much less Bassanio, can meet her wit, subtlety, and cunning, which are peerless in the comedy.

Rather than attacking or dismantling the premises of revenge, she transmutes revenge into a subtle tactic. Like Shylock, Portia resorts to revenge as a stance against the degrading or devaluing of human worth. If the play opens with Antonio's mysterious sadness, it closes with an even more disquieting sadness, for Portia's actions show us that ultimately there is no getting free of the bonds of exchange: gifts can no more be freely given than freely accepted, and no smart woman would give all without setting up the conditions of such a gift, in effect turning the gift into a loan that can be rendered forfeit.[10] Portia's secret resources lie in spiritual usury and "mercifixion," to use Harry Berger Jr.'s coinage, by which he means a show of mercy that wounds where it bestows charity.[11] Through Portia, Shakespeare shows how love becomes a problem rather than a solution in the fallen world of materialism, and that love comes "dear bought" (3.2.312) despite one's finer spiritual or romantic aspirations. Like Antonio, Portia faces this reality head-on, but she is better equipped than he to deal with reality. The Pauline resonance in Portia's "dear bought" gets at the troubling bind she is in, yet also points to her awareness of marriage as both material *and* spiritual. St. Paul tells the Corinthians, "For ye are boght for a price: therefore glorifie God in your bodie, and in your spirit: for they are Gods" (1 Cor. 6:20). Portia's awareness of the spiritual claims of love undergirds her seemingly crass economic language, making clear that Love is the elusive Other to which she aspires.

Thus, in *The Merchant* debt and revenge bind characters together: both are structures of obligation involving two parties in a relationship with a strict sense of what is due, or what is deserved, to echo the silver casket ("Who chooseth me, shall have as much as he deserves"). At root, revenge is an urgent demand for a moral debt to be repaid, and in that repayment there is a sense of justice at work. Shylock's insistence upon his pound of flesh takes on this urgency, as well as a pedagogic function. The creditor-avenger will *teach* the debtor to understand the nature of his debt, and why he is deserving of the avenger's aggression—why the debtor must pay with his flesh and blood, with his life, for example, rather than by a more benign form of repayment, like money with interest, a formal apology, or a bestowal of gifts. Only the strictest terms of foreclosure will satisfy the debt. As Linda Woodbridge argues, "In a world where revenge is a shadow system of debt, this play offers the quintessential form of revenge: foreclosure."[12] What plays out in the trial scene is a subtle, strange form of doubling with Shylock and Portia both standing for law, insisting upon foreclosure. Yet just as tensions reach their most severe point, Portia turns upon Shylock, refuses to allow him to collect monetary repayment of his loan, shames him, and throws him upon the mercy of the Duke and Antonio. The end effect of the trial scene is that Portia puts Shylock in an abject position, and he loses much of his life and living. With the loss of his legal advantage as creditor, he must concede Portia's advantage. She, the Duke, and Antonio follow the logic of the silver casket, giving Shylock what they think he deserves. They make him pay in every conceivable manner, except with blood.

The trial scene brings to an explosive conclusion a plot fueled by mutual hatred and moral debt, yet *The Merchant of Venice* investigates the nature of debt in mutually loving relationships, as well. Indeed, the play's first scene impresses upon us how tightly interlaced love and debt are. The seeds for Bassanio's marital difficulties and Portia's ethical challenges are planted firmly in this scene where we see the charming profligate Bassanio approach his friend, the prominent royal merchant Antonio, to ask for yet another loan, this time to woo Portia, the rich heiress in Belmont. He confesses, "to you Antonio / I owe the most in money and in love, / And from your love I have a warranty / To unburthen all my plots and purposes / How to get clear of all the debts I owe" (1.1.130–34). What the aristocrat Bassanio faces is the difficult, even embarrassing, prospect of ever-mounting debt, and marriage to the wealthy Portia seems his best chance at repaying that debt. His courtship, then, is a "plot" with a seemingly ethical purpose—an honorable man repays his debts and repairs his "disabled . . . estate" (1.1.123)—yet his intention to be clear of *all* debt is mere fantasy in the early modern economy Shakespeare lived in and depicted so vividly. In late sixteenth-century Venice and Belmont, all human interactions are defined according to economic principles of ongoing exchange: borrowing and lending, crediting and profiting, hazarding and forfeiting.[13]

Bassanio's declaration that he owes Antonio not only money but *love* presents us with the true stakes here, the reality of *emotional* debt, which in its immateriality remains incalculable and perhaps always in excess of complete reciprocity. Antonio willingly overextends his credit—he "rack[s]" it, or tortures it, to the "uttermost" (1.1.181)—by allowing himself to be bound to the "usurer" Shylock as surety in a loan for Bassanio. This desperate bond he forges with his enemy betrays the lengths Antonio will go not necessarily to see his friend well married, but to keep Bassanio perpetually indebted to him. Here lies the dark seat of Antonio's generosity, a seeming virtue that fails to meet a high ethical standard. He does not truly benefit Bassanio, for such excessive loans do not help instill the virtues of self-control or fiscal responsibility in his friend. Rather than curbing Bassanio's profligacy, the merchant is willing to risk his own livelihood, reputation, and even his life to continue lending to his friend and to reap what emotional benefits come from such profligate lending. Antonio impresses upon Bassanio that he has "unlocked" his purse, person, and "extremest means" (1.1.139, 138) to his friend. Such extravagance—his loaning and giving all and then some—implicitly binds Bassanio to him, ensuring strong feelings of gratitude, guilt, and, Antonio can only hope, love. For even if Bassanio is able to use Portia's riches to discharge all financial debt, the less-tangible moral and emotional obligations to his friend will remain.

The emotionally charged dialogue between Antonio and Bassanio prepares audiences for an exploration of how obligations of financial, spiritual, and emotional kinds merge, complicating, if not making impossible in the play's world, the endeavor "to get clear of all the debts [one] owe[s]." Financially speaking, clearing material debts for many people living in early modern Europe was nearly impossible, for the economy ran largely on credit rather than cash. Craig Muldrew's study of the culture of credit and social relations in early modern England demonstrates how the "market was not only a structure through which people exchanged material goods, but was also a way in which social trust was communicated. . . . Such trust was interpersonal and underpinned by emotional relations between individuals communicated in the form of reputation."[14] Credit operated as the currency of reputation, and risk in financial matters (rather than usury, which guaranteed profit) gained men moral credit. Conceiving personal relationships in economic terms of debt and credit reflected the everyday financial realities of material existence, of marriage negotiation, and other social exchanges, but it also reflected the social ethic of trust between parties, and individuals' or families' reputations.[15]

Economic metaphors were central, too, to the mind-set of the medieval church and to the language of early English literature. We need think only of the pervasive commercial language of Chaucer's *Canterbury Tales* (for example, the Wife of Bath's insistence on the marriage "debt") to recall the truth of this. The mercantile language of *The Merchant of Venice* is especially attuned to nuances in relationships; the play's vocabulary of obligations and transactions is radically woven into its linguistic texture, as Ralph Berry, Lars Engle, and others have noticed. Even when characters express their affection and love for one another, they resort to talk of riches, of buying and venturing, indebtedness and credit. Their talk reflects a mind-set unmistakably marked by an ethic that aligns social worth and trust with credit. The characters' economic rhetoric insists that we see Venice and Belmont as sites of giving and receiving, loaning and forfeiting, hazarding and losing, satisfying and accruing debt.[16]

Certainly on the Rialto and in business transactions, being creditworthy defined the value of a man. Shylock understands Antonio to be a "good" man; he is a trustworthy borrower and creditor. His reputation is sound. The "good" man Antonio passionately decries the practice of usury, reviling Shylock publicly for his practice. This economic practice of making money from money, of taking advantage of and from a debtor, is brought up as an issue in the play in seeming juxtaposition with Antonio's interest-free loans to Bassanio. When Shylock recognizes that Antonio does not lend or borrow "Upon advantage" (1.3.65), he uses the suggestive early modern term *advantage,* which means interest on a loan.[17] The play's rich economic rhetoric suggests that moral and emotional undercurrents run through all human exchanges. Indeed, the play seems most concerned with the pressures exerted by credit and debt. Since emotional debts are incalculable, extremely difficult to satisfy, and exacerbated by financial debt, creditors implicitly take interest upon their loans through receipt of emotional dues. The play explores the nature of debts that accrue in moral and emotional terms, debts that demand satisfaction that no amount of money could buy. Thus, Antonio's moral debt to Shylock, Bassanio's debt of love to Antonio, Bassanio's marital debt to Portia, and Antonio's debt of life and living to Portia all involve intricate negotiations "Upon advantage."

How, then, are debts of the intangible kind ever to be satisfied? How exactly does one repay debts of love from a friend, or the extravagant gifts of a rich wife? The financial situation of debt, forfeit, and penalty is analogous to the ethical situation of revenge in which moral debts accrue and demand repayment.[18] The debtor lies at the mercy of the creditor. Creditors in this play have emotional needs and moral requirements, which they try to fulfill through means that bind their debtors to them. Paying what is due may mean paying in blood to satisfy the vengeful heart of the creditor. Paying what is due may involve suffering humiliation. Economic metaphors for revenge reach back to the mind-set of *talionic* cultures where revenge was an integral aspect of justice, valuation, and the economy of bodies, goods, and moneys. As a cultural practice, revenge is a model of exchange that binds individuals, households, and communities in reciprocal relationships. Revenge is a reckoning, a calling to account for an outstanding balance. The avenger claims what is due, often "upon advantage." Revenge is an act of reciprocity, giving back as good as one gets, with the goal of bringing things back to even. To bring things back to even, however, is as much a fantasy as clearing all debt, for in the moral calculus of love and enmity, how does one measure precisely the weight of those balances?

If credit, loans, debts, and bonds are established from the start of *The Merchant* as means by which love and hate thrive, gift-giving, too, is deeply implicated in the Venetian and Belmontian structures of exchange. We might think of Marcel Mauss's observations of gift-exchange in archaic societies, and how the gift creates mutual obligations and interests between donor and recipient.[19] As with loans or the extending of credit, gifts demand reciprocity as well. Like the gift-giving of Pacific coast chiefs or the Big Man of Highland Papua New Guinea, Antonio maintains power and prestige by giving more than can be repaid. Furthermore, he is willing to destroy his own life to give the appearance that he wishes nothing in return from Bassanio, that all debts are rendered gifts in need of no repayment.[20] This kind of debt-incursion might be called mental usury, a concept drawn from Scholastic theology, which referred to the often unspoken expectation of material or immaterial gain on a loan.[21] Antonio surely expects intangible returns such as gratitude and continued intimacy from Bassanio.

Antonio is not the play's only mental usurer, for *The Merchant of Venice* is equally concerned with how its female protagonist manages her credit and gives with the expectation of return. Portia, too, gives gifts for which she can never be repaid in full. In this respect, she is Antonio's feminine counterpart and competitor in love, credit, and debt-making. In effect, she also gives and lends "Upon advantage" (1.3.65).[22] By the play's end, Bassanio finds himself in debt not only to Antonio, but to Portia as well, now owing *her* the most "in money and in love" (1.1.131). Although we are more accustomed to viewing Portia as a generous female who gives gifts *unconditionally,* the text suggests a rather different view of her character, for she employs a precise language of accounting and fiscal credit in negotiating her marital bond, treating it as an "oath of credit" (5.1.246), and maneuvers both Bassanio and Antonio into a position of perpetual indebtedness to her. Her mental usury, or "negative usury," as Harry Berger Jr. calls it, inspires emotional and moral obligations, with financial obligations never far from the picture.[23] Seen from an anthropological perspective, Portia's usury reflects her aspiration to be the Big Man in her culture's terms and, as Karen Newman argues, in achieving this status with gifts that cannot be reciprocated fully, she successfully "short-circuits the system of exchange and the male bonds it creates, winning her husband away from the arms of Antonio."[24]

Indeed, Portia *masters* the male forms of exchange in her culture, for she can do what Antonio and Shylock do—make bonds, instill a sense of obligation, extend credit—but she *betters* the instruction she implicitly receives from men. As Lars Engle states, "[M]ore than any other Shakespearean play, *The Merchant of Venice* shows a woman triumphing over men and male systems of exchange: the male homosocial desire of Antonio is almost as thoroughly thwarted in the play as Shylock's vengefulness."[25] As wife, she appears to give all to Bassanio, in accordance with the common law of *femme couvert:* "Myself, and what is mine, to you and yours / Is now converted" (3.2.166–67). Yet she effectively renders these gifts as loans when she maintains control of her finances and the management of her household and, furthermore, when she gives her ring with its attendant symbolism and conditions to Bassanio.[26] As Mauss observed in his study of the gift, there are "mechanisms of obligation which are resident in the gifts themselves."[27] Portia articulates the consequences of Bassanio's failure to meet his obligations to her, a failure symbolized in his giving away of that all-important gift, the ring. When Antonio fervently swears that he and Bassanio "stand indebted over and above / In love and service to you evermore" (4.1.409–10) to Balthazar/Portia, he directs his friend to give Portia's ring as repayment for the service of the doctor of laws. When Bassanio complies, Antonio ironically has set the stage for Portia's renegotiation of his bond of friendship with Bassanio on *her* terms.

In male guise, Portia's prestige and power become manifest in terms her culture can recognize and legitimate. Her gender exchange enables her to take the role of an exacting minister of justice in a social arena larger than her own, yet related to it through a network of financial and emotional bonds. As "doctor," she achieves the position of teacher; her work in Venice aims at educating her audience. She achieves a stunning victory in debtor's court, doing a great deed for her husband and his friend, and displaying to all of Venice the price to be paid when a man does not forgive a debt whose terms will destroy a life. She is able to retain her social and moral advantage when she steps out of her disguise, for her achievement in court as a doctor of laws must be acknowledged later by Antonio and Bassanio and is of a piece with her ethical practice as a wife and household governor. She reflects the shrewd intelligence of those early modern English wives who sought to wage law to maintain financial independence from their husbands. Historical evidence shows that rulings from the Chancery favored women in their attempts to protect their financial interests from husbands, so such a practice would have seemed familiar to Shakespeare and his audience.[28] While Antonio staked his claim in Bassanio through insurmountable debt, sacrifice, and loss, Portia stakes her claim in Bassanio through a mastery of the conditions of obligation. Her gift-giving and extension of credit come with conditions that are realistic and ethical; failure to reciprocate and forfeiting a bond are met with imaginative responses designed to inspire moral reflection and changed behavior.

Her mastery depends to some extent on the security of her riches and property, but more so on her keen understanding of where her challenges lie and how to meet them with intelligence and an exacting shrewdness. The comic riches invested in her character—wit, articulate speech, self-awareness, and disguise—allow Portia to give ethical shape to her own fate and the play's action. Furthermore, such reserves allow her to profit from the economic conditions of her culture. Portia's actions and reflections bring into play the ethical challenges of a woman determined to maintain credit and advantage in the early modern world. Her ultimate challenge in the comedy lies in making a good marriage, one that does not rob her coffers or devalue her spiritual or wifely worth. To do this, Portia must work around the law of *femme couvert,* which she herself expresses in lines such as "if mine then yours, / And so all yours" (3.2.17–18), to find an advantageous position in the marriage. The groundwork for establishing her "vantage" needs to be laid, and this proves complex work in human terms because of the kinds of debt Bassanio brings with him, his sense of masculine honor, which he places above honoring his wife, and the questionable nature of his credit. How Portia stands in relation to men's debts and creditworthiness, how she seizes and establishes her "vantage," defines her ethical position as a woman in the men's world of bonds, a world that would seem to exclude women as agents in their own interest.[29]

Portia's ethical position requires a keen sense not only of how to manage and increase her credit, but how to pay back those who default on their loans. Her strategizing with loan defaults brings us to the realm of revenge. In both plots, Portia first pleads for altering the values of masculine exchange: to Shylock, she holds up the prospect of mercy, or forgiving debt, instead of vengeance, and to the grateful Antonio and Bassanio, she refuses the ring, claiming their debt is "well paid," as she is "well satisfied" in "delivering" Antonio (4.1.411, 412). In other words, saving a man's life is reward in itself. None of the men accept her terms. When they insist upon pursuing their own terms of exchange, Portia must respond to their choices as a moral agent in her own right. She becomes the feminine pedagogue, the master-mistress who teaches lessons in reciprocity. First, in entering the male domain of the Venetian court, she plays a heroic role, countering the terrifying prospect of lawful blood revenge with retributive justice. When Shylock refuses to show mercy, when he refuses to forgive a debt, she shows him the consequences of his stony position. She turns the tables upon Shylock, throwing him upon the mercy of Antonio and the court. He receives little mercy for his no mercy. When Antonio insists that Bassanio give Balthazar/Portia the ring as repayment for their debt, the husband loses credit with his wife, and she has cause to distrust him and "exclaim on" him. When she returns to Belmont, Portia orchestrates her wifely revenge through an imagined cuckoldry: "by this ring the doctor lay with me" (5.1.259). In this manner, she repays his dishonoring and devaluing of their marriage bond. In both cases, Portia's character is defined not by the quality of mercy, but rather by the quality of revenge. Her revenges are, of course, bloodless, and they are designed to provoke moral awareness. But they are not entirely harmless, and in the harm she must do to negotiate the terms of her marriage lies a painful awareness of the costs of love, bound up as love is with the problems of debt and trustworthiness.

In paying close attention to revenge in the play, we must return again to René Girard and his unflinching perspective on the "truth" of *The Merchant of Venice:* no matter how extravagantly characters mask their intentions and actions with the rhetoric of heroism, charity, and mercy, "[t]he truth of the play is revenge and retribution."[30] In Girard's psychoanalytic reading, this truth is a terrible one, acknowledged only by Shylock, the scapegoat created by Christian hatred, who willingly confesses "a lodg'd hate, and a certain loathing" for Antonio (4.1.60) and unapologetically demands his lawful revenge through the flesh bond. The Christians, too, are vengeful, but their revenge is "almost invisible"; it is driven underground, denied, and rhetorically masked as charity, moral righteousness, and mercy.[31] As the alien in Venice, the one who has been notoriously abused and oppressed by members of the dominant culture, Shylock feelingly speaks of Christian hypocrisy and cruelty. When he speaks of revenge, he looks to the Christians to provide justification for such "villainy," for they have "instructed" him in hatred and malicious behavior. Shylock's appeal to the audience's sympathy lies in his abject position. What recourse does he have, he implicitly asks us, to gain back his integrity and professional legitimacy? Where is the Jew to find justice in the community of Christians?

Girard's argument is seductive for post-Holocaust audiences, for it uncovers the lies and psychological violence a dominant culture lives by, and it lends a degree of necessity, if not inevitability, to retaliation. Shylock's sense of self-justification, righteousness, and cruelty are shown to grow out of his ugly dealings with one Christian in particular, the merchant Antonio, from whom he suffers public humiliation and professional setbacks. To continue to lie down and take it or to forgive again and again, as the play's Christians and some critics believe Shylock should do, are not necessarily the best moral responses, and these responses are certainly at odds with a man's desire to defend personal, familial, or communal honor. Girard's view of *The Merchant* emphasizes the scapegoating of Shylock and the discreet ironies that can strip away the audiences' defenses and comfortable illusions. In this respect he joins critics such as Leslie Fiedler, Harold Goddard, and A. D. Moody, whose views unsettle a tradition of liberal humanist and idealist readings of the play.[32]

An ironic *Merchant* seems decidedly modern; such a vision has much to show us post–World War II readers and theatergoers about ourselves—our racism, intolerance, vengefulness, greed, and so on. But it also brings to light the rich ambivalences and subversions at work in Shakespeare's early modern text. The play is so terribly powerful in the theater because, in truth, it does possess unsettling ironies, veiled realities, and irresolvable tensions. Moody is right when he observes how romantic and idealist interpretations of the play are "at odds with the experience it actually offers."[33] Yet how well does Girard's reading of revenge's insidious underground presence work in relation to Portia's character? He conflates Portia with the other Christians, as if there is no discernible difference. Is Portia complicit in a "sad," cruel system "in which even the difference between revenge and charity has been abolished"?[34] Is she an unreflective, implacable revenger, who calls revenge by other names? To address these troubling questions in the sections that follow, we must examine not only cultural values and gender issues, but also the deeper structural, linguistic, and mythological resonances at work in the drama.

Portia's Name

As with Ophelia's name, Shakespeare seems to have chosen Portia's name with a sense of its generative possibilities. Bassanio is first to mention her name, and he associates her with a famous classical namesake: "Her name is Portia, nothing undervalu'd / To Cato's daughter, Brutus' Portia" (1.1.165–66). Traces of the Roman Portia (Porcia in Latin) can be found in Portia's character, urging comparison. Bassanio is quick to arrive at the notion of *value* in his comparison, though his emphasis is made grammatically through the opposing ideas of "nothing" and "undervalu'd," which form a resonant phrase forecasting precisely what is at stake for Shakespeare's Portia. She will need to prove her value in an extravagant, shrewd, and binding manner, which will teach her husband to regard her as his equal, if not better. Shakespeare depicts Brutus's Portia in *Julius Caesar* as a devoted wife who insists to her husband, by his vows of love and "that great vow / Which did incorporate and make us one," "unfold to me, your self, your half, / Why you are heavy" (2.1.271–74). She invokes the "bond of marriage" (line 279) to remind Brutus of his husbandly debt—he owes her his confidence and allegiance, his very self if he regards her truly as a wife (and not merely as a harlot). Shakespeare has the classical Portia claim worth, too, from being the daughter of the honorable, morally strict Cato (Marcus Porcius Cato Uticensis, after whom she is named), who killed himself rather than submit to the rule of Caesar. A more distant Cato in Portia's family wrote against usurers, claiming they were murderers that destroyed their debtors' livings; this Cato rid Sardinia of usurers.[35] Portia's declaration of her rights when Bassanio is "heavy" with Antonio's misfortunes echoes the language and situation of this scene, though Portia's reputation derives largely from her father's riches and the casket lottery rather than from his virtue and ethical action, which only Nerissa seems to remember. The Roman Portia proved her constancy and trustworthiness by wounding herself in the thigh. Belmont's Portia need not resort to self-wounding, for she has other resources, comic resources, available to prove her value and creditworthiness.

Portia's name strongly suggests *portion,* both as an aural pun and, more obscurely, as an echo of the classical Latin *portio* (share, part, proportion). The association with a marriage portion and daughter's inheritance can be seen readily here. The standard cultural practice in early modern Western cultures was for the father to give a dowry, a gift, or settlement to a woman's husband upon marriage, and the groom's father would give a jointure (a widow's allowance) to protect the wife's interests in the future. As Bassanio's father must be dead, Antonio steps in to provide the jointure, which turns out to be no financial arrangement, but rather spiritual surety for Bassanio's oath: "My soul upon the forfeit" (5.1.252). Portia's name, then, has inscribed within it her riches, which are to be paid to her husband as part of her marriage settlement. *Portion* also suggests "the means to relieve debts (of various sorts)," as Lars Engle astutely notes, which is what Portia, like many rich Elizabethan wives, offers to provide for her indebted husband.[36] But we are directed, as well, to contemplate the deeper spiritual reality of Portia herself comprising the marriage portion, or the gift. As the King of France movingly exclaims about the dispossessed Cordelia in *King Lear,* "She is herself a dowry" (1.1.239). Scriptural resonances can be heard in Portia's name: "A verteous woma[n] is a good portio[n] which shalbe giuen for a gift vnto suche as feare the Lord" (Ecclus. 26:3). And "The Lord *is* the porcion of mine inheritance and of my cup: thou shalt mainteine my lot" (Ps. 16:5).

Thus, Portia's name signifies not only the material exchanges involved in marriage negotiations, but the possibility of spiritual exchange as well. Yet the latter form of exchange—the exchange of selves as gifts—is not so easily rendered, for Portia is, in crass material terms, entirely *possessed* of and by her fortune; there is no escaping her riches, her earthly inheritance, which have attracted her suitors, including Bassanio, to her port. Bassanio's first words about Portia tell us precisely why he woos her: "In Belmont is a lady richly left" (1.1.161). We recall his words to Antonio, which reveal that his "chief care" (1.1.127) lies in repaying his debts to his friend. Portia is perceived internationally not as a dowry unto herself, but as a rich heiress who represents the promise of relief from debt to bankrupt aristocrats such as Bassanio. Riches, therefore, constitute Portia's reputation. Her beauty and virtues are secondary attributes, as Bassanio attests: "And she is fair," he adds, "and (fairer than that word), / Of wondrous virtues" (1.1.162–63). Portia's challenge lies in how to establish her reputation based on qualities of character, rather than on her renowned material wealth.

Acoustically present in Portia's name, as well, is the term *port* (Latin, *portus*), which refers to a grand, expensive style of living. The notion of port connects Portia and Bassanio, as does *portion,* for she will be his means to regain his "estate," and to live in the grand style to which he is accustomed. Bassanio claims to have "disabled mine estate, / By something showing a more swelling port / Than my faint means would grant continuance" (1.1.123–25). His lavish "port" has drained his own noble estate and racked up debt with creditors, primarily Antonio. Shakespeare echoes his Italian source *Il Pecorone* (Milan, 1558), in which Gionetto, the suitor of the fair lady of Belmont, returns three times to his lady's port. In Ser Giovanni Fiorentino's tale, the port is dangerous and alluring, the site of masculine loss and the lady's trickery. Belmont's port in Shakespeare's play attracts suitors who risk and lose much, but Bassanio is the fortunate one. He, too, travels three times to the port of Belmont; his second time there wins him the lady, and the third time represents a return to a safe harbor in which the losses of his great friend Antonio are returned. When Portia mysteriously produces a letter that restores Antonio's fortune, she exclaims, "There you shall find three of your argosies / Are richly come to harbour suddenly" (5.1.276–77). It is Portia who seems to restore Antonio's losses; it is her harbor to which he has come to hear of his restoration. A *port* was known as well to be a merchant's settlement.[37] The various meanings of *port* then suggest that for Bassanio and the merchant Antonio, Portia will provide safety and a haven from the risks of their business dealings. But it is here that Antonio will have to pay his "settlement" in the form of surety for Portia and Bassanio's bond.

Since classical antiquity, *portion* could refer to one's lot or fate. This connection, rooted in Portia's name, is expressed through the fairy-tale-like "lott'ry" (1.2.28) established by her "holy" father upon his deathbed. The word *lottery* derives from the Old English *hlot,* which is a rendering of the Latin *portio,* and from the Old Norse *hlaut,* which means "blood of sacrifice." *Lottery* describes "that which is given to a person by fate or divine providence, one's destiny, fortune, or 'portion' in this life."[38] Through these etymological relationships, Portia is defined—she is bound to her father's lottery and bound to the choice of the "right" suitor. Bassanio literally engages in a ritual choosing of lots to win his prize. While lotteries and lots are often associated with chance, Nerissa makes clear that this lottery is of the providential kind: "Your father was ever virtuous, and holy men at their death have good inspirations,—therefore the lott'ry that he hath devised in these three chests of gold, silver, and lead, whereof who chooses his meaning chooses you, will no doubt never be chosen by any rightly, but one who you shall rightly love" (lines 27–32). Right choosing and right loving are linked here and, in Nerissa's mysterious estimation, made possible by a virtuous father's inspiration. This fairy-tale gloss on the caskets conveys the comforting promise that Portia "shall rightly love," yet it succeeds only in mystifying the situation in which Portia finds herself. Portia does indeed love one of her suitors. While that alone should determine the outcome, according to Nerrisa, Portia wisely sets about negotiating the terms of her fate, for Portia has chosen Bassanio as her fate, and she exerts a subtle force through speech and song to help shape the outcome of the lottery.

The notion of Portia as *porta* (gate) is suggestive, subtly invoking the Roman god Janus, guardian of the doorways of houses and city gateways. He was distinguished by his double face, which during the Renaissance was allegorized as a symbol of past and future, or of prudence. At the start of the play, Portia is situated between past and future, facing both directions as it were, and she is trapped indefinitely in the present. In her reflection on wise conduct, she exhibits knowledge of prudence, though her constrained situation hardly calls for any exercise of virtue. The audience encounters a weary Portia, who sighs in her opening line, "my little body is aweary of this great world" (1.2.1–2). Only mockery of her suitors relieves the tedium: "in truth I know it is a sin to be a mocker, but he!" (line 54). Her double face, however, can be seen explicitly embodied when she trades her womanly guise for the doctor of laws disguise. In becoming male, she may take the name Balthazar and be called a second Daniel, but she is fulfilling meanings lodged in her own name—she brings to Venice an interpretation of law that metes out portions. In doing so, she attempts to exemplify prudence, apportioning lots for the future.

In his dictionary published in 1611, John Florio defined *portione* as "a portion, a share, a parcell, a part, a rate, a quantitie, a measure or peece, a partage."[39] The quantitative meanings of *portion* can thus be seen to relate to justice and bonds—the parceling out of shares and quantities, the establishing of measure and rate, the exact meting out of justice. The idea of proportion is implicit here, and certainly appears woven into Portia's name. *Proportion* expresses the fitting or appropriate relationship between things, a relationship of equivalence, balance, symmetry, harmony.[40] In a play of extremes—cruelty and kindness, risk and loss, hatred and love, vengefulness and mercy, sacrifice and self-interest—Portia gives voice to proportion, balance, and exactitude, much as Cordelia does in the opening scene of *King Lear.* Shylock and Antonio are both figures of excess, locked in mortal hatred of one another, driven to extremes by their passions. Bassanio, too, tends toward excess in running up debt and his willingness to sacrifice himself for Antonio. Portia's function is to bring the action to a point of balance. As Ralph Berry has argued, Portia is a "stable center of values, to which the action relates."[41] Portia seeks to restore an equilibrium in each of the play's central relationships, and this equilibrium is justice, as she sees it.

Mythological Resonances and Subtexts

There has been some effort on the part of later twentieth-century directors, actresses, and literary critics to acknowledge the contradictions and ambiguities that define Portia's character—her comic *and* tragic aspects, her graciousness *and* cruelty, her wisdom *and* folly.[42] Often, actresses have been at the mercy of the actor playing Shylock and a director who typically holds Shylock as the play's center of gravity. Actresses such as Deborah Findlay speak of their frustration in trying unsuccessfully to accommodate their interpretations of Portia to their male colleagues' more extreme views.[43] On the one hand, there are many who wish to uphold a traditionally romantic view of her character as a witty, resourceful heroine; even recent literary criticism continues to portray Portia as "the wisest character in the play" whose values are "humility, hazard, and self-sacrifice."[44] On the other

hand, some recent interpretations of Portia have characterized her as cal-
culating, power-hungry, castrating, and vindictive.[45] One reviewer of Bill
Alexander's 1987 RSC production found Deborah Findlay's Portia "as
nasty as she ought to be but so rarely is."[46] Playing Portia as nasty and cruel
may not have been the actress's choice, but clearly the performance struck
a chord with some viewers. An acknowledgment of Portia's moral complexity can help us achieve a more balanced view of character and a deeper
understanding of the play's action and catharsis. She is a character defined
by doubleness and contradiction—male and female, active and passive,
dominant and submissive, doctor of laws and lawfully wedded wife, merciful judge and revenger. Like the other characters, Portia is passionate, and
her passions run high and resonate deeply, yet she does not exhibit a hot
temper or rashness. Portia is not a bored, spoiled heiress transformed into
a supremely confident comic heroine; nor is she the cruel, castrating bitch
of some contemporary productions. In the character, what we find represented is an ethical struggle to make right choices; one might say the casket
lottery confronts Portia with the ground of her being—that right choosing
will matter tremendously to herself and those whose lives she affects.

Portia's character develops over time to show her function in the ethical
dispensation of the drama: from a melancholic virgin prized for her wealth,
she emerges as a shrewd judge who holds the lives of others in the balance,
and then must sustain herself, her husband, his friend, and her household
as a smart wife who insists upon her moral and social worth. Portia's transformations are charted through shifting mythological associations that reflect her growth in agency and competency—from the relative passivity of
Penelope and Hesione to the heroic strength of Hercules and the mysterious powers of Medea. The subtexts that resonate in the comedy show us
how Shakespeare constructs Portia's negotiation with her fate, aligning her
with ancient figures, yet distancing her so as to avert disaster or diminished
integrity.

Submerged sources and allusions come into play from the start, underlying images and rhetoric in the opening three scenes of the play. In visual
terms, these scenes form an intricate Renaissance triptych for the reader's
imagination: to the left, we have the return of the prodigal, a lavishly dressed
young lord appealing to the goodwill of a wealthy merchant-benefactor; to
the right, we see the men again, this time in intense negotiation with the
Jewish moneylender, who appears in his gabardine robe, holding a balance;
in the central panel we see a golden-haired, reclining lady, a Penelope with
suitors overrunning her opulent estate. My description is intended to draw
to the surface mythic residues in the language and situations presented in
the play. Shakespeare's suggestive dramatic structuring of scenes, like my
painterly analogue, gives Portia the central position, which reflects her

function in the drama: she lies in the midst of men's affairs. Yet her riches and golden beauty should not mislead us, as they do the men in the play and critics who focus merely on her exchange value. Indeed, Portia's symbolic function as a "golden fleece" in an exchange between men is rendered of little importance when the moral stakes of the play's central relationships come to light. Portia's value lies in deeper forms of engagement and satisfaction, which come into play when she takes on the moral debts incurred in both the men's scenes of loan negotiations. In time, the men will all wish for satisfaction, but money turns out to be hardly what they are after. Portia will play a significant part in negotiating not the financial, but rather the legal and ethical, terms of these relationships and in bringing satisfaction to all of them. To do this, she will leave Penelope behind to assume the Odyssean role of an adventuring male, who according to his legend faces perils, takes a disguise, and exhibits cunning. I shall return to this point later.

If the first scene of this drama represents the threshold over which we travel to arrive in mercantile Venice, we are presented, not surprisingly, with a figure of the threshold god, Janus: the "merchant of Venice" exudes a mysterious sadness that marks him as so "marvellously chang'd" (1.1.76) that his friend Solanio invokes the "two-headed Janus" to swear by (line 50). The assumption is that Antonio is typically a merry merchant who, of a sudden, has been struck with melancholy: "In sooth I know not why I am so sad, / It wearies me, you say it wearies you," he sighs (lines 1–2). A sense of weariness is conveyed in one of the Elizabethan meanings of sadness: "having had one's fill, satisfied, sated, weary or tired (of something)."[47] This meaning counters the notion of melancholy, which suggests loss or lack. Perhaps both senses apply to Antonio, for he has great wealth and reputation in Venice, yet he is on the verge of losing a great friend to a foreign wife. What is most evident is that he is shaken out of his melancholy or weariness only by the strongest sentiment of love, which comes into play when Antonio meets with Bassanio, and of hatred, when they meet with Shylock.

The second scene opens with a repeated note of sadness, followed by an intimate exchange of wit between women. "By my troth Nerissa, my little body is aweary of this great world" (1.2.1–2), sighs Portia, who like Antonio suffers from a paradoxical mix of surfeit and lack. In their sadness, wealth, and emotional interest in Bassanio, Portia and Antonio strike audiences as doubles. Antonio's sighs give way in his emotionally charged conversation with Bassanio, while Portia's desolation begins to lift with the mention of Bassanio, the "best deserving a fair lady," as Nerissa says, and "worthy of thy [i.e., Nerissa's] praise," as Portia confirms (1.2.113, 114–15). "I remember him well," Portia says, for Bassanio's visit some time ago when her father was living clearly left its impression. She has been faith-

ful to that memory and to the hope that Bassanio will prove himself creditworthy. The source of Portia's desolation is made clear: she is a "living
daughter curb'd by the will of a dead father" (1.2.24–25). Her agency, *her
will,* is held at bay by her father's lottery. Her submission to the lottery reflects Portia's debt to the dead; not until she discharges that debt will she
be free. She may have abundant good fortune, but she is, in a sense, absent
from life, in a state of perpetual waiting and ennui. Furthermore, she is subject to the intrusions of countless suitors who have overrun her household.
In this respect, she resembles the ancient Greek Penelope, plagued by suitors while she waited years for Odysseus's return. Bassanio fulfills the
Odyssean role in his return to Belmont, and in time frees Portia from the
endless intrusion of suitors vying to win her and possess her fortune.

A possible source for this classical resonance may come from Robert
Greene's *Penelope's Web* (1587). In this prose work, Greene celebrates
women's virtues, especially chastity, through his representation of Penelope at the loom. As she weaves to keep her suitors at a distance, she and
her women converse about feminine virtues, marriage, and the "shipwreck
of love" her swarming suitors intend to make (7).[48] They discuss as well
"the proportion of reason" in love (7) and choosing men for their "inward
substance," rather than their outward attractions (8). Penelope tells two stories that demonstrate the hidden powers of chastity, self-restraint, and obedience. Her first story deals with the profaning of the marriage bed and a
rejected wife's obedient patience, which repays her with the gods' revenge:
"Now, Barmenissa," the heroine counsels herself, "thou seest that delay in
revenge is the best physic, that the gods are just and have taken thy quarrel as advocates of thine injury; now shalt thou see wrong overruled with
patience, and the ruin of thine enemy with the safety of thine own honour;
time is the discoverer of mishap, and fortune never ceaseth to stretch her
strings till they crack; shame is the end of treachery, and dishonour ever
fore-runs repentance" (17). In Penelope's story, patience and chastity,
while seemingly passive, require active virtue and self-counseling. "Delay
in revenge" is the virtuous path, for the gods will take up the betrayed
woman's cause. Like the female protagonist of the tale, like Penelope, Portia respects the value of an oath; she is chaste, indisputably, but in time she
will have to weigh the ethics of vengeance, and find her own path for dealing with marital shame and dishonor.

Like Nerissa, Penelope's maid Eubola expounds upon moderation, exclaiming, "extremity is ever a vice, too much in everything is hurtful" (6).
In *The Merchant of Venice* Nerissa says, "You would be [weary] (sweet
madam), if your miseries were in the same abundance as your good fortunes are: and yet for aught I see, they are as sick that surfeit with too much,
as they that starve with nothing" (1.2.3–6). Nerissa suggests that unhappiness lies in excess; to be "seated in the mean," to achieve moderation

("competency"), is to find "no mean happiness" (lines 7, 8–9). Portia registers the difficulty of practicing such wisdom, yet she understands the value of the mean, of measure and moderation, quite well. In material terms, she has "too much," which makes her sick. In spiritual terms, she is perhaps starved, which adds to her sickness. She knows what she should be aiming for—what her function in the comedy will be. Her function, as we have determined, is inscribed in her name: Portia, portion, proportion, apportioning lots. But such a function for Portia will require that she absorb the wisdom of Penelope and then make choices Homer's and Greene's heroines were not equipped to make.

While the ancient Penelope's craft lay in unthreading her tapestry so that she never fulfills her promise to give herself to a suitor, Portia's craft lies in wit, which weaves a thin web of psychological protection about her and gives her the capacity to triumph in her fate. Mysteriously, she seems to have been able to steer a plethora of unworthy suitors away from the correct casket. None of them love her "rightly," nor does she "rightly love" any of them (1.2.32), until Bassanio (her Odysseus) returns, and he is the one she chooses to direct discreetly and virtuously toward right choosing and right loving. When her chosen suitor becomes her husband, he will break his oath to her, and she will change Barmenissa's story: she will take revenge, for she represents justice in her marriage and household, and she must take up her own quarrel.

One of Portia's mock portraits of the suitors anticipates her future engagement with the ethic of revenge and her departure from the passive stances of Penelope and her heroine, Barmenissa. The humiliation of the Scottish lord makes for a colorful, instructive tale: He "hath a neighborly charity in him," Portia exclaims, "for he borrowed a box of the ear of the Englishman, and swore he would pay him again when he was able: I think the Frenchman became his surety, and seal'd under for another" (1.2.75–79). The humiliation of the Scotsman leads to the desire for revenge, which is couched in the language of charity, borrowing, paying back, surety, and sealing bonds, all central to the play's ethos and Portia's function. Portia's words recall Girard's point about how Christian revenge is masked in the rhetoric of charity. Portia seems aware of such self-delusion and finds male behaviors driven by honor and revenge to be ridiculous. In time, she will have to contend with a serious form of revenge and vengeful intentions of her own, for opting out of the vengeance ethic altogether will render Portia at a serious disadvantage in love.

The third scene introduces a far more literal case of charity masking revenge, and it is *Shylock's* supposed charity, rather than Christian charity, on display here. This scene introduces Shylock in negotiation with Bassanio over a bond for a loan. While the three thousand ducats and terms of the bond are highlighted, the emotions fueling the scene are on display, both through rhetoric and performance. Shylock confesses to the audience from the start of the scene his desire to "catch" Antonio "upon the hip" to "feed fat the ancient grudge I bear him" (1.3.41–42). Indeed, once Antonio appears, he cannot resist emphasizing the irony of their situation, for "the shames that you have stain'd me with" (line 135) imply that Antonio is in a hypocritical, even shameful, position, now that he must ask his enemy for money. Antonio has insulted Shylock repeatedly in the Rialto, treating him like a dog, spitting on him, spurning him, and kicking him in contempt. While Antonio claims that such treatment arises from his moral opposition to usury, perceived in Shakespeare's time as theft and lack of charity, Shylock perceives Antonio's behavior as morally intolerable and shameful. A moral debt has accrued, and in the economy of revenge, Antonio owes him. Antonio's unexpected need for a loan from Shylock offers the moneylender a chance for revenge. It is a long shot, as Antonio is a "good" man who should be able to repay the debt in time, but *if* he were to forfeit the loan, Shylock could *force* him to clear his debt on whatever terms Antonio had agreed to. Their bond is legally binding; he makes sure of that. It is not the monetary value of the debt that counts so much as the moral value of a long-standing debt (one Antonio in his righteousness is willfully ignorant of) that must be repaid, with steep interest.

Shylock's language and expressed intent insistently call to mind the values Bassanio and Antonio claim to espouse. He appears to gain the upper hand morally by extending friendship, kindness, and an interest-free loan to Antonio:

> I would be *friends* with you, and have your love,
> *Forget the shames* that you have stain'd me with,
> Supply your present wants, and take *no doit*
> *Of usance* for my moneys, and you'll not hear me,—
> This is *kind* I offer.
>
> (lines 134–38, my emphases)

Is this a sincere desire to renovate their relationship through a loan that is really a gift? One suspects not, yet the exchange is equivocal. Shylock continues with his negotiations, adding, as if an afterthought, a final term: "in a merry sport," he playfully concludes, "let the forfeit / Be nominated for an equal pound / Of your fair flesh" (lines 141, 144–46). Antonio takes the bond with the words "Content in faith" (line 148), and overrules Bassanio's words of protest. Shylock makes clear that the bond will bear no profit (the pound of flesh is not profitable as the flesh of animals is); therefore, his advantage must lie in reaping other kinds of interest. He is "buy[ing] his favour," "extend[ing] this friendship," "And for my love I pray you wrong me not" (1.3.164, 166). Shylock indeed argues for a new kind of reciprocity: favor, friendship, and love for a return of the same. Antonio rejects this offer, making clear that the loan is to be between enemies. Underlying this "kind" talk lies the old animosity between enemies, and the lingering disease created by the entanglement of flesh in a legal bond.

With the money Bassanio receives from this potentially fatal bond, he sails to Portia's port to win his fortune. He comes bearing "Gifts of rich value" (2.9.91), which have been subsidized by the loan, but, the source notwithstanding, his intent is to give and hazard all in this venture. He is to play "Bassanio, Lord Love," as Nerissa calls him (2.9.101), and he is to be most fortunate, as he himself has predicted. The casket scene (3.2) represents an early climax in the play's romantic bond plot, which is bound subliminally to the friendship/flesh bond plot. The passionate conversation between Portia and Bassanio echoes motifs from Bassanio's earlier conversation with Antonio. Here Portia is in Antonio's position, a rich creditor who desires the love of a profligate young lord. Portia, however, though she loves him, dares to question Bassanio's creditworthiness. When Bassanio insists that he "live[s] upon the rack," Portia finds his metaphor troubling: "Upon the rack Bassanio? then confess / What treason there is mingled with your love" (3.2.25, 26–27). The motif of Antonio's credit, "rack'd even to the uttermost" (1.1.181), resurfaces, but Portia has the wisdom to suspect treason or some element of falseness underlying Bassanio's motives. Bassanio's debts of love and money to Antonio have bound him already to another; thus, the indebted Bassanio's expressions of love to Portia are, indeed, mingled with treason. Before he approaches the caskets, Portia asserts, "I am lock'd in one of them,— / If you do love me, you will find me out" (3.2.40–41). The metaphor of locking and unlocking the self comes into play again. We recall that Antonio had proclaimed his generosity as an *unlocking* of purse, person, and means—all for Bassanio's use. Portia reverses the conceit by giving Bassanio the potential to unlock her—that is, free her—by unlocking the correct casket in which she has been locked figuratively since her father's death. In her metaphor lies hope for reciprocity and its necessary condition: "*If* you do love me" (my emphasis).

As Bassanio approaches the caskets to cast his lot, as it were, Portia figures his venturing in light of Hercules' heroic redemption of the virgin Hesione. This allusion to the Ovidian tale taps into major motifs in *The Merchant:* contracts, broken faith, refused reciprocity, blood sacrifice for the indebted, and revenge.[49] That Portia brings such serious motifs into play as Bassanio is about to make his choice reveals her wary stance and her sense of risk and hazard. The Hercules-Hesione tale in Ovid's *Metamorphoses,* book 11, recounts the building of Troy and its imperilment due to broken faith. The tale involves the will and wrath of the gods. Apollo and Neptune have aided King Laomedon in building Troy. Disguised as men, they negotiate a sum of gold in payment from the King for their tremendous service. When Laomedon refuses to pay, swearing oaths that are false, Neptune cries, "Thou shalt not mock us unrevendgd" (Golding's translation, 11.231). Neptune floods Troy and demands as "pennance for the falsehod" (line 236) the sacrifice of Hesione, the King's daughter, to the sea monster. Hercules appears on the scene to take on the redemption of the virgin. He saves her from the beast, with his reward in mind. When Laomedon refuses to pay the hero "of so great desert" (line 240), Hercules takes his revenge and sacks Troy. Hesione becomes the wife of Telamon, King of Salamis, who is rewarded with the lady for "honour of his service" (line 242). This tale depicts the realm of epic warfare, heroic exploits, masculine adventure, and feminine sacrifice. Portia's invoking of this ancient tale binds together the risks of romantic love with the heroic actions of Hercules, yet her recounting of the tale's distinctive violence done to the helpless Hesione and to the city of Troy, and the threat of broken faith exhibited by the father, betrays her uneasiness with her own father's contract and Bassanio's venture.

"Now he goes," Portia proclaims,

> With no less presence, but with much more love
> Than young Alcides, when he did redeem
> The virgin tribute, paid by howling Troy
> To the sea-monster: I stand for sacrifice,
> The rest aloof are the Dardanian wives,
> With bleared visages come forth to view
> The issue of th'exploit: go Hercules!
> Live thou, I live—with much much more dismay,
> I view the fight, than thou that mak'st the fray.
>
> (3.2.53–62)

The transmutation of Ovid's figurative language is revelatory: "presence," "love," "redeem," "tribute," "paid," "stand for sacrifice," "exploit," "fight," and "fray" help to rework Ovid's tale, imaginatively deepening the mercantile and heroic motifs. The images of "howling Troy" and the "bleared visages" of the Trojan wives are not in the source, yielding the scene from Portia's perspective. What she sees is the catastrophe of the situation and the grief of women, who appear to be the only audience weeping before the tragic scene. That they are wives is a clue to Portia's thinking: these women, further along in their life cycles than Hesione, bear witness to the unnaturalness of the sacrifice, to the virgin girl waiting to be devoured by a monster due to her father's false oaths and reneging of a bargain made with the gods. While Portia's father has been represented as holy by Nerissa, his will nonetheless robs his daughter of her own—she is a sacrifice to the lottery he has established. Portia's identification with Hesione suggests that she is as bound to the caskets as Hesione is to the rock.

Portia's cheering for Hercules/Bassanio wills into existence the heroic strain in Ovid's tale, yet colors it with fervent, romantic desire. Like Hercules, Bassanio must redeem the virgin, but with a significant difference. It is in the dialectical play between source and allusion that Shakespeare's drama takes place. Portia is insistent on "much more love," signaling her awareness that love was not a motive at all for Hercules. The ancient hero bargained for his "hyre," and desired Laodemon's horses, not his daughter. Portia herself is to be the prize won in the casket lottery, which means that her challenge, as she understands it, is to revise the source text to suit her own story. The line linking Bassanio's life to hers ("Live thou, I live") evidences another important revision, reminding us that Bassanio's choice is an ethical one that carries consequences. She figures it as a fatal choice of life or death. More dire than the penalty in *Il Pecorone* (loss of riches), wrong choice for Portia's suitors results in loss of future happiness and a legacy—no Portia, no wife, no lawful children, no lineage. This is a figurative death, and Portia, too, will suffer a figurative death if she loses the only suitor she loves.

It is no small irony that Bassanio's speech rejects the heroic mode in favor of a meditation on outward shows that "entrap the wisest" (3.2.101). "The beards of Hercules and frowning Mars" are exposed as masks for the cowardly heart; "snaky golden locks," a "dowry" for a skull; and gold, the "hard food" of Midas (lines 85, 92, 95, 102). These thoughts seem to reflect tremendous moral growth in Bassanio, for not long ago he had confessed to Antonio that he was seeking Portia's gold, her dowry, to repay his debts. "[H]er sunny locks / Hang on her temples like a golden fleece," he exclaimed, and he felt certain that he would be the "fortunate" Jason in his "quest" (1.1.169–70, 176, 172). His newfound wisdom, however, distinctly echoes the moral sentiments he received from Portia herself. Her language, which emphasized the values of the lead casket, has subtly schooled him in right thinking in order to prepare for his right choosing; thus, without being forsworn, or violating the letter of her father's law, this Hesione has conveyed the wisdom her Hercules needs to undergo his ordeal.[50] Her tremendous emotional response upon his correct choosing demonstrates that real risk was involved: "O love be moderate, allay thy extasy, / In measure rain thy joy, scant this excess! / I feel too much thy blessing, make it less / For fear I surfeit" (3.2.111–14). Bassanio might not have been swayed by the subtle instruction Portia gave him, and therefore might have lost her forever. Portia's emphasis on moderation and measure—on a proportionate relationship between feeling and reason—prepares her for the important task she then faces in negotiating the terms of her marriage. She cannot afford to be overwhelmed by the ecstasy of love.

Indeed, Portia is ready for Bassanio when he turns to her to say, "doubtful whether what I see be true, / Until confirm'd, sign'd, ratified by you" (lines 147–48). That he renders back to her the right to choose him as husband rather than assert his claim bespeaks his potential worthiness. Her speech possesses touches of modesty, yet with its accounting rhetoric ("account," "sum," "gross") it conveys an awareness of the stakes in the marital bond. Her wish "to stand high" in Bassanio's "account" means that she will "in virtues, beauties, livings, friends" have to "Exceed account" (lines 155–57). The "full sum" of Portia is yet to be disclosed. Bassanio has credited Portia with riches, beauty, and virtue, in that order, but now Portia is schooling him again in the necessity to look more deeply than her worldly reputation. Portia's concern lies in Bassanio's creditworthiness, for he has only begun to establish credit with her. Where her new husband stands in Portia's account is yet to be determined.

When she gives "all" to Bassanio, as the early modern wife must to her "lord" under the laws of *femme couvert,* Portia makes clear that *she* has been "lord / Of this fair mansion, master of my servants, / Queen o'er myself" (lines 167–69). In conveying her powers to Bassanio, she skillfully renders the gift conditional.[51] Those powers come with the ring she gives him, and this ring has mysterious powers, for Bassanio's fortune (material and spiritual) rides on that ring: "when you part from, lose, or give away, / Let it presage the ruin of your love, / And be my vantage to exclaim on you" (lines 171–73). Loss of the ring means ruin, and Bassanio understands the terms, for he echoes them back to Portia: "but when this ring / Parts from this finger, then parts life from hence,— / O then be bold to say Bassanio's dead!" (lines 183–85). As one critic asserts, this is Portia's means "to establish Bassanio's trustworthiness, in order to 'credit' him with honor in their marriage."[52] She, rather than Bassanio, is the source of credit in their marriage, and she will choose to bestow credit upon him not once, but twice, in order to make the marriage fast.

Portia's second trial with Bassanio presents itself hard upon the heels of their oath-taking and complicates the matter of credit. If Portia's giving of her ring marks the beginning of their marital negotiations and nuptial rites, such rites are interrupted. The intrusion of bad news from Venice—"Some dear friend dead," as Portia intuits with almost uncanny exactness—prompts a confession from Bassanio: "I have engag'd myself to a dear friend, / Engag'd my friend to his mere enemy / To feed my means" (lines 244, 260–62). This chain of "engagements" bodes catastrophe, with Bassanio's fault shining bleakly in the greater light of his newest engagement. Antonio's ventures have been dashed upon the "merchant-marring rocks" (3.2.270), and his letter reveals that his loan from Shylock is forfeit. He wishes to clear "*Sweet Bassanio*" from debt, and wishes only that he "*might but see*" his dear friend "*at my death*" (lines 314, 318). He attaches a condition to Bassanio's freedom, then, which is designed to show his friend the ultimate sacrifice of love—Antonio will die for love of Bassanio. To show the utter magnanimity of his position, Antonio appears to release Bassanio even from that one condition: "[I]f your love do not persuade you to come, let not my letter" (lines 319–20). Yet such a despairing gesture could only inspire an answering guilt and urgency in Bassanio to see his friend, to show great love in return. The emotional tenor of the letter is in fact communicated to exact reciprocity, for the very abject position Antonio adopts implicitly lays a burden of gratitude and love upon Bassanio. The moral and emotional stakes here are high, and Bassanio's worth and his reputation depend on how he responds to the man who tortured his credit for him, and will now, it appears, lose his life for him.

Portia must handle this unexpected situation with ingenuity and delicacy, for she is suddenly faced with the prospect of a husband who has a prior obligation not only of a steep financial kind, but even more importantly, a profound emotional kind. Indeed, both financial and emotional debts bind Bassanio morally to Antonio. Portia wisely understands that the debt to his friend now overwhelms the debt he owes to his soon-to-be wife. When Bassanio at first reads the letter from Antonio silently, she insists, "I am half yourself, / And I must freely have the half of anything / That this same paper brings you" (lines 247–49). As something of a paradox, she asserts her right to demand that her husband give freely to her half of what is his. The Pauline concept of "due benevolence" or conjugal debt (1 Cor. 7:1–5) underlies this exchange, even though the issue is not explicitly that of sexual debt in marriage. Portia instructs Bassanio in the fuller implications of due benevolence: he cannot withhold himself; he must give Portia what is hers by right. This is not only the right over his body, but over his business affairs and troubles, as well. The contents of the "paper" bring Portia, figuratively speaking, not Bassanio's body as in conjugal debt, but rather "the body of my friend, / And every word in it a gaping wound / Issuing life-blood" (32.263–65). Since everything that Bassanio has is on loan from Antonio, Portia's jointure is, in effect, Antonio. Portia immediately exclaims that she will "deface the bond" that holds Antonio's life in the balance (line 298). Bassanio must marry her first, and then she will send countless ducats to Venice with him to "pay the petty debt twenty times over" (line 306). This grand gesture of generosity pits the enormity of Portia's riches against the "petty debt," as if it could be easily crushed under the weight of ducats. Portia exalts momentarily in her wealth, for it promises to redeem the lives of two men.

But there are some debts money cannot buy back, and Portia has silently acknowledged this truth as she absorbs the shock of hearing the extent of Bassanio's indebtedness to his "dear friend" (line 290). Further sacrifice and risk are called for on her part. Her odd profession that she and Nerissa "Will live as maids and widows" (line 309) while the men do business in Venice indicates the precariousness of her role as *wife,* the unuttered word lying in the gap between maid and widow. She has entered a liminal state, which will demand a heroic effort to make possible a successful transition into wifehood. She intuits much about the nature of her husband's debts to his friend. Salerio and Jessica make clear to her the cruelty of Shylock, so Portia understands that Antonio's creditor may not be satisfied even with sixty thousand ducats. Portia understands that she has work to do, a "device" (3.4.81) to carry out, if she is to pass happily over the threshold into marriage. Her disguise as a male doctor of laws manifests her liminality; here is a form that allows her to cross boundaries of gender, social status, and place to face her new husband, his "bosom lover" (3.4.17), and his enemy in the Venetian court. All of their fates hang in the balance here: the court trial is indeed the ultimate liminal rite in which all of the characters participate, and once over the threshold they are utterly changed by the choices they make in the courtroom. Here we see Portia part company with Penelope and Hesione to assume roles akin to those of Odysseus and Hercules, the adventuring males who exhibit courage in the face of arduous trials.

THE DEBTOR'S TRIAL: THE BLOODY CREDITOR AND PORTIA'S HERCULEAN ORDEAL

Harold C. Goddard claims that the casket scene is replayed in the trial scene, only this time Portia is tested—and she fails. Her failure lies in her painfully and unnecessarily drawing out the trial for the sake of "spectacle, a dramatic triumph with herself at the center."[53] Goddard is certainly right that Portia is on trial in this scene, as are Antonio, Bassanio, and Shylock, but he is unnecessarily cynical about how Portia plays her hand as doctor of laws, and he is unnecessarily focused on Portia's theatricality, which he deems narcissistic. There are subtler points to be made about the nature of Portia's trial, and one way to get at them is to ask in what other guises the casket scene is replayed. While the theatrical dimension strikes some viewers, as it did Goddard, others have been attuned to the rich biblical and theological meanings informing the language and allegorical meaning of the scene.[54] Attention to mythic dimensions is less in evidence, yet such an approach promises to repay investigation.

Let us return to the myth of Hercules and Hesione, first elicited through Portia's anxious imagination. This Ovidian tale continues to resonate subliminally here, but the roles have been recast. Hercules' rescue of the Trojan princess Hesione recurs with Portia assuming the role of Hercules and Antonio that of the feminine sacrifice; he insists that he is a "wether," the "weakest kind of fruit" (4.1.114, 115). Shylock, then, takes on the role of the sea monster, ready to devour the sacrifice. "[T]hy desires / Are wolvish, bloody, starv'd, and ravenous," Gratiano cries out (lines 137–38). Earlier, we heard of Shylock's appetite for revenge: he swore to Salerio that he would take Antonio's flesh to "feed [his] revenge" (3.1.48). He is associated, too, with the angry god Neptune demanding the price of blood for a forfeited oath. The tale remains submerged, to be sure, but resemblances linger from Portia's strongly imagined scenario. That she, who formerly positioned herself as the sacrifice Hesione, can now act as the redeemer of the sacrifice, that she assumes Hercules' role to undertake a dangerous labor, is a telling inversion and an assumption of agency that she formerly lacked. She has seized the opportunity to fulfill an alternate meaning in "I stand for sacrifice": she now *defends* the sacrifice, and will submit herself to the trial or ordeal of freeing the one who is to be sacrificed.

In performance, there should be no glib knowingness in Portia, for the enactment of justice is unstable and uncertain in the worldly Venetian court. Tensions run high, for Antonio expects to die, and the audience at court fears a bad outcome to the trial. There is intense work involved, and the strength of Portia's character and the force of her rhetoric need to be conveyed as if they have been mustered for all they are worth. The actress playing Portia might sweat; she might show her mental labor. She might appear dumbfounded; she might show exasperation, anger, ruthlessness, and pity at different moments. The actress playing Portia (Derbhle Crotty) in Trevor Nunn's 1999 Royal National Theatre production showed just such an emotional range in the character. As it became apparent that a mortal struggle was unfolding, she appeared to be under tremendous pressure. There was no *sprezzatura* in her Portia's performance; the victory was hard-won. Crotty's high-stakes performance revealed a Portia at odds with traditional romanticized interpretations of character. In the Venetian court, Portia's labor is tremendous; yet, like Hercules, she is peculiarly equipped to redeem the blood sacrifice intended to appease a powerful enemy. However, she does not know at every moment precisely how she will get through the ordeal. Portia's hope is for a reward greater than Hercules was to receive, yet less tangible, and her pursuit of nonmaterial satisfaction seems bound up with moral principles. Indeed, her association by name with the biblical Balthazar/Daniel suggests that she stands for and receives "no treasure," the meaning of "Balthazar," and appears to function as the "judgment of God," the meaning of Daniel's name.

Indeed, scriptural allusions abound in this scene and cannot be ignored, even when our interpretation is not geared explicitly toward allegorical or religious meanings. A number of significant texts from both Old and New Testaments bear on the crucial themes of debt, forgiveness, mercy, judgment, and vengeance. Derived from both Christian and Jewish traditions, the Lord's Prayer underlies Portia's speech—"we do pray for mercy, / And that same prayer, doth teach us all to render / The deeds of mercy" (4.1.196–

98). The Geneva translation of the well-known prayer reads "And forgiue vs our dettes, as we also forgiue our detters" (Matt. 6:12). The Semitic and Hebraic image of sin was debt—owing something to someone.[55] The ancient concept of sin as debt survives in most late medieval translations of the Bible and in some major early modern English versions, such as the Coverdale, the Geneva, the Bishops', and the King James Bibles. From a religious perspective, as Barbara K. Lewalski observes, "the debtor's trial in the court of Venice [is] a precise analogue of the sinner's trial in the court of Heaven."[56] Portia's awareness of the greater spiritual stakes in this earthly court comes into play with her allusions to the Lord's Prayer, as well as Old Testament and Apocryphal verses that attest to God's mercy, forgiveness, and vengeance. Ecclesiasticus, in particular, resonates in Portia's "quality of mercy" speech: "Oh, how faire a thing is mercie in the time of anguish and trouble! It is like a cloude of raine, that cometh in the time of a drought" (35:19). And most potently, we hear echoes from the following passage: "He that seketh vengeance, shal finde vengeance of the Lord. . . . / Forgiue thy neighbour the hurt that he hathe done to thee, so shal thy sinnes be forgiuen thee also, when thou praiest. / Shulde a man beare hatred against man, and desire forgiuenes of the Lord?/ He wil shewe no mercie to a man, which is like him self: and wil he aske forgiuenes of his owne sinnes?" (Ecclus. 28:1–4). Shakespeare slyly has Portia appeal to this Jewish book of wisdom to make her case for mercy.

Seen in the best light, Portia advocates restorative justice. An authentic show of mercy and forgiveness, she suggests, will reflect Shylock's godlike virtue and bless the community. Her opening argument in favor of mercy does not fall on deaf ears, but the reciprocity Balthazar/Portia urges (mercy for mercy) is based on the assumption that Shylock places the value of forgiveness from God above the bond's legality and whatever satisfaction he hopes to attain from seeing his enemy punished. Portia is blind to Shylock's victimization and to the just anger he feels in his abject position. She sees only the implacable will of the avenger who perverts law to his own advantage. Shylock, in turn, is blind to any sense of himself as a sinful creature, for it seems beside the point here in a court of law. He is filled with righteousness and a zeal for the law. He claims to have done no wrong. Much wrong has been done *to him*. It is a point of integrity and principle now for Shylock to withhold forgiveness. He demonstrates clearly that mercy and forgiveness cannot be commanded, any more than love or hate can be. Indeed, Portia's "quality of mercy" speech is inspired by Shylock's question, "On what compulsion must I [show mercy]? tell me that" (4.1.179). For she has made the error in insisting that the Jew "must . . . be merciful" (line 178). In response to Portia's speech, he then proclaims with vehemence, "My deeds upon my head! I crave the law, / The penalty and forfeit of my bond" (4.1.202–3). His words call to mind the Jews' cry for the crucifixion of Christ: "His blood *be* on vs, and on our children" (Matt. 27:25). Thus, he is bent on "law," "penalty," and "forfeit"—the legality of his position—and any sense that he has debts as well that need to be forgiven is utterly abolished from his thinking.

Shylock's word "crave," however, betrays what lies beneath his insistence on the law. *Crave* suggests a primal need, an appetite driven by addiction, a hunger that has intensified since he first claimed to Salerio that Antonio's flesh would "feed [his] revenge" (3.1.48). Shylock's moral position is hidden from the court, but as his audience we know what has produced the insatiable craving. Shylock's whole being is now focused on Antonio's debt, his enemy's sins, for Antonio has treated Shylock in a shameful fashion, abusing and reviling him in public. To forgive Antonio and to forgive his debts would be akin to accepting the violation and devaluing of his self that he has endured for so long. For these sins against him, Shylock becomes a "bloody creditor" (3.3.34) who seeks his enemy's life.

It is Antonio who identifies Shylock as "bloody," a point that holds great significance in relation to Old Testament law, for Shylock should know that shedding the blood of a man is strictly forbidden by God (e.g., Ps. 5:6, Prov. 29:10). Shylock's intent to pursue his bond may seem morally and psychologically necessary to him, but this action would break the letter of Judaic law. Portia's insistence that he shed not a "jot of blood" (4.1.302) calls attention to this violation.[57]

Portia's legal stipulation calls vividly to mind Shylock's intent; his harping on *flesh* is hardly a cover for his bloodthirstiness. Shylock's preoccupation with the legitimacy of the bond gives way to the reality of bloodlust and his choice of blood revenge as the punishment for wrong. The stage image of the avenging Jew sharpening the knife, which he readies to plunge into his victim's chest to take a pound of flesh nearest the heart, is a terrifying spectacle, not only because of the threatened violence, but also because of the seeming helplessness of the court. Shylock's revenge is so alarming because it appears to be as lawful as it is merciless. His bond is a cunning use of the law to catch his mortal enemy Antonio on his hip. Turning the other cheek in the marketplace has achieved nothing. The bond promises to achieve a perverse kind of moral satisfaction for Shylock. With his bond Shylock would appear to have a stranglehold on the law.

Shylock's refusal to forgive a debt, or to accept three times the payment owed, reflects a shocking moral position for early modern Christian audiences. In practical economic terms, too, Shylock's position establishes an entirely uncharitable relationship to his debtor. Here is a man so radically violated, we must conclude, so humiliated and loveless, that he can find no feeling response toward his debtor other than righteous bloodthirstiness. When Portia says to Antonio, "You stand within his danger" (4.1.176), she touches upon the relationship between danger and debt, for *danger* referred explicitly to being in the debt of a powerful individual who can inflict harm.[58] For a while, Shylock is that powerful enemy who thinks he has the authority of Venetian law in his favor. He enters the court of justice with the advantage of a legally binding document in a city that places a premium on the law, the safeguard of trade and all economic exchanges. The audience has witnessed Shylock's mounting rage and his insistence in 3.1 that he will demand a fleshly repayment of his bond. Yet only when Shylock suffers loss upon loss, including his daughter and his ducats (3.1), does he speak of revenge as if it were a necessity. In this respect, Antonio is to be punished for *all* of Shylock's losses, *all* of his humiliations. We see Antonio's function as scapegoat emerging, and Shylock's desire for a compensatory restoration of all losses through the sacrifice of his enemy. The question of how much and exactly what Antonio owes Shylock and for which sins and whose debts arises with stark urgency.

The excessiveness in the revenge and Shylock's own admission of villainy increase the shock value of his actions and the radical ambivalence we feel in acknowledging his moral position as the victim of Christian hatred. "The villainy you [Christians] teach me I will execute, and it shall go hard but I will better the instruction" (lines 65–66): The coupling of revenge and villainy is straightforward here, for the oath he swears to himself comes at the end of his revenge speech. "If you wrong us shall we not revenge?" he cries out bitterly (line 60). He swears he will "resemble" the Christian in his revenge, for Christians, as far as he can see, do not suffer humility when Jews wrong them, but rather take their revenge. He has not cast revenge in a good light here—it is no virtue, by his own admission. And in his own experience, he feels he has suffered at the hands of Christian vengeance. If this is the way of the world, he reasons, and if this is the only way he can fight injustice, so be it, for Antonio has plagued Shylock mercilessly; therefore, in Shylock's estimation he *deserves* revenge. He now may demand that "dearly bought" (4.1.100) pound of flesh and stand by the "oath in heaven" (line 224), which he claims has sealed this bond.

A tragic gulf opens in the comedy as Shylock's wrath and sense of injury overcome him, transforming him into a hate-driven avenger. Yet, by the time he steps into court, revenge has become synonymous in his mind with justice, not villainy. Neither, however, prove to be a virtue as he practices them. The coupling of revenge and justice is shown in its most extreme form as a perverse violation of moral codes. A just vengeance for Shylock will be a shocking blood sacrifice to his people and to his God. His desire to make Antonio pay for his sins and to have Venice witness this scene of violence sanctioned by law overwhelms him. Shylock's revenge, legally tied to the bond's terms of forfeiture, will enact an ancient Greek scene of sacrifice in an early modern, "civilized" court of law.

Terrifying as Shylock is, he has more than met his match in Portia, whose appearance may be in the form of the diminutive Balthazar, but whose intelligence and cunning make her as formidable an opponent as Hercules. His fantasy of payback is forestalled—there will be no figurative feeding on flesh in her courtroom—and the debts owed him are irrevocably canceled. The undoing of Shylock's revenge fantasy comes about ironically through the mechanism of revenge itself. "My deeds upon my head" could not have been a more blindingly ironic statement. If we look at how Portia manipulates the law and places Shylock at the mercy of his enemies, we see that her skills get *her* (and Venice) precisely what Shylock desired— lawful revenge. Few critics have been willing to assert Portia's vengefulness so baldly, yet her words and actions support such a view.[59] While Portia advocates mercy as a noble response that can bend an unforgiving law, she also allows that justice can be a harsh, retributive force that can be used against the man who fails to show mercy. Her intention in giving Shylock strict justice, all justice, is to instruct him feelingly and ethically. Furthermore, as Stephen Orgel points out, Portia allows "*us* to have *our* revenge," while at the same time allowing for a "degree of mercy to be shown to Shylock far greater than any he was willing to extend to Antonio."[60] "The quality of mercy" speech is a piece of resplendent rhetoric, shimmering in its ethical knowingness, but as the scene gets thoroughly underway the quality of mercy seems to have turned into its opposite, revenge, for Portia's justice turns Shylock's vengeful stance back upon him. She redeems Antonio's life, but in the process pays back Shylock. As William Ian Miller suggests, "Perhaps the perfect Shakespearean revenge takes place in a play that denies that revenge is taking place, and there the culprit is given his life but is systematically humiliated and unmanned, kept alive to suffer his shame, all in the name of mercifulness."[61]

The quality of revenge is not strained, and, as Portia demonstrates to Shylock, revenge can be a bitter pouring rain that carries no blessing to the avenger or the avenged. As the actress Deborah Findlay concluded in Bill Alexander's 1987 RSC production, Portia "follows a simple rule of thumb: mercy, or justice. . . . She holds scrupulously to the letter of the law, since that is what Shylock has chosen. . . . Hers is an act of strict impartiality, explaining the law to everyone present. If you reject human mercy then there is only the implacable face of justice to fall back on."[62] The irony in this sentiment is stunning: here is the notion of justice with a vengeance, a harsh justice that recoils back on the so-called just.

Portia's use of impartial law does, however, work in favor of her hidden partiality for Antonio and Bassanio's interests, and her own. Indeed, in protecting her own interests so boldly, we might conclude that Portia has failed to recognize what is owed the Jew: she does not address the underlying moral debt incurred by Antonio in his treatment of Shylock. Although she would not know necessarily about the history between the merchant and the Jew, this painful lack is what the audience perceives: the law does not deal with many wrongs that disgrace and humiliate people. Shylock is able to bring his enemy to court, not for the long history of abuses he suffered, but for the forfeiture of a legal bond. This proves to be Shylock's only means to punish his enemy—to take him to court. Outside the law, he is helpless; only through exploiting the law can he find an instrument of revenge. And this instrument fails him when he encounters a more masterful avenger in Portia.

Portia's challenge in the Venetian court lies not only in releasing Antonio from the danger of Shylock's nefarious bond, but also in defusing the emotional threat Antonio represents to her new marriage. Portia's understanding of how debt works encompasses both Antonio's sacrificial position, which binds his beloved friend to him, and Shylock's legalistic position, which seeks the life of a man who merely defaults on a loan. Portia stands for sacrifice *and* law in this scene, defending both, yet working to undo the powers of each—of Antonio's emotional grip on Bassanio through his death, and Shylock's legalism that gives him the authority to kill a man. Portia's liminal persona allows her to negotiate her way out of her earlier sacrificial position, and around the laws governing wives' subordination to husbands. Upon becoming a wife, she recognizes quickly that loving relationships must be negotiated as rigorously as legal bonds are. Shylock's literal balance, brought to court to weigh the pound of flesh, is parodic of Portia's figurative balance in which she weighs the value of the men with whom she deals. As the Daniel figure, she can look both to Shylock and Bassanio and say, as it were, "thou art wayed in the balance, and art founde to light" (Dan. 5:27). While Bassanio gained credit with Portia when he chose the right casket and took a solemn oath to her, he loses credit when he gives away her ring, "A thing stuck on with oaths upon [his] finger, / And so riveted with faith unto [his] flesh" (5.1.168–69). These are Portia's words, emphasizing "oaths," "faith," and "flesh."

Lurking here in both visual and acoustical memory is Antonio's "dearly bought" flesh (4.1.100), which Portia triumphantly redeemed in the Venetian court; now Bassanio's symbolic sundering of his own "dear bought" flesh (3.2.312)—of his "one flesh," as Saint Paul deems the union of husband and wife—becomes the issue. He defends his action by invoking a powerful trinity—shame, courtesy, and honor—claiming to Portia that he was forced to give the ring away: "I was beset with shame and courtesy, / My honour would not let ingratitude / So much besmear it" (5.1.217–19). His loving debt to Antonio lies behind this claim, for Antonio applies pressure to his friend's sense of honor and obligation, urging: "My Lord Bassanio, let him have the ring, / Let his deservings and my love withal / Be valued 'gainst your wife's commandement" (4.1.445–47). Antonio wins over Bassanio, who already declared publicly how much less he valued his wife than his most "esteem'd" friend: "Antonio, I am married to a wife," he begins, "Which is as dear to me as life itself. . . . I would lose all, ay sacrifice them all / Here to this devil [Shylock], to deliver [Antonio]" (4.1.281, 278–79, 282–83). This intensely emotional declaration makes his choice clear: he may have chosen the right casket, but he loves Antonio above all else. It is not for Portia that he fulfills the credo for wise loving on the lead casket: "Who chooseth me, must give and hazard all he hath" (2.7.9).

MEDEAN MOTIFS: OUTFACING AND OUTSWEARING THE MEN

The comedy's final scene taps into the mythic dimension of the play, once more exploring the tragic undercurrents of broken faith and undeserved credit. The lovers are all married and reunited, but they are on uncertain ground with each other. They must look to their bonds. At the scene's opening, Shylock's daughter, Jessica, and her new husband, Lorenzo, engage in a melancholic lyrical contest, attempting to "out-night" (5.1.23) each other with tragic examples of classical lovers. After Lorenzo's invocation of the sighing Troilus, the focus moves to heroines—Cressida, Thisbe, Dido, Medea. The most beguiling and ominous of the group is Medea, the example Jessica invokes to outnight Lorenzo's Dido. Why Medea trumps Dido is a question worth pursuing, particularly in relation to the women's situations in the play. One might observe immediately that Dido despairs over the loss of faithless Aeneas, killing herself in a spectacular funeral pyre, whereas Medea triumphs through revenge.

But Jessica's focus is trained on the magical Medea who "gathered the enchanted herbs" in the moonlight to "renew old Æson" (5.1.13, 14) rather than the betrayed lover and avenging wife. Her brief rendering of Ovid's tale captures Medea as a dark figure of regeneration, restoring the youth of her beloved husband's father. Medea's motive is worth remembering, for it is significant in relation to key motifs in *The Merchant*. When Jason asks for Medea's help, wishing to give years from his life to his father, Medea proclaims that she can give "a greater gift than you require and more for your behoofe" (Golding's translation, 7.239). Medea is an extraordinary gift-giver, who does magical deeds for her husband's good, indebting him to her. This gift follows upon others Medea had given to Jason when he came to her homeland of Colchis on a quest to win the golden fleece. Her magical interventions allowed him to pass her father's tests, to win the fleece, and to acquire a heroic reputation. In Ovid's tale, she bestows yet another gift: the death of Jason's uncle and enemy, King Pelia. She tricks the old king's daughters into shedding his blood, promising they can revitalize him as she did old Jason. But then she refuses to use her magical powers, allowing the daughters to slaughter their father. Her final gifts to Jason are as gruesome as this one. When he violates their marriage oath, she sends a poisoned gift to Jason's new wife, which destroys her, and then she commits infanticide to avenge his faithlessness. The killing of their children takes from Jason his future line and essentially ruins him. Through the destruction of his fame, glory, and progeny, she takes back her gifts to Jason.

From the Medea allusion emerge dark motifs of unreciprocated gift-giving, debt, broken faith, and revenge, which reach through the whole network of relationships in *The Merchant*. The allusion offers two potent prototypes: the faithless, venturing husband and the resourceful, avenging wife. Lorenzo's response to the image of Medea's dark gift to Jason is to call up Jessica's gift-giving in the form of reckless or "unthrift love" and theft—"In such a night / Did Jessica steal from the wealthy Jew, / And with an unthrift love did run from Venice, / As far as Belmont" (5.1.14–17). The coarse mercantile puns on "steal" and "unthrift" cast Jessica's actions in a rather bad light. Jessica's response is to transfer the emphasis from unthrifty feminine love to faithless masculine vows and thievery, when she asserts: "In such a night / Did young Lorenzo swear he loved her well, / Stealing her soul with many vows of faith, / And ne'er a true one" (lines 17–20). Jessica's words are wise, knowing, and perhaps sad, expressing her anxious uncertainty about Lorenzo's faithfulness and her risk-taking. In calling Lorenzo "young," she associates him with immaturity, and with the young Jason who "stole" Medea's soul to get what he wanted. Like the other young, venturing Venetian lovers, Lorenzo is a Jason figure, which suggests his dependence on a cunning woman to whom he is indebted and with whom he may break faith.

Like Medea, Jessica forsakes everything for love. In disguise and with her father's fortune in hand, she has fled everything she knows to make a transgressive marriage, in the hope of gaining love, a husband, a new life, and a new faith. But in this fragile moment in the moonlight, her gains seem as tenuous as Medea's were; for Jessica, the future remains an open question with the threat that her dearly bought Lorenzo and his vows of faith might be false. Jessica has risked everything for love, as did Medea, but her resources are fewer. Her claim that she can "out-night" Lorenzo when they are alone suggests that her wit may be her best resource in their marriage. She perhaps can get the better of Lorenzo in using classical precedents to instruct him in the value of oaths. Ancient stories possess dark knowledge, spiritual anguish, and tragic loss for women, but women can strive to transcend or renovate these models in their relationships, and even "slander" men in order to provoke in their chosen audience an ethical response.

If the Medea myth serves as a threatening undercurrent in Jessica's fate, it does so as well for Portia, though she negotiates her interactions with the myth to her distinct advantage.[63] Indeed, the very act of magical renewal Jessica focuses on finds its parallel in Portia's renewal of Antonio's life, an act she performs for her Jason, Bassanio.[64] As John W. Velz rightly claims, the Medea myth "underpins the role" of Portia and the play's "action."[65] Direct allusions to the tale of Jason and the Argonauts, however, come from the venturing male characters, who explicitly associate Portia not with Medea, but rather with the valuable prize to be won in Colchis, the golden fleece. In viewing themselves as Jasons, they see only the heroic male figure who triumphs. They neglect the terrible ironies in Jason's story and the feminine perspectives offered by his wives: Hypsipyle, Medea, and Creusa. Shakespeare and some members of his audience would have been familiar with the wives' laments in Ovid's *Heroides*. With the exception of Jessica's evocation, the figure of Medea is suppressed, so that male ventures can be celebrated without any threatening intrusion from the female.

The first Jason/fleece reference comes early in the play from Bassanio, who describes Portia to Antonio as a lady "richly left" whose "sunny locks / Hang on her temples like a golden fleece, / Which makes her seat of Belmont Colchos' strond, / And many Jasons come in quest of her" (1.1.161, 169–72). The second reference occurs when Bassanio opens the lead casket to find Portia's portrait; he see the image of her hair painted as "A golden mesh t'entrap the hearts of men" (3.2.122). Here the golden fleece appears to be a snare, for he seems under the spell of Portia's wise instruction and now wishes to think of her as more than her riches. But after Gratiano too has won his "fleece," he boasts, in the play's third reference, "We are the Jasons, we have won the fleece" (3.2.240), to which Salerio sardonically replies, "I would you had won the fleece that he hath lost" (line 241). The pun on fleece/fleets and the reference to Antonio's losses associate the valuable prize of Colchis explicitly with Venetian venturing.

Yet the Medea myth runs far deeper in the subterranean element of Shakespeare's comedy, offering a disturbing tragic vision of how broken faith in marriage can lead to great suffering and the ruin of a man. While in his *Metamorphoses* Ovid focuses on the anguished self-division of the young, passionate Medea, who uses sorcery to aid Jason and win his love, in his *Heroides* he portrays an angry, rational Medea who focuses on Jason's debt; she recounts all she did for him, all she gave up for him, and then she connects the marriage dowry with her gifts to him: "Where is my dowry, you ask? On the field I counted it out—that field which you had to plough before you could bear away the fleece. The famous golden ram, sightly for deep flock, is my dowry—the which should I say to you, 'Restore it!' you would refuse to render up. My dowry is yourself—saved; my dowry is the band of Grecian youth! . . . you owe me" (12.199–203, 206).[66]

In the Ovidian Medea's calling Jason to account, we hear the strong influence of economic metaphors of reciprocity and revenge. Shakespeare, as I have been arguing, pursues economic metaphors thoroughly in his depiction of social relations in *The Merchant,* giving Portia a Medea-like power in her handling of men.

In Seneca's play, translated by the Elizabethan John Studley, Shakespeare also would have found a maddened Medea speaking in overwrought language of the outrages she has suffered. The linguistic texture and thematic concerns of *The Merchant* can be heard in Studley's Chorus: "*How deerley was that wicked journey bought? / Medea accurst, and eke the golden Fleece, / That greater harme then storme of seas hath wrought / Rewarded well that voyage first of Greece*" (act 2). Medea's Nurse proclaims, "Of all the wealth and worldly mucke wherewith thou didst abounde / No porcion remaynes at all, whereby some helpe is founde" (act 2). Medea's retort reveals how her "porcion" resides in her own magical self, the elements, and the gods: "Medea yet is left, (to much) and here thou mayst espy / The Seas to succour us in flyght, and landes aloofe that ly: / Yea yron tooles, with burning brands we have to worke them woe, / And Gods that with the thunder dint shall overquell our foe" (act 2). When Jason faces the wrathful Medea, he curses his "lucklesse lot" and swears that to get back into the "good deserts" of Fortune, he should "hazard" his "ventrous lyfe to leese it for her sake" (act 3).

Medea joins the Furies as an archetypal avenger, capable of the harshest of punishments in the face of a broken oath. In the Medea myth lies the extreme example of masculine faithlessness met with feminine vengeance. Neither Jessica nor Portia approach the terrifying grandeur of Medea, for they are comic women who commit no physical violence, much less kinslaying. Indeed, Portia prevents the bloodshed of a fellow Christian (whom we might see as a kinsman in her religious community). Yet, like Medea, Portia is highly skilled and associated with mysterious powers. She, too, protects the marriage bed and the oath that binds a husband and wife. She, too, takes revenge on her husband, only her intent is not to destroy him, but rather to regenerate him with the possibility of her renewed faith. What is unsalvageable to the tragic Medea is redeemable to the comic Portia.

As part of the comic dispensation in *The Merchant,* the heroine's stronger passions do not overcome her, nor does she suffer in relative isolation. Unlike Medea (and unlike Jessica), Portia has a feminine accomplice and ally in her devices and revenges. Medea had her Nurse, who counseled her against violent action and shared with the audience her dread of what her mistress might be capable of, and Euripides' Medea had the chorus of Corinthian wives whom she manipulates into sympathizing with her. But

Medea is essentially friendless and acts alone. Nerissa is Portia's wise and loving companion, whose significance can be understood through her name and mythological association. *Nerissa* derives from the Latin *nereid* and *nereis*, who are sea nymphs and the daughters of the sea-god Nereus.[67] Nereus was an ancient Titan and son of the Sea, associated with Proteus, and known to have aided Hercules. In his *Theogony*, Hesiod describes Nereus as "unerring and truthful," and as one who "does not forget established customs but contrives just and gentle plans" (lines 233–35). Nerissa embodies this ethical disposition in her friendship with Portia.

The significance of Nerissa's function might be understood better if we consider how feminine friendship is represented in contrast to masculine friendship in the play. Antonio and Bassanio may protest their love for one another and may both assume the sacrificial position in spectacular fashion, but Nerissa and Portia demonstrate values of a more stable, measured, Aristotelian kind. Their affection is mutual, as is their respect; they support each other with wisdom and wit; and they play their cards well so that they need never forfeit on their debt to each other, nor compromise their honor and integrity. Their friendship is secure and trustworthy, and an exemplary Renaissance model of prudent relations. While Antonio has helped mire his friend in debt, Nerissa has been a wise counselor to Portia, such that her mistress will confess, "Nerissa teaches me what to believe" (5.1.207). While the male friendship modeled in the play is cast in the extremes of indebtedness, risk, and danger, the female friendship displays the virtues of measure, balance, and mutual ethical instruction. Indeed, it is a friendship in proportion. Nerissa accompanies and aids Portia in necessary ways for the trial, but in the marital bond/ring plot, she is a full-blown collaborator, doubling the force of Portia's instruction.

The women offer a double portrait of feminine revenge that rejects elements of the Medean prototype. In the courtroom Portia ended up resembling Shylock (and Medea) in her pitilessness and ruthlessness, but in the domestic sphere, she is not the dispenser of harsh justice. Pitted against the men's false "swearing," the women "outface them, and outswear them too" (4.2.15, 17). When Portia, still in disguise as Balthazar, says to Bassanio, "I pray you know me when we meet again" (4.1.415), her word "know" reverberates meaningfully later in the disclosures made during their reunion in Belmont. Bassanio exclaims in wonder, "Were you the doctor, and I knew you not?" (5.1.280). Lori Schroeder Haslem argues that in Portia's riddling words "one senses [that] the inevitable uncloaking of Portia will bring an even fuller acknowledgement of her relinquished autonomy," for female authority and autonomy are not viable in the world of the play.[68] The final scene of the play, however, explicitly counters such a view, for there we see Portia fully in possession of self, property, husband, and friends. The laws of *femme couvert* may apply technically to Portia in her status as wife, but these patriarchal laws seem to be little in evidence as Portia "exclaims upon" Bassanio, produces the letter that holds news of Antonio's financial recovery, "drop[s] manna" upon Jessica and Lorenzo, and promises that all will be "satisfied / Of these events at full" (5.1.294, 296–97).

Portia ushers everyone into her estate with a legal promise: "charge us there upon inter'gatories, / And we [she and Nerissa] will answer all things faithfully" (lines 298–99). Just as witnesses in a lawsuit were asked questions before trials in the Chancery Court, the women promise to answer all questions put before them by the men. Thus, the final words of the avenging Portia in *her* comedy—her journey into marriage—emphasize satisfaction, oaths, and faithfulness, all promoted in the legal atmosphere of a domestic court established on her estate. Ovid's Penelope in his *Heroides* imagined herself "hang[ing] on the tale that falls from her husband's lips" (1.30), but we can see how roles have been exchanged here as the husband hangs on the wife's tale.

Barbara K. Lewalski suggests that "[t]he ring episode is, in a sense, a comic parody of the trial scene," with explicit legal language calling attention to the parody.[69] Yet to call Portia's comic revenge and wifely redemption of Bassanio's credit a parody devalues the underlying seriousness of Portia's work. If we think again of her Herculean labor as an ethical agent in the courtroom, we might see how she continues to deal with the ways that men have undervalued or falsified their oaths. Shylock's "oath to heaven" was a debased oath based on willful blindness to Mosaic Law. Now, Portia faces Bassanio, as Nerissa faces Gratiano, knowing full well that the men have broken their marital oaths. To Bassanio, Portia insists on "the virtue of the ring," and "her worthiness that gave the ring," and "your own honour to contain the ring" (5.1.199, 200, 201). These teachings he accepts as fundamental to their marriage, for he must learn what honor in marriage means. The Belmontian community re-forms to include part of the Venetian community. The legal decisions, the bonds, the debts, and the credit from Venice carry over into Belmont in real and lasting ways, but they are translated into terms negotiable by Portia. When Antonio discovers her identity as Balthazar, he acknowledges his everlasting debt to Portia by offering his very soul as surety for Bassanio's marital bond. Antonio make his final loan to his friend: "I dare be bound again, / My soul upon the forfeit, that your lord / Will never more break faith advisedly" (lines 251–53). In a significant gesture, Portia gives her ring to Antonio to return to Bassanio.

To gain her advantage, Portia has upset the traditional Pauline notion of due benevolence, or reciprocal debt. If the common law of *femme couvert* supported the husband's collection of wifely debt, converting her assets into his power, Portia's position as creditor and subtle avenger works to ensure husbandly debt and to accept surety from her husband's former creditor.[70] Portia may return the ring to Bassanio as a symbol of renewed reciprocity and faith, but she controls the terms of renewal. She has chastised Bassanio before her household and guests: when Bassanio begs her forgiveness and attempts to swear an oath by her fair eyes, she relishes the irony here and mocks him: "Mark you but that!" she says to her audience, "In both my eyes he doubly sees himself: / In each eye one,—swear by your double self, / And there's an oath of credit" (5.1.243–46). Like Medea, she credits him with nothing at this point, except his faithlessness, or doubleness. When Antonio gives the ring to Bassanio, Portia brings down the house with her revelation: "I had it of [the doctor]: pardon me Bassanio, / For by this ring the doctor lay with me" (lines 258–59). Nerissa echoes this bombshell to her husband, Gratiano.

The prospect of cuckoldry conjured by Portia and Nerissa is as playful as it is punitive, and once uttered as a real possibility, it cannot be forgotten. It is a warning for the future. Portia just as quickly restores the women's virtue by confessing to their disguises, but not before the men have been drawn into Portia's power, recognizing that she has hidden resources they could not have imagined. Above all, her witty deployment of revenge places Portia in a commanding position in marriage. Unlike Shylock, who virtually destroys himself in his pursuit of vengeance, Portia uses a vengeful tactic in a constructive manner to assert her rights as wife and to teach a lesson in the fruits of faithlessness. When she releases Bassanio from his mock punishment, Portia gives him more than he deserves; she has some grace, yet she has had her revenge too.

CUCKOLDRY AS WOMEN'S REVENGE

Most Shakespearean female characters do not engage in adulterous relations for any reason, but the prospect of cuckoldry comes into play time and again. Male and female characters alike are aware of this dark specter that threatens the imagination and well-being of married people. Long feared as a feminine mode of revenge, cuckoldry has the power to ruin a man's reputation and his sense of personal honor. Thus, the adulterous wife can do irreparable damage to her husband. In *Othello* Emilia's speech on fallen wives justifies such revenges in a passionate argument that echoes Shylock's speech justifying his revenge. She responds to Desdemona's naïveté about adulterous wives by insisting that there are "a dozen, and as many to th'vantage as would / store the world they played for" (4.3.83–84). She imagines sexually liberal women gambling to make their own world where they have the power to make right any small wrong they might commit. Her speech quickly moves to the wrongs men do women and men's failure to attribute human qualities like "sense," "affections," "Desires for sport," and "frailty" to their wives (lines 93, 99, 100, 100). This all-too-human portrait of women should garner them sympathy and affection from their husbands and should move them to "use us well," Emilia exclaims, "else let them know," and she threatens, "The ills we do, their ills instruct us so" (lines 101–2). Those "ills" refer to adultery, and the misuse of sexuality to take revenge. "Why, we have galls: and though we have some grace / Yet have we some revenge," Emilia asserts (lines 91–92).

The sharpest weapon Emilia can think of lies in the sexual dishonoring of the husband. But just as Shylock in his gall, or resentment, coupled revenge and villainy, Emilia thinks of ills: ill return for ill use. Their very words explicitly confess the truth about their intentions. When played out literally with the sexual transgressions of the body and a shedding of blood, revenge is a lowering of one's humanity and a spiritual degradation. Yet Emilia does not take revenge in this manner; rather, she turns upon her vile husband to expose his villainy through the liberality of words, not flesh. Rather than pay him back with her ill deeds, she chooses a virtuous revenge —to speak the truth, and thereby let justice be done.

In *The Merchant of Venice,* Shakespeare imagines the wife's playful exploitation of cuckoldry, a revenge motif typically found in Continental drama, fabliaux, and novelle. Portia's disguise and her creation of a "fantas[y] of cuckoldry and forgiveness," to use Marilyn L. Williamson's words, show her determination to retain some control in her marriage.[71] She would not deem to lower herself by performing a dishonorable deed, but she is clever enough to seize and maintain her advantage by raising the specter of cuckoldry. Through his imaginative and emotional participation in the cuckoldry fantasy, the young husband receives ethical instruction from his wife: he cannot get away with deflating the value of his wife (for he would not want his value, his honor, deflated through cuckoldry), and he must treat his oath to his wife as solemn and binding.

In *Cymbeline,* Shakespeare raises the question of a wife's revenge upon her husband through cuckoldry once again. The newly married Imogen is confronted with the prospect of a faithless husband and a willing lover who wishes to help her take revenge. The prospect, however, is a false portrait painted by the corrupt Iachimo, who wishes to win a wager on Imogen's virtue. Her husband, Posthumous, foolishly has wagered the precious ring Imogen gave him, accepting Iachimo's challenge that he can steal the young wife's virtue. When Imogen gave the ring to Posthumous, she solemnly said, "keep it till you woo another wife, / When Imogen is dead" (1.2.44–45). Now with her husband's approval, Iachimo assaults Imogen's virtue. Iachimo first leads Imogen to question Posthumous's fidelity and moral character. He then trains her mind on revenge, exclaiming, "Be reveng'd, / Or she that bore you was no queen, and you / Recoil from your great stock" (1.7.126–28). His emphasis here lies in the prerogative of great ones to defend their honor and punish wrongs.

Imogen is horrified, though, at the thought of revenge and cries out,

> Reveng'd!
> How should I be reveng'd? If this be true,
> (As I have such a heart that both mine ears
> Must not in haste abuse) if it be true,
> How should I be reveng'd?
>
> (1.7.128–32)

The repetitions here suggest not only distress, but caution as well; *if* this unbelievable thing be true, she repeats, then *how* should I be revenged? Iachimo responds immediately by calling her to "Revenge it" by allowing him to give her "sweet pleasure, / More noble than that runagate to your bed" (lines 135, 136–37). Imogen refuses to debase and dishonor herself and her husband through a corrupt form of revenge. For Imogen, revenge is not sweet. With the offer of adultery, Imogen understands instinctually that he has "told this tale" (line 143) not for virtuous, but for base, dishonorable ends. Her virtue proves unassailable, and it is Iachimo's chosen mode for her revenge, cuckoldry, that signals the falseness of his tale.

In the characters of Portia, Emilia, and Imogen, we see how women's virtue comes into play when they deal with the question of revenge. They each find the grace to choose wisely in how they respond to male faithlessness and deception. In all three cases, the women confront the prospect of cuckoldry as a mode of feminine revenge, though only Portia finds herself in circumstances that warrant making her husband believe she has done the deed to punish him. In the next chapter we will see how Emilia's words ring true—how the female avenger has gall, yet grace as well. The ethics of revenge lies in just such a seeming paradox.

9

Women's Gall, Women's Grace: Female Friendship, Moral Rebuke, and the Vindictive Passions

> We all have a duty to support—both intellectually and emotionally—the moral order, an order represented by clear understandings of what constitutes unacceptable treatment of one human being by another. If we do not show some resentment to those who, in victimizing us, flout those understandings, then we run the risk—in Aurel Kolnai's words—of "being complicitous in evil."
>
> —Jeffrie G. Murphy, *Getting Even*

> Morality requires not only a firm hand but a loud and clear voice.
>
> —Peter A. French, *The Virtues of Vengeance*

> *Emilia.* Why we have galls: and though we have some grace
> Yet have we some revenge.
>
> —Shakespeare, *Othello*

Aᴄᴄᴏʀᴅɪɴɢ ᴛᴏ ᴛʜᴇ *ᴏxғᴏʀᴅ ᴇɴɢʟɪsʜ ᴅɪᴄᴛɪᴏɴᴀʀʏ, ɢᴀʟʟ* ɪs ʙɪʟᴇ, ᴏʀ ᴛʜᴇ secretion of the liver; it also refers to bitterness of spirit, rancor, and the "Spirit to resent injury or insult."[1] Emilia's well-known words, quoted above, align gall and revenge, reflecting early modern belief, inherited from an Aristotelian- and Galenic-based medicine, that the gall bladder was the seat of resentment, anger, and bitterness, which is to say, the seat of revenge. To lack gall, as Hamlet says he does, is to be without bile, or the natural, inward spur to anger or resentment. To desire gall, as Lady Macbeth does, is to wish for a rancorous spirit that will course through the body and spur action. Avengers need gall to provide the passion that will drive them to give voice to outrages done by their enemies, to plot against them, and possibly to slaughter them. The concept of gall is set provocatively in the balance with grace in Emilia's formulation, urging Shakespeare's audiences to contemplate the co-existence of seemingly opposite dispositions

262

within the female self. Just as Salome, the "custom-breaker" in Elizabeth
Cary's *The Tragedy of Miriam,* asks, "Are men, than we, in greater grace
in heaven, / Or cannot women hate as well as men?" (1.309, 307–8),[2] Emilia
too works to collapse binaries implicit in early modern discourses on
women. Gall and hate would seem to express negative passions in women,
but Emilia's lines urge us to ask whether there can be a positive function
to the vindictive passions. We are prodded to think about the ethics of gall
—that is to say, the ethics of women's revenge and its attendant passion,
anger.

Thus far, in this book's investigation into Shakespeare's complex handling of women's revenge, we have addressed ethical dimensions of the
subject, but begged questions of a specifically religious nature. I have been
making an argument for women's ethics on grounds not entirely removed
from the religious, but more properly understood in relation to humanist
and virtue-based ethics drawn from the Aristotelean-Thomistic tradition.
The concept of grace has secular connotations such as attractiveness,
charm, propriety, and favor, but equally important for Shakespeare's contemporaries were the moral connotations of grace, conveyed most explicitly through religious discourses of the culture; whenever uttered, the word
carried a moral charge. *Grace* referred to the monarch's divine right and
authority, blessings from God, "a mark of divine favor," an "individual
virtue or excellence, divine in its origin," and "Mercy, clemency; hence,
pardon or forgiveness."[3] To be in a state of grace, or to possess grace, was
to be favored by and influenced by God, even to be godlike in one's behavior. Grace had to do with the condition and fate of one's soul. Emilia's
formulation seems, then, to articulate a conventional antithesis: personal
revenge (women's revenge) stands in opposition to grace—that is, God's
favor—and therefore constitutes a graceless or godless act. In the antithetical positioning of "gall" and "grace" lies a moral antithesis early modern
English people would have been exhorted to accept as true; homilies, moral
philosophy, and tracts on the passions all reinforced such thinking.

Early modern writers tended to exaggerate the dangers of women's gall,
using extreme examples to illustrate their point.[4] Peter de la Primaudaye
uses the murderous Clytemnestra as a figure of the provoked wrathful wife
who takes revenge upon her husband, Agamemnon, by committing adultery and consenting to his death. He concludes, "This sexe is fraile, spite-
full, and giuen to reuenge: and therefore men are to vse the greater prudence
in the gouerning and managing of them."[5] A similar view can be found in
the French writer Nicholas Caussin's *The Holy Court,* where the author
blames Eleanor of Aquitaine for instigating the three hundred years of war
and the ruin of England. "The anger of potent women," he exclaims, "is
above all dreadfull, when they are not with held by considerations of conscience, because they have a certaine appetite of revenge, which exceedeth

all may be imagined."[6] Such disturbing representations of angry women, without conscience and hungry for vengeance, underlie Emilia's sentiments and her warning to husbands, but it is surely a view she contests, simply in her allowing grace into the moral equation. Her words bring to light the shortcomings of a moral position that does not square with women's suffering and men's unjust treatment of them.

In the defiant voice of this angry wife, Shakespeare calls to mind a conventional fearful and moralistic view of women's anger and revenge, but he does so in order to trouble the legitimacy of its logic—if gall, then no grace? Surely sympathetic listeners are moved to ask: Are there not circumstances in which one finds grace in gall, or virtue in vengeance? What ethical sentiments might underlie the expression of anger? Is there a nobility in anger and revenge if they are directed rightfully toward one's enemies, to invoke Aristotle's argument in *Rhetoric* (1367a)? Can we not extend Aristotle's defense of just anger and vengeance to women? What morally allowable recourse does a wife have when her enemy is her husband? Might Shakespeare not be following Erasmus in locating the blame for women's weaknesses in the immorality of men? In his *Encomium Matrimonii,* Erasmus exclaims, "Believe me, an evil wife is not wont to chance, but to evil husbands. . . . We blame wives falsely. No man . . . had ever a shrew to his wife, but through his own default."[7] Can there not be a moral force in women's revolt against wayward and abusive men?

We have established in previous chapters conditions under which vindictiveness and vengeance express virtue and ethical plenitude, rather than vice and mere destructiveness. These conditions often complicate, and even challenge, the foundation of conventional Christian morality and Stoic thought. The case of Emilia can help us bring this argument into focus as we move toward our conclusion. The legal philosopher Jeffrie G. Murphy offers a helpful defense of vindictiveness that we can apply here. He makes his case along Aristotelian lines, countering the Stoic-Christian tradition, which tends to represent the vindictive passions of anger, resentment, and vengefulness as irrational, unnatural, and evil. Murphy first asserts that moral commitment demands not only an intellectual allegiance, but an emotional one as well.[8] He follows the contemporary philosopher Robert C. Solomon in acknowledging an emotional dimension to justice and views vengeance as an intrinsically justice-seeking passion. One common emotional response to the "unacceptable treatment of one human being by another" is vindictiveness. An angry resistance to inhumane actions, to injustice, expresses an allegiance to a moral order.[9] Murphy's and Solomon's views recall Aristotle's position: vindictiveness is morally appropriate when the expression of anger and resentment is fitting to its object, does not run to excess and become self-destructive, and has a beneficial purpose.[10] Importantly, too, vindictiveness can express self-worth, by virtue of the authority one allows oneself in judging another's conduct.[11]

The merry wives of Windsor, for example, fulfill Murphy's requirements for a proportionate vindictiveness: their passions and their actions reflect a commitment to a morally ordered society. Their outrage expressed against their would-be seducer, Falstaff, emanates both from feelings of self-worth and an appropriate defensiveness regarding community values. If the passion for vengeance can be held in balance with reason, if vindictiveness confirms a person's (or character's) commitment to a moral order, then its expression may suit with justice. Vengeance need not be a blinding, destructive passion that comes to dominate a life, as it is in some literary works, such as *Moby-Dick* and *Michael Kohlhass,* or as it appears in the psychoanalytic thought of Karen Horney, who writes of the pathology of vindictiveness. To avenge oneself or one's friend may be "just, and the just is noble," as Aristotle argued; "not to surrender" to one's enemies who have committed wrongs "is a mark of courage." To surrender is the mark of a slave (*Rhetoric* 1367b).

To return to Emilia, the well-known lines quoted above are drawn from her private conversation with Desdemona in the willow-song scene of *Othello*. In the intimacy of Desdemona's bedchamber, the women speak frankly of sexual infidelity. The threat of male betrayal and slander weighs heavily upon them as Emilia helps prepare Desdemona for bed. Othello's irrational, angry treatment of Desdemona has provoked fear and sadness in the innocent young wife, and anger in her more worldly friend, Emilia. While Desdemona sings plaintively of love's sorrow and betrayal—"*If I court moe women, you'll couch with moe men*" (4.3.56)—she hardly believes adultery possible. Emilia counters Desdemona's naïveté playfully at first, imagining cuckoldry as the wife's revenge. She entertains the possibility of her "own world" in which sexual equality is possible, and a wrong lies within a woman's power to "quickly make . . . right" (lines 81–82). Her words, however, turn bitter as she begins to contemplate the pain not only of infidelity, but also of husbands' daily abuses of wives: women are subjected to their husbands' irrational jealousies, their violence ("they strike us"), and the restraints they place on women's freedom (lines 87–90). She essentially catalogues the unjust treatment she and Desdemona have received from their husbands. She insists that women are as *human* as men are, with affections, desires, and frailty, and therefore deserving of humane treatment, protection, and care. And, like men, women should not have to suffer silently and passively as men injure their bodies and sense of self-worth. In anger, she ends her speech with a warning to men: "Then let them use us well: else let them know, / The ills we do, their ills instruct us so" (lines 101–2). The unmistakable threatening note of revenge has been sounded, as it was by a rightfully angry Shylock in *The Merchant of Venice:* the victim will get his or her own back by following the villain's lead, returning ill for ill.

Yet this is not what Emilia does. She takes her revenge on a wicked husband, but far from returning ill for ill, she rises to the occasion of justice and appeals to a higher good in what might be perceived as a paradoxical state of grace and righteous gall. The ethic of revenge she practices is not unreflectively mimetic, the product of a debased male pedagogy; rather, she reveals a moral capacity to take a stance in her marriage, in her friendship, and in the political community represented by Venetian males. She courageously takes the part of her wronged friend, Desdemona, and refuses to surrender her agency and speech to male authorities. As Desdemona has no male kin to avenge her murder, Emilia takes on the role of her avenger. Her revenge comes neither in the form of cuckoldry nor violence. Her revenge comes not for a personal injury, but rather for the harm done her beloved friend. Her revenge comes in the verbal defeat of her enemies through the disclosure of the truth. She is the logos required to bring justice to Cyprus and Venice. She fulfills the expressive function of revenge, denouncing and condemning the wrongdoing of her husband and the formerly great general, Othello. Only Emilia can attest to Desdemona's chastity and faithfulness; only Emilia can reveal Iago's villainy and Othello's ignorance and folly. Only Emilia can reside in that paradoxical moral space in which vengeance is exercised through the agency of grace. Against Desdemona's bewildered, self-effacing loyalty to Othello, against forgiveness, Emilia asserts an ethic of vindictiveness.

As Kenneth Burke argues, the play needs Emilia, for she takes on the essential "vindictive role": "Because of her relation to Iago within the conditions of the play, because of the things she alone knows, she is in the best position to take over the vindictive role we eagerly require of *someone* at this point. Or, you could state it thus: some disclosures are due, she is in a position to make them venomously, she will do best by our pent-up fury, a fury still further heightened by the fact that Desdemona died Christlike."[12] Burke's analysis confirms the structural and ethical functions of the vindictive character. He confirms, as well, that Emilia's revenge connects feelingly with the audience's passions and expectations: her revenge is *our* revenge. Her fury gives livid expression to our fury, erupting as a morally legitimate response to Iago's evil. When Iago insists that she "charm" her tongue into silence, she insists, "I will not charm my tongue, I am bound to speak: / My mistress here lies murdered in her bed" (5.2.179, 180–81). In her word "bound" lies an ethical imperative: both character and action are brought to the ground of truth here. The proverbial "Murder will out" is implied, but no "miraculous organ" is required, to echo Hamlet (2.2.529), for murder finds its tongue in Emilia who names both deed and the wicked doers of the deed.

Burke is right to emphasize that there is no one but Emilia to bring us to this point of disclosure in the play. But Shakespeare has taken pains to show us, too, that Emilia functions as an agent of true friendship, honesty, and love, and, furthermore, as a female hero whose virtue lies in her courage. Her ethics places the sanctity of female friendship and the honor of women above all negative or ambivalent cultural expectations regarding women's behavior, speech, and passions. Carole McKewin rightly hears in Emilia's speech to Desdemona "the preparation and warning for her cleansing fury in the final act."[13] When that fury is unleashed, it burns through falsehood and seeks to assert an ethical balance in the play's morally disordered world. As Kent says in *King Lear,* "Anger hath a privilege" (Folio, 2.2.64), and here it is the anger of the nonaristocratic, subordinate female that rises to a heroic pitch. Gwynne Kennedy makes the case that in early modern discourses, "[j]ust anger is either explicitly or implicitly gendered masculine. The result is a presumption of legitimacy for certain types of anger in men that is not extended to women. Women who claim the right to just anger consequently have a large obstacle to overcome."[14] Shakespeare's portrayal of a morally justified angry Emilia challenges cultural assumptions about gendered passions and the questionable ethical benefit of women's anger. Emilia is aware, certainly, of her insubordination to patriarchal authority, but feels a moral obligation to give expression to her outrage. Her commitment is to fundamental human decency, to justice, to women's honor. Silence and obedience to her husband would be far more morally egregious than disobeying societal norms. She would be "complicitous in evil," to invoke Aurel Kolnai's words.[15] Emilia refuses to accept such a graceless state.

We could say, then, that Emilia's anger does essential cultural and ethical work in *Othello,* and that she is the only grace offered in the midst of the catastrophe brought on by the men. Only Emilia can defend, with complete conviction, Desdemona's honor, for she knows her friend's mind from their intimate exchanges. Only Emilia can step forward, defiant before the jaws of death, to speak her mind and do figurative battle with the men. To Othello, she exclaims, "Thou art rash as fire to say / That she was false. O, she was heavenly true!" (5.2.132–33). When Othello wishes to stop her tongue with a show of his sword, she scornfully says, "I care not for thy sword, I'll make thee known / Though I lost twenty lives. Help, help, ho help! / The Moor hath killed my mistress! Murder, murder!" (lines 161–63). She names the villains: "'Twill out, 'twill out! I peace?" "No," she exclaims, as she outfaces Iago's command, "Zounds, hold your peace!" (lines 217–18, 216). She accuses Iago publicly of lying and villainy, and insists to Graziano and Montano, the Venetian ambassadors, "Good gentlemen, let me have leave to speak. / 'Tis proper I obey him—but not now. / Perchance, Iago, I will ne'er go home" (lines 192–94). Her condemnation of the men's villainy is absolute, and she insists that she will "speak as liberal as the north. / Let heaven and men and devils, let them all, / All, all cry shame against me, yet I'll speak" (lines 218–20). After blazoning forth the guilt of the men, Emilia becomes Iago's target and dies for her cause.

But it is not before she performs the function of lamenter over the body of her lady. One could argue that her cries against injustice have been motivated by grief and have laid the emotional and ethical groundwork for vengeance, as did feminine lamentation in ancient Greek drama. This final movement in her lamentation provokes pity, but it works, as well, to provoke revenge. When Emilia expresses her wish to be laid by Desdemona's body, the actors onstage are called forth to lay her on the bed. In performance, the uniting of the women in death offers an emblem of true friendship that is honorable and sacrificial. Emilia picks up a strain of the willow song as a lamentation for her friend and for herself. As she dies, however, Emilia speaks boldly, wishing her own "soul to bliss as I speak true! / So speaking as I think, alas, I die" (lines 248–49). The assertion of her righteousness—indeed, of her *right* to or expectation of bliss after death—is nothing short of astonishing. Her final words reflect her defiant position against the Venetian patriarchy, against early-modern religious authority, and against social mores regarding women's behavior. These words, finally, constitute Emilia's ethic of revenge. Emilia has spoken and acted from the moral ground of her being. She outfaces the men and their wickedness to women with bravery and conviction; her payback lies in being right.

I have offered many of Emilia's lines as evidence for the virtue in her vindictiveness, which blazes forth as a beacon of justice, both domestic and worldly, and offers something more than simply the structural functionality Burke perceives. If we look to the Folio text, we note that while she lives, Emilia's speech dominates the climactic scene at the play's end (5.2), where eighty-five lines belong to her. Eleven lines were added to Emilia's speech from the earlier Quarto text of *Othello*. If the Folio text reflects Shakespeare's revision of the Quarto, then we see an enhancement of Emilia's part, and the dramatist's recognition of its centrality. One added speech in particular gives Emilia the forceful rhetoric of anger and grief, as she repeats the word *villainy* six times in four lines, and laments that she will kill herself. Her husband murders her in a horrifying replication of Othello's crime, but her grief is so great that she must articulate how far she would go to express such sorrow. This outrage makes clear Emilia's part as a female tragic hero, for in this final scene, under terrific pressure, she exhibits heroic qualities similar to those of a classical warrior like Achilles—wrath, courage, mettle (in her tongue), nobility in spirit, and vindictiveness—and like Achilles she pays for her ethical stance with her life. Importantly, we might observe how she upstages the male revengers in this final scene by altering the ethics of revenge. If Iago avenges himself upon Othello with malice and envy, if Othello avenges himself upon Desdemona out of jealousy and shame, Emilia avenges herself upon the men and patriarchal authority out of a sense of moral outrage.

We might say that this scene gives extended articulation to the values Emilia possesses as those that *should* constitute the moral order in Venice and Cyprus. Emilia's honor is not lodged exclusively or even primarily in her sexual chastity, but rather in her commitment to justice and truth. The women's friendship, based on truth-telling, wifely suffering, and a desire for domestic justice, displaces the men's perverse, jaundiced friendship, which has wrought nothing but destruction, all—for Othello—in the name of masculine honor, or reputation. As Sandra Clark rightly asserts, "[T]he strength of the women's bond is startlingly vindicated."[16] In Emilia, the passions of vindictiveness—anger, resentment, vengefulness—have joined with the passion for justice, and they have carried the day in *Othello*. When Emilia speaks, she brings down the illusory artifice holding together male friendship and male-defined values in the play. Herein lies Emilia's grace.

Shakespeare invests a surprising degree of authority in female friendships and alliances, often revealing in women an integrity, moral capacity, and constancy lacking in men. In some of his plays, women seek to redress the terrible wrongs their sex has endured from men. Feminine outrage can be heard in characters who are passionately determined not to let the slandering or the death of a beloved female friend go unpunished. Characters such as Emilia, Beatrice from *Much Ado About Nothing,* and Paulina from *The Winter's Tale* take up the cause of a victimized woman, becoming her avenger. Their angry words are potent and just, for they name wrongdoers and bring to light the crimes of men against women. Indeed, anger in women can be a precondition of heroism, rather than a sign of moral weakness and thoughtless insubordination to authority. Anger can lead to revenge, but neither anger nor revenge are, by definition, intrinsically morally wayward, petty, or malicious; rather, such strong passions can be the foundation of an ethical response to injustice.

While in their anger, Shakespeare's women sometimes desire blood vengeance, some examples represent women rejecting, transcending, or sidestepping bloody solutions to injustice. Ironically, genre may not always be an accurate gauge for our expectations of what a female avenger's choice of weapon or punishment might be. The question of blood revenge seems to hover even at the periphery of comedy's borders. Emilia, for example, wants the death of Desdemona avenged, and one could argue that she knows the fatal consequence for Iago once he is exposed, but she does not cry out explicitly for blood. The comic heroine Beatrice, on the other hand, clearly wants blood repayment for Hero's slander; we can hear it in her explosive instruction to Benedick: "Kill Claudio" (4.1.288). Typically, however, comedy calls for "Craft against vice," to use Duke Vincenzio's phrase from *Measure for Measure* (3.2.270), or moral "physic," another apt metaphor, to apply to the wrongdoer.

In *The Winter's Tale,* a late romance that incorporates elements of comedy and tragedy, we find again the presence of a vocal female who brings gall and grace into play in the same ethical field. Paulina is perhaps Shakespeare's most morally creative experiment with feminine revenge. Through the moral style, inner strength, and function of this character, Shakespeare displays the work of revenge as ethically warranted, and shows how "the office / Becomes a woman best" (2.2.31–32). A righteous feminine vindictiveness is woven into the ethical pattern of *The Winter's Tale,* preparing the way for grace. Paulina's gall—her anger and moral rebuke of the irrational, punitive husband—is essential to laying the groundwork for the "quickening" of moral regeneration. Not only that, Paulina's vindictiveness keeps alive the memory of Hermione, the abused wife, in the mind of her cruel husband, Leontes. He is not allowed to forget his crime and must endure a purgatorial period before he satisfies the demands of virtuous vengeance. In the end, grace rains down upon the royal household, but only after the moral work of revenge has been done.

"Some new grace will be born": Paulina's Vengeance

The Winter's Tale offers a happy ending of sorts to our narrative of women and revenge in Shakespeare. In this play, we find various strands of our narrative brought together: mythological resonances, the moral force of vindictiveness, the expressive function of revenge, shame, and honor, and finally, the ethics of revenge wedded to an aesthetic project. Salman Rushdie's words, which serve as an epigraph for this book, find fulfillment in this dark romance, which starts as "an almost excessively masculine tale, a saga of sexual rivalry . . . betrayal, death, revenge." While the women speak up in the first half of *The Winter's Tale,* it is not until the fifth act that it becomes apparent that they "have taken over; they [have] marched in from the peripheries of the story to demand" that the "'male' plot" be "refracted, so to speak, through the prisms of its reverse and 'female' side." Shakespeare's audience might join Rushdie's narrator in realizing "that the women knew precisely what they were up to—that their stories explain, and even subsume, the men's."[17] To say this is to challenge a dominant view in Shakespearean scholarship that argues for women's subordinate or ancillary position in relation to the male protagonist. To say this is to assert the interests and values of the female characters as fundamentally in line with the plays' ethical dispositions, to say that women's functions, their speeches, their ethical work, and their presence onstage through actors' embodiments can "reverse" the perspective much literary criticism has taught us to expect. Leontes may be the guilty, remorseful male upon whom Paulina works, but her "work" lies at the ground of the drama. Furthermore, the extraordinary final scene of *The Winter's Tale* features the affections and alliances of women, the triumph of women whose stories emerge forcefully in the minds of readers and spectators.

In *The Winter's Tale*, feminine revenge reaches perhaps its greatest ethical potential, for Shakespeare has imagined revenge not only as a morally expressive force, a rebuke delivered to an offender, but also as an action more sublime than the artful trick or social drama we saw in *Twelfth Night* and *The Merry Wives of Windsor*. The play asserts revenge as a radical form of grace and Paulina as the avenging "physician" (2.3.54) who ministers to the sick (both Leontes and Hermione) and finally shows herself to be a benevolent or kindly Fury in her gift of Hermione's return. The romance addresses the deepest fantasy of revenge: that by doing harm, harm can be undone. Paulina's revenge plot acts as an antidote, undoing the potent forces of jealousy, slander, vengeance, and murder that poison the masculine "tale." Although Paulina's vindictive rebukes act upon Leontes as a harsh physic, a medicine that punishes the offender much as a Fury would hound a wrongdoer, such a tactic serves an essential and necessary process to achieve a just end. The play is a dramatic argument for the place of revenge in bringing about justice and for the ethical use of both punitive and restorative acts of revenge. In the character of Paulina, Shakespeare has raised the specter of the classical Fury, but she possesses the double character of the Furies, who in time were transformed by Athena into the Eumenides, or the "Kindly Ones." Like the Furies, Paulina grows from pursuer of the guilty to kindly healer.[18]

Paulina's revenge has its purpose in fulfilling the romance genre's requirement to restore what has been lost. Apollo's oracle has given voice to this expected pattern and aligned it with the gods' will, but it is left to Paulina to make of this design something intrinsically meaningful not only for Leontes, but also for the women in the play and for the play's audience. She practices what might be called *restorative vengeance*. Such a paradoxical phrase captures the peculiar blending of restoration and revenge found in romance. I have invoked here the modern idea of *restorative justice*, which involves a process of cooperation between the offender and the community, a meting out of punishment through which redemption is earned, and a reintegration of the offender into the community. The goal of this practice is to make the violator human again, to redeem the violator's humanity and, by doing so, to restore dignity to all members of the com-

munity. Thus, it is a form of justice focused on the dignity and moral requirements of both the individual and the community. Modern theories of
restorative justice distinguish this concept and practice from those of retributive justice and revenge, yet these practices all share a fundamental belief that wrongdoing should be met with a moral response and some form
of punishment.

In this final exploration of feminine revenge in Shakespeare, we shall
look at the question of how women's responses to injustice can not only
express agency and moral force, but also achieve constructive results for
the individuals involved (both violator and violated) and the community. It
is a question that transcends genre, yet seems best answerable in comedy
and romance. It is a question of human dignity and justice. It is a question
of great urgency for female characters who are subjected to violations of
many kinds from men.

In some of his plays, Shakespeare pairs a womanly paragon of virtue
who has been subjected to moral outrage with a passionate female friend
who comes to her defense. In such a pairing, we see that the inspiration for
feminine vindictiveness often lies in moral outrage against injustices done
to other women.[19] Paulina resembles Emilia in her fierce defense of her
friend's honor, and, like Emilia, she serves the vindictive function in the
play. If Hermione's position, like Desdemona's, is "pity, not revenge!"
(3.2.123), the counterprinciple, equally concerned with justice, is to be
found in the vibrant, angry, socially and ethically engaged character who
challenges masculine authority and gives voice to moral outrage. In her
moving self-defense at her trial, Hermione imagines "powers divine / Behold[ing] our human actions" and asserts the virtues of innocence, patience, and chastity (3.2.28–29). She claims to have acted always within
the "bound of honour," and appeals to Leontes' "own conscience" in
weighing her honor (lines 51, 46). She movingly appeals to the ghost of her
father to look down upon her, but only with eyes of pity, not vengeance.
Her just words, however, fail to alter Leontes' diseased mind; only the
death of his son, felt to be a punishment from Apollo for his sacrilegious
disregard of the oracle, can move him to relent. And soon thereafter,
Hermione dies (or appears to die) as well.

It is left to Paulina, then, to unleash vindictiveness upon Leontes, and
she does so with the full force of moral rebuke. From her first angry words
spoken in defense of her friend Hermione to her final staging of reconcili-
ations in the royal family, Paulina expresses an ethical stance in the play
that encompasses both gall and grace. In the romance genre, Shakespeare's
handling of the expression, means, and ends of vindictiveness differs in significant ways from its function in tragedy. For one, the crimes against
Hermione and the eruption of Paulina's gall occur early in the play, leaving much time for the avenger to work her physic upon the guilty husband,

Leontes. Slander, "Whose sting is sharper than the sword's" (2.3.86), is the painful wrong Hermione suffers, and her suffering leads to death. *The Winter's Tale* equivocates upon this pattern, which we see played out in *Much Ado About Nothing* (with the figurative death and resurrection of Hero) and *Othello* (with the literal death of Desdemona). Whether Hermione literally dies is an irresolvable question in the play, yet she does appear as a ghost and she does disappear from court for sixteen years. In effect, she is dead to Leontes and the court.

In Paulina's first encounter with Leontes, she has taken upon herself the "office" that "Becomes a woman best" (2.2.31, 32)—to rebuke the King for his fits of lunacy and to defend Hermione's honor. Hermione's attendant, Emilia, attests to Paulina's moral character: "Your honour and your goodness is so evident . . . there is no lady living / So meet for this great errand" (lines 43, 45–46). Knowing that she is an "audacious lady" (2.3.42), fearless and outspoken, Leontes has ordered Paulina's husband, Antigonus, to keep her from him. He is right to fear Paulina, for in "red-look'd anger" (2.2.34) she will champion the Queen and her newborn girl as an "advocate to th' loud'st" (2.2.39). In matters of honor and moral commitment, Paulina refuses to be ruled by her husband (2.3.50); her agency and integrity are one and lie within her own self-government. She deems herself the King's "loyal servant," "physician," and "obedient counsellor" (lines 54, 54, 55), yet she "dares" (line 55) define each role in relation to a higher good than she finds reflected in the King. She serves the "good," but she makes clear where she finds it located by repeating the word seven times in seven lines—in reference to Hermione. In Hermione's defense, Paulina fiercely claims heroic mettle in her desire to prove the Queen's virtue in a trial by combat: "Good queen, my lord, good queen: I say good queen, / And would by combat make her good, so were I / A man" (2.3.59–61).

Such vaulting heroism represents only a momentary gesture or fantasy, for the image and function Paulina fits most consistently is that of a moral physician. Such a metaphoric description was used by the Reformers Calvin and Luther to justify the bitter medicine preachers must use necessarily for curing the ailments of those who are morally sick.[20] Paulina's forceful rebuke of Leontes can been understood in relation to Saint Paul and the early modern Reformers' cultivation of the Pauline paradigm for preachers. As Huston Diehl astutely observes, Reformers such as Calvin and Luther wrote commentaries on Saint Paul's Acts and Epistles that "call attention to the way Paul rebukes the men he would convert" with bitter, sharp, discomforting words.[21] The state of discomfort, which we see painfully exhibited in the character of Leontes, is essential for provoking moral quickening and reformation. When Paulina asserts, "I'll use that tongue I have: if wit flow from't / As boldness from my bosom, let't not be doubted / I shall do good" (2.2.52–54), she makes a claim for the ethical intention of her speech, though it is far from "honey-mouth'd" (line 33). She claims the authority and wisdom of a moral physician, whose words are "as medicinal as true, / Honest, as either, to purge [Leontes] of that humour," "his tyrannous passion" (2.3.37–38, 28). Her counseling, then, obeys a higher good—the good she seeks to find in Leontes—and her words, like performatives, have force, eventually catching the conscience of the King. Such performatives are purgatives, working inwardly in Leontes' mind, releasing the bad humors, and bringing him back into a balance that accords with reason and morality.

She also will fulfill Paul's paradoxical injunction against revenge, which apparently leaves vengeance to the Lord, while allowing the would-be avenger the satisfaction that arises when one can "ouercome euil with goodnes" (Rom. 12:21). Such satisfaction Paul renders through an image of cruel punishment, which the victim metes out figuratively: the heaping of coals of fire on one's enemy's head. Ironically, the schadenfreude achieved here is the result of an act of *kindness:* "if thine enemie hunger, feede him: if he thirst, giue him drinke" (12:20). Paul urges his audience to "Abhorre that which is euil, and cleaue vnto that which is good" (12:9), yet surely the repayment of evil with good (a good that is received like scalding coals) is a strange kind of virtuous vengeance. Paulina follows Paul in not recompensing evil for evil (12:17), but she rains the painful truth upon Leontes' head, and he can only grope for cover, lodging misogynist names like bullets at the source of truth: "mankind witch," "most intelligencing bawd," "gross hag" (2.3.67, 68, 107). If sin is the suppression of grace, as Paul defines it, then Leontes' early attempts to suppress Paulina and then his subsequent embrace of her indicate her function as grace in his moral life. Paulina rebukes Leontes' failure to serve as a minister of God or the gods, who practice just vengeance upon those who do evil (Rom. 13:4). His revenge upon Hermione abuses his office as a divine minister of vengeance, and the appropriation of this office is left to the good, honorable Paulina, whose spiritual authority has been figured in her name.

In Paulina's second meeting with Leontes, she delivers the message of Hermione's death. For such a crime, she can only think of punishment, of the gods' vengeance: "The sweet'st, dear'st creature's dead: and vengeance for't / Not dropp'd down yet" (3.2.201–2). Earlier, the King's counselor Camillo wishes vengeance upon whoever slanders Hermione: "I would not be a stander-by, to hear / My sovereign mistress clouded so, without / My present vengeance taken" (1.2.279–81). Like Camillo, Paulina articulates what is just: for a "sin" (line 283) such as slander or murder, which are virtually equivalent socially speaking, vengeance is required. Camillo indicates that he would take the task of vengeance upon himself, even if the slanderer were the King. Paulina, in contrast, seems to be leaving vengeance to the gods. Yet as the play progresses, ironically, Camillo flees Bohemia and Paulina stays to conspire with the gods, as it were, against the slanderer-murderer Leontes. Her revenge is conjunctive with the gods' will and unfolds over time.

As in other plays such as *The Merchant of Venice,* this play's language is steeped in economic metaphors related to revenge: debt, recompense, loss, and redeem are the most obvious examples. Act 5 opens with explicit references to redeeming faults and paying down debt, or paying with interest as his counselor Cleomenes claims Leontes has done. Such metaphors lead Cleomenes to advise Leontes that he has suffered enough; the gods have forgiven you, he proclaims, so it is now time to "forgive yourself" (5.1.6). Leontes does not believe he is worthy of forgiveness, and Paulina, to whom Leontes has given over the care of his soul, agrees. Over the course of sixteen years, Leontes has been paying for his egregious sins. In committing a terrible offense against his wife and their children, he had been willfully deaf to the wise counsel of anyone in his kingdom. Upon Paulina, he poured venom, falling into a furious, misogynist rant, but when he suffers the total loss of his family, his delusions crumble, his rage dissipates, and he turns himself over to her. At first Paulina is merciless, cursing him in her despair. He accepts her bitterness, now saying, "Thou canst not speak too much; I have deserv'd / All tongues to talk their bitt'rest" (3.2.215–16). When she sees that he "is touch'd / To th' noble heart" (lines 221–22), Paulina relents, begs his forgiveness, and says she will speak no more of Hermione and their dead son. "What's gone and what's past help / Should be past grief. . . . Let me be punish'd, that have minded you / Of what you should forget" (lines 222–23, 225–26). Yet she does not hold to what she says here. Indeed, she will subscribe to the precise opposite view on matters: she will ensure that the past stays ever present, that grief is ever renewed, that Hermione's memory is ever living, and that Leontes suffers perpetual punishment.[22]

Sixteen years later, at the start of act 5, Leontes speaks of remembering Hermione, and Paulina reinforces his lament by speaking of "[her] you killed" (5.1.15). This reminder of his sin reopens the still-fresh wound, a wound Paulina has fed salt: "it is as bitter / Upon thy tongue as in my thought. Now, good now, / Say so but seldom" (lines 18–20). Memory, as we see in countless examples from literature, ethnography, and psychology, plays a crucial role in revenge: remembrance keeps the mind fixated on its object, revenge, whereas forgetting shifts attention away from revenge. It is Paulina's memory that serves her revenge; her gall is an ever-present moral irritant. While Leontes' counselors Cleomenes and Dion would speak for the gods ("Do as the heavens have done, forget your evil; / With them, forgive yourself" [5.1.5–6]), Paulina speaks for Hermione and for the oracle; her remembrance counters the lords' "remembrance" of the "present comfort, and . . . future good" of their sovereign, Leontes (5.1.25,

32). Leontes makes this concession to Paulina: "Good Paulina, / Who hast the memory of Hermione, / I know, in honour,—O, that ever I / Had squar'd me to thy counsel!" (lines 49–52). His regret is profound.

Paulina's position of moral authority and political power is striking; she has risen to become Leontes' most trusted counselor. She feeds his image of Hermione's perfection and gains from him an oath to never marry without her consent. In the fifth act, an odd piece of dialogue gives us a sense of Paulina's hold over Leontes' imagination and passions. Paulina and Leontes imagine a supernatural occurrence in which the ghost of Hermione appears to chastise Leontes for taking another wife. Paulina claims that Hermione would have "just cause" for chastisement, and Leontes says, she "would incense me / To murder her I married" (lines 61, 61–62). A murderous Hermione must strike listeners as entirely uncharacteristic, for Hermione's virtuous patience and restraint from revenge distinguished her while she lived, and marked her character as in conformity with essential Christian values. But such murderousness might be seen as the extreme end of *Paulina's* passions. Paulina responds by figuring herself in the position of ghost, with herself urging Leontes' murder of a second wife:

> *I* should so:
> Were *I* the ghost that walk'd, *I'd* bid you mark
> Her eye, and tell *me* for what dull part in't
> You chose her: then *I'd* shriek, that even your ears
> Should rift to hear *me;* and the words that follow'd
> Should be "Remember *mine."*
>
> (lines 62–67, my emphases)

Paulina's graphic imagination betrays her punitive function as a Fury, which takes the form of the vengeful ghost that Hermione refuses to be. Shrieking in Leontes' ear, striking his guilty conscience, she would go so far as to drive him to murder.

The specter of vengeance recalls the earlier reported appearance of Hermione's ghost to Antigonus: he sees a figure "in pure white robes, / Like very sanctity," a "vessel of . . . sorrow" (3.3.22–23, 21). She does not come in fury, he notes, for in her sorrowing aspect, she names her child *Perdita* (the Lost One), declares that because of "this ungentle business, / Put on thee by my lord" (lines 34–35), he will never see his wife, Paulina, again, and then "with shrieks, / . . . melt[s] into air" (lines 36–37). Hermione may have been the vessel of sorrow and patience, but Paulina is the vessel of vindictiveness.

As the revenge nears its wondrous end, the royal party is drawn away from the patriarchal site of the palace to a feminine space, Paulina's separate lodging, where, one might gather, she and Hermione have secretly lived in friendship for the past sixteen years. Paulina has orchestrated an unveiling, a showing, which is made possible by the return of Hermione's daughter, Perdita. Now that one loss has been restored, in fulfillment of the oracle's word, Paulina can work to restore other losses. All along, she has served the vindictive function in the play—her just anger has simmered and kept alive Hermione's image in Leontes' mind and our minds; it has worked like gall, keeping his remorse and self-chastisement active. The association between Paulina and Saint Paul continues to resonate in this final scene. As Huston Diehl sees it, we are invited to participate in a wonder distinctly marked as Pauline, "born of rebuke and remembrance."[23] In Paulina's character, Shakespeare has given full play to the vindictive passions, and his character has performed her charge brilliantly. Not only does she give moral force to rebuke, but she molds her stone into the material form and artistic articulation of rebuke, for as Leontes perceives, "the stone rebuke[s] me . . . " (5.3.37).

Leontes gazes upon the stone, and the passion that arises in him is shame:

> I am asham'd: does not the stone rebuke me
> For being more stone than it? O royal piece!
> There's magic in thy majesty, which has
> My evils conjur'd to remembrance. . . .
>
> (5.3.37–40)

In his book on shame in Shakespeare, Ewan Fernie has anatomized shame brilliantly, arguing that early modern Christian writers would recognize the spiritual value of shame. As he puts it, "[S]hame is an approach to truth, a self-realisation. It is the shattering of the false self, the end of illusion. . . . Shakespearean shame is the beginning of a spiritual journey." Shame "performs . . . ethical work," he asserts.[24] Paulina is instrumental in maintaining the conditions under which shame can thrive and do its work. Her rebuke, sustained over time and now embodied in Hermione's form, calls to mind the memory of Leontes' evils. He has been visiting the grave of Hermione and his son on a daily basis, feeling "Our shame perpetual" and shedding tears as his "recreation" (3.2.238, 240). The play shows us that he cannot be fully "re-created" until he has been shattered by shame, cleansed by tears, and invited back into the moral community through a ritual conducted by Paulina.

Shakespeare displays the painfully slow process of justice unfolding through time at the very ground of a character's being. Justice is not simply an abstract quality of the universe, tied inextricably to the oracle and the gods' will. "Justice is a matter of personal character," Robert C. Solomon argues, of what one does and how one directs one's passions.[25] Justice is expressed, then, in the fitting repayment for wrongful actions and passions. In that respect, the aims of vengeance meet those of justice, for they are inextricably bound up together, and designed to bring a self or soul back into moral balance. Paulina's vengeance upon Leontes is ethically productive, a matter of *her* character, as much as of Leontes' character.

In her compassion, Paulina is almost sorry for the pain she inflicts, but she is aware of the greatness of her task: "I am sorry, sir, I have thus far stirr'd you: but / I could afflict you farther" (5.3.74–75). Leontes responds by begging her, "Do, Paulina; / For this affliction has a taste as sweet / As any cordial comfort" (lines 75–77). There is an unexpected sweetness in gall; the "cordial comfort"—the medicine applied to his stony heart—has been painful, but it has acted upon him as a healing grace. In the stony Hermione, there seems to arise a spiritual manifestation of grace come to earth. The final "affliction" Leontes must endure is the "awakening" of the stone—Hermione and his heart—which comes with the awakening of his faith. Hermione calls upon the gods to pour graces upon her daughter; she has been transformed by Paulina into a conduit of grace. In this appeal, we see how Paulina's gall has been transmuted into grace.

When she shows the statue of Hermione, she insists "the stone is mine" (5.3.58). She has imagined herself as Hermione's punitive ghost, and here she takes possession of Hermione / the stone. The work is hers, Hermione's justice is hers, the moral outrage is hers. Hermione's cause has been Paulina's life's cause: without children, without husband, she has had only Hermione, her beloved friend. But the work she does in this final scene will bring an end to the roles they have all played in this revenge drama. Harry Keyishian argues, "[T]hough [Leontes' punishments] are not, strictly speaking, revenges, since they do not issue from human agencies, Paulina's role in prolonging and enforcing Leontes' suffering does the work of a revenge that redeems both revenger and offender."[26] This sort of redemptive work, I argue, lies at the heart of Paulina's restorative vengeance. Her satisfaction as an avenger will lie not only in punishment, but also in reconciliation.

The moment when Leontes crosses over the threshold (*limen*) into Paulina's house signals a shift into the liminal space of transformation. The dialogue between the restorative avenger and the criminal reveals to us the success of Paulina's preparatory work. She has provided not only rebuke, but comfort as well, and paradoxically comfort in rebuke. Leontes cannot refrain from exclaiming to her, "O grave and good Paulina, the great comfort / That I have had of thee!" (5.3.1–2). Her reply insists upon the reciprocity of the arduous moral process they have undertaken together: "What, sovereign sir, / I did not well, I meant well. All my services / You have paid home" (lines 2–4). Paulina acknowledges not only Leontes' reward to her for service, but his repayment of a moral debt. Her expression "paid home" recalls various early modern meanings of *home,* which I explored in an earlier chapter on *King Lear.* Like Lear, Leontes violates the moral order with his extreme passion and, in doing so, he shatters home. Both monarchs must accept service and instruction of a most bitter kind to help bring them "home," or into intimate contact with their own moral beings. Paulina speaks of Leontes' visit to her house in surprising terms as "a surplus of your grace, which never / My life may last to answer" (lines 7–8). She revives the language of subject to monarch because, in her judgment, he once more warrants the royal title "Grace." Her answering grace will come in the multivalent form of Hermione's stone, which rebukes even as it awakens faith, provokes shame as surely as it does wonder, creates hope where there realistically should be none, and (miraculously) comes to life, which seems to defy the laws of nature.

While Paulina has worked toward a final restorative vengeance, treating Leontes as a moral agent who can be reformed, Hermione has been shrouded in silence and absence. The women's friendship has unfolded beyond our sight, evidenced only in their joint effort at raising the dead in this final scene. When she is shown as a statue, Hermione's silent form provokes silence, at least momentarily, and Paulina approves of the spectators' wondering silence. The realm we find ourselves in is rendered in distinctly visual and performative terms.[27] The very text itself, in the words of the Third Gentleman, says that if you are merely reading or hearing the words, "Then have you lost a sight which was to be seen, cannot be spoken of" (5.2.43–44). The final scene, then, engages all of the senses, but to see it is to be in the presence of a visual wonder, to enter into a liminal space that promises to be transformative. And it is a wonder to see Paulina in the role of avenger, ministering to the royal family and orchestrating the final restorations, the promised end of revenge. Earlier she had sworn to Leontes that Hermione was dead, and cruelly challenged him to "bring / Tincture, or lustre in her lip, her eye / Heat outwardly or breath within" (3.2.204–6). If he could perform such a godly act, she claims, she would serve him. But because he kills rather than revives, he is a tyrant worth "nothing but despair" (line 210). She claimed at the time of Hermione's death that not even ten thousand years of penance would move the gods (or her) to forgiveness. In time she relents; in time she brings tincture and heat to Hermione. In time she performs the godly act. In time, she exhibits the Pauline principle: "by grace through faith" (Eph. 2.8).

When Hermione finally speaks, she has words only for the gods and her daughter; indeed, she claims to have "preserv'd" herself only "to see the issue" (5.3.127, 128). She claims agency in choosing to live and to wait for a time when the tenuous condition in which her family exists will be altered. "Issue" suggests her patient expectation, fed by the oracle's word, in seeing Perdita, her progeny, and in finding what fortune has befallen her. She has not a single word for Leontes, yet she can bear witness to the "issue" Paulina's medicine has extracted from his diseased mind. The evidence flows forth from his humbled, shamed form, which in its every aspect bespeaks remorse, grief, and newfound joy. As Stanley Cavell enigmatically writes, "The first move of revenge it seems easy to determine; the first move to set aside revenge, impossible."[28] At what point do vindictive feelings abate? At what point does the specter of vengeance melt away?

The final scene generates the pleasure and rich satisfaction of reconciliation, wonder, and joy, yet nowhere do we find forgiveness named, begged for, or spoken with words. Why the absence of such words? Shakespeare's concern seems to be with the enactment of forgiveness as a transcendent, moving "action," in the Aristotelian sense, as a moral force working its way outward through the final stage of revenge. Years before, Hermione met Leontes' accusations against her not with words of resentment and hatred, but with incomprehension: "You speak a language that I understand not" (3.2.80). In the end, Hermione does not use language to forgive him, nor does Leontes need to ask for forgiveness. In the end, the long drawn-out process of forgiveness (or Leontes' becoming worthy of forgiveness) and the enactment of its final rite lie in the hands of the avenger, who presides over the ethical domain of the kingdom and the souls of its suffering monarchs. Through her years of rebuke, she has not only kept Leontes' conscience vitally active; she has helped him achieve self-forgiveness, which allows him to become fully human once more in the presence of the benevolent Hermione. Furthermore, the play enacts a tough morality of forgiveness, insisting that the Christian virtue of forgiveness is earned—and desired by theater audiences—only *after* revenge.[29]

Paulina, then, has been a most virtuous avenger, steadfast in her goal of restoring losses in the kingdom. In the end, she can proclaim triumphantly that the members of the royal family are "precious winners all" (5.3.131). She turns to them—and to the audience—and says, "your exultation / Partake to every one" (lines 131–32). *The Winter's Tale* displays the genuine positive effects of vengeance, as its restorative force is felt on the stage and in the theater. Paulina's rebukes constitute the necessary moral groundwork to prepare the way for restored joy and harmony in the royal family. What has been severed will be joined again. Paulina is the constant reminder, the prod to remembrance in the palace, ensuring that Hermione's image does not fade. She performs the positive function of revenge, though not without some of revenge's capacity for harm. But Leontes welcomes the pain, and embraces the affliction that eventually leads to a re-creation of his moral self, showing how forceful the battering of a stony heart must be, to echo John Donne's famous sonnet.

The story of Paulina, however, is not without pathos, for at the end of the play, after her work is done, her haunting words remind us of *her* dead husband, "that's never to be found again" (line 134), whom she will "Lament, till I am lost" (line 135). Functioning as the avenger has had its personal costs. The loss of her husband years ago is a still-open wound, so painful it promises to crush her. By reminding the kingdom and us of her loss, of death as the absolute, Paulina is cast as Leontes' double. In a sense, what she has lost, he has found. She, too, has suffered the death of a spouse for sixteen years, but unlike Leontes, there is no benevolent force to raise him seemingly from the dead. Her husband, Antigonus, is "never to be found again," she laments (line 134). Leontes attributes to Paulina the power of "finding" Hermione: "Thou hast found mine" (line 138), and he moves quickly to reciprocate in the only way he can, by insisting that Paulina accept "a husband . . . by my consent, / As I by thine a wife: this is a match, / And made between 's by vows" (lines 136–38). He wishes to give return for the good she has done (good for good), but surely his offer sounds as strange and bewildering to Paulina and to an audience as the Duke's offer of marriage to Isabella at the end of *Measure for Measure*. The male protagonist's use of marriage to make all's well that ends well suits the genres of comedy and romance, but the woman's particular emotional and ethical constitution seems to be ignored. When Paulina calls herself an old turtle-dove (line 132) in this scene, she means to characterize herself as a constant, faithful wife, who like the proverbial turtle mates for life.

What matters most in Leontes' final speech to Paulina, however, is his acknowledgment of her virtues: her "worth and honesty / Is richly noted; and here justified / By us, a pair of kings" (lines 144–46). Here Shakespeare vindicates the outspoken, justice-minded woman. No longer must such a woman sustain slanderous abuse, being called a lewd woman, as Paulina is, or a "callat / Of boundless tongue, who late hath beat her husband, / And now baits me" (2.3.90–92). He who spoke such venomous words is made to acknowledge such a woman's fundamental worth, her rightness, her moral integrity. Indeed, in the final moments of the drama, Leontes looks to Paulina as the leader of their newly formed community: "Lead us from hence," he says to her, to a place where they will exchange tales of their "part[s] / Perform'd in this wide gap of time, since first / We were dissever'd" (5.3.152, 153–55). His words resonate in interesting ways: "part" and "perform'd" bring to our awareness the theatrical nature of this event. "Gap" and "dissever'd" convey the various kinds of distance and severings that have marked the ethical shape of the play. Camillo's image from early in the play of two friends shaking hands "as over a vast" (1.1.30) comes full circle. Figuratively speaking, it is not a question of whether Paulina accepts the hand of Camillo, which Leontes is advocating, but rather the resolution of the question of how enemies can shake hands as friends. The two friends shaking hands "as over a vast" are, finally, Paulina and Leontes. In this image, we find Shakespeare's moving portrayal of the avenger spanning that vast moral ground to reach her enemy in peace.

Conclusion

Cᴀɴ ᴛʜᴇʀᴇ ʙᴇ ᴀ ᴠɪʀᴛᴜᴇ ɪɴ ᴠᴇɴɢᴇᴀɴᴄᴇ? Cᴀɴ ʀᴇᴠᴇɴɢᴇ ᴅᴏ ᴇᴛʜɪᴄᴀʟ ᴡᴏʀᴋ? Can revenge be the obligation of women? I have been rather bold in offering answers to such questions in relation to Shakespeare's women. By uncovering positive functions in female characters' speech and actions and marshaling arguments from a variety of quarters—Aristotle, Saint Paul, Thomas Aquinas, Francis Bacon, Peter A. French, Robert C. Solomon—I have made the case for Shakespeare's women as ethical agents who articulate fundamental experiences with injustice and revenge. In his dramas, Shakespeare discloses how vengeful women take upon their "shoulders the moral duty of empowering what is right," to quote Peter A. French.[1] Through their agency and moral courage, avenging women do not permit the unjust to get away with stealing the honor or lives of kin, of the innocent, of women and children, through slander, rape, and murder. As the early modern meanings of *revenge, vengeance, retaliation,* and *retribution* all affirm, wrongdoers incur moral and social debts, and the avenger's job is to make them pay. The claims of justice are not necessarily at odds with the motives and ends of vengeance.

Virtuous female avengers such as Paulina and Emilia might be understood as pursuing what Peter de la Primaudaye has called "the best reuenge": "[T]he best reuenge and most honorable victorie, which we can carie away from our enimies, will be to surpasse them in diligence, bountie, magnanimitie, good-turnes, and in all vertuous actions: whereby they wil sooner perceiue and confesse them selues vanquished & constrained to stop their mouth, and to represse their toong, than by any other force, which we can oppose against them."[2] De la Primaudaye's book of moral philosophy, *The French Academie,* translated into English in 1586, shares the conservative Stoic-Christian position against revenge commonly found in early modern discourses on the subject. Yet there is a paradoxical quality to his idea of "revengeless revenge," as Harry Keyishian rightly calls it.[3] What he describes is not only the principle of virtue as its own reward, but virtue as a kind of revenge-driven activity. The intent behind virtue is to exhibit itself forcefully so that the wrongdoer eventually undoes himself. This is a subtle transmutation of revenge, or an appropriation of revenge's capacity by the virtuous, who amazingly do not have to pick up a weapon to foil a villain. We might think of the conceit of "killing" someone with "kindness," to echo the title of an Elizabethan play. Or Saint Paul's famous letter to the Romans: in the very passage where he reinforces that vengeance belongs to God, he advocates giving the hungry enemy food, and the thirsty enemy drink, "for in so doing, thou shalt heape coles of fyre on his head" (Rom. 12:19–20). This sounds like nothing so much as the moral and emotional *satisfaction* of revenge. Furthermore, it is a figurative revenge particularly suitable to the sociocultural and moral circumstances in which Shakespeare depicts many of his female characters. Saint Paul does not argue away the satisfaction achieved through imagining the burning coals descending on one's enemy's head. The moral problem does not lie in vengefulness itself, but rather the mode of vengeance. If one can find a virtuous path to revenge, if one can "ouercome euil with goodness" (Rom. 12:21) by schooling one's enemy through rebuke, reinforcing the honor of women and marriage, bringing a beloved friend back from the dead, then revenge possesses a moral force. The vindictive passions have served a virtuous function, and gall and grace emerge together in a felicitous paradox.

In light of Primaudaye's "best reuenge," I wish to look at a final play, one of Shakespeare's so-called problem comedies. *Measure for Measure* explicitly foregrounds problems of reciprocity in the moral realm, and places its female characters in ethically challenging positions that require them to make decisions about what constitutes a just measure in response to vice. The cases of the wronged women in *Measure for Measure* offer subtle counterpoints to those of the women in *Othello, Much Ado About Nothing,* and *The Winter's Tale.* While women in all of these plays are subjected to men's slander, irrational jealousy, and murderousness, there are examples in each play of a strong woman (Emilia, Beatrice, Paulina) who speaks defiantly and does what she can to fight injustice. These women are avengers, if not entirely in their actions, then in their speech and intention at the very least. In *Measure for Measure,* the women exercise their agency and give voice to vindictiveness through bold speech and the infamous bedtrick, yet they are caught up in the Duke's plot. The question of how the women participate in the Duke's "Craft against vice" (3.2.270) and how they function overall in Shakespeare's comedy has divided critics radically. Are the female characters merely "instruments of some more mightier member / That sets them on" (5.1.236–37)? Are their words and actions manipulated to the point where they become no more than the Duke's "victims," "puppets," or at best "cooperative pawns" in a masculine master plot?[4] Do we witness the tragedy of Isabella, as at least one critic argues?[5]

Clearly, Isabella and Mariana possess reason and speak feelingly onstage. Claudio credits Isabella rightly with "prosperous art" (1.2.174), by which he means the ability to use reason and discourse to persuade her audience. The women may be drawn into the Duke's plot, and their actions sanctioned by the religious authority he pretends to possess, but they do not function *merely* as his mouthpiece and his agents. They act in their own interests and in the interest of moral restitution. They make visible and audible to the theater audience the extraordinary pressures placed on virtuous women whose honor is compromised and whose words and actions can be turned against them. We might join Richard Wheeler in pointing out that sexual degradation is the greatest threat to characters in this play's world; such a threat lies disturbingly at "the very center of the comic action."[6] But we should go further and state that the significance of sexual degradation lies in its power to shatter integrity and moral wholeness. Isabella cries out fiercely against this degradation of the moral self through forced sexual union. Her appeal to chastity as an ultimate personal and social good is central to the play's ethos. This appeal does not function to characterize Isabella as prideful, morally zealous, selfish, or eccentric, but rather to give the audience a moral gauge in the play's world. As Barbara Baines helpfully points out, "[T]he priority Isabella places on chastity reflects the values of the entire society that the play depicts. . . . Society, not scripture, defines chastity as the definitive virtue that gives identity and place to women and to men. . . . [S]ecular law prescribes [chastity] as a remedy for the diseased state."[7]

While the male characters are equally vulnerable to sexual degradation, the women feel more keenly the choices involving their chastity (sexual purity) and honor (personal integrity). Far more than the men, they elicit sympathy from the audience for the moral outrages they must bear. As an abandoned fiancée, the grieving Mariana appears pitiful to the Duke and Isabella, yet also as righteous and empowered in her willing pursuit of domestic justice. It is no small irony, however, that Mariana's act of prenuptial sex is potentially degrading to herself. But she chooses not to see it that way, and to enter Angelo's bed with chaste intentions. That the Duke, Isabella, Angelo, and Mariana herself do not question the morality of what she does suggests the play's complicity with a form of justice that is poetic and retributive. Craft against vice carries the day. And ultimately, chastity will be regulated by the state when the Duke enforces Angelo's marriage to Mariana.

As the novice who becomes an object of desire, Isabella finds herself in a deeply ironic, compromised position. While she had sought refuge from the urban corruption of Vienna in the convent, at the start of the play, she finds herself drawn reluctantly back into worldly business. She is confronted directly with the horrifying prospect of her own sexual degradation when Angelo insists that she must give her chastity as the price for her brother Claudio's life. In a display of power, Angelo attempts to "arrest" her words, even as he would arrest her body. Isabella threatens revenge:

> I will proclaim thee, Angelo, look for't.
> Sign me a present pardon for my brother,
> Or with an outstretch'd throat I'll tell the world aloud
> What man thou art.
>
>   (2.4.150–53)

He responds swiftly with menacing words: "Who will believe thee, Isabel?" (2.4.153). He successfully arrests her words here as he thwarts her just revenge, and shows himself pitiless and cruel in his assertion of power. This scene, including Isabella's plaintive soliloquy—"To whom should I complain? Did I tell this, / Who would believe me?" (2.4.170–71)—encourages the audience's harsh judgment of Angelo.

Indeed, the play's rhetoric of judging and measuring indicates the problematic relationship between justice and law, which have been so utterly debased in Vienna that "the rod" is "more mock'd than fear'd" and "decrees, / Dead to infliction, to themselves are dead, / And Liberty plucks Justice by the nose" (1.3.26, 27, 27–29). The first word of the play is "Escalus," which means "scales," and the sense one gets very quickly as the play unfolds is that the scales of justice have tipped too far in the drection of leniency. When Angelo becomes deputy, however, they tip too far the other way. Ironically, his enforcement of the law shows not so much how "hideous" (1.4.63), "biting" (1.3.19), and "angry" (3.1.201) Viennese law is, but rather how hypocritical the judge's moral code is. In its examination of ethical questions related to judgment and justice, *Measure for Measure* shares concerns with *The Merchant of Venice* and *The Tempest*. These three plays try the moral power of characters, particularly when the opportunity for revenge arises. Shylock, Portia, Prospero, Angelo, the Duke, Isabella, and Mariana all find themselves with a degree of power and an opportunity to act and speak decisively. They each stand in judgment of wrongdoers, and each contends with questions of mercy, revenge, and justice. None of these characters entirely rejects revenge; rather, each believes that he or she pursues justice through a morally instructive vengeful plot or device. Shylock and Angelo offer foils to the others, for they would go so far as to take a life for a sin or debt, unbalancing the *talionic* equation altogether. The women join the Duke in striving for a justice that balances mercy and revenge, not so that justice and mercy become "almost indistinguishable," as Linda Anderson argues,[8] but so that these forces can act together to achieve the greatest social good.

For the female characters, honor and justice are essential virtues. In *Measure for Measure,* violations against women's honor prove to be the sticking point in the renewal of justice in the state. The Duke places much stock in the women's virtue, admiring "the truth of honour" in Isabella (3.1.163), whose virtue remains intact during Angelo's "assault," as the

Duke himself calls it (line 183). In the trial scene (5.1) he emphasizes how
Angelo "hath wrong'd" Isabella's "well defended honor" (lines 399, 400),
and he places Angelo's very life in Isabella's hands. Indeed, he declares
himself "Attorneyed at your service" (line 383), meaning that he appears
as Isabella's agent. When Isabella approaches the Duke in this scene, she
repeats the word *justice* five times in her first speech alone. The Duke seems
prepared to give her justice in the form of Angelo's execution, which would
represent the state's retribution against a criminal.

When the audience first meets Isabella, she is a novice in a convent of
the Poor Clares, begging for "a more strict restraint / Upon the sisters"
(1.4.4–5). She is "precise," or puritanical, not only in her religious practice, but also in her perceptions of human behavior and in her conduct in
the world. When Lucio visits her in the convent, imploring her to "Assay
the power you have" (1.4.76) to save Claudio's life, Isabella is confronted
with the prospect of her brother's death and her need to find "grace" to
"soften" (1.4.69, 70) the authority who has ordered this harsh sentence.
When Isabella moves from the secluded convent into the world, she finds
herself subject to the kinds of passions and crises she wished to avoid
through "strict restraint." Her intervention on behalf of her brother leads
Isabella to moments of moral crisis that try her virtue in ways she could not
have imagined as a cloistered nun. These ethically precarious moments are
opportunities for her to "Assay" her "power," a power she initially "doubt[s]"
(lines 76, 77) she has. Under extreme pressure, she must choose whether
to save Claudio's life or her chastity; to avenge or not to avenge the wrong
Angelo has done her (first through the bed-trick, and then through his execution); and, finally, to accept or refuse the Duke's proposal of marriage.

Isabella's encounters with Angelo and the Duke (and the Duke-as-friar)
display her capacity for grace and reason, as well as for revenge and mercy.
Like Portia, who must work against the seemingly inevitable death of Antonio, Isabella uses her "prosperous art" to try to win back life. When she
meets with Angelo, the deputy who has condemned her brother to death,
she appeals first to his sense of mercy. When Angelo insists there is "no
remedy" (2.2.48), Isabella invokes the seventh book of Matthew, reminding Angelo of a God, the ultimate judge, who will "judge you as you are."
"O, think on that," she says, "And mercy then will breathe within your lips,
/ Like man new made" (lines 77–79). To this vision of a newly made Angelo, she adds the uncanny suggestion of a sexual fault lying within Angelo's heart: "authority," she insists, "though it err like others,"

> Hath yet a kind of medicine in itself
> That skins the vice o'th'top. Go to your bosom,
> Knock there, and ask your heart what it doth know
> That's like my brother's fault. If it confess

> A natural guiltiness, such as is his,
> Let it not sound a thought upon your tongue
> Against my brother's life.
>
> (lines 135–42)

Angelo finds himself utterly subdued by the moral clarity and rationality of her argument, which has pierced to the truth of his "natural guiltiness," and by the sensuality expressed in her form and voice. He registers his response to her in private words that play on the word *sense;* it is a sensuality beyond reason that has quickened in Angelo.

When Angelo and Isabella meet again, the audience encounters a man steeped so deeply in lust that he appears to enjoy striking a vicious bargain with the novice to give his vice free reign: "either / You must lay down the treasures of your body / To this suppos'd, or else to let him suffer: / What would you do?" (2.4.95–98). Angelo wishes to take Isabella's chastity in exchange for Claudio's life. Isabella recognizes a paradox in this situation, as she finds a "devilish mercy in the judge" (3.1.64). Isabella finds herself in the ethical bind of this paradox—her decision is a matter of life and death for her brother and for herself. Isabella equates chastity with eternal life, which means that she would die spiritually so that Claudio can resume his earthly existence: life for life. It is a sacrifice that anguishes Isabella and drives her to a stark position: "More than our brother is our chastity" (2.4.184). What she faces is a collapse of all values into appetite. Mercy has been perverted by lust, which now seems to govern right and wrong, law and justice, with a tyranny of its own. She holds firm before this moral chaos, and invests all authority in chastity. She will appeal to her brother's "mind of honour" (2.4.178), which she hopes will be devoutly opposed to the pollution of his sister's body.

It takes a clever comic device to offer an alternative to this ethical dilemma. And it is a device Shakespeare did not find in the play's major source, Giraldi Cinthio's *Hecatommithi* 8.5, where the lady sadly gives herself to the lustful governor of Innsbruck. Shakespeare's alteration of that Italian tale lies in his use of a classic revenge plot in which the villain is hoisted upon his own petard.[9] The Duke concocts a bed-trick designed to ensnare Angelo in the nets of his own desire. Disguised as Isabella, Mariana will visit Angelo's bed, where sexual consummation will work to reseal a broken bond. If in Angelo "Virtue itself turns vice being misapplied," then in the Duke's plot and the women's actions "vice sometime [is] by action dignified" (*Romeo and Juliet*, 2.3.17, 18). Herein lies the equivocal morality of the revenge trick. However, in the exchange of women's bodies, a Mariana for an Isabella in Angelo's bed, four goods are apparently to be gained, which the Duke emphasizes: Isabella's "honour" will remain "untainted," Mariana will have Angelo in her debt, Claudio's life will be saved, and "the corrupt deputy" will be "scaled" (*Measure for Measure*, 3.1.254, 255, 256). The Duke recounts to Isabella the story of "dejected Mariana" (line 266), who was cast aside by Angelo when her brother and her dowry were lost in a shipwreck. To negate the premarital contract, Angelo "swallowed his vows whole, pretending in her discoveries of dishonour" (3.1.226–27). In declaring that Angelo acts with "unjust unkindness" (line 240), the Duke emphasizes both injustice and the betrayal of kindness or a kinship bond with Mariana. With Angelo's slander of her honor and rejection of marriage, Mariana has fallen into perpetual lamentation; her love has become "violent and unruly" (line 243).

Isabella responds to Mariana's plight with anger and outrage. When the Duke tells her that it is in her power to "cure" and "heal" the "rupture" (3.1.236, 235) in this relationship without blemishing her honor, Isabella is ready to take Mariana's part. Through the substitution of Mariana's body for Isabella's, they and the Duke will "compel" Angelo to give Mariana "recompense" (3.1.253). The economic metaphor here points up Angelo's debt to Mariana; the Duke gives her the power to exact her revenge and make him pay. In his disguise as a friar, the Duke absolves Mariana of sin by noting that Angelo is already her husband by "pre-contract," and that the "justice of your title to him / Doth flourish the deceit" (4.1.72, 74-75). The precontract aside, the whole circumstance of the bed-trick, however, seems fraught with ethical ambivalence, which gets "flourished" or decoratively embellished by the tricksters' intentions to see justice done. The Duke uses his disguise to lend moral authority to the trick. Angelo will be allowed to play out his fantasy of polluting a virgin. Mariana will have to subject her body to the man's lust. Isabella's consent betrays a contradiction in her ethics: the strictness of her observance of chastity has suddenly relaxed. She supports a sexual union of the kind her brother Claudio had with Juliet, for which he is facing a death sentence she admits to be "just" (2.2.41). Isabella has asserted, "I have spirit to do anything that appears not foul in the truth of my spirit" (3.1.205-7). How is it that the bed-trick "appears not foul" to her? She and Mariana both seem to accept this sexual liaison as a necessary evil, or a kind of virtuous vengeance that will help redeem their honor and "arrest" Angelo. The Duke acknowledges to Isabella that the success of the trick "lies much in your holding up" (3.1.262). Her authority, the stamp of her moral approval, seems to matter the most here, for she supports the authority of chastity, which is utterly beleaguered in Vienna. As Barbara Baines argues, "[A]uthority [the Duke] privileges chastity and depends in turn upon chastity to authorize authority."[10]

After supporting the ambiguous ethics of the bed-trick, Isabella is shocked then to hear the Duke's message that Claudio has been executed. Angelo's deceit and hypocrisy seem to strike a mortal blow to Isabella, and she cries out in fury, "O, I will to him [Angelo], and pluck out his eyes!"

(4.3.119). The eye is a crucial image here, subtly getting at the problems of judgment and justice. The sudden eruption of vengefulness in Isabella resonates with Hecuba's violent revenge for her son's murder. Euripides and Ovid both depict Hecuba and her women gouging out the eyes of King Polymestor as part of his punishment for an unspeakable crime. The eye also recalls the biblical equation of an eye for an eye (vengeance as justice) and the "mote in the eye" from Matthew, which appears in a passage essential to *Measure for Measure:* "Ivdge not, that ye be not iudged. For with what iudgement ye iudge, ye shal be iudged, and with what measure ye mette, it shal be measured to you againe. And why seest thou the mote, that is in thy brothers eye, and perceiuest not the beame that is in thine owne eye?" (Matt. 7:1–3). The tension between *talionic* law and Christian restraint/humility is enacted in the play: the central characters are measured and forced to acknowledge the beam in their own eyes.

Mariana's revenge bears fruit when she looks Angelo in the eye and confronts him publicly with his wrongdoing and his hypocrisy. In the trial scene she unveils to reveal herself as Angelo's wife and as the woman he took to bed:

> My husband bids me; now I will unmask.
> This is that face, thou cruel Angelo,
> Which once thou swor'st was worth the looking on:
> This is the hand which, with a vow'd contract,
> Was fast belock'd in thine: this is the body
> That took away the match from Isabel
> And did supply thee at thy garden-house
> In her imagin'd person.
>
> (5.1.205–12)

The force of Mariana's words strike Angelo to the quick with shame. He wishes devoutly for death. While Angelo does not exhibit love for Mariana, he does display remorse and the potential for a "cure."[11] With the aid of Isabella and the Duke, Mariana has enforced *her will* and used both body and voice to avenge herself. The vengeance is just, for she asserts her right as a wife by "vowed contract" to demand due recompense.

The specter of vengeance arises yet again in the play's most famous passage, where the Duke follows the *talionic* principle in condemning Angelo to death. As the minister of Justice who bears the "sword of heaven" (3.2.254), he has the authority to pursue retribution, and he sounds like he is urging vengeance upon Isabella. Even mercy, he proclaims, demands strict requital:

> The very mercy of the law cries out
> Most audible, even from his proper tongue:

> "An Angelo for Claudio; death for death.
> Haste still pays haste, and leisure answers leisure;
> Like doth quit like, and Measure still for Measure."
>
> (5.1.405–9)

The Duke states that Isabella must pardon the wrong Angelo has done to her honor, but for her brother's life, she may take revenge, which he will support with the authority of his position. When Mariana implores Isabella to beg for Angelo's life, the Duke invokes the belief that the ghost of the murdered Claudio will haunt his duty-bound sister if his death is not avenged. He appeals to Isabella as if they were in the world of Aeschylus:

> Against all sense you do importune her.
> Should she kneel down in mercy of this fact,
> Her brother's ghost his paved bed would break,
> And take her hence in horror.
>
> (5.1.431–34)

Mariana's exclamation rides immediately on the heels of this vision; she cries out, "Isabel! / Sweet Isabel, do yet but kneel by me" (lines 434–35). Isabella chooses to listen to Mariana here, the living woman present before her, rather than some imagined, punitive ghost reminiscent of an old ethic of revenge.

Her response is carefully calibrated to the demands of virtue, justice, and mercy. She argues that Claudio "had but justice / In that he did the thing for which he died" (lines 446–47), but Angelo, since he sinned only in intent and found himself distracted from "due sincerity" (line 444) by Isabella, does not deserve death. Her closing statement carries political overtones, registering the limitations in the Duke's jurisdiction: "Thoughts are no subjects; / Intents, but merely thoughts" (lines 451–52). This speech marks a sublime degree of tolerance on Isabella's part, and perhaps a mind attuned to legal technicalities more than newfound wisdom. A number of ironies unsettle her argument. First, it seems less than believable that Isabella would place blame upon herself for Angelo's fall. His criminal desire for her virgin body is morally repulsive. Second, if it had not been for the women's involvement in the bed-trick, an act of comic restorative vengeance, Angelo would have sinned in flesh as well as mind. It would appear, then, that Isabella has made the choice here to align herself with Mariana and to sacrifice her own satisfaction for Mariana's. In the end, Isabella relinquishes revenge—what she must, on some level, believe to be justice—for the sake of another woman's happiness and livelihood.

Ultimately, this careful speech reflects nothing so much as Isabella's grace. Though she might want revenge for herself, and for her brother, she has considerations that transcend her own needs. She argues for mercy be-

cause that is the right virtue to apply here and, in the end, her strict morality favors mercy. She returns to the grounds of the argument she made for
her own brother's life. The irony here is rather stunning, though, for not
only is Isabella's appeal rejected by the Duke, such grace seemingly crushed
by justice's sword, but also not long thereafter, Angelo's life is spared after the "miraculous" appearance of Claudio. An enforced marriage between
Angelo and Mariana will complete the bed-trick, uniting revenge, justice,
and mercy. It may not be a mercy Angelo desires, but he receives it from
Isabella and from the Duke nonetheless. For both characters, there must be
something of the Pauline satisfaction at work here that in giving mercy, the
offender will feel the "hot coals" of his sin and shame. Angelo suffers disgrace publicly. His dishonor is so profoundly shameful that he wishes only
for death. Thus, this marriage may very well be a punishment worse than
death. For Mariana, again, it is a risk she takes to redeem her honor, and
perhaps out of the inexplicable depths of love she possesses for Angelo,
she desires him as her husband. While Angelo is radically unworthy of her,
Mariana wants him nonetheless, and Isabella assays what power she has to
try to save this woman's husband.

Finally, we have the strange matter of the Duke's proposal to Isabella
and her profound silence. For a character who has spoken so passionately
with eloquence and reason, her silence is rather deafening and suggests
Shakespeare's interest in leaving audiences unsettled about her fate. In a
play that explores the dialectic of justice and mercy, the comic resolution
brought about by the Duke's justice appears in an oddly ambivalent light.
At the comedy's conclusion, four couples are presented to the audience.
The only mutually happy couple is Claudio and Juliet; Claudio has escaped
the harsh rule of law, and his "crime" of premarital sex has been forgiven
by the Duke. Two couples are forced to marry; Angelo and Lucio are forced
to give "recompense" to women with their flesh—sins of the flesh are paid
by arresting the flesh and forcing flesh to regulate itself through marital
chastity. The joys of marriage are entirely lost on them, for marriage is a
punishment rather than a cure for these sexually wayward men.[12] Thus we
see a painful reality about marriage exposed here, that as a social institu-
tion it does not have the power to redeem what is corrupted, and that sexual union can be forced in unpleasant ways that are considered good for the
state.

The fourth couple is not a couple at all, for Isabella and the Duke have
not undertaken a courtship together or taken an oath, and the woman is virtually a nun. Isabella's silence indicates a radical uncertainty about her fate
and a pressing decision that needs making almost immediately. The proposal comes hard on the heels of the appearance of Claudio as if from the
dead. Is marriage to be a form of recompense here—Isabella's life for Claudio's life? Does the Duke manage, strangely enough, to get what Angelo

292 WOMEN AND REVENGE IN SHAKESPEARE

was after, the violation of Isabella's sanctity?[13] Has Isabella's integrity been destroyed with her voice in the end by patriarchal encroachments upon her spirit, particularly through the manipulation of the Duke-as-friar?[14] Marilyn Williamson's response to such questions is quite appealing: "[S]ilence after eloquence may signify not acquiescence, but defiance of an urgent authority."[15] We might conclude that Isabella has been challenged over the course of the drama to practice an ethics more flexible than that which she could have imagined at the start of the play. She has learned through painful experience the difficulties that can arise in the world when a woman seeks to defend cherished values such as honor, chastity, justice, and mercy. Her defiant silence in the end may reflect, quite simply, the wisdom in keeping her own counsel in the face of yet another ethical challenge.

Isabella's defiant spirit, like that of all the female inciters and avengers I have brought to bear in this book, is an expression of her agency and her ethics. She has felt the passions associated with revenge—just anger, hatred, vindictiveness, and a love of justice—participated in the bed-trick, and advocated a revengeless revenge (ironically, mercy) for Angelo. She has assayed what power she has, given the painful circumstances she finds herself in. Like many of the cases in Shakespeare's dramas, Isabella's approach to justice shows us that revenge's place in the proceedings of justice need not be destructive and morally misguided. Revenge and its attendant passions erupt when injustice prevails. Women often direct these passions toward exposing vice and restoring justice to individuals and their communities.

In representing bold, courageous, vengeful women, Shakespeare used the virtue ethics tradition, classical mythology, and European revenge tales to confer upon these characters and their social circumstances a nuanced, gender-sensitive ethics. Shakespeare challenged conservative religious, social, and political views by depicting and exploring the conditions under which vengeance becomes a cultural norm practiced in defense of honor, an ethical necessity, and a choice that serves the good of women and the moral order. Shakespeare understood that a passion for justice lies at the root of women's vengefulness. Shakespeare's women raise their voices, exercise their wills, and exact revenge in response to wrongs, often grievous wrongs, committed against family members, friends, and their community. The stakes are high, for wrongs such as slander, murder, rape, attempted seduction, and oath-breaking compromise women's bodies, minds, and reputations in fundamental ways. Women express outrage against wrongdoers (and violations of the moral order) through specific means: they incite men to revenge; they lament corruption and wrongful death; they rebuke sinners; they pursue vendettas or warfare; and they play tricks or stage revenge scenes with the intention of teaching a lesson. Thus, in the pursuit of just revenge, Shakespeare's women take on the roles of inciters, lamenters, rebukers, scourges, warriors, moral physicians, amateur dramatists, pedagogues, and vindicators of women's honor. These roles, as we have seen, bespeak a degree of moral authority in women's motives and actions.

My aim with this book has been to do justice to women's stories of revenge, to let them march in from the peripheries of revenge literature and criticism into the spotlight. As my epigraph from Salman Rushdie predicted, the women's stories have explained and subsumed the men's stories to some extent: the famous stories of Hamlet, Titus, Lear, and Shylock are refracted through the prisms of the women's narratives. Beyond doubt, Shakespeare's contributions to the Western revenge narrative were extensive and subtle, and particularly so in relation to women. His dramas uncover the exceptionally rich, varied, and controversial nature of women's roles in that narrative. In Shakespeare's plays, irrespective of genre, women's concerns with revenge and justice, honor and shame, crime and punishment are central to the plots and cultural worlds depicted. Shakespeare was deeply invested in exploring the artistic and ethical possibilities of feminine vengeance. The ethical work of Shakespeare's female avengers highlights the function of women in literature as vindicators of their own sex. Shakespeare's fierce, resourceful, avenging women—Margaret, Cordelia, Portia, Paulina, Emilia, and the rest—show us that justice is always at stake for women in their personal relationships and in society, and that women in literature as in life are far from silent and passive in their fight against injustice.

Notes

All quotations from Shakespeare's plays have been taken from Arden editions, unless otherwise noted. All quotations from the Bible have been taken from the 1560 edition of the Geneva Bible. All definitions and etymologies from the *Oxford English Dictionary* have been taken from the online edition: http://www.dictionary.oed.com.

PREFACE

1. For an analysis of "grief and mourning as a site of important cultural work performed by women" (17) in Anglo-Saxon poetry, see Patricia Clare Ingham's excellent study, "From Kinship to Kingship: Mourning, Gender, and Anglo-Saxon Community," in *Grief and Gender, 700–1700,* ed. Jennifer Vaught and Lynne Dickson (Hampshire, England: Palgrave Macmillan, 2003): 24.

2. Quotations from *Beowulf* have been taken from Howell D. Chickering Jr.'s dual-language edition (New York: Anchor Books, 1977).

3. See John M. Hill, "The Ethnopsychology of In-Law Feud and the Remaking of Group Identity in *Beowulf*: The Cases of Hengest and Ingeld," *Philological Quarterly* 78, nos. 1–2 (Winter-Spring 1999): 97–123; and Hill, "Feud Settlements in *Beowulf*," in *The Cultural World in "Beowulf"* (Toronto: University of Toronto Press, 1995), 25–37.

4. The definitions for these terms found in the *Oxford English Dictionary* demonstrate a range of related meanings in their sixteenth-century usage. Punishment for a wrong or injury is given as a definition for each. For clarification on historical word usage, see also the verbal forms *to avenge* and *to revenge* and the terms *justice* and *vindication.*

INTRODUCTION

1. Homer, *The Iliad,* trans. Robert Fitzgerald (1974; repr., New York: Farrar, Straus and Giroux, 2004).

2. This Old English phrase appears in line 1142 of the narrative account of the Finnsburh episode in *Beowulf.*

3. Salman Rushdie, *Shame* (New York: Picador, 1983), 180.

4. Harry Keyishian, *The Shapes of Revenge: Victimization, Vengeance, and Vindictiveness in Shakespeare* (Amherst, NY: Humanities Books, 2003), 26.

5. Ibid. I have emphasized Keyishian's word coinage here.

6. Alison Findlay, *A Feminist Perspective on Renaissance Drama* (Oxford: Blackwell, 1999), 49. Findlay argues a point that may apply in some, but not all, cases of feminine revenge: "The use of violence by female revengers, even to redress the wrongs suffered by

the sex, is deeply problematic from a feminist point of view since it often reproduces masculine modes of oppression and possibly even the dominant modes of patriarchy" (72).

7. Crucial texts from philosophers include Aristotle's *Nicomachean Ethics* and *Rhetoric;* and Thomas Aquinas's *Summa Theologica.* Other significant philosophical works include Peter A. French, *The Virtues of Vengeance* (Lawrence: University Press of Kansas, 2001); Robert C. Solomon, *A Passion for Justice: Emotions and the Origins of the Social Contract* (Reading, MA: Addison-Wesley Publishing Company, 1990); and Jeffrie Murphy, *Getting Even: Forgiveness and Its Limits* (Oxford: Oxford University Press, 2003). For other important critical works that acknowledge the element of justice in revenge, see Susan Jacoby, *Wild Justice: The Evolution of Revenge* (New York: Harper and Row, 1983); and Pietro Marongiu and Graeme Newman, *Vengeance: The Fight Against Injustice* (Totowa, NJ: Rowman and Littlefield, 1987).

8. Kenneth Burke, *The Philosophy of Literary Form: Studies in Symbolic Action,* 3rd ed. (Berkeley and Los Angeles: University of California Press, 1973), 23.

9. René Girard, *Violence and the Sacred,* trans. Patrick Gregory (1972, repr., Baltimore: Johns Hopkins University Press, 1977), 14.

10. Catherine Belsey, *The Subject of Tragedy: Identity and Difference in Renaissance Drama* (London: Routledge, 1985), 5. See also Christy Desmet, *Reading Shakespeare's Characters: Rhetoric, Ethics, and Identity* (Amherst: University of Massachusetts Press, 1992).

11. Girard, *Violence and the Sacred,* 21.

12. A significant study that has laid essential groundwork for this effort is Linda Anderson, *A Kind of Wild Justice: Revenge in Shakespeare's Comedies* (Newark: University of Delaware Press, 1987). Studies of revenge in early modern plays typically center on revenge tragedy, a genre (or subgenre) first identified and categorized by A. H. Thorndike in "The Relations of *Hamlet* to Contemporary Revenge Plays," *PMLA* 17 (1902): 125–220. Lily B. Campbell's "Theories of Revenge in Renaissance England" (*Modern Philology* 28, no. 3 [1931]: 281–96) and Fredson Bowers's influential *Elizabethan Revenge Tragedy, 1587–1642* (Princeton, NJ: Princeton University Press, 1940) established negative Elizabethan attitudes toward revenge, which generations of Shakespeare scholars have accepted uncritically. They also gave tragedy center stage in the study of literary revenge, and men the role of protagonist. Important later studies of revenge tragedy include Jagannath Chakravorty, *The Idea of Revenge in Shakespeare* (Calcutta: Jadavpur University Press, 1969); Eleanor Prosser, *"Hamlet" and Revenge* (Stanford, CA: Stanford University Press, 1967); Ronald Broude, "Revenge and Revenge Tragedy in Renaissance England" (*Renaissance Quarterly* 28, no.1 [Spring 1975]: 38–58); Charles A. Hallett and Elaine S. Hallett, *The Revenger's Madness: A Study of Revenge Tragedy Motifs* (Lincoln: University of Nebraska Press, 1980); Peter Mercer, *"Hamlet" and the Acting of Revenge* (Iowa City: University of Iowa, 1987); Keyishian, *Shapes of Revenge;* and John Kerrigan, *Revenge Tragedy: Aeschylus to Armageddon* (Oxford: Clarendon Press, 1996). Only within the past few decades have critical studies on revenge shifted attention to other genres and the other sex. The scholarship on women and revenge is of recent origin, motivated in part by the critical assumptions governing feminist and gender-oriented criticism. See, for example, Findlay, *Feminist Perspective;* essays in *Revenge Tragedy,* ed. Stevie Simkin (Houndmills, England: Palgrave Macmillan, 2001); essays in *The Female Tragic Hero in English Renaissance Drama,* ed. Naomi Conn Liebler (New York: Palgrave Macmillan, 2002); and Carol Fisher Sorgenfrei, "Unsexed and Disembodied: Female Avengers in Japan and England," in *Revenge Drama in European Renaissance and Japanese Theatre,* ed. Kevin J. Wetmore Jr. (New York: Palgrave Macmillan, 2008), 45–73.

13. Girard, *Violence and the Sacred,* 47.

14. French, *Virtues of Vengeance.* For a thorough discussion of the conditions of virtuous vengeance, see chaps. 4–7, pp. 112–229.

15. David N. Beauregard, *Virtue's Own Feature: Shakespeare and the Virtue Ethics Tradition* (Newark: University of Delaware Press, 1995), 14. For evidence of the virtue ethics tradition in England, see esp. his chap. 2, "'Aristotle and the rest': The Aristotelian-Thomistic Tradition of Moral Philosophy," 36–57.

16. Quotations from Aristotle's *Rhetoric* are taken from W. Rhys Roberts's translation in *The Complete Works of Aristotle: The Revised Oxford Translation,* ed. J. Barnes, vol. 2 (Princeton, NJ: Princeton University Press, 1984).

17. French, *Virtues of Vengeance,* 225.

18. Solomon, *Passion for Justice,* 140. He discusses three of these metaphors for vengeance (140–143). I add the metaphor of appetite to his list, as it occurs frequently in Shakespeare's plays and in the literature of revenge.

19. Ibid., 143.

20. This phrase occurs in Anthonie Marten's translation of Peter Martyr Vermigli's *Common Places* (London, 1583), a well-known Protestant text in early modern England.

21. Quotations from John Studley's 1566 translation of Seneca's *Medea* are taken from Thomas Newton, *Seneca, His Tenne Tragedies, Translated into English* (1581; repr., Bloomington: Indiana University Press, 1960).

22. Beauregard, *Virtue's Own Feature,* 104. As Beauregard rightly notes, Anderson's book *A Kind of Wild Justice* offers a flexible ethical understanding of revenge.

23. Christopher Boehm, *Blood Revenge: The Enactment and Management of Conflict in Montenegro and Other Tribal Societies* (Lawrence: University Press of Kansas, 1984; repr. with an expanded preface, Philadelphia: University of Pennsylvania Press, 1987). Citations are to the Pennsylvania edition.

24. Ibid., 47.

25. Ibid., 55.

26. Ibid., 57. Mary Edith Durham tells of another case in Montenegro in *Some Tribal Origins: Laws and Customs of the Balkans* (London: George Allen and Unwin, 1928). "But in Montenegro there was a woman living in Antivari, when I was there, who had taken blood. She learnt that a certain man, when drinking at the han, had boasted that he knew both her and her sister to be no better than they should be. While her husband was out she borrowed his rifle and waited for this man outside his own door. When he came out she cried: 'You shall never tell another lie!' and shot him dead. Taken before the court, she not only said she had done it, but expressed her readiness to kill anyone else who maligned her, and was enthusiastically acquitted" (171).

1. WOMEN AND REVENGE

1. French, *Virtues of Vengeance,* 3.

2. Ibid., 17.

3. Froma Zeitlin makes a similar point in her early work when she insists that the suppression and undermining of the Furies in Aeschylus's conclusion to the *Oresteia* supports a patriarchal gender ideology. Zeitlin, "The Dynamics of Misogyny in the *Oresteia,*" *Arethusa* 11 (1978): 149–84.

4. Quotations from Aeschylus's *Oresteia* (*Agamemnon, The Libation Bearers, The Eumenides*) have been taken from Richmond Lattimore's translation (Chicago: University of Chicago Press, 1953).

5. French, *Virtues of Vengeance,* 4. For the myth of Gaia's revenge, see Hesiod *Theogony* 154–210, in *Theogony, Works and Days, Testimonia,* trans. Glenn W. Most (Cambridge, MA: Harvard University Press, 2006). Further quotations from *Theogony* will refer to this edition.

6. William Smith, ed., *A Dictionary of Greek and Roman Biography and Mythology,* vol. 3 (New York: AMS Press, 1967), 91.

7. Ruth Padel, *In and Out of the Mind: Greek Images of the Tragic Self* (Princeton, NJ: Princeton University Press, 1992), 175.

8. Smith, *Dictionary,* 2:92. See also Richard Buxton, *The Complete World of Greek Mythology* (New York: Thames and Hudson, 2004), 86. For a classical example of the representation of three Furies, see Allen Mandelbaum's translation of Virgil's *Aeneid* (1961; repr., Toronto: Bantam Books, 1981), 6.755–59, 7.431–751, 12.1122–77.

9. This quotation from *Gismond of Salerne* is taken from John W. Cunliffe's edition, *Early English Classical Tragedies* (Oxford: Oxford University Press, 1912).

10. For image and text, see Leslie Thomson, ed., *Fortune: "All is but Fortune,"* Folger Shakespeare Library Exhibition, January 18–June 10, 2000 (Seattle: University of Washington Press, 2000), 36.

11. Francis Bacon, *The Wisdome of the Ancients,* trans. Sir Arthur Gorges Knight (London: John Bill, 1619), E2r, E2r, E4r.

12. See Ruth Padel, *Whom Gods Destroy: Elements of Greek and Tragic Madness* (Princeton, NJ: Princeton University Press, 1995), esp. 167–92.

13. Helene P. Foley, *Female Acts in Greek Tragedy* (Princeton, NJ: Princeton University Press, 2001), 151.

14. Ibid., 151, 150, 169.

15. Ibid., 171. Here Foley argues a similar point to mine regarding Sophocles' character Electra.

16. Christian M. Billing, "Lament and Revenge in the *Hekabe* of Euripides," *New Theatre Quarterly* 23, no. 1 (2007): 50.

17. Ibid.

18. Padel, *In and Out of the Mind,* 177.

19. Ibid., 167.

20. Nicole Loraux, *The Mourning Voice: An Essay on Greek Tragedy,* trans. Elizabeth Trapnell Rawlings (Ithaca, NY: Cornell University Press, 2002), 97.

21. For scholarship on female goading, see Carol Clover, "Hildigunnr's Lament," in *Cold Counsel: Women in Old Norse Literature and Mythology,* ed. Sarah M. Anderson with Karen Swenson (New York: Routledge, 2002), 15–54; Jenny Jochens, "The Medieval Icelandic Heroine: Fact or Fiction?" *Viator* 17 (1986): 35–50; Jochens, *Old Norse Images of Women* (Philadelphia: University of Pennsylvania Press, 1996); William Ian Miller, *Bloodtaking and Peacemaking: Feud, Law, and Society in Saga Iceland* (Chicago: University of Chicago Press, 1997), 211–14; Miller, "Choosing the Avenger: Some Aspects of the Bloodfeud in Medieval Iceland and England," *Law and History Review* 1, no. 2 (1983): 159–204; and R. George Thomas, "Some Exceptional Women in the Sagas," *Saga-Book of the Viking Society* 13 (1952–53): 307–27.

22. Quotations from "The Whetting of Gudrun" and other Gudrun lays are taken from Carolyne Larrington's translation of *The Poetic Edda* (Oxford: Oxford University Press, 1996).

23. See Clover, "Hildigunnr's Lament."

24. Ibid., esp. 36.

25. Judith Jesch, *Women in the Viking Age* (Woodbridge, England: Boydell Press, 1991), 190, 191.

26. Jochens, *Old Norse Images of Women,* 175.

27. Thomas, "Some Exceptional Women in the Sagas," 316, 317.

28. Miller, "Choosing the Avenger," 181.

29. Ibid., 185.

30. Clover, "Hildigunnr's Lament," 17, my emphasis.

31. Nicole Loraux, *Mothers in Mourning with the Essay "Of Amnesty and Its Opposite,"* trans. Corinne Pache (Ithaca, NY: Cornell University Press, 1998), 1–7.

32. Quotations from George Chapman's *The Revenge of Bussy D'Ambois* are taken from Katharine Maus's edition of *Four Revenge Tragedies* (Oxford: Oxford University Press, 1995).

33. This quotation is taken from Arthur Golding's 1567 translation of Ovid's *Metamorphoses* in John Frederick Nims's edition (Philadelphia: Paul Dry Books, 2000). All further quotations from Golding's translation are indicated through line numbers in my text. For Ovid's *Tristia,* see Arthur Leslie Wheeler's translation in vol. 6 of *Ovid in Six Volumes,* rev. ed. G. P. Goold (Cambridge, MA: Harvard University Press, 1988).

34. In Euripides' *Hecuba,* translated numerous times during the sixteenth century, Jasper Heywood's translation of Seneca's *Troas,* and Golding's rendition of Ovid's *Metamorphoses,* Shakespeare and his contemporaries could find versions of Hecuba's tragic tale. See Emrys Jones, *The Origins of Shakespeare* (Oxford: Clarendon Press, 1977); Judith Mossman, *Wild Justice: A Study of Euripides' "Hecuba"* (London: Bristol Classical Press, 1999); and Lizette I. Westny, "Hecuba in Sixteenth-Century English Literature," *CLA Journal* 27, no. 4 (June 1984): 436–59.

35. Antonio Tempesta illustrated the figure of Revenge in nine of the etchings in his prose narrative entitled *Historia septem infantium de Lara.* Of note, as well, is his illustration of Procne and Philomela's revenge on Tereus in his series for Ovid's *Metamorphoses.*

36. Kevin Dunn, "'Action, Passion, Motion': The Gestural Politics of Counsel in *The Spanish Tragedy,"* *Renaissance Drama* 31 (2002): 41.

37. See Frederick Kiefer, *Shakespeare's Visual Theatre: Staging the Personified Characters* (Cambridge: Cambridge University Press, 2003), chap. 2, "Revenge, Murder, and Rape in *Titus Andronicus,"* 41–62. In "Action, Passion, Motion," Dunn mentions another woodcut of this kind, which features a male figure seated in his study biting his finger. The image, called "La Meditatione, ouero la vendetta," appeared in Valeriano's *I ieroglifici* (1625).

38. *Oxford English Dictionary,* s.v. "Habiliment," 3.b.

39. The quotation from Thomas Norton and Thomas Sackville's *Gorboduc* is taken from *Drama of the English Renaissance I: The Tudor Period,* ed. Russell A. Fraser and Norman Rabkin (New York: Macmillan, 1976).

40. Quotations from Francis Beaumont and John Fletcher's *The Maid's Tragedy* are taken from the Revels Plays edition, ed. T. W. Craik (Manchester: Manchester University Press, 1988).

41. Quotations from John Ford's *The Broken Heart* are taken from T. J. Spencer's edition (Baltimore, MD: Johns Hopkins University Press, 1981). These words of warning come from the philosopher Tecnicus to the revenger Orgilus, who then echoes them twice in the tragedy (4.1.139, 4.1.152, 5.2.147). This sentiment about revenge functions as a proverb or an epigram in the play, suggesting its familiarity to English audiences fed on a theatrical diet of revenge tragedies.

42. Karen Horney, "The Value of Vindictiveness" (1948), in *New Perspectives in Psychoanalysis,* ed. Harold Kelman (New York: W. W. Norton, 1965), 27–51.

43. Quotations from Francis Bacon's "Of Revenge" are taken from *Essays, Advancement of Learning, New Atlantis, and Other Pieces,* ed. Richard Foster Jones (New York: Odyssey Press, 1937). This reference appears on page 14.

44. The phrase is drawn from Tudor Reformer and church authority Thomas Cranmer's "A Sermon concerning the Time of Rebellion," published by the Parker Society of Cambridge University in *Miscellaneous Writings and Letters of Thomas Cranmer,* ed. John Edmund Cox (Cambridge: Cambridge University Press, 1846), 193.

45. Nicholas Stratford, *A Dissuasive from Revenge* (London: Richard Chiswell, 1684),

quoted in Lily B. Campbell, "Theories of Revenge in Renaissance England," *Modern Philology* 28, no. 3 (1931): 290.

46. Girard, *Violence and the Sacred,* 15.

47. Bacon, "Of Revenge," 13.

48. Ibid., 14.

49. Robert Ashley, *Of Honour,* ed. Virgil B. Heltzel (San Marino, CA: Huntington Library, 1947).

50. Julius R. Ruff, *Violence in Early Modern Europe* (Cambridge: Cambridge University Press, 2001), 75.

51. See William Ian Miller, *Humiliation and Other Essays on Honor, Social Discomfort, and Violence* (Ithaca, NY: Cornell University Press, 1993).

52. Martin Luther, *Temporal Authority: To What Extent it Should be Obeyed* (1523), trans. J. J. Schindel, rev. Walther I. Brandt, in *Luther's Works,* ed. Walther I. Brandt, vol. 45 (Philadelphia: Muhlenberg Press, 1962), 101, 103.

53. Beauregard, *Virtue's Own Feature,* 109 n. 43, 229. For evidence of Martyr's importance to the English Church, Beauregard cites Patrick Collinson's important essay, "England and International Calvinism," in *International Calvinism, 1541–1715,* ed. Menna Prestwich (Oxford: Clarendon Press, 1985).

54. Peter Martyr Vermigli, "Of Reuenge," in *The Common Places,* trans. Anthonie Marten, part 2, chap. 9, quoted in Beauregard, *Virtue's Own Feature,* 109.

55. Beauregard, *Virtue's Own Feature,* 109.

56. Thomas Aquinas, *Summa Theologica,* trans. Fathers of the English Dominican Province, vol. 3. (Westminster, MD: Christian Classics, 1948). This quotation comes from 2-2.108.2 ("Of Vengeance").

57. Juan Luis Vives, *The Office and Duty of an Husband,* trans. Thomas Paynell (London, 1555?), in *Daughters, Wives, and Widows: Writings by Men about Women and Marriage in England, 1500–1640,* ed. Joan Larsen Klein (Urbana: University of Illinois Press, 1992), 125.

58. Gwynne Kennedy, *Just Anger: Representing Women's Anger in Early Modern England* (Carbondale: Southern Illinois University Press, 2000), 15–20.

59. Nicholas Caussin, *The Holy Court,* trans. Thomas Hawkins (London, 1638), 316. Kennedy cites Caussin's text, a Christian account of the four passions of love, desire, anger, and envy, in *Just Anger* as an example of the reputed dangers of women's anger (Kennedy, *Just Anger,* 18–19).

60. The quotation from John Reynolds's *The Triumph of Gods Revenge* is taken from Joan M. Walmsley's edition (Lewiston, NY: Edwin Mellen Press, 2004).

61. Findlay, *Feminist Perspective,* 54. Findlay's argument is compelling: "It is not surprising that revenge is feminized since it is diametrically opposed to the paternal Word, the Law of the Father" (52).

62. Ibid., 51.

63. Solomon, *Passion for Justice,* 42.

64. Marongiu and Newman, *Vengeance,* 9.

65. Keyishian, *Shapes of Revenge,* 2.

66. Bruce Lenman and Geoffrey Parker, for example, use this term in their essay "The State, the Community and the Criminal Law in Early Modern Europe," in *Crime and the Law: The Social History of Crime in Western Europe since 1500,* ed. V. A. C. Gatrell, Bruce Lenman, and Geoffrey Parker (London: Europa, 1980), 11–48. See also Ruff, *Violence in Early Modern Europe,* 73–75.

67. Ruff, *Violence in Early Modern Europe,* 73.

68. "The Instrument of an Association for the Preservation of Her Ma(jes)ties Royall Persone" (October, 1584), in *Elizabethan England: Being the History of This Country "In*

Relation to all Foreign Princes," by Eva Mabel Tenison, vol. 5 (1932; rpt., England: Obscure Press, 2006), app. B, 206, 207.

69. Tim Stretton, *Women Waging Law in Elizabethan England* (Cambridge: Cambridge University Press, 1998). See especially his chap. 3, "Female Litigants and the Culture of Litigation," 43–69.

70. Ibid. See especially his chap. 2, "Women, Legal Rights and Law Courts," 21–42.

71. Kennedy, *Just Anger.*

72. French, *Virtues of Vengeance,* x.

2. VALOROUS TONGUES, LAMENTING VOICES

1. Edward Muir, *Mad Blood Stirring: Vendetta and Factions in Friuli during the Renaissance* (Baltimore, MD: Johns Hopkins University Press, 1993), 73. See especially 72–76. Fiona McHardy examines evidence for the use of exile as a response to homicide in the ancient Greek world. See her *Revenge in Athenian Culture* (London: Duckworth, 2008), 15–25.

2. Muir, *Mad Blood Stirring,* 76. Muir presents a number of reasons why outlawing failed in Renaissance Friuli: the administrators of justice were at a distance in Venice; local administrators were participants in feuds and thus less likely to enforce outlaw proclamations; and Venetian law was not as threatening as local dangers arising from feuds. He concludes that in Friuli "vendetta constituted the real law and often the only justice" (76).

3. Thomas Nashe, *Pierce Penilesse His Svpplication to the Divell* (1592), in *The Works of Thomas Nashe,* ed. Ronald B. McKerrow, vol. 1 (Oxford: Basil Blackwell, 1958), 186.

4. Prosser, *"Hamlet" and Revenge,* 79.

5. See Coppélia Kahn, *Man's Estate: Masculine Identity in Shakespeare* (Berkeley and Los Angeles: University of California Press, 1981), and an opposing view from Richard Levin, "Feminist Thematics and Shakespearean Tragedy," *PMLA* 103, no. 2 (March 1988): 125–38.

6. Jenny Jochens's research subject is Old Nordic historiography and literature. See *Old Norse Images,* 175.

7. J. L. Austin, *How to Do Things with Words,* ed. J. O. Urmson (Cambridge, MA: Harvard University Press, 1962).

8. Dianne Hunter, "Doubling, Mythic Difference, and the Scapegoating of Female Power," in *The Persistence of Myth: Psychoanalytic and Structuralist Perspectives,* ed. Peter L. Rudnytsky (New York: Guilford Press, 1988), 131, 129. Hunter's fascinating psychoanalytic reading of *Macbeth* shows how the structure of crime and punishment in the play "dramatizes the reflexivity of the revenge motive: Do unto others what they have done unto you; or in psychoanalytic terms, undo unto others what has been undone to you. Revenge is a magical form of undoing in which the original victim exchanges roles with the original aggressor, and repeats the original crime in order to undo it and gain mastery of its psychological and concrete effects" (131–32).

9. Quotations from Raphael Holinshed's *"Chronicles"* are taken from *Shakespeare's Holinshed: An Edition of Holinshed's Chronicles (1587),* ed. Richard Hosley (New York: G. P. Putnam's Sons, 1968), 10.

10. Ibid., 18.

11. Ibid., 15, 19.

12. Hunter, "Doubling, Mythic Difference," 135. I am indebted to Hunter's illuminating discussion of Scottish history.

13. Muriel C. Bradbrook, "The Sources of *Macbeth*," *Shakespeare Studies* 4 (1951), rpt. in *Aspects of "Macbeth*,*"* ed. Kenneth Muir and Philip Edwards (Cambridge: Cambridge University Press, 1977), 17. Citations are to the Cambridge edition.

14. *The Description of Scotland*, trans. from the Latin of Hector Boethius by William Harison, chap. 13, prefixed to Holinshed, *Historie of Scotland* (1577), quoted in Bradbrook, "Sources of *Macbeth*," 17.

15. Bradbrook, "Sources of *Macbeth*," 16.

16. Quotations from Euripides' *Medea* are taken from Eleanor Wilner and Inés Azar's translation in *Euripides, I,* ed. David R. Slavitt and Palmer Bovie (Philadelphia: University of Pennsylvania Press, 1998).

17. Yves Peyré, "'Confusion Now Hath Made his Masterpiece': Senecan Resonances in *Macbeth*," in *Shakespeare and the Classics,* ed. Charles Martindale and A. B. Taylor (Cambridge: Cambridge University Press, 2004), 141. See also Inga-Stina Ewbank, "The Fiend-like Queen: A Note on *Macbeth* and Seneca's *Medea*," *Shakespeare Studies* 19, rpt. in *Aspects of "Macbeth*,*"* ed. by Kenneth Muir and Philip Edwards (Cambridge: Cambridge University Press, 1977), 53–65. Citations are to the Cambridge edition.

18. James Stuart, *Daemonologie in Forme of a Dialogue* (Edinburgh: Robert Waldegraue, 1597).

19. Harriet Walter, *Macbeth* (London: Faber and Faber, 2002), 32. Walter surmises that Lady Macbeth's childlessness (perhaps her miscarriages) leaves her bereaved, "truly blighted and perhaps vengeful against the world" (32). She needs *something,* some achievement, something of worth in life, so she seizes upon status and power. This generalized sense of vengeance, however, lacks the social and ethical dimensions that typically define revenge in honor-shame cultures.

20. As Janet Adelman argues, Lady Macbeth infantilizes Macbeth. Adelman, *Suffocating Mothers: Fantasies of Maternal Origin in Shakespeare's Plays, "Hamlet" to "The Tempest"* (London: Routledge, 1992).

21. Quotations from Euripides' *Electra* are taken from John Davie's translation in *Electra, and Other Plays* (London: Penguin Books, 1998).

22. Stuart Sillars, *Painting Shakespeare: The Artist as Critic, 1720–1820* (Cambridge: Cambridge University Press, 2006), 226–27.

23. Ibid., 227.

24. Julian Pitt-Rivers, "Honour and Social Status," in *Honour and Shame: The Values of Mediterranean Society,* ed. J. G. Peristiany (Chicago: University of Chicago Press, 1966), 37.

25. Richard A. Levin, *Shakespeare's Secret Schemers: The Study of an Early Modern Literary Device* (Newark: University of Delaware Press, 2002), 44.

26. Keyishian, *Shapes of Revenge,* 26.

27. The quotation from John Webster's *The White Devil* is taken from F. L. Lucas's edition (New York: Macmillan, 1959).

28. Quotations from *The Spanish Tragedy* are taken from J. R. Mulryne's second edition (London: A and C Black, 1989).

29. Austin, *How to Do Things with Words.*

30. Katharine Goodland, *Female Mourning in Medieval and Renaissance English Drama: From the Raising of Lazarus to "King Lear"* (Aldershot, England: Ashgate, 2005), 133.

31. See Levin, *Shakespeare's Secret Schemers,* 44. For an extensive discussion of "monstrous mourning" and critical perceptions of the excessiveness of maternal grief, see Goodland, *Female Mourning.*

32. Goodland, *Female Mourning,* 22.

33. Levin, *Shakespeare's Secret Schemers,* 45.

3. Reporting the Women's Causes Aright

1. In his excellent reading of *Hamlet* in *Issues of Death: Mortality and Identity in English Renaissance Tragedy* (Oxford: Clarendon Press, 1997), Michael Neill focuses on death and narrative. He argues that the Ghost "speaks the master-narrative from which all others in the play in some sense derive" (223). Death is the abruption of narrative, and revenge becomes "the only kind of reckoning that can perfect this broken narrative" (218). Yet there is always the sense in *Hamlet* of "other stories which stubbornly resist telling—tales which remain either untold, or beyond completion even in the triumphant consummation of revenge" (218). See especially his chapter 6, "'To Know My Stops': *Hamlet* and Narrative Abruption," 216–42.

2. Critics who focus on Ophelia, particularly in relation to mourning and song, include Susan Letzler Cole, Christy Desmet, Leslie C. Dunn, Nona Fienberg, Sandra K. Fischer, Jacqueline Fox-Good, Katharine Goodland, Cherrell Guilfoyle, and Lois Potter. As Fox-Good maintains, in Ophelia's songs we find "her own story"; she "us[es] her own voice for her grief, and for rage and protest." See Fox-Good, "Ophelia's Mad Songs: Music, Gender, Power," in *Subjects on the World's Stage: Essays on British Literature of the Middle Ages and Renaissance,* ed. David G. Allen and Robert A. White (Newark: University of Delaware Press, 1995), 222. In a reading that resonates with my own, Potter argues that "Ophelia is as much a revenger of her father as Laertes, using her madness—and her songs—to say things as provocative as Hamlet's." See Potter, "Shakespeare and the Art of Revenge," *Shakespeare Studies* 32 (1994): 45. Critics who focus on Gertrude include Carolyn Heilbrun, G. B. Shand, Richard Levin, and Rebecca Smith.

3. Adrian Poole notes Ophelia's connection with the Ghost in *Tragedy: Shakespeare and the Greek Example* (Oxford: Basil Blackwell, 1987), but his emphasis lies mainly in how both Old Hamlet and Ophelia need to be recognized and remembered (123).

4. The first set of quoted definitions is offered by Murray J. Levith, *What's in Shakespeare's Names* (North Haven, CT: Archon Books, 1978), 52.

5. For a brief discussion of Ophelia's name in light of the Lord's Prayer, sin, and forgiveness, see Gene Fendt, *Is "Hamlet" a Religious Drama?* (Milwaukee, WI: Marquette University Press, 1998), 82–84.

6. William Ian Miller, *Eye for an Eye* (Cambridge: Cambridge University Press, 2006), 152.

7. At least one critic, Murray J. Levith, sees the Greek serpent in Ophelia's name, but Levith's conclusion differs from mine in that he finds in this disturbing resonance "the taint of circumstance" (*What's in Shakespeare's Names,* 52).

8. Padel, *In and Out of the Mind,* 167.

9. Keyishian, *Shapes of Revenge,* 26, 26–28.

10. Leslie C. Dunn, "Ophelia's Songs in *Hamlet:* Music, Madness, and the Feminine," in *Embodied Voices: Representing Female Vocality in Western Culture,* ed. Leslie C. Dunn and Nancy A. Jones (Cambridge: Cambridge University Press, 1994), 50.

11. While Judith Weil has located "descendants of Hecuba" in Shakespeare's Constance and Volumnia, I contend that Ophelia, too, revives Hecuba's memory. See Weil, "Visible Hecubas," in *The Female Tragic Hero in English Renaissance Drama,* ed. Naomi Conn Liebler (New York: Palgrave Macmillan, 2002), 67. In *Female Mourning,* Katharine Goodland connects the Player's enactment of Hecuba's grief with Ophelia's mourning by pointing out that the word *nothing* is used by Hamlet and by the Gentleman to describe both performances of grief (182). Christy Desmet detects that "Hecuba also resembles Ophelia as a choric figure who can do nothing but mourn her dead. Hecuba, like Ophelia, perceives a mad world" and "solemnizes the end with an outburst of grief" (*Reading Shakespeare's Characters,* 14).

12. Mossman, *Wild Justice*, 2.

13. Richard Rainolde, *The Foundation of Rhetoric* (1563; rpt., Menston, England: Scolar Press, 1972), N1r–3r.

14. In *Female Mourning,* Goodland argues that Hamlet "resists identifying with Hecuba's grief, a resistance to female sorrow that will, in the end, place him in a superior moral position to his rival avenger Laertes" (162). In *Hamlet* feminine grief is "disparaged" (160), she argues, as a dangerously excessive show of passion. I would suggest, however, that in his soliloquy, Hamlet responds to the Player's tears for Hecuba by seeing himself in competition with the Hecuba figure; he imagines that his story—if the Player were to speak feelingly for him—might inspire a great deal more passion from auditors and spectators than does the woeful account of the fallen Trojan queen.

15. See Susan Letzler Cole, *The Absent One: Mourning Ritual, Tragedy, and the Performance of Ambivalence* (University Park: Pennsylvania State University Press, 1985), 56, and the discussion that follows (56–58).

16. Ibid., 58.

17. In her cross-cultural study, Gail Holst-Warhaft observes that lament is a woman's art form practiced widely throughout time in countless cultures. Women's lament has been perceived as dangerous because of its challenge to state authority and "has been almost eliminated from the modern western world." Gail Holst-Warhaft, *Dangerous Voices: Women's Laments and Greek Literature* (London: Routledge, 1992), 6. She regards ancient Greek tragedy and the early Christian fathers' "symbolic substitution" of the Virgin's grief for her dead son for personal grief as two significant diversions of women's lament into a male-controlled domain (6). See also Goodland, *Female Mourning,* esp. 12–13.

18. Dunn, "Ophelia's Songs," 52, 61.

19. The quotation from Euripides' *Hecuba* is taken from John Davie's translation in *Electra and Other Plays* (London: Penguin Books, 1998).

20. Poole, *Tragedy,* 122.

21. Louise Schleiner, "Latinized Greek Drama in Shakespeare's Writing of *Hamlet,*" *Shakespeare Quarterly* 41, no. 1 (Spring 1990): 45. The English translations from 1599 were *Agamemnon* and *Orestes' Furies*.

22. Ibid., n. 55.

23. *Oxford English Dictionary,* s.v. "Yield," 7.a, b.

24. See *Hamlet,* ed. Anne Thompson and Neil Taylor, The Arden Shakespeare (London: Thomson Learning, 2006), nn. 42–43 at 4.5.

25. *Oxford English Dictionary,* s.v. "Table," 1.b, 7.a.

26. Loraux, *Mourning Voice,* 33.

27. Cole, *Absent One,* 9.

28. Richard Levin, "Gertrude's Elusive Libido and Shakespeare's Unreliable Narrators," *Studies in English Literature* 48, no. 2 (Spring 2008): 323.

29. Carolyn Heilbrun, "The Character of Hamlet's Mother" (1957), repr. in *Hamlet's Mother and Other Women* (New York: Columbia University Press, 1990), 11. Fendt emphasizes this point, as well, in *Is "Hamlet" a Religious Drama?* (15).

30. G. B. Shand, "Realizing Gertrude: The Suicide Option," in *The Elizabethan Theatre XIII,* ed. A. L. Magnusson and C. E. McGee (Toronto: P. D. Meany, 1994), 105.

31. Erwin Fernie, *Shame in Shakespeare* (London: Routledge, 2002), 17, 21.

32. Ibid., 8.

33. *Oxford English Dictionary.* s.v. "Mouse," 2.a, 3.a.

34. Poole, *Tragedy,* 122–23.

35. Goodland, *Female Mourning,* 197.

36. René Girard, *A Theater of Envy: William Shakespeare* (South Bend, IN: St. Augustine's Press, 2004), 275–76. Girard reads *Hamlet* in light of our modern-day nuclear threat;

revenge can only be "sick revenge" and destructive. He is perplexed by critics who insist on justifying the ethics of revenge.

37. Fendt, *Is "Hamlet" a Religious Drama?* 130.

38. In *An English Dictionary,* first published in 1676, Elisha Coles offers this definition for the name Gertrude, which is of Saxon origin.

39. *Oxford English Dictionary,* s. v. "Sweet."

40. Mercer, *"Hamlet" and the Acting of Revenge,* 258.

41. For readings that diminish Lavinia's agency and participation in revenge, see, for example, Carolyn Asp, "'Upon Her Wit Doth Earthly Honor Wait': Female Agency in *Titus Andronicus,"* in *Titus Andronicus: Critical Essays,* ed. Philip C. Kolin (New York: Garland Publishing, 1995), 333–46; Derek Cohen, *Shakespeare's Culture of Violence* (New York: St. Martin's Press, 1993); Sara Eaton, "A Woman of Letters: Lavinia in *Titus Andronicus,"* in *Shakespearean Tragedy and Gender,* ed. Shirley Nelson Garner and Madelon Sprengnether (Bloomington: Indiana University Press, 1996), 54–74; and Douglas E. Green, "Interpreting 'Her Martyr'd Signs': Gender and Tragedy in *Titus Andronicus,"* *Shakespeare Quarterly* 40 (1989): 317–26.

42. Deborah Willis, "'The Gnawing Vulture': Revenge, Trauma Theory, and *Titus Andronicus,"* *Shakespeare Quarterly* 53, no. 1 (2002): 32.

43. Ibid., 33.

44. D. J. Palmer emphasizes the turn to ritual throughout *Titus,* arguing that "the response to the intolerable is ritualised, in language and action, because ritual is the ultimate means by which man seeks to order and control his precarious and unstable world." Palmer, "The Unspeakable in Pursuit of the Uneatable: Language and Action in *Titus Andronicus,"* *Critical Quarterly* 14 (1972): 321–22.

45. See Howard Baker, *Induction to Tragedy* (Baton Rouge: Louisiana State University Press, 1939); Barbara Mowat, "Lavinia's Message: Shakespeare and Myth," *Renaissance Papers* (1981): 55–69; and Karen Robertson, "Rape and the Appropriation of Progne's Revenge in Shakespeare's *Titus Andronicus,* or 'Who Cooks the Thyestean Banquet?'" in *Representing Rape in Medieval and Early Modern Literature,* ed. Elizabeth Robertson and Christine M. Rose (New York: Palgrave Macmillan, 2001), 213–37. The tale of Philomel, Procne, and Tereus can be found in Ovid, *Metamorphoses,* 6.401–674.

46. Robertson, "Rape and Appropriation," 215, 214.

47. Ibid., 227.

48. Ibid.

49. See Ovid's *Metamorphoses* for the tale of Io (1.568–746).

50. Seneca, *Hippolytus,* in *Seneca's Tragedies,* trans. Frank Justus Miller (Cambridge, MA: Harvard University Press, 1917).

51. See Heather James's perceptive reading of *Titus Andronicus* in *Shakespeare's Troy: Drama, Politics, and the Translation of Empire* (Cambridge: Cambridge University Press, 1997). As James argues, Lavinia is "Shakespeare's extreme image of Rome's cultural disintegration" (44). Lavinia's rape recalls the role of rape in the foundation of Rome: the rapes of the Sabine women, Lucrece, Ilia, and, more subtly, Aeneas's marriage to Lavinia, "which threatened to repeat the rape of Helen of Troy" (44). By splicing the Ovidian Philomel's rape onto the others, and invoking Dido's story, as well, in the representation of Lavinia's rape, Shakespeare offers an Ovidian critique of Rome: he "suggests that the founding acts of empire contain the seeds of its ruin" (44).

52. Mowat, "Lavinia's Message," 58–59.

53. Kahn, *Man's Estate,* 63.

54. Ibid., 65.

55. See Jonathan Bate's introduction to the Arden edition of *Titus Andronicus* (London: Routledge, 1995), 83–92.

56. Linda Woodbridge, "Palisading the Body Politic," in *True Rites and Maimed Rites: Ritual and Anti-Ritual in Shakespeare and His Age,* ed. Linda Woodbridge and Edward Berry (Urbana: University of Illinois Press, 1992), 291.

57. William Proctor Williams, "*Titus Andronicus* in Washington, D.C.," *Shakespeare Newsletter* (Spring/Summer 2007): 12.

58. Linda Anderson, *Kind of Wild Justice,* 97.

59. French, *Virtues of Vengeance,* chap. 5, "The Avenger: The Authority Condition," 118–72.

60. Fernie, *Shame in Shakespeare,* 88.

61. S. P. Cerasano, "Half a Dozen Dangerous Words," in *Much Ado About Nothing and The Taming of the Shrew,* ed. Marion Wynne-Davies (Houndmills, England: Palgrave Macmillan, 2001), 40.

62. See, for example, Fernie, *Shame in Shakespeare,* 85–88; and Robert Lane, "'Foremost in Report': Social Identity and Masculinity in *Much Ado About Nothing,*" *Upstart Crow* 16 (1996): 31–47.

63. Anderson regards their verbal combat as "a series of comic revenges" (*Kind of Wild Justice,* 93), but notes that they are capable equally of imagining themselves as the objects of revenge (94–95).

64. R. W. Maslen, *Shakespeare and Comedy* (London: Thomson Learning, 2006), 156.

65. Maggie Steed, "Beatrice in *Much Ado About Nothing,*" in *Players of Shakespeare 3,* ed. Russell Jackson and Robert Smallwood (Cambridge: Cambridge University Press, 1993), 45, 46.

66. Barbara Everett, "*Much Ado About Nothing:* The Unsociable Comedy," in *English Comedy,* ed. Michael Cordner, Peter Holland, and John Kerrigan (Cambridge: Cambridge University Press, 1994), 73, 74.

67. On the Hercules/Alcestis subtext, see Jonathan Bate, "Dying to Live in *Much Ado About Nothing,*" in *Surprised by Scenes: Essays in Honour of Professor Yasunari Takahashi,* ed. Yasunari Takada (Tokyo: Kenkyusha, 1994), 69–85.

68. Everett, "*Much Ado About Nothing,*" 83.

69. Marilyn Williamson, *The Patriarchy of Shakespeare's Comedies* (Detroit: Wayne State University Press, 1986), 48.

70. Homer, *Iliad.,* trans. Richmond Lattimore (Chicago: University of Chicago Press, 1951).

71. *The True Tragedie of Richard the Third* (London: Richard Creede, 1594).

72. Anderson, *Kind of Wild Justice,* 97. On mixed responses in the theater to the line "Kill Claudio," see J. F. Cox, "The Stage Representation of the 'Kill Claudio' Sequence in *Much Ado About Nothing,*" *Shakespeare Survey* 32 (1979): 27–36.

73. Friedrich Nietzsche, *Beyond Good and Evil: Prelude to a Philosophy of the Future,* trans. and ed. Marion Faber (Oxford: Oxford University Press, 1998), aphorism 139.

4. Hecuba's Legacy

1. For one example of criticism that focuses on Margaret's femaleness as opposed to her usurped maleness, see Naomi C. Liebler and Lisa Scancella Shea, "Shakespeare's Queen Margaret: Unruly or Unruled?" in *Henry VI: Critical Essays,* ed. Thomas A. Pendleton (New York: Routledge, 2001). Liebler and Shea take a Jungian approach to Margaret's character in order to establish an "alternative discourse of power" (95). They argue against the view that Margaret violates gender roles and adopts masculine traits. Rather, "By performing archetypal feminine roles, the dramatic figure of Margaret—neither submissive nor necessarily subversive—directs our attention to the power inherent in those roles" (95).

2. See, for example, David Bevington, "The Domineering Female in *1 Henry VI,*" *Shakespeare Studies* 2 (1966): 51–58; Sigurd Burckhardt, *Shakespearean Meanings* (Princeton, NJ: Princeton University Press, 1968), 47–77; David Scott Kastan, *Shakespeare and the Shapes of Time* (Hanover, NH: University Press of New England, 1982), 116; Jean E. Howard and Phyllis Rackin, *Engendering a Nation: A Feminist Account of Shakespeare's English Histories* (London: Routledge, 1997); and Nina S. Levine, *Women's Matters: Politics, Gender, and Nation in Shakespeare's Early History Plays* (Newark: University of Delaware Press, 1998).

3. Loraux, *Mothers in Mourning,* 49. I am indebted to Loraux's provocative insights into how "the mourning of mothers" can become a "challenge to political life as it is defined by the city-state" (7).

4. Barthélemy Aneau, *Picta poesis* (Lyons: Macé Bonhomme, 1552), digitized on the Web site French Emblems at Glasgow, http://www.emblems.arts.gla.ac.uk/french/books .php?id=FANa&o=. The section of the Latin motto I have translated appears as follows: "Dilaniat Tigris rabiosam Hyrcana seipsam./ Et lacerat carnis propria membra suae. . . . O sexus cupiens vindictae, at viribus impos, / Hyrcana mulier Tigride saeva magis!" In his *Metamorphoses,* Ovid, too, compares Procne to a tiger (6.636–37): "nec mora, traxit Ityn, veluti Gangetica cervae / lactentem fetum per silvas tigris opacas. . . ."

5. Quotations from John Studley's *Medea* are taken from Thomas Newton's *Seneca, His Tenne Tragedies, Translated into English* (1581; repr. Bloomington: Indiana University Press, 1960).

6. The quotation from Virgil's *Aeneid* is taken from *P. Vergili Maronis: Opera,* ed. R. A. B. Mynors (Oxford: Oxford University Press, 1969). See also Henry Howard, Earl of Surrey's sixteenth-century English translation: "Faithlesse, forsworn, ne Goddesse was thy dam, / Nor Dardanus beginner of thy race, / But of hard rockes mount Caucase monstruous / Bred thee, and teates of Tyger gaue thee suck" (4.477–80). *The "Aeneid" of Henry Howard, Earl of Surrey,* ed. Florence H. Ridley (Berkeley and Los Angeles: University of California Press, 1963).

7. The quotation from Christopher Marlowe's *Dido, Queen of Carthage* is taken from C. F. Tucker Brooke's edition in *The Works and Life of Christopher Marlowe,* ed. R. H. Case, vol. 1 (New York: Gordian Press, 1966).

8. See, for example, Juliet Dusinberre, *Shakespeare and the Nature of Women,* 3rd ed. (New York: Palgrave Macmillan, 2003), 299–304.

9. See Patricia-Ann Lee's excellent assessment of the historical record on Queen Margaret, which demonstrates how gender was a primary category of criticism against the early modern female ruler. Lee, "Reflections of Power: Margaret of Anjou and the Dark Side of Queenship," *Renaissance Quarterly* 39, no. 2 (Summer 1986): 183–217. The quotations are drawn from Richard Grafton, *A Chronicle at Large and Meere History of the Affayres of England and Kinges of the Same* (1569), ed. Henry Ellis (London: J. Johnson et al., 1809), 1: 670, 655; and Edward Hall, *Hall's Chronicle; containing the history of England, during the reign of Henry the Fourth, and the succeeding monarchs, to the end of the reign of Henry the Eighth* (original title, *The Union of the Two Noble and Illustre Famelies of Lancastre and Yorke . . .,* 1548), ed. Henry Ellis (London: J. Johnson et al., 1809), 249, 234.

10. Dusinberre's conflation of adultery, vengefulness, and murderousness in immoral female characters in Elizabethan drama fails to offer nuanced interpretations in each case (*Shakespeare and the Nature of Women,* 301–3). She observes rightly that "The violent woman in Shakespeare's theatre is nearly always an adulteress" (301–2), but the adultery is not necessarily the symbolic root or first step toward further taboo-breaking, as she suggests.

11. Robert Greene, *Groats-Worth of Witte, bought with a million of Repentance* (London: John Lane, 1592), 45–46. See Carol Chillington Rutter's excellent article, "Of Tygers' Hearts and Players' Hides," in *Shakespeare's Histories and Counter-Histories,* ed. Dermot

Cavanagh, Stuart Hampton-Reeves, and Stephen Longstaffe (Manchester: Manchester University Press, 2007), 182–98.

12. Jones, *Origins of Shakespeare,* 185.

13. Dusinberre, *Shakespeare and the Nature of Women,* 299.

14. Howard and Rackin, *Engendering a Nation,* 94.

15. Nina S. Levine argues that many critics have evaluated Queen Margaret negatively in accordance with traditional gender norms and argues sensibly that "just because the plays support censure of Margaret's rule, they do not necessarily endorse the gendered terms of York's attack" (*Women's Matters,* 68).

16. Steven Urkowitz, "Five Women Eleven Ways: Changing Images of Shakespearean Characters in the Earliest Texts," in *Images of Shakespeare: Proceedings of the Third Congress of the International Shakespeare Association, 1986,* ed. Werner Habicht, D. J. Palmer, and Roger Pringle (Newark: University of Delaware Press, 1988), 297.

17. Ibid.

18. Penny Downie, "Queen Margaret in *Henry VI* and *Richard III,*" in *Players of Shakespeare 3,* ed. Russell Jackson and Robert Smallwood (Cambridge: Cambridge University Press, 1993), 115.

19. See, for example, Patricia Silber, "The Unnatural Woman and the Disordered State in Shakespeare's Histories," *Proceedings of the PMR Conference* 2 (1977): 87–95; Bevington, "Domineering Female"; and Lee, "Reflections of Power," 216. Silber emphasizes, without critical nuance, that "unnatural women dominate men, follow masculine rather than feminine pursuits, and substitute cruelty and hatred for womanly tenderness" (88). Furthermore, the unnatural usurpation of men's roles by women in *1 Henry VI* serves as "certain indication of grave turmoil" (87) in the country. She couples Margaret and Joan La Pucelle as unnatural women, the former replacing the latter in the symbolic dispensation of the plays. The view that Margaret is Joan's adjunct can be found, as well, in William M. Hawley, *Critical Hermeneutics and Shakespeare's Plays* (New York: Peter Lang, 1992), 26; Barbara Hodgdon, *The End Crowns All: Closure and Contradiction in Shakespeare's History* (Princeton, NJ: Princeton University Press, 1991), 69; Gabriele Bernhard Jackson, "Topical Ideology: Witches, Amazons, and Shakespeare's Joan of Arc," *English Literary Review* 18 (1988): 40–65; Leah Marcus, *Puzzling Shakespeare: Local Reading and Its Discontents* (Berkeley and Los Angeles: University of California Press, 1988), 66–89; and Angela Pitt, *Shakespeare's Women* (Newton Abbot, England: David and Charles, 1981), 150–57.

20. Downie, "Queen Margaret," 119, 122, 135.

21. Elizabeth Schafer, *Ms-Directing Shakespeare: Women Direct Shakespeare* (New York: St. Martin's Press, 2000), 172.

22. Ibid.

23. Antonio Tempesta, "Hecuba trucidatum a Polymnestore Polydorum reperit" [Hecuba discovering Polydorus' Body], plate 123 in *Metamorphoseon . . . Ovidianarum* (c. 1585, 1606).

24. A somewhat distant, though not forgotten, stage model for scenes depicting a mother's lament over her dead son can be found in the Virgin's laments in the English mystery cycles. In the *Ludus Coventriae,* in particular, Mary makes impassioned outbursts before the cross, begs for death to take her, and, upon the removal of the body, holds her son's corpse in her lap as she gives a brief lament. See Rosemary Woolf, *The English Mystery Plays* (Berkeley and Los Angeles: University of California, 1972), esp. 262–66.

25. Schafer, *Ms-Directing Shakespeare,* 171.

26. See Roger Virgoe, "The Death of William de la Pole, the Duke of Suffolk," *Bulletin of the John Rylands Library* 47 (1964–65): 489–502.

27. Dusinberre, *Shakespeare and the Nature of Women,* 299.

28. In Edward Hall's *Chronicle,* which Holinshed follows and elaborates upon, Margaret

does not kill anyone, much less the Duke of York or his son, the Earl of Rutland. Lord Clifford cruelly kills the twelve-year-old Rutland; after decapitating the dead York, Clifford places a paper crown on the head, and then affixes the head to a pole to present to Margaret (250–51).

29. Holinshed, *Shakespeare's Holinshed,* 215, echoes E. Hall, *Hall's Chronicle,* 301.

30. E. Hall, *Hall's Chronicle,* 301.

31. Dusinberre, *Shakespeare and the Nature of Women,* 300. Similarly, in "Of Tygers' Hearts and Players' Hides," Rutter comments that in *Richard III,* "like Alecto, she [Margaret] distributes discord and, like Nemesis, presides as vengeance descends upon the House of York" (190).

32. Margaret makes an unhistorical appearance in *Richard III.* After being imprisoned in London and ransomed by her father, she returns to France and dies in 1482.

33. A. P. Rossiter, *Angel with Horns, and Other Shakespeare Lectures,* ed. Graham Storey (New York: Theatre Arts Books, 1961), 13–14.

34. Ibid., 14.

35. Jessica Lange played Tamora in Julie Taymor's 1990 film production, and Estelle Kohler played Tamora in Deborah Warner's 1987 RSC production.

36. Loraux, *Mothers in Mourning,* 49.

37. Brian Cox, "Titus Andronicus," in *Players of Shakespeare 3,* ed. Russell Jackson and Robert Smallwood (Cambridge: Cambridge University Press, 1993), 174–88, 178, 179.

38. Willis, "'Gnawing Vulture,'" 37.

39. Ronald Broude, "Four Forms of Vengeance in *Titus Andronicus,*" *Journal of English and Germanic Philology* 78 (1979): 495–97. Broude's identification of four kinds of revenge in *Titus Andronicus* makes useful distinctions: human sacrifice, vendetta, state justice, and divine retribution.

40. See, for example, Robert Parker, *Miasma: Pollution and Purification in Early Greek Religion* (Oxford: Clarendon Press, 1983), 11–12.

41. Pliny the Elder, *Natural History,* trans. H. Rackham, vol. 8 (Cambridge, MA: Harvard University Press, 1963), 30.3.12. He notes that a senatorial decree in 97 BCE formally abolished human sacrifice.

42. See Broude's brief, enlightening discussion of this scene in "Four Forms," 496–97.

43. Willis, "'Gnawing Vulture,'" 35.

44. See Mowat, "Lavinia's Message." Mowat observes, "The general shape of *Titus Andronicus* is that of the destruction of a noble house where the parent is destroyed through the destruction of the children" (61). Tamora is reminiscent of the avenging Ovidian goddesses that destroy houses: Juno and the Fury she calls up to destroy the house of Cadmus, and Latona who destroys the house of Thebes (61).

45. Ibid., 58.

46. The quotation from Seneca's *Thyestes* is taken from the Loeb edition of *Seneca in Nine Volumes,* vol. 9 (Cambridge, MA: Harvard University Press, 1917).

47. Willis, "'Gnawing Vulture,'" 41.

48. In *The Origins of Shakespeare,* Jones argues, "We shall not properly appreciate the play unless we see that Shakespeare's Titus is in essence nothing else than a male Hecuba" (101). See also Mowat, "Lavinia's Message," 58–62.

49. Jeanne Addison Roberts, "Sex and the Female Tragic Hero," in *The Female Tragic Hero in English Renaissance Drama,* ed. Naomi Conn Liebler (New York: Palgrave Macmillan, 2002), 199–216.

50. Shakespeare alludes directly to Tomyris in *1 Henry VI* when the Countess of Auvergne plots to entrap and defeat Talbot, the "bloodthirsty" "scourge of France" (2.3.33, 14), as she calls him. She has prepared her revenge: "The plot is laid. If all things fall out right / I shall be as famous by this exploit / As Scythian Tomyris by Cyrus' death" (2.3.4–

6). She aspires to the heroism of an avenging Tomyris, who was capable of defeating a powerful male enemy.

51. Herodotus *Histories* 1.212. For the story of Tomryis and Cyrus, see 1.201–14. Herodotus claims, "Many stories are related to Cyrus' death; this, that I have told, is the worthiest of credence" (1.214).

52. Ibid., 1. 214.

53. James Hall, *Dictionary of Subjects and Symbols in Art,* rev. ed. (Boulder, CO: Westview Press, 1979), 305.

54. Findlay, for example, refers to Kyd's "male personification of Revenge" in *Feminist Perspective,* 52. See Kiefer's discussion of the gender of Kyd's Revenge in *Shakespeare's Visual Theatre,* 47–48.

55. J. Hall, *Dictionary of Subjects,* 304.

5. "REVENGING HOME"

1. As Robert S. Miola has observed, "[T]hough the revenge dynamic—rending and integration—is enormously complicated in *Lear* (and, finally, subverted), rhetoric and action bear continual witness to its presence." See Miola, *Shakespeare and Classical Tragedy: The Influence of Seneca* (Oxford: Clarendon Press, 1992), 144. Miola characterizes *King Lear* as a "tragedy of wrath" (Thomas Nashe's phrase), wrath being "the archetypal Senecan passion" (151). He follows a host of critics from the eighteenth century (e.g., Charles Gildon, Aaron Hill) through the twentieth century, with later seminal studies including Lily B. Campbell, *Shakespeare's Tragic Heroes: Slaves of Passion* (Cambridge: Cambridge University Press, 1930); and Gordon Braden, *Renaissance Tragedy and the Senecan Tradition: Anger's Privilege* (New Haven, CT: Yale University Press, 1985). None of these scholars, however, pursue the question of revenge's complex presence in *King Lear.*

2. See especially his chapter 2, "'Aristotle and the rest': The Aristotelian-Thomistic Tradition of Moral Philosophy," 36–57, in Beauregard's *Virtue's Own Feature.*

3. Thomas Aquinas, *Summa Theologica,* 2-2.108.4. In "Of Vengeance," a brief section of the *Summa,* Aquinas follows Augustine in arguing that sin is voluntary; "Therefore vengeance should be taken only on those who have deserved it voluntarily. . . . [P]unishment is not due save for sin, because by means of punishment the equality of justice is restored, in so far as he who by sinning has exceeded in following his own will suffers something that is contrary to his will" (108.4).

4. Ibid., 2-2.108.1. "[I]n the matter of vengeance, we must consider the mind of the avenger. For if his intention is directed chiefly to the evil of the person on whom he takes vengeance, and rests there, then his vengeance is altogether unlawful: because to take pleasure in another's evil belongs to hatred, which is contrary to the charity whereby we are bound to love all men. . . . If, however, the avenger's intention be directed chiefly to some good, to be obtained by means of the punishment of the person who has sinned (for instance, that the sinner may amend, or at least that he may be restrained and others be not disturbed, that justice may be upheld, and God honored), then vengeance may be lawful, provided other due circumstances be observed" (108.1).

5. Ibid., 2-2.108.2. Following Tully who argues that men use vengeance for the good to resist force and wrong, Aquinas makes the case for vengeance as a "special virtue."

6. Quotations from Aristotle, *Nicomachean Ethics* come from W. D. Ross and J. O. Urmson's translation in *The Complete Works of Aristotle: The Revised Oxford Translation,* ed. J. Barnes, vol. 2 (Princeton, NJ: Princeton University Press, 1984).

7. Unless otherwise noted, quotations from and references to *King Lear* are taken from

the 1623 Folio text in *The Norton Shakespeare*, ed. Stephen Greenblatt (New York: W. W. Norton, 1997). The 1608 Quarto text, when quoted, is from *The Norton Shakespeare*, as well.

8. *Oxford English Dictionary*, s.v. "Home," adv. 5.a. Further commentary on the word *home* reflects various definitions found in the *OED*.

9. In "The War in *King Lear*," *Shakespeare Survey* 33 (1980): 27–34, Gary Taylor demonstrates how, unlike the Quarto, the Folio text envisions Cordelia as head of a war or a rebellion with few reminders of the French force cropping up. The omissions from the Quarto text "clearly and strongly establish the narrative expectation of war," and Cordelia "as the sole representative of that apocalyptic counter-movement which culminates disastrously, in V, ii" (29, 32). Some notable productions of *King Lear* have emphasized the war and Cordelia's strength as a military leader or warrior (e.g., the Royal Shakespeare Company 1950 production with Peggy Ashcroft armed and dressed in a breastplate, reminiscent of Joan of Arc; and the 1973 Joseph Papp production with Lee Chamberlin as a militant, fierce Cordelia).

10. A number of critics have discussed Cordelia's attempt to fulfill the role of a male heir. See especially Barbara C. Millard, "Virago with a Soft Voice: Cordelia's Tragic Rebellion in *King Lear*," *Philology Quarterly* 68, no. 2 (Spring 1989): 143–65; and Gayle Whittier, "Cordelia as Prince: Gender and Language in *King Lear*," *Exemplaria* 1, no. 2 (October 1989): 367–99.

11. See two excellent studies that explain how Shakespeare raises and defeats romantic and comic generic expectations in *King Lear*: Michael L. Hays, *Shakespearean Tragedy as Chivalric Romance: Rethinking "Macbeth," "Hamlet," "Othello," and "King Lear"* (Cambridge: D.S. Brewer, 2003); and Susan Snyder, *The Comic Matrix of Shakespeare's Tragedies* (Princeton, NJ: Princeton University Press, 1979).

12. William R. Elton, *"King Lear" and the Gods* (San Marino, CA: Huntington Library, 1966), 123, 121.

13. *Oxford English Dictionary*, s.v. "Rest," 6.a, b, 7.a–f. "To set my rest" means "to stake all."

14. *Oxford English Dictionary*, s.v. "Nursery," 2.a.

15. In *What's in Shakespeare's Names*, Murray J. Levith notes the Greek root in Cordelia's name (*delos*) and suggests, as well, that *cœur de leon* would spring to mind because she marries the King of France (57).

16. Braden, *Renaissance Tragedy*, 216. Jasper Heywood translates the beginning of Atreus's speech in *Thyestes* as follows: "Above the reache that men are woont to worke, / begins to swell: / And slayeth with slouthfull hands. What thinge it is I cannot tell: / But great it is . . ." (act 2). See *Seneca: His Tenne Tragedies Translated into English*, ed. Thomas Newton (1581; rpt., Bloomington: Indiana University Press, 1960).

17. Text from vol. 7 of Geoffrey Bullough, ed., *Narrative and Dramatic Sources of Shakespeare*, 8 vols. (London: Routledge, 1957–75).

18. Girard, *Theater of Envy*, 182.

19. Thomas Aquinas, *Summa Theologica*, 2-2.108.2.

20. J. Hall, *Dictionary of Subjects*, 238.

21. Millard, "Virago with a Soft Voice," 144.

22. Ibid.

23. Girard, *Violence and the Sacred*, 21.

24. See Prosser, *"Hamlet" and Revenge;* and Bowers, *Elizabethan Revenge Tragedy.*

25. Thomas Aquinas, *Summa Theologica*, 2-2.108.1.

26. Thomas Cranmer, "A Sermon concerning the Time of Rebellion," in *Miscellaneous Writings and Letters of Thomas Cranmer*, ed. John Edmund Cox (Cambridge: Cambridge University Press, 1846), 193.

27. Martin Luther, *Temporal Authority: To What Extent It Should be Obeyed* (1523), trans. J. J. Schindel, rev. Walther I. Brandt, in *Luther's Works*, ed. Walther I. Brandt, vol. 45 (Philadelphia: Muhlenberg Press, 1962), 101, 103.

28. Stanley Cavell, *Disowning Knowledge in Seven Plays by Shakespeare*, updated ed. (Cambridge: Cambridge University Press, 2003), 80.

29. Thomas Aquinas, *Summa Theologica*, 2-2.108.2.

30. Keyishian, *Shapes of Revenge*, 68, 76. Keyishian argues that Lear "*finally gets it right:* he is angry at last (Aristotle would have approved) at the right person, at the right time, for the right reason; and he takes the right revenge" (68). He calls Lear's revenge "wonderful, exhilarating, heroic" and argues that it affords Lear a "momentary regeneration" (76).

31. See Girard, *Violence and the Sacred*, esp. 1–27.

32. Snyder, *Comic Matrix*, 179.

6. *TWELFTH NIGHT*

1. In *Shakespeare's Festive Comedy: A Study of Dramatic Form and Its Relation to Social Custom* (Cleveland: World Publishing Company, 1959), C. L. Barber makes the saturnalian case for comedy and the positive functions of socially disruptive activities. The result of irreverently mocking or turning over normative laws is a final clarification of social restrictions and a renewed sense of self and community. Following Barber, a plethora of critics have taken up the saturnalian interpretation of *Twelfth Night*, arguing essentially that "Pleasure . . . becomes the touchstone for judgment of what bars it or is incapable of it" (Barber, *Shakespeare's Festive Comedy*, 8). See also Northrop Frye, *A Natural Perspective* (New York: Columbia University Press, 1965). More recently, in *A Kind of Wild Justice* Linda Anderson pursues the saturnalian interpretation by focusing specifically on how vengeful actions in comedy create intrigue and conflict, which necessitate a healthy, morally edifying reconciliation. Unsaturnalian interpretations of *Twelfth Night* began to appear in the 1970s as correctives to the festive view of the play. See, for example, F. H. Langman, "Comedy and Saturnalia: The Case of *Twelfth Night*," *Southern Review* 7 (1974): 102–22. Ralph Berry notes the earlier critics' "imperviousness to the ending" of *Twelfth Night* in his critique of festive readings. Berry, "*Twelfth Night:* The Experience of the Audience," *Shakespeare Survey* 34 (1981): 117. Linda Woodbridge insightfully suggests that rather than a *festive* comedy, *Twelfth Night* is at heart a "corrective comedy . . . that basically enacts the inadvisability, not the therapeutic benefits, of excess" (289). Woodbridge, "'Fire in Your Heart and Brimstone in Your Liver': Towards an Unsaturnalian *Twelfth Night*," *Southern Review* 17 (November 1984): 270–91.

2. Berry, "*Twelfth Night*," 117. I am indebted to Berry's excellent critique of the festive view of *Twelfth Night*. Other critics who emphasize darker, anticomic tones and generic complexity in *Twelfth Night* include Julian Markels, "Shakespeare's Confluence of Tragedy and Comedy: *Twelfth Night* and *King Lear*," *Shakespeare Quarterly* 15 (1964): 75–88; Clifford Leech, "*Twelfth Night*" *and Shakespearian Comedy* (Toronto: University of Toronto Press, 1965), esp. 29–55; Anne Barton, "*As You Like It* and *Twelfth Night:* Shakespeare's Sense of an Ending," in *Shakespearian Comedy*, ed. Malcolm Bradbury and David Palmer, Stratford-upon-Avon Studies 14 (London: Edward Arnold, 1972): 160–80; and Maslen, *Shakespeare and Comedy*, 192–210.

3. Stephen Booth's self-conscious discomfort regarding this speech is worth noting here. He claims, while "Fabian and his peacemaking speech ask us to take them as furniture of the play as play—as stuff in a comedy," he cannot help pursuing a line of thought "entirely alien to the spirit generically appropriate to an audience listening while a playwright brings his comic machine to rest." Booth, *Precious Nonsense: The Gettysburg Address, Ben Jonson's Epitaphs on his Children, and "Twelfth Night"* (Berkeley and Los Angeles: University of California Press, 1998), 179, 178–79.

4. Kerrigan, *Revenge Tragedy,* 194.

5. Ibid., 216.

6. Ibid.

7. Jagannath Chakravorty, for example, assures us that "Maria's 'revenge' is, of course, good-hearted—nothing more than a desire to teach him a lesson" (*Idea of Revenge in Shakespeare,* 257). Harold C. Goddard, on the other hand, regards Maria as a practical joker with a "cruel streak"; he detects ambition and envy in her, as well as a desire to show off her talents to Sir Toby. Goddard, *The Meaning of Shakespeare,* vol. 1 (Chicago: University of Chicago Press, 1951), 298. Similarly, in *"Twelfth Night,"* Berry emphasizes Maria's social resentment; he notes, "she endures the classic ambivalence of the lady-in-waiting, above the servants but not ranking with the great" (114). Harold Bloom argues that Maria is sadistic, calling her "the only truly malicious character in *Twelfth Night.*" Bloom, *Shakespeare, Invention of the Human* (New York: Riverhead Books, 1998), 238.

8. Michael Billington, ed., *Approaches to "Twelfth Night,"* by Bill Alexander, John Barton, John Caird, Terry Hands. RSC Directors' Shakespeare (London: Nick Hern Books, 1990), 87, 86. As John Barton insightfully argues, "The way you take Maria is one of the big interpretive choices because it is open-ended: it's not textually defined how old she is or what she is at all" (85).

9. In *The Meaning of Shakespeare,* Goddard finds a "vague premonition of the Iago-Cassio theme" in Maria's simile, "I have dogged him like his murderer," and asserts that her intelligence and the constraints of a servile position have led to her ambition and envy (298).

10. Cristina Malcolmson, "'What You Will': Social Mobility and Gender in *Twelfth Night,*" in *Twelfth Night,* ed. R. S. White (New York: St. Martin's Press, 1996), 186.

11. Penny Gay, *As She Likes It: Shakespeare's Unruly Women* (London: Routledge Press, 1994), 18.

12. While directors tend to present Maria as a maid or housekeeper onstage, a careful examination of the text makes clear the error of too lowly a social designation for Maria. Olivia and Malvolio both call her a "gentlewoman" (1.5.165, 166), establishing her gentility at an early point in the play. Perhaps Sir Toby Belch's phrase, "My niece's chambermaid" (1.3.50) and Valentine's reference to "handmaid" (1.1.25) have misled readers and directors. The *Oxford English Dictionary,* however, confirms that the Elizabethan terms *chambermaid* and *handmaid* may refer to a gentlewoman who attends an aristocratic lady. Richard A. Levin suggests that the term is used as a private witticism exchanged between Sir Toby and Maria; Sir Toby calls her "My niece's chambermaid" to confuse Sir Andrew and to play on Maria's social aspirations. See Levin, *Love and Society in Shakespearean Comedy: A Study of Dramatic Form and Content* (Newark: University of Delaware Press, 1985), 132.

13. See Elliott Krieger, *"Twelfth Night:* 'The Morality of Indulgence,'" in *Twelfth Night,* ed. R. S. White (New York: St. Martin's Press, 1996), 60. About Maria, he rightly observes, "Through her service to Sir Toby she transcends service, rises to a higher social position. Her vocation allows her to express and to fulfill herself." See also Levin, *Love and Society,* where he argues that Maria serves as Sir Toby's "self appointed steward" (138).

14. The directors John Caird and Bill Alexander regard this moment as the pivotal one for Maria, for she must choose whether or not to align herself publicly with Sir Toby Belch. See Billington, *Approaches to "Twelfth Night,"* 86.

15. Mark Thornton Burnett makes a similar point in *Masters and Servants in English Renaissance Drama and Culture* (New York: St. Martin's Press, 1997), 142.

16. Laurie E. Osborne makes a similar point, referring to Maria's "occupation" of Olivia's position in "Letters, Lovers, Lacan: Or Malvolio's Not-So-Purloined Letter," *Assays* 5 (1989): 70–71.

17. In *Precious Nonsense,* Stephen Booth notes that Shakespeare does not waste "the inherent energy of *hand*" as a frequently repeated metaphor and body part in *Twelfth Night*

(201–2). Geoffrey H. Hartman comments that in the "dark room" scene words such as *hand* suddenly receive their full value. Hartman, "Shakespeare's Poetical Character in *Twelfth Night*," in *Shakespeare and the Question of Theory*, ed. Patricia Parker and Geoffrey Hartman (New York: Methuen, 1985), 50.

18. Here and elsewhere I am indebted to Karen Robertson's excellent article, "A Revenging Feminine Hand in *Twelfth Night*," in *Reading and Writing in Shakespeare*, ed. David Bergeron (Newark: University of Delaware Press, 1996), 123.

19. Inge Leimberg argues, "Malvolio, for all his passionate efforts to 'see . . . see . . . see', is blind to what everyone else sees clearly because it is indeed as revealing as 'Daylight and champaign'; he is virtually illiterate, unable to read the very ABC of self-knowledge spread before his eyes." Leimberg, "'M.O.A.I.': Trying to Share the Joke in *Twelfth Night* 2.5 (A Critical Hypothesis)," *Connotations*, no. 1 (1991): 82.

20. *Oxford English Dictionary*, s.v. "Baffle," v., etymology.

21. Berry, "*Twelfth Night*," 119.

22. Jason Scott-Warren notes Bill Alexander's directorial choice in his excellent article, "When Theaters Were Bear-Gardens; or What's at Stake in the Comedy of Humors," *Shakespeare Quarterly* 54, no. 1 (2003): 65. Scott-Warren belongs to a group of scholars (e.g., John R. Ford, Stephen Dickey, Ralph Berry) who have pursued links between bearbaiting and theater in *Twelfth Night*. As Scott-Warren argues, "For a while, Shakespeare's comedy is propelled by the violent energies of the bear-garden; finally, it almost comes to grief on them" (80).

23. *Oxford English Dictionary*, s.v. "Physic," 5.b, 4.a, 3.a.

24. John R. Ford, *Twelfth Night: A Guide to the Play* (Westport, CT: Greenwood Press, 2006), 58.

25. Chakravorty believes that Malvolio is "at last cured of his 'self-love'" (*Idea of Revenge in Shakespeare*, 258). Markels credits Feste, not Maria, with curing Malvolio, claiming that the Fool purges the steward's pride with a set catechism in the dark room scene ("Shakespeare's Confluence," 85–86). Ruth Nevo also focuses on Feste, claiming that Feste's ministrations to Malvolio in prison "travesty cure," but end up having a "rough curative effect." Nevo, *Comic Transformations in Shakespeare* (London: Methuen, 1980), 214. In *William Shakespeare: The Comedies*, Ronald R. Macdonald argues, "No matter how we experience the tone of the joke played on Malvolio . . . the fact remains that insofar as it is aimed at bringing him to his senses and giving him a more workable sense of the self, it is a failure." Macdonald, *William Shakespeare: The Comedies* (New York: Twayne Publishers, 1992), 118.

26. French, *Virtues of Vengeance*, 85.

27. In *Shakespeare's Festive Comedy*, Barber slyly gets at what Malvolio desires: "His secret wish is to violate decorum himself, then relish to the full its power over others" (255).

28. I have borrowed this felicitous term from Ruth Nevo, "Shakespeare's Comic Remedies," *New York Literary Forum* 5–6 (1980), 8.

29. Thomas Aquinas, *Summa Theologica*, 2-2.108.2.

30. See Camille Wells Slights, *Shakespeare's Comic Commonwealths* (Toronto: University of Toronto, 1993) for an enlightening discussion of how mutual dependence and continuing obligations define the comic world.

31. Léon Wurmser, *The Mask of Shame* (Baltimore: Johns Hopkins University Press, 1981), 81, my emphasis.

32. Bacon, "Of Revenge," 14.

33. The law student John Manningham attended the 1601 Middle Temple performance, recording in his diary how he relished the "good practise" of making the "steward beleeue his Lady widdowe was in Loue wth him by counterfayting a lett^r / as from his Lady in generall tearmes / telling him what shee liked best in him / and prescribing his gesture in smiling his apparraile / &c. /. And then when he came to practise making him beleeue they tooke

him to be mad." Quoted in the Arden edition of *Twelfth Night* ed. J. M. Lothian and T. W. Craik (London: Routledge, 1995), xxvi.

34. Francis Bacon, *The Philosophical Works of Francis Bacon,* ed. John M. Robertson (Freeport, NY: Books for Libraries Press, 1970), 555.

7. FEMININE VINDICATION

1. *Oxford English Dictionary,* "Vindication," etymology, 1.a, b; 2, 3.

2. Victor Turner, "Social Dramas in Brazilian Umbanda: The Dialectics of Meaning," in *The Anthropology of Performance* (New York: PAJ Publications, 1987), 33–71.

3. Ibid., 34.

4. Ibid.

5. Ibid.

6. Ibid., 35

7. K. M. Lea, *Italian Popular Comedy: A Study in the Commedia Dell' Arte, 1560– 1620, with Special Reference to the English Stage,* vol. 2 (New York: Russell and Russell, 1962), 431–34.

8. Turner, "Social Dramas," 35.

9. Ibid., 33.

10. Anne Barton, "Falstaff and the Comic Community," in *Shakespeare's "Rough Magic": Renaissance Essays in Honor of C. L. Barber,* ed. Peter Erickson and Coppélia Kahn (Newark: University of Delaware Press, 1985), 139.

11. On the deceit of women, see Pamela Allen Brown, *Better a Shrew than a Sheep: Women, Drama, and the Culture of Jest in Early Modern England* (Ithaca, NY: Cornell University Press, 2003), 47. Brown cites Abraham Vele's *Deceyte of women* (1563) as an "exhaustive" early modern source on the subject (47 n. 52).

12. Leslie S. Katz, "*The Merry Wives of Windsor:* Sharing the Queen's Holiday," *Representations* 51 (Summer 1995): 83.

13. Brown, *Better a Shrew,* 44.

14. Anne Parten, "Falstaff's Horns: Masculine Inadequacy and Feminine Mirth in *The Merry Wives of Windsor,*" *Studies in Philology* 82, no. 2 (Spring 1985): 188.

15. The quotation is taken from Jacob Black-Michaud, *Cohesive Force: Feud in the Mediterranean and the Middle East* (New York: St. Martin's Press, 1975), 179. See also Pitt-Rivers, "Honour and Social Status," 24–25.

16. Leo Salingar, *Shakespeare and the Traditions of Comedy* (Cambridge: Cambridge University Press, 1974), 233.

17. See ibid., 228–38; and Lea, *Italian Popular Comedy,* 2:432–33. Lea mentions *The Merry Wives* in light of *Li Tre Becchi,* a highly farcical scenario that involves a lady, Franceschina, tricking her husband by hiding her lover, Pantalone, in a tub of dirty clothing. Other examples include tales from the *Decameron* and Italian carnival plays such as *La Calandria.* For the influence of New Comedic conventions deriving from Plautus's *Casina,* see Bullough, *Narrative and Dramatic Sources,* 2:8–9; and Robert Miola, "*The Merry Wives of Windsor:* Classical and Italian Intertexts," *Comparative Drama* 27, no. 3 (Fall 1993): 364– 76. On Shakespeare's "reformation" of narrative traditions of sexual intrigue, see Richard Helgerson, "The Buck Basket, the Witch, and the Queen of Fairies: The Women's World of Shakespeare's Windsor," in *Renaissance Culture and the Everyday,* ed. Patricia Fumerton and Simon Hunt (Philadelphia: University of Pennsylvania Press, 1999): 170–71.

18. Studies that foreground revenge include Anderson, *Kind of Wild Justice;* and W. L. Godshalk, "An Apology for *The Merry Wives of Windsor,*" in *Renaissance Papers* (Durham,

NC: Southeastern Renaissance Conference, 1973), 97–108. In *Shakespeare's Comedies: Explorations in Form* (Princeton, NJ: Princeton University Press, 1972), Ralph Berry suggestively entitles his chapter on *The Merry Wives* "The Revengers' Comedy," yet does not develop the concept of revenge in his analysis.

19. Godshalk, "Apology," 100.

20. Nevo, "Shakespeare's Comic Remedies," 9.

21. For the play's association with skimmington rituals, see Parten, "Falstaff's Horns," 185–88.

22. Brown, *Better a Shrew*, 41.

23. Jeanne Addison Roberts, *Shakespeare's English Comedy: "The Merry Wives of Windsor" in Context* (Lincoln: University of Nebraska Press, 1979), 75.

24. Ibid.

25. John Kerrigan writes compellingly about the intimate relationship between drama and revenge in *Revenge Tragedy*. Following Aristotle, he demonstrates how "theatrical 'doing' gravitates, quite naturally, towards revenge," expressing the "radically dramatic power of revenge" (4, 5). Kerrigan's argument can be applied to comedy, as well. On the dramaturgic skill and collaboration of the wives, see, for example, Sandra Clark, "'Wives May Be Merry and Yet Honest Too': Women and Wit in *The Merry Wives of Windsor* and Some Other Plays," in *Fanned and Winnowed Opinions: Shakespearean Essays Presented to Harold Jenkins,* ed. John W. Mahon and Thomas A. Pendleton (London: Methuen, 1987), 260–63, and the early work on play and theatrical metaphor in Shakespeare done by Anne Righter Barton in her seminal study, *Shakespeare and the Idea of Play* (Harmondsworth, England: Penguin Books, 1967), esp. 130–31.

26. Bullough raises the possibility that the medieval romance of Virgilius, which derives from Socrates' humiliation in Aristophanes' *The Clouds,* exerted direct or indirect influence on *The Merry Wives*. See *Narrative and Dramatic Sources,* 2:8. John Steadman argues that the basket-story would have offered Shakespeare's audiences a suggestive parallel for Falstaff's humiliation: "First, Virgil had long since become a conventional example of the power of love and man's vulnerability to women's wiles. Second, several versions of the basket-story include the motif of the husband's sudden return. Third, certain variants incorporate the motif of punishment by water." Steadman, "Falstaff as Actaeon: A Dramatic Emblem," *Shakespeare Quarterly* 14, no. 3 (Summer 1963): 238.

27. Katz, "*Merry Wives of Windsor,*" 83.

28. Friedrich Nietzsche, *On the Genealogy of Morals,* trans. Walter Kaufmann and R. J. Hollingdale, in *On the Genealogy of Morals; Ecce Homo,* ed. Walter Kaufmann (New York: Vintage Books, 1969), 2.6.

29. See Bullough, *Narrative and Dramatic Sources,* 8 vols., passim; and Salingar, *Shakespeare and the Traditions of Comedy,* esp. 188–90.

30. See D. P. Rotunda, *Motif-Index of the Italian Novella in Prose* (Bloomington: Indiana University Press, 1942) for numerous examples of Italian novellas that contain the interrelated motifs of deception and revenge.

31. Shakespeare may have known *Le Piacevole Notti* in its original Italian, in a French translation, or in William Painter's English translation.

32. See Bullough, *Narrative and Dramatic Sources,* 2:6–7.

33. See, for example, Berry, *Shakespeare's Comedies,* 146.

34. Ralph Berry, ed., *On Directing Shakespeare: Interviews with Contemporary Directors* (London: Hamish Hamilton, 1989), 179.

35. Berry, *Shakespeare's Comedies,* 147, 146.

36. Roberts, *Shakespeare's English Comedy,* 69–70.

37. Trudy Govier, *Forgiveness and Revenge* (London: Routledge, 2002), 20.

38. Kerrigan, *Revenge Tragedy,* 210.

39. Ibid., 211.

40. Berry, *Shakespeare's Comedies,* 146. The idea of Falstaff as the *pharmakos* or scape-goat is suggested by Northrop Frye in *The Anatomy of Criticism* (Princeton, NJ: Princeton University Press, 1957), 45, and developed by a number of scholars, including J. A. Bryant Jr., "Falstaff and the Renewal of Windsor," *PMLA* 89 (1974): 296–301; and Jan Lawson Hinely, "Comic Scapegoats and the Falstaff of *The Merry Wives of Windsor,*" *Shakespeare Studies* 15 (1982): 37–54. Barbara Freedman counters the view of Falstaff as scapegoat in "Falstaff's Punishment: Buffoonery as Defensive Posture in *The Merry Wives of Windsor,*" *Shakespeare Studies* 14 (1981): 163–74.

41. Steadman, "Falstaff as Actaeon."

42. George Gordon Byron, *Don Juan,* in *Byron's Poetry,* ed. Frank D. McConnell (New York: W. W. Norton, 1978), canto 1, stanza 124.

8. The Quality of Revenge

1. Girard, *Theater of Envy,* 254.

2. On covert usury, see Joan Ozark Holmer, *The Merchant of Venice: Choice, Hazard and Consequence* (New York: St. Martin's Press, 1995), 170–71.

3. Critics who see parallels between Portia and Shylock are in the minority. Critics who emphasize similarities based on economic practices include Harry Berger Jr., "Marriage and Mercifixion in *The Merchant of Venice:* The Casket Scene Revisited," *Shakespeare Quarterly* 32, no. 2 (1981): 155–62; and Natasha Korda, "Dame Usury: Gender, Credit, and (Ac)counting in the Sonnets and *The Merchant of Venice,*" *Shakespeare Quarterly* 60, no. 2 (2009): 143. As Korda points out, "Critics who read Portia as Shylock's antithesis have difficulty with the terminology of credit and accounting that characterizes her speech, which is replete with references to accounts, full sums, terms in gross, oaths of credit, sureties, and the like" (143). For critics who find the characters' similarities lying in their oppression and their marginalized positions, see Keith Geary, "The Nature of Portia's Victory: Turning to Men in *The Merchant of Venice,*" *Shakespeare Survey* 37 (1984): 66; and Susan Oldrieve, "Marginalized Voices in *The Merchant of Venice,*" *Cardozo Studies in Law and Literature* 5 (1993): 87.

4. *Oxford English Dictionary,* s.v. "Quality," 1.b.

5. Ibid., 7.c, 1.d, 2.b, 8.a.

6. Williamson, *The Patriarchy of Shakespeare's Comedies,* 29–30.

7. *Oxford English Dictionary,* s.v. "Vantage," 1.a, b, 3.a, 4.b.

8. In "Dame Usury," Natasha Korda offers a compelling reading of Portia's character in light of "the emergent figure of the female moneylender" in early modern England (130).

9. Miller, *Eye for an Eye,* 83.

10. Sean Lawrence points out how selfless love "threatens to violate the exchange mechanisms by which characters and critics understand the fictive world." When Portia gives her ring with her love, she "imposes reciprocal bonds of loyalty and debt." Lawrence, "'To Give and to Receive': Performing Exchanges in *The Merchant of Venice,*" in *Shakespeare and the Cultures of Performance,* ed. by Paul Yachnin and Patricia Badir (Aldershot, England: Ashgate, 2008), 46.

11. Berger, "Marriage and Mercifixion," 160. Ralph Waldo Emerson has observed a similar point about the nature of gift-giving in his essay "The Gift" (1844).

12. Linda Woodbridge, "Payback Time: On the Economic Rhetoric of Revenge in *The Merchant of Venice,*" in *Shakespeare and the Cultures of Performance,* ed. Paul Yachnin and Patricia Badir (Aldershot, England: Ashgate, 2008), 39.

13. I am indebted to numerous critics who have offered insightful economic readings of *The Merchant of Venice:* Lars Engle, *Shakespearean Pragmatism: Market of His Time* (Chicago: University of Chicago Press, 1993); Lawrence, "'To Give and to Receive'"; Korda, "Dame Usury"; Karen Newman, "Portia's Ring: Unruly Women and Structures of Exchange in *The Merchant of Venice," Shakespeare Quarterly* 38, no. 1 (1987): 19–33; and Woodbridge, "Payback Time."

14. Craig Muldrew, *The Economy of Obligation: The Culture of Credit and Social Relations in Early Modern England* (New York: St. Martin's Press, 1998), 5.

15. Ibid., see esp. his chapter 6.

16. For critical interpretations that support this view, see Berry, *Shakespeare's Comedies,* 11–45; Engle, *Shakespearean Pragmatism,* 77–106; and Woodbridge, "Payback Time," 29–40.

17. *Oxford English Dictionary,* s.v. "Advantage," 7.

18. Woodbridge, "Payback Time," 37–40.

19. Marcel Mauss, *The Gift: The Form and Reason for Exchange in Archaic Societies,* trans. W. D. Halls (New York: W.W. Norton, 1990).

20. For an anthropological context that bears upon gift-giving and exchanges in *The Merchant,* see Mauss's discussion of the system of gift-giving, or potlatch, in the American Northwest, and the balance between self-interest and disinterestedness in extravagant or destructive gift-giving (ibid., 71–78). Antonio's extreme, sacrificial generosity short-circuits honorable exchange between himself and Bassanio. As Mauss explains, "The obligation to reciprocate worthily is imperative. One loses face for ever if one does not reciprocate, or if one does not carry out destruction of equivalent value" (42).

21. In *Merchant of Venice,* Joan Ozark Holmer cites Miles Mosse's six sermons published in 1595 as evidence of the Protestant teaching against mental usury, the "serpent in the bosom" (Mosse's colorful metaphor). Holmer paraphrases Mosse's definition of mental usury as "a kind of usury committed in the mind of the lender, no actual contract with the borrower being made; it is simply the *expectation* (intent or hope) of *gain* on a loan" (240). See also Marc Schell, "The Wether and the Ewe: Verbal Usury in *The Merchant of Venice," Kenyon Review,* n.s., 1, no. 4 (Autumn 1979): 86.

22. I echo Natasha Korda who makes the same claim in "Dame Usury" when she characterizes Portia as a "skillful lender upon advantage" (153).

23. Berger, "Marriage and Mercifixion," 161.

24. Newman, "Portia's Ring," 26.

25. Engle, *Shakespearean Pragmatism,* 97–98.

26. Berger, "Marriage and Mercifixion," 161; and Korda, "Dame Usury," 142.

27. Mauss, *Gift,* 21.

28. See Stretton, *Women Waging Law,* esp. chap. 3, "Female Litigants and the Culture of Litigation," 43–69.

29. For a critical discussion of the privileged nature of male "homosocial" bonds in society, which exclude women as agents yet traffic in their exchange, see Eve Kosofsky Sedgwick, *Between Men: English Literature and Male Homosocial Desire* (New York: Columbia University Press, 1985). As Engle points out in *Shakespearean Pragmatism,* "the wooing of Portia can be seen as an instance of what Eve Kosofsky Sedgwick has defined as 'male homosocial desire,'" and therefore "part of a complex erotic and economic transaction between two males." Yet "no male seems thoroughly to control" the "economic patterns of the play" (85).

30. Girard, *Theater of Envy,* 247.

31. Ibid.

32. Leslie Fiedler, *The Stranger in Shakespeare* (New York: Stein and Day, 1972); Harold Goddard, *The Meaning of Shakespeare* (Chicago: University of Chicago Press,

1951); and A. D. Moody, *Shakespeare: "The Merchant of Venice"* (London: Edward Arnold, 1964).

33. Moody, *Shakespeare,* 17.

34. Girard, *Theater of Envy,* 247.

35. On names, see Holmer, *Merchant of Venice,* 89.

36. Engle, *Shakespearean Pragmatism,* 92.

37. *Oxford English Dictionary,* s.v. "Port," n. 4, etymology: "revenues of a port." Norman Nathan emphasizes the aural relationship between *port* and *Portia* in "Portia, Nerissa, and Jessica—Their Names," *Notes* 34, no. 4 (December 1986): 425–29.

38. *Oxford English Dictionary,* s.v. "Lottery," etymology, 2.d. We might recall how Octavia was called a blessed lottery to Antony in *Antony and Cleopatra,* which proves to be ironic given that Antony's lot lay in his fatal embrace of Cleopatra.

39. John Florio's definition from his Italian-English dictionary (1611) is quoted in Levith, *What's in Shakespeare's Names,* 81.

40. *Oxford English Dictionary,* s.v. "Proportion," 1.a.

41. Berry, *Shakespeare's Comedies,* 141.

42. In the English theater, the former RSC director John Barton has exercised a tremendous influence on actors' and directors' approaches to character. His focus on the nuances, rhythms, and ambiguities of language has offered a methodology for unpacking characters' complexities and contradictions. A character such as Portia tends to polarize critics; Barton's formalist approach suggests a meeting ground for radically divergent interpretations. On Portia's character in the theater, see Penny Gay's survey of actresses who have played Portia, from Ellen Terry to Derbhle Crotty: Gay, "Portia Performs: Playing the Role in the Twentieth-Century English Theater," in *The Merchant of Venice: New Critical Essays,* ed. John W. Mahon and Ellen MacLeod Mahon (New York: Routledge, 2002), 431–54.

43. See Deborah Findlay, "Portia in *Merchant of Venice,*" in *Players of Shakespeare 3,* ed. Russell Jackson and Robert Smallwood (Cambridge: Cambridge University Press, 1993), 52–67.

44. Holmer, *Merchant of Venice,* 99, 100.

45. Thomas C. Bilello, "Accomplished with What She Lacks: Law, Equity, and Portia's Con," *Law and Literature* 16, no. 1 (2004): 11–32; Vera M. Jiji, "Portia Revisited: The Influence of Unconscious Factors upon Theme and Characterization in *The Merchant of Venice,*" *Literature and Psychology* 26, no. 1 (1976): 5–15; and Jalal Toufic, "If You Prick Us, Do We Not Bleed?" *Discourse: Berkeley Journal for Theoretical Studies in Media and Culture* 20, no. 3 (Fall 1998): 165–69.

46. Critic of the *Financial Times* (April 30, 1987), quoted in James C. Bulman, *The Merchant of Venice: Shakespeare in Performance* (Manchester: Manchester University Press, 1991), 135.

47. *Oxford English Dictionary,* s.v. "Sad," 1.a.

48. Robert Greene, *Penelope's Web* (London, 1587). A transcription by Nina Green (2003) can be found at http://www.oxford-shakespeare.com/Greene/Penelopes_Web.pdf.

49. For interpretations of Shakespeare's use of this Ovidian myth, see Berger, "Marriage and Mercifixion," 156; Macdonald, *William Shakespeare,* 63–64; and Michael Zuckert, "The New Medea: On Portia's Comic Triumph in *The Merchant of Venice,*" in *Shakespeare's Political Pageant: Essays in Literature and Politics,* ed. Joseph Alulis and Vickie Sullivan (Lanham, MD: Rowman and Littlefield Publishers, 1996), 10.

50. Zuckert, "New Medea," 11–13; Holmer, *Merchant of Venice,* 101–2.

51. See Korda's discussion of Portia's rhetoric of coverture in "Dame Usury," 141–44.

52. Jill Phillips Ingram, *Idioms of Self-Interest: Credit, Identity, and Property in English Renaissance Literature* (New York: Routledge, 2006), 113.

53. Goddard, *Meaning of Shakespeare,* 107, 109.

54. See Lawrence Danson, *The Harmonies of "The Merchant of Venice"* (New Haven, CT: Yale University Press, 1978); Holmer, *Merchant of Venice;* and Barbara K. Lewalski, "Biblical Allusion and Allegory in *The Merchant of Venice," Shakespeare Quarterly* 13, no. 3 (1962): 327–43.

55. Kenneth W. Stevenson, *The Lord's Prayer: A Text in Tradition* (Minneapolis, MN: Fortress Press, 2004), 20, 225.

56. Lewalski, "Biblical Allusion," 338.

57. See Holmer, *Merchant of Venice,* 203–7.

58. *Oxford English Dictionary,* s.v. "Danger," 1.a, b.

59. Miller, *Eye for an Eye,* 152.

60. Stephen Orgel, *Imagining Shakespeare: A History of Texts and Visions* (New York: Palgrave Macmillan, 2003), 160.

61. Miller, *Eye for an Eye,* 152.

62. Findlay, "Portia in *The Merchant of Venice,"* 64.

63. On the importance of Ovid's Medea to *The Merchant of Venice,* see John W. Velz, "Portia and the Ovidian Grotesque," in *The Merchant of Venice: New Critical Essays,* ed. John W. Mahon and Ellen MacLeod Mahon (New York: Routledge, 2002), 179–86; and Zuckert, "New Medea."

64. Zuckert, "New Medea," 26.

65. Velz, "Portia and the Ovidian Grotesque," 180.

66. The quotation from Ovid's *Heroides* is taken from Grant Showerman's translation, which appears in volume 1 of *Ovid in Six Volumes,* rev. ed. G. P. Goold (Cambridge, MA: Harvard University Press, 1977).

67. See Nathan, "Portia, Nerissa, and Jessica," 427.

68. Lori Schroeder Haslem, "'O Me, the Word Choose!': Female Voice and Catechetical Ritual in *The Two Gentlemen of Verona* and *The Merchant of Venice," Shakespeare Studies* 22 (1994): 133.

69. Lewalski, "Biblical Allusion," 342.

70. Korda, "Dame Usury," 153; and Ingram, *Idioms of Self-Interest,* 99.

71. Williamson, *Patriarchy of Shakespeare's Comedies,* 51.

9. WOMEN'S GALL, WOMEN'S GRACE:

1. *Oxford English Dictionary,* s.v. "Gall," 1.a., 3.a., 3.b.

2. The quotation from Elizabeth Cary's *The Tragedy of Miriam, The Fair Queen of Jewry* (London, 1613) is taken from *Renaissance Drama by Women: Texts and Documents,* ed. S. P. Cerasano and Marion Wynne-Davies (New York: Routledge, 1996).

3. *Oxford English Dictionary,* s.v. "Grace," 8.d, 11.e, 15.a.

4. See Kennedy, *Just Anger,* 18–20.

5. Peter de La Primaudaye, *The French Academie* (1586), a facsimile ed. (Hildesheim: Georg Olms Verlag, 1972), 503–4.

6. Nicholas Caussin, *The Holy Court: The Command of Reason over the Passions,* trans. Thomas Hawkins (London, 1638), 316.

7. Desiderius Erasmus, "A Right Fruitful Epistle . . . in Laud and Praise of Matrimony," trans. Richard Taverner (1536?), in *Daughters, Wives, and Widows: Writings by Men about Women and Marriage in England,* ed. Joan Larsen Klein (Urbana: University of Illinois Press, 1992), 84.

8. Murphy, *Getting Even,* 19.

9. Ibid., 20.

10. Ibid., 22.

11. Elizabeth Spelman makes the case for women's anger as a just vindictive passion when expressed in the context of unequal power relations; see Spelman, "Anger and Insubordination," in *Women, Knowledge, and Reality: Explorations in Feminist Philosophy*, ed. Ann Garry and Marilyn Pearsall (Boston: Unwin Hyman, 1989), 266.

12. Kenneth Burke, "*Othello:* An Essay to Illustrate a Method," in *Kenneth Burke on Shakespeare*, ed. Scott L. Newstok (West Lafayette, IN: Parlor Press, 2007), 81.

13. Carole McKewin, "Counsels of Gall and Grace: Intimate Conversations between Women in Shakespeare's Plays," in *The Woman's Part: Feminist Criticism of Shakespeare*, ed. Carolyn Ruth Swift Lenz, Gayle Greene, and Carol Thomas Neely (Urbana: University of Illinois Press, 1980), 117–32.

14. Kennedy, *Just Anger*, 12.

15. Aurel Kolnai, quoted in Murphy, *Getting Even*, 20. Emilia's and Paulina's condemnation of wrong might be understood in relation to Aurel Kolnai's argument in "Forgiveness," *Proceedings of the Aristotelian Society* 74 (1973–74): 91–106.

16. Clark, "'Wives May Be Merry,'" 267.

17. Rushdie, *Shame*, 180–81, 181.

18. My point echoes a similar one made by Janet S. Wolf in "'Like an Old Tale Still': Paulina, 'Triple Hecate,' and the Persephone Myth in *The Winter's Tale*," in *Images of Persephone: Feminist Readings in Western Literature*, ed. Elizabeth T. Hayes (Gainesville: University Press of Florida, 1994), 35–36. Wolf, however, views Paulina as a Hecate figure.

19. In *The Shapes of Revenge*, Harry Keyishian observes, "A characteristic Shakespearean strategy for portraying victimized women whose virtue lies in enduring their martyrdoms without complaint is to pair them with aggressive women who articulate their grievances for them" (156).

20. Huston Diehl, "'Dost Not the Stone Rebuke Me?': The Pauline Rebuke and Paulina's Lawful Magic in *The Winter's Tale*," in *Shakespeare and the Cultures of Performance*, ed. Paul Yachnin and Patricia Badir (Aldershot, England: Ashgate, 2008), 74.

21. Ibid., 73.

22. Surely Harry Keyishian is right in observing that Paulina keeps alive the memory of Leontes' crimes, and that her indignation persists, despite her earlier vow to "say nothing" (3.2.232). Keyishian goes so far as to suggest that Hermione is "kept alive by Paulina's indignation" (*Shapes of Revenge*, 158).

23. Diehl, "'Dost Not the Stone Rebuke Me?,'" 80.

24. Fernie, *Shame*, 225–26, 228.

25. Solomon, *Passion for Justice*, 20.

26. Keyishian, *Shapes of Revenge*, 157.

27. Charles Frey, *Shakespeare's Vast Romance: A Study of "The Winter's Tale"* (Columbia: University of Missouri Press, 1980), 154.

28. Cavell, *Disowning Knowledge*, 220.

29. I echo Lois Potter's fine point here about revenge tragedies and their audiences in Potter, "Shakespeare and the Art of Revenge," 34.

Conclusion

1. French, *Virtues of Vengeance*, 85.

2. La Primaudaye, *French Academie*, 383.

3. Keyishian, *Shapes of Revenge*, 156.

4. See, for example, Marsha Riefer, "'Instruments of Some Mightier Member': The Constriction of Female Power in *Measure for Measure*," *Shakespeare Quarterly* 35, no. 2

(Summer 1984): 161; Harriet Hawkins, *Measure for Measure* (Boston: Twayne Publishers, 1987), 104; William Empson, *The Structure of Complex Words* (London: Chatto and Windus, 1951), 283; and Janet Adelman, "Bed Tricks: On Marriage as the End of Comedy in *All's Well That Ends Well* and *Measure for Measure*," in *Shakespeare's Personality,* ed. Norman N. Holland, Sidney Homan, and Bernard J. Paris (Berkeley and Los Angeles: University of California Press, 1989), 174.

5. Riefer, "'Instruments of Some Mightier Member,'" 167.

6. Richard Wheeler, *Shakespeare's Development and the Problem Comedies: Turn and Counter-Turn* (Berkeley and Los Angeles: University of California Press, 1981), 102.

7. Barbara Baines, "Assaying the Power of Chastity in *Measure for Measure*," *SEL* 30, no. 2 (Spring 1990): 284.

8. Anderson, *Kind of Wild Justice,* 157.

9. Anderson makes this same observation in her discussion of how the Duke's treatment of Angelo "is compounded of justice, mercy, and revenge" (ibid., 165).

10. Baines, "Assaying the Power," 299.

11. Adelman argues the opposite case in "Bed Tricks," 167, 172–73.

12. Adelman observes, "In *All's Well* marriage is a cure, even if an enforced cure; in *Measure for Measure* it is a punishment" (ibid., 173–74).

13. Hans Sachs argues that the Duke commits, "in a legitimate and honorable way, the crime which Angelo attempted in vain." Sachs, "The Measure in *Measure for Measure*," in *The Design Within,* ed. Melvin D. Faber (New York: Science House, 1970), 495–96.

14. In "'Instruments of Some Mightier Member,'" Riefer claims unequivocally that Isabella's "sense of self is undermined and finally destroyed through her encounters with patriarchal authority, an authority represented emphatically, but not exclusively, by the insensitive Duke" (162–63).

15. Williamson, *Patriarchy of Shakespeare's Comedies,* 104.

Bibliography

Adelman, Janet. "Bed Tricks: On Marriage as the End of Comedy in *All's Well That Ends Well* and *Measure for Measure.*" In *Shakespeare's Personality,* edited by Norman N. Holland, Sidney Homan, and Bernard J. Paris, 151–74. Berkeley and Los Angeles: University of California Press, 1989.

———. *Suffocating Mothers: Fantasies of Maternal Origin in Shakespeare's Plays, "Hamlet" to "The Tempest."* London: Routledge, 1992.

Aeschylus. *Oresteia.* Translated by Richmond Lattimore. Chicago: University of Chicago Press, 1953.

Anderson, Linda. *A Kind of Wild Justice: Revenge in Shakespeare's Comedies.* Newark: University of Delaware Press, 1987.

Aneau, Barthélemy. *Picta poesis.* Lyons: Macé Bonhomme, 1552. French Emblems at Glasgow. http://www.emblems.arts.gla.ac.uk/french/books.php?id=FANa&o=.

Aristotle. *Nicomachean Ethics.* Translated by W. D. Ross. Revised by J. O. Urmson. In vol. 2 of *The Complete Works of Aristotle,* edited by Jonathan Barnes. Princeton, NJ: Princeton University Press, 1984.

———. *Rhetoric.* Translated by W. Rhys Roberts. In vol. 2 of *The Complete Works of Aristotle,* edited by Jonathan Barnes. Princeton, NJ: Princeton University Press, 1984.

Ashley, Robert. *Of Honour.* Edited by Virgil B. Heltzel. San Marino, CA: Huntington Library, 1947.

Asp, Carolyn. "'Upon Her Wit Doth Earthly Honor Wait': Female Agency in *Titus Andronicus.*" In *Titus Andronicus: Critical Essays,* edited by Philip C. Kolin, 333–46. New York: Garland Publishing, 1995.

Austin, J. L. *How to Do Things with Words.* Edited by J. O. Urmson. Cambridge, MA: Harvard University Press, 1962.

Bacon, Francis. *Essays, Advancement of Learning, New Atlantis, and Other Pieces.* Edited by Richard Foster Jones. New York: Odyssey Press, 1937.

———. "Of Revenge." In *Essays, Advancement of Learning, New Atlantis, and Other Pieces,* edited by Richard Foster Jones, 13–14. New York: Odyssey Press, 1937.

———. *The Philosophical Works of Francis Bacon.* Edited by John M. Robertson. Freeport, NY: Books for Libraries Press, 1970.

———. *The Wisdome of the Ancients.* Translated by Arthur Gorges Knight. London: John Bill, 1619.

Baines, Barbara. "Assaying the Power of Chastity in *Measure for Measure.*" *SEL* 30, no. 2 (Spring 1990): 283–301.

Baker, Howard. *Induction to Tragedy.* Baton Rouge: Louisiana State University Press, 1939.

Bamber, Linda. *Comic Women, Tragic Men: A Study of Gender and Genre in Shakespeare.* Stanford, CA: Stanford University Press, 1982.

Barber, C. L. *Shakespeare's Festive Comedy: A Study of Dramatic Form and Its Relation to Social Custom.* Cleveland, OH: World Publishing Company, 1959.

Barton, Anne Righter. "*As You Like It* and *Twelfth Night:* Shakespeare's Sense of an Ending." In *Shakespearian Comedy,* edited by Malcolm Bradbury and David Palmer, 160–80. Stratford-upon-Avon Studies 14. London: Edward Arnold, 1972.

———. "Falstaff and the Comic Community." In *Shakespeare's "Rough Magic": Renaissance Essays in Honor of C. L. Barber,* edited by Peter Erickson and Coppélia Kahn, 131–48. Newark: University of Delaware Press, 1985.

———. *Shakespeare and the Idea of the Play.* Harmondsworth, England: Penguin Books, 1967. First published 1962 by Chatto and Windus.

Bate, Jonathan. "Dying to Live in *Much Ado About Nothing.*" In *Surprised by Scenes: Essays in Honour of Professor Yasunari Takahashi,* edited by Yasunari Takada, 69–85. Tokyo: Kenkyusha, 1994.

———. Introduction to *Titus Andronicus.* Arden ed. London: Routledge, 1995.

———. *Shakespeare and Ovid.* Oxford: Clarendon Press, 1993.

Beaumont, Francis, and John Fletcher. *The Maid's Tragedy.* Edited by T. W. Craik. Manchester: Manchester University Press, 1988.

Beauregard, David N. *Catholic Theology in Shakespeare's Plays.* Newark: University of Delaware Press, 2008.

———. *Virtue's Own Feature: Shakespeare and the Virtue Ethics Tradition.* Newark: University of Delaware Press, 1995.

Belsey, Catherine. *The Subject of Tragedy: Identity and Difference in Renaissance Drama.* London: Routledge, 1985.

Benston, Alice N. "Portia, the Law, and the Tripartite Structure of *The Merchant of Venice.*" *Shakespeare Quarterly* 30, no. 3 (Summer 1979): 367–85.

Berger, Harry, Jr. "Marriage and Mercifixion in *The Merchant of Venice:* The Casket Scene Revisited." *Shakespeare Quarterly* 32, no. 2 (Summer 1981): 155–62.

Berry, Ralph, ed. *On Directing Shakespeare: Interviews with Contemporary Directors.* London: Hamish Hamilton, 1989.

———. *Shakespeare's Comedies: Explorations in Form.* Princeton, NJ: Princeton University Press, 1972.

———. "*Twelfth Night:* The Experience of the Audience." *Shakespeare Survey* 34 (1981): 111–19.

Bevington, David. "The Domineering Female in *I Henry VI.*" *Shakespeare Studies* 2 (1966): 51–58.

Bilello, Thomas C. "Accomplished with What She Lacks: Law, Equity, and Portia's Con." *Law and Literature* 16, no. 1 (2004): 11–32.

Billing, Christian M. "Lament and Revenge in the *Hekabe* of Euripides." *New Theatre Quarterly* 23, no. 1 (2007): 49–57.

Billington, Michael, ed. *Approaches to "Twelfth Night."* By Bill Alexander, John Barton, John Caird, Terry Hands. RSC Directors' Shakespeare. London: Nick Hern Books, 1990.

Black-Michaud, Jacob. *Cohesive Force: Feud in the Mediterranean and the Middle East.* New York: St. Martin's Press, 1975.

Bloom, Harold. *Shakespeare: The Invention of the Human.* New York: Riverhead Books, 1998.

Boehm, Christopher. *Blood Revenge: The Enactment and Management of Conflict in Montenegro and Other Tribal Societies.* Lawrence: University Press of Kansas, 1984. Reprinted with an expanded preface, Philadelphia: University of Pennsylvania Press, 1987. Citations are to the Pennsylvania edition.

Booth, Stephen. *Precious Nonsense: The Gettysburg Address, Ben Jonson's Epitaphs on his Children, and "Twelfth Night."* Berkeley and Los Angeles: University of California Press, 1998.

Bowers, Fredson. *Elizabethan Revenge Tragedy, 1587–1642.* Princeton, NJ: Princeton University Press, 1940.

Bradbrook, M. C. "The Sources of *Macbeth.*" *Shakespeare Studies* 4 (1951). Reprinted in *Aspects of "Macbeth,"* edited by Kenneth Muir and Philip Edwards, 12–25. Cambridge: Cambridge University Press, 1977. Citations are to the Cambridge edition.

Braden, Gordon. *Renaissance Tragedy and the Senecan Tradition: Anger's Privilege.* New Haven, CT: Yale University Press, 1985.

Broude, Ronald. "Four Forms of Vengeance in *Titus Andronicus.*" *Journal of English and Germanic Philology* 78 (1979): 494–507.

———. "Revenge and Revenge Tragedy in Renaissance England." *Renaissance Quarterly* 28, no.1 (Spring 1975): 38–58.

Brown, Pamela Allen. *Better a Shrew than a Sheep: Women, Drama, and the Culture of Jest in Early Modern England.* Ithaca, NY: Cornell University Press, 2003.

Bryant, J. A., Jr. "Falstaff and the Renewal of Windsor." *PMLA* 89 (1974): 296–301.

Bullough, Geoffrey, ed. *Narrative and Dramatic Sources of Shakespeare.* 8 vols. London: Routledge and Kegan Paul, 1957–75.

Bulman, James C. *The Merchant of Venice: Shakespeare in Performance.* Manchester: Manchester University Press, 1991.

Burckhardt, Sigurd. *Shakespearean Meanings.* Princeton, NJ: Princeton University Press, 1968.

Burke, Kenneth. "*Othello:* An Essay to Illustrate a Method." In *Kenneth Burke on Shakespeare,* edited by Scott L. Newstok, 65–100. West Lafayette, IN: Parlor Press, 2007.

———. *The Philosophy of Literary Form: Studies in Symbolic Action.* 3rd ed. Berkeley and Los Angeles: University of California Press, 1973.

Burnett, Anne Pippin. *Revenge in Attic and Later Tragedy.* Berkeley and Los Angeles: University of California Press, 1998.

Burnett, Mark Thornton. *Masters and Servants in English Renaissance Drama and Culture.* New York: St. Martin's Press, 1997.

Bush, Geoffrey. *Shakespeare and the Natural Condition.* Cambridge, MA: Harvard University Press, 1956.

Buxton, Richard. *The Complete World of Greek Mythology.* New York: Thames and Hudson, 2004.

Byron, George Gordon. *Byron's Poetry.* Edited by Frank D. McConnell. New York: W. W. Norton and Company, 1978.

Campbell, Lily B. *Shakespeare's Tragic Heroes: Slaves of Passion.* 1930. Reprint, New York: Barnes and Noble, 1952.

———. "Theories of Revenge in Renaissance England." *Modern Philology* 28, no. 3 (1931): 281–96.

Cary, Elizabeth. *The Tragedy of Miriam, The Fair Queen of Jewry.* London, 1613. In *Renaissance Drama by Women: Texts and Documents,* edited by S. P. Cerasano and Marion Wynne-Davies. London: Routledge, 1996.

Caussin, Nicholas. *The Holy Court: The Command of Reason over the Passions.* Translated by Thomas Hawkins. London, 1638.

Cavell, Stanley. *Disowning Knowledge in Seven Plays of Shakespeare.* Updated edition. Cambridge: Cambridge University Press, 2003.

Cerasano, S. P. "Half a Dozen Dangerous Words." In *Much Ado About Nothing and The Taming of the Shrew,* edited by Marion Wynne-Davies, 31–50. Houndmills, England: Palgrave Macmillan, 2001.

Chakravorty, Jagannath. *The Idea of Revenge in Shakespeare.* Calcutta: Jadavpur University Press, 1969.

Chapman, George. *Chapman's Homer: The "Iliad," the "Odyssey," and the Lesser Homerica.* Edited by Allardyce Nicoll. 2nd ed. 2 vols. Princeton, NJ: Princeton University Press, 1967.

———. *The Revenge of Bussy D'Ambois.* In *Four Revenge Tragedies,* edited by Katharine Maus. Oxford: Oxford University Press, 1995.

Chickering, Howell D., trans. *Beowulf.* New York: Anchor Books, 1977.

Clark, Sandra. "'Wives May Be Merry and Yet Honest Too': Women and Wit in *The Merry Wives of Windsor* and Some Other Plays." In *Fanned and Winnowed Opinions: Shakespearean Essays Presented to Harold Jenkins,* edited by John W. Mahon and Thomas A. Pendleton, 249–67. London: Methuen, 1987.

Clover, Carol J. "Hildigunnr's Lament." In *Cold Counsel: Women in Old Norse Literature and Mythology.* edited by Sarah M. Anderson with Karen Swenson, 15–54. New York: Routledge, 2002.

———. "Maiden Warriors and Other Sons." *Journal of English and Germanic Philology* 85, no. 1 (1986): 35–49.

Cohen, Derek. *Shakespeare's Culture of Violence.* New York: St. Martin's Press, 1993.

Cole, Susan Letzler. *The Absent One: Mourning Ritual, Tragedy, and the Performance of Ambivalence.* University Park: Pennsylvania State University Press, 1985.

Coles, Elisha. *An English Dictionary.* London: J. Walthoe et al., 1717.

Cook, Robert, trans. *Njál's Saga.* London: Penguin Books, 2002.

Cox, Brian. "Titus Andronicus." In *Players of Shakespeare 3,* edited by Russell Jackson and Robert Smallwood, 174–88. Cambridge: Cambridge University Press, 1993.

Cox, J. L. "The Stage Representation of the 'Kill Claudio' Sequence in *Much Ado About Nothing.*" *Shakespeare Survey* 32 (1979): 27–36.

Cranmer, Thomas. "A Sermon concerning the Time of Rebellion." In *Miscellaneous Writings and Letters of Thomas Cranmer,* edited by John Edmund Cox. Cambridge: Cambridge University Press, 1846.

Cunliffe, John W., ed. *Gismond of Salerne.* In *Early English Classical Tragedies.* Oxford: Oxford University Press, 1912.

Danson, Lawrence. *The Harmonies of "The Merchant of Venice."* New Haven, CT: Yale University Press, 1978.

Dante Alighieri. *Inferno.* Translated by Allen Mandelbaum. Toronto: Bantam Books, 1982.

Desmet, Christy. *Reading Shakespeare's Characters: Rhetoric, Ethics, and Identity.* Amherst: University of Massachusetts Press, 1992.

Diehl, Huston. "'Dost Not the Stone Rebuke Me?': The Pauline Rebuke and Paulina's Lawful Magic in *The Winter's Tale.*" In *Shakespeare and the Cultures of Performance,* edited by Paul Yachnin and Patricia Badir, 69–82. Aldershot, England: Ashgate, 2008.

Downie, Penny. "Queen Margaret in *Henry VI* and *Richard III.*" In *Players of Shakespeare 3,* edited by Russell Jackson and Robert Smallwood, 114–39. Cambridge: Cambridge University Press, 1993.

Dunn, Kevin. "'Action, Passion, Motion': The Gestural Politics of Counsel in *The Spanish Tragedy.*" *Renaissance Drama* 31 (2002): 27–60.

Dunn, Leslie C. "Ophelia's Songs in *Hamlet:* Music, Madness, and the Feminine." In *Embodied Voices: Representing Female Vocality in Western Culture,* edited by Leslie C. Dunn and Nancy A. Jones, 50–64. Cambridge: Cambridge University Press, 1994.

Durham, Mary Edith. *Some Tribal Origins, Laws and Customs of the Balkans.* London: Allen and Unwin, 1928.

Dusinberre, Juliet. *Shakespeare and the Nature of Women.* 3rd ed. New York: Palgrave Macmillan, 2003.

Eaton, Sara. "A Woman of Letters: Lavinia in *Titus Andronicus.*" In *Shakespearean Tragedy and Gender,* edited by Shirley Nelson Garner and Madelon Sprengnether, 54–74. Bloomington: Indiana University Press, 1996.

Elton, William R. *"King Lear" and the Gods.* San Marino, CA: Huntington Library, 1966.

Empson, William. *The Structure of Complex Words.* London: Chatto and Windus, 1951.

Engle, Lars. *Shakespearean Pragmatism: Market of His Time.* Chicago: University of Chicago Press, 1993.

Erasmus, Desiderius. "A Right Fruitful Epistle . . . in Laud and Praise of Matrimony." Translated by Richard Taverner. [1536?] In *Daughters, Wives, and Widows: Writings by Men about Women and Marriage in England,* edited by Joan Larsen Klein. Urbana: University of Illinois Press, 1992.

Euripides. *Electra, and Other Plays.* Translated by John Davie. London: Penguin Books, 1998.

———. *Medea.* Translated by Eleanor Wilner and Inés Azar. In *Euripides I,* edited by David R. Slavitt and Palmer Bovie. Philadelphia: University of Pennsylvania Press, 1998.

Everett, Barbara. *"Much Ado About Nothing:* The Unsociable Comedy." In *English Comedy,* edited by Michael Cordner, Peter Holland, John Kerrigan, 68–84. Cambridge: Cambridge University Press, 1994.

Ewbank, Inga-Stina. "The Fiend-like Queen: A Note on *Macbeth* and Seneca's *Medea.*" *Shakespeare Studies* 19. Reprinted in *Aspects of "Macbeth,"* edited by Kenneth Muir and Philip Edwards, 53–65. Cambridge: Cambridge University Press, 1977. Citations are to the Cambridge edition.

Fendt, Gene. *Is "Hamlet" a Religious Drama?* Milwaukee, WI: Marquette University Press, 1998.

Fernie, Ewan. *Shame in Shakespeare.* London: Routledge, 2002.

Fiedler, Leslie A. *The Stranger in Shakespeare.* New York: Stein and Day, 1972.

Fienberg, Nona. "Jephthah's Daughter: The Parts Ophelia Plays." In *Old Testament Women in Western Literature,* edited by Raymond-Jean Frontain and Jan Wojcik, 128–43. Conway, AR: UCA Press, 1991.

Findlay, Alison. *A Feminist Perspective on Renaissance Drama.* Oxford: Blackwell, 1999.

Findlay, Deborah. "Portia in *The Merchant of Venice.*" In *Players of Shakespeare 3,* edited by Russell Jackson and Robert Smallwood, 52–67. Cambridge: Cambridge University Press, 1993.

Fischer, Sandra K. "Hearing Ophelia: Gender and Tragic Discourse in *Hamlet.*" *Renaissance and Reformation* 14, no. 1 (1990): 1–10.

Foley, Helene P. *Female Acts in Greek Tragedy.* Princeton, NJ: Princeton University Press, 2001.

Ford, John. *The Broken Heart.* Edited by T. J. Spencer. Baltimore: Johns Hopkins University Press, 1981.

Ford, John R. *Twelfth Night: A Guide to the Play.* Westport, CT: Greenwood Press, 2006.

Fox-Good, Jacquelyn A. "Ophelia's Mad Songs: Music, Gender, Power." In *Subjects on the World's Stage: Essays on British Literature of the Middle Ages and Renaissance,* edited by David G.Allen and Robert A. White, 217–38. Newark: University of Delaware Press, 1995.

Freedman, Barbara. "Falstaff's Punishment: Buffoonery as Defensive Posture in *The Merry Wives of Windsor.*" *Shakespeare Studies* 14 (1981): 163–74.

French, Peter A. *The Virtues of Vengeance.* Lawrence: University Press of Kansas, 2001.

Frey, Charles. *Shakespeare's Vast Romance: A Study of "The Winter's Tale."* Columbia, MO: University of Missouri Press, 1980.

Frye, Northrop. *The Anatomy of Criticism.* Princeton, NJ: Princeton University Press, 1957.

———. *A Natural Perspective.* New York: Columbia University Press, 1965.

Gay, Penny. *As She Likes It: Shakespeare's Unruly Women.* London: Routledge Press, 1994.

———. "Portia Performs: Playing the Role in the Twentieth-Century English Theater." In *The Merchant of Venice: New Critical Essays,* edited by John W. Mahon and Ellen MacLeod Mahon, 431–54. New York: Routledge, 2002.

Geary, Keith. "The Nature of Portia's Victory: Turning to Men in *The Merchant of Venice.*" *Shakespeare Survey* 37 (1984): 55–68.

The Geneva Bible. A facsimile of the 1560 edition with an introduction by Lloyd E. Berry. Madison, WI: University of Wisconsin Press, 1969.

Girard, René. *A Theater of Envy: William Shakespeare.* South Bend, IN: St. Augustine's Press, 2004.

———. *Violence and the Sacred.* Translated by Patrick Gregory. Baltimore: Johns Hopkins University Press, 1977.

Goddard, Harold C. *The Meaning of Shakespeare.* 2 vols. Chicago: University of Chicago Press, 1951.

Godshalk, W. L. "An Apology for *The Merry Wives of Windsor.*" In *Renaissance Papers,* 97–108. Durham, NC: Southeastern Renaissance Conference, 1973.

Golding, Arthur. *Ovid's Metamorphoses: The Arthur Golding Translation of 1567.* Edited by John Frederick Nims. Philadelphia: Paul Dry Books, 2000.

Goodland, Katharine. *Female Mourning in Medieval and Renaissance English Drama: From the Raising of Lazarus to "King Lear."* Aldershot, England: Ashgate, 2005.

Govier, Trudy. *Forgiveness and Revenge.* London: Routledge, 2002.

Grafton, Richard. *A Chronicle at Large and Meere History of the Affayres of England and Kinges of the Same.* Edited by Henry Ellis. 1569, Reprint, London: J. Johnson et al., 1809.

Green, Douglas E. "Interpreting 'Her Martyr'd Signs': Gender and Tragedy in *Titus Andronicus.*" *Shakespeare Quarterly* 40 (1989): 317–26.

Greene, Robert. *Groats-Worth of Witte, bought with a million of Repentance.* London: John Lane, 1592.

———. *Penelope's Web.* 1587. Transcribed by Nina Green, 2003. http://www.oxford-shakespeare.com/Greene/Penelopes_Web.pdf.

Guilfoyle, Cherrell. "'Ower Swete Sokor': The Role of Ophelia in *Hamlet.*" *Comparative Drama* 14 (1980): 3–17.

Hall, Edward. *Hall's Chronicle; containing the history of England, during the reign of Henry the Fourth, and the succeeding monarchs, to the end of the reign of Henry the Eighth.* Edited by Henry Ellis. London: J. Johnson et al., 1809. (Original title, *The Union of the Two Noble and Illustre Famelies of Lancastre and Yorke . . .,* 1548.)

Hall, James. *Dictionary of Subjects and Symbols in Art.* Rev. ed. Boulder, CO: Westview Press, 1979.

Hallett, Charles A., and Elaine S. Hallett. *The Revenger's Madness: A Study of Revenge Tragedy Motifs.* Lincoln: University of Nebraska Press, 1980.

Hartman, Geoffrey H. "Shakespeare's Poetical Character in *Twelfth Night.*" In *Shakespeare and the Question of Theory,* edited by Patricia Parker and Geoffrey Hartman, 37–53. New York: Methuen, 1985.

Haslem, Lori Schroeder. "'O Me, the Word Choose!': Female Voice and Catechetical Ritual in *The Two Gentlemen of Verona* and *The Merchant of Venice.*" *Shakespeare Studies* 22 (1994): 122–40.

Hawkins, Harriet. *Measure for Measure.* Boston: Twayne Publishers, 1987.

Hawley, William M. *Critical Hermeneutics and Shakespeare's Plays.* New York: Peter Lang, 1992.

Hays, Michael L. *Shakespearean Tragedy as Chivalric Romance: Rethinking "Macbeth," "Hamlet," "Othello," and "King Lear."* Cambridge: D.S. Brewer, 2003.

Heilbrun, Carolyn G. "The Character of Hamlet's Mother." 1957. Reprinted in *Hamlet's Mother and Other Women.* New York: Columbia University Press, 1990.

Helgerson, Richard. "The Buck Basket, the Witch, and the Queen of Fairies: The Women's World of Shakespeare's Windsor." In *Renaissance Culture and the Everyday,* edited by Patricia Fumerton and Simon Hunt, 162–82. Philadelphia: University of Pennsylvania Press, 1999.

Herodotus. *The Histories.* In vol. 1 of *Herodotus,* translated by A. D. Godley. Rev. ed. Cambridge, MA: Harvard University Press, 1990.

Hesiod. *Theogony.* In *Theogony, Works and Days, Testimonia,* translated by Glenn W. Most. Cambridge, MA: Harvard University Press, 2006.

Hill, John M. *The Cultural World in "Beowulf."* Toronto: University of Toronto Press, 1995.

———. "The Ethnopsychology of In-Law Feud and the Remaking of Group Identity in *Beowulf:* The Cases of Hengest and Ingeld." *Philological Quarterly* 78, nos. 1–2 (Winter-Spring 1999): 97–123.

Hinely, Jan Lawson. "Comic Scapegoats and the Falstaff of *The Merry Wives of Windsor.*" *Shakespeare Studies* 15 (1982): 37–54.

Hodgdon, Barbara. *The End Crowns All: Closure and Contradiction in Shakespeare's History.* Princeton, NJ: Princeton University Press, 1991.

Holinshed, Raphael. *Shakespeare's Holinshed: An Edition of Holinshed's "Chronicles" (1587).* Selected, edited, and annotated by Richard Hosley. New York: G. P. Putnam's Sons, 1968.

Holmer, Joan Ozark. *The Merchant of Venice: Choice, Hazard and Consequence.* New York: St. Martin's Press, 1995.

Holst-Warhaft, Gail. *Dangerous Voices: Women's Laments and Greek Literature.* London: Routledge, 1992.

Homer. *The Iliad.* Translated by Robert Fitzgerald. New York: Farrar, Straus and Giroux, 2004.

———. *The Iliad.* Translated by Richmond Lattimore. Chicago: University of Chicago Press, 1951.

Hoover, Claudette. "Goneril and Regan: 'So Horrid as in Woman.'" *San Jose Studies* 10, no. 3 (1984): 49–65.

Horney, Karen. "The Value of Vindictiveness." In *New Perspectives in Psychoanalysis,* edited by Harold Kelman, 27–51. New York: W. W. Norton and Company, 1965. Originally published in 1948.

Howard, Henry, Earl of Surrey. *The "Aeneid" of Henry Howard, Earl of Surrey.* Edited by Florence H. Ridley. Berkeley and Los Angeles: University of California Press, 1963.

Howard, Jean E., and Phyllis Rackin. *Engendering a Nation: A Feminist Account of Shakespeare's English Histories.* London: Routledge, 1997.

Hunter, Dianne. "Doubling, Mythic Difference, and the Scapegoating of Female Power in *Macbeth.*" In *The Persistence of Myth: Psychoanalytic and Structuralist Perspectives,* edited by Peter L. Rudnytsky, 129–52. New York: Guilford Press, 1988.

Ingham, Patricia Clare. "From Kinship to Kingship: Mourning, Gender, and Anglo-Saxon Community." In *Grief and Gender, 700–1700,* edited by Jennifer Vaught and Lynne Dickson, 17–32. Hampshire, England: Palgrave Macmillan, 2003.

Ingram, Jill Phillips. *Idioms of Self-Interest: Credit, Identity, and Property in English Renaissance Literature.* New York: Routledge, 2006.

Jackson, Gabriele Bernhard. "Topical Ideology: Witches, Amazons, and Shakespeare's Joan of Arc." *English Literary Review* 18 (1988): 40–65.

Jacoby, Susan. *Wild Justice: The Evolution of Revenge.* New York: Harper and Row, 1983.

James, Heather. *Shakespeare's Troy: Drama, Politics, and the Translation of Empire.* Cambridge: Cambridge University Press, 1997.

Jesch, Judith. *Women in the Viking Age.* Woodbridge, England: Boydell Press, 1991.

Jiji, Vera M. "Portia Revisited: The Influence of Unconscious Factors upon Theme and Characterization in *The Merchant of Venice.*" *Literature and Psychology* 26, no. 1 (1976): 5–15.

Jochens, Jenny. "The Medieval Icelandic Heroine: Fact or Fiction?" *Viator* 17 (1986): 35–50.

———. *Old Norse Images of Women.* Philadelphia: University of Pennsylvania Press, 1996.

Jones, Ann Rosalind. "Revenge Comedy: Writing, Law, and the Punishing Heroine in *Twelfth Night, The Merry Wives of Windsor,* and *Swetnam the Woman-Hater.*" In *Shakespearean Power and Punishment,* edited by Gillian Murray Kendall, 23–38. Madison, NJ: Fairleigh Dickinson University Press, 1998.

Jones, Emrys. *The Origins of Shakespeare.* Oxford: Clarendon Press, 1977.

Kahn, Coppélia. *Man's Estate: Masculine Identity in Shakespeare.* Berkeley and Los Angeles: University of California Press, 1981.

———. *Roman Shakespeare: Warriors, Wounds, and Women.* London: Routledge, 1997.

Kastan, David Scott. *Shakespeare and the Shapes of Time.* Hanover, NH: University Press of New England, 1982.

Katz, Leslie S. "*The Merry Wives of Windsor:* Sharing the Queen's Holiday." *Representations* 51 (Summer 1995): 77–93.

Kennedy, Gwynne. *Just Anger: Representing Women's Anger in Early Modern England.* Carbondale: Southern Illinois University Press, 2000.

Kerrigan, John. *Revenge Tragedy: Aeschylus to Armageddon.* Oxford: Clarendon Press, 1996.

Keyishian, Harry. *The Shapes of Revenge: Victimization, Vengeance, and Vindictiveness in Shakespeare.* 1995. Reprint, Amherst, NY: Humanities Books, 2003.

Kiefer, Frederick. *Shakespeare's Visual Theatre: Staging the Personified Characters.* Cambridge: Cambridge University Press, 2003.

Klein, Joan Larsen, ed. *Daughters, Wives, and Widows: Writings by Men about Women and Marriage in England.* Urbana: University of Illinois Press, 1992.

Korda, Natasha. "Dame Usury: Gender, Credit, and (Ac)counting in the Sonnets and *The Merchant of Venice.*" *Shakespeare Quarterly* 60, no. 2 (2009): 129–53.

Krieger, Elliott. *"Twelfth Night:* 'The Morality of Indulgence.'" In *Twelfth Night,* edited by R. S. White, 37–71. New York: St. Martin's Press, 1996.

Kyd, Thomas. *The Spanish Tragedy.* Edited by J. R. Mulryne. 2nd ed. London: A and C Black, 1989.

Langman, F. A. "Comedy and Saturnalia: The Case of *Twelfth Night.*" *Southern Review* 7 (1974): 102–22.

La Primaudaye, Peter de. *The French Academie.* 1586. A facsimile edition. Hildesheim: Georg Olms Verlag, 1972.

Larrington, Caroline, trans. *The Poetic Edda.* Oxford: Oxford University Press, 1996.

Lawrence, Sean. "'To Give and to Receive': Performing Exchanges in *The Merchant of Venice.*" In *Shakespeare and the Cultures of Performance,* edited by Paul Yachnin and Patricia Badir, 41–51. Aldershot, England: Ashgate, 2008.

Lea, K. M. *Italian Popular Comedy: A Study in the Commedia Dell'Arte, 1560–1620 with Special Reference to the English Stage.* 2 vols. New York: Russell and Russell, 1962.

Lee, Patricia-Ann. "Reflections of Power: Margaret of Anjou and the Dark Side of Queenship." *Renaissance Quarterly* 39, no. 2 (Summer 1986): 183–217.

Leech, Clifford. *"Twelfth Night" and Shakespearian Comedy.* Toronto: University of Toronto Press, 1965.

Leimberg, Inge. "'M.O.A.I.': Trying to Share the Joke in *Twelfth Night* 2.5 (A Critical Hypothesis)." *Connotations* 1, no. 1 (1991): 78–95.

Lenz, Carolyn Ruth Swift, Gayle Greene, and Carol Thomas Neely, eds. *The Woman's Part: Feminist Criticism of Shakespeare.* Urbana: University of Illinois Press, 1980.

Levin, Richard. "Feminist Thematics and Shakespearean Tragedy." *PMLA* 103, no. 2 (March 1988): 125–38.

———. "Gertrude's Elusive Libido and Shakespeare's Unreliable Narrators." *Studies in English Literature* 48, no. 2 (Spring 2008): 305–26.

Levin, Richard A. *Love and Society in Shakespearean Comedy: A Study of Dramatic Form and Content.* Newark: University of Delaware Press, 1985.

———. *Shakespeare's Secret Schemers: The Study of an Early Modern Literary Device.* Newark: University of Delaware Press, 2002.

Levine, Nina S. *Women's Matters: Politics, Gender, and Nation in Shakespeare's Early History Plays.* Newark: University of Delaware Press, 1998.

Levith, Murray J. *What's in Shakespeare's Names.* North Haven, CT: Archon Books, 1978.

Lewalski, Barbara K. "Biblical Allusion and Allegory in *The Merchant of Venice.*" *Shakespeare Quarterly* 13, no. 3 (1962): 327–43.

Liebler, Naomi Conn, ed. *The Female Tragic Hero in English Renaissance Drama.* New York: Palgrave Macmillan, 2002.

Liebler, Naomi Conn and Lisa Scancella Shea. "Shakespeare's Queen Margaret: Unruly or Unruled?" In *Henry VI: Critical Essays,* edited by Thomas A. Pendleton, 79–96. New York: Routledge, 2001.

Loomba, Ania. "Women's Division of Experience." In *Revenge Tragedy,* edited by Stevie Simkin, 41–70. New York: Palgrave Macmillan, 2001.

Loraux, Nicole. *Mothers in Mourning with the Essay "Of Amnesty and Its Opposite."* Translated by Corinne Pache. Ithaca, NY: Cornell University Press, 1998.

————. *The Mourning Voice: An Essay on Greek Tragedy.* Translated by Elizabeth Trapnell Rawlings. Ithaca, NY: Cornell University Press, 2002.

Luther, Martin. *Temporal Authority: To What Extent It Should be Obeyed.* Translated by J. J. Schindel. Revised by Walther I. Brandt. In vol. 45 of *Luther's Works,* edited by Walther I. Brandt. Philadelphia: Muhlenberg Press, 1962.

Macdonald, Ronald R. *William Shakespeare: The Comedies.* New York: Twayne Publishers, 1992.

Mahon, John, and Ellen MacLeod Mahon, eds. *The Merchant of Venice: New Critical Essays.* New York: Routledge, 2002.

Malcolmson, Cristina. "'What You Will': Social Mobility and Gender in *Twelfth Night.*" In *Twelfth Night,* edited by R. S. White, 160–93. New York: St. Martin's Press, 1996.

Marcus, Leah. *Puzzling Shakespeare: Local Reading and Its Discontents.* Berkeley and Los Angeles: University of California Press, 1988.

Markels, Julian. "Shakespeare's Confluence of Tragedy and Comedy: *Twelfth Night* and *King Lear.*" *Shakespeare Quarterly* 15 (1964): 75–88.

Marlowe, Christopher. *The Life of Marlowe and The Tragedy of Dido Queen of Carthage.* Edited by C. F. Tucker Brooke. Vol.1, *The Works and Life of Christopher Marlowe,* edited by R. H. Case. 1930. Reprint, New York: Gordian Press, 1966.

Marongiu, Pietro, and Graeme Newman. *Vengeance: The Fight against Injustice.* Totowa, NJ: Rowman and Littlefield, 1987.

Maslen, R. W. *Shakespeare and Comedy.* The Arden Critical Companions. London: Thomson Learning, 2006.

Maus, Katharine. Introduction to *Four Revenge Tragedies.* Edited by Katharine Maus. Oxford: Oxford University Press, 1995.

Mauss, Marcel. *The Gift: The Form and Reason for Exchange in Archaic Societies.* Translated by W. D. Halls. New York: W. W. Norton and Company, 1990.

McHardy, Fiona. *Revenge in Athenian Culture.* London: Duckworth, 2008.

————. "Women's Influence on Revenge in Ancient Greece." In *Women's Influence on Classical Civilization,* edited by Fiona McHardy and Eireann Marshall, 92–114. London: Routledge, 2004.

McKewin, Carole. "Counsels of Gall and Grace: Intimate Conversations between Women in Shakespeare's Plays." In *The Woman's Part: Feminist Criticism of Shakespeare,* edited by Carolyn Ruth Swift Lenz, Gayle Greene, and Carol Thomas Neely, 117–32. Urbana: University of Illinois Press, 1980.

Mercer, Peter. *"Hamlet" and the Acting of Revenge.* Iowa City: University of Iowa, 1987.

Millard, Barbara C. "Virago with a Soft Voice: Cordelia's Tragic Rebellion in *King Lear.*" *Philology Quarterly* 68, no. 2 (Spring 1989): 143–65.

Miller, William Ian. *Bloodtaking and Peacemaking: Feud, Law, and Society in Saga Iceland.* Chicago: University of Chicago Press, 1990.

————. "Choosing the Avenger: Some Aspects of the Bloodfeud in Medieval Iceland and England." *Law and History Review* 1, no. 2 (1983): 159–204.

————. *Eye for an Eye.* Cambridge: Cambridge University Press, 2006.

————. *Humiliation and Other Essays on Honor, Social Discomfort, and Violence.* Ithaca, NY: Cornell University Press, 1993.

Miola, Robert S. *"The Merry Wives of Windsor:* Classical and Italian Intertexts." *Comparative Drama* 27, no. 3 (Fall 1993): 364–76.

———. *Shakespeare and Classical Tragedy: The Influence of Seneca.* Oxford: Clarendon Press, 1992.

Montaigne, Michel de. *The Essays.* Translated by John Florio. Edited by Adolph Cohn. New York: G. P. Putnam's, 1907.

Moody, A. D. *Shakespeare: "The Merchant of Venice."* London: Edward Arnold, 1964.

Mossman, Judith. *Wild Justice: A Study of Euripides' "Hecuba."* London: Bristol Classical Press, 1995.

Mowat, Barbara. "Lavinia's Message: Shakespeare and Myth." *Renaissance Papers,* 1981, 55–69.

Muir, Edward. *Mad Blood Stirring: Vendetta and Factions in Friuli during the Renaissance.* Baltimore: Johns Hopkins University Press, 1993.

Muldrew, Craig. *The Economy of Obligation: The Culture of Credit and Social Relations in Early Modern England.* New York: St. Martin's Press, 1998.

Murphy, Jeffrie G. *Getting Even: Forgiveness and Its Limits.* Oxford: Oxford University Press, 2003.

Nashe, Thomas. *Pierce Penilesse His Svpplication to the Divell.* 1592. In vol. 1 of *The Works of Thomas Nashe,* edited by Ronald B. McKerrow. Oxford: Basil Blackwell, 1958.

Nathan, Norman. "Portia, Nerissa, and Jessica—Their Names." *Notes and Queries* 34, no. 4 (December 1986): 425–29.

Neill, Michael. *Issues of Death: Mortality and Identity in English Renaissance Tragedy.* Oxford: Clarendon Press, 1997.

Nevo, Ruth. *Comic Transformations in Shakespeare.* London: Methuen, 1980.

———. "Shakespeare's Comic Remedies." *New York Literary Forum* 5–6 (1980): 3–15.

Newman, Karen. "Portia's Ring: Unruly Women and Structures of Exchange in *The Merchant of Venice.*" *Shakespeare Quarterly* 38, no. 1 (1987): 19–33.

Newton, Thomas, ed. *Seneca, His Tenne Tragedies, Translated into English.* 1581. Reprint, Bloomington: Indiana University Press, 1960. (First published 1927 by Constable and Co., and Alfred A. Knopf.)

Nietzsche, Friedrich. *Beyond Good and Evil: Prelude to a Philosophy of the Future.* Translated and edited by Marion Faber. Oxford: Oxford University Press, 1998.

———. *On the Genealogy of Morals.* Translated by Walter Kaufmann and R. J. Hollingdale. In *On the Genealogy of Morals; Ecce Homo,* edited by Walter Kaufmann. New York: Vintage Books, 1969.

Norton, Thomas, and Thomas Sackville. *Gorbuduc.* In *Drama of the English Renaissance I: The Tudor Period,* edited by Russell A. Fraser and Norman Rabkin. New York: Macmillan, 1976.

Okayama, Yassu. *The Ripa Index: Personifications and their Attributes in Five Editions of the Iconologia.* Doornspijk, Netherlands: Davaco, 1992.

Oldrieve, Susan. "Marginalized Voices in *The Merchant of Venice.*" *Cardozo Studies in Law and Literature* 5 (1993): 87–105.

Orgel, Stephen. *Imagining Shakespeare: A History of Texts and Visions.* Houndmills, England: Palgrave Macmillan, 2003.

Osborne, Laurie E. "Letters, Lovers, Lacan: Or Malvolio's Not-So-Purloined Letter," *Assays* 5 (1989): 63–89.

Ovid. *Heroides and Amores.* Translated by Grant Showerman. Vol. 1 of *Ovid in Six Volumes.* Rev. ed. by G. P. Goold. Cambridge, MA: Harvard University Press, 1977.

———. *Metamorphoses.* Translated by Frank Junius Miller. Vols. 3 and 4 of *Ovid in Six Volumes.* Rev. ed. by G. P. Goold. Cambridge, MA: Harvard University Press, 1977.

———. *Tristia and Ex Ponto.* Translated by Arthur Leslie Wheeler. Vol. 6 of *Ovid in Six Volumes.* Rev. ed. by G. P. Goold. Cambridge, MA: Harvard University Press, 1988.

Padel, Ruth. *In and Out of the Mind: Greek Images of the Tragic Self.* Princeton, NJ: Princeton University Press, 1992.

———. *Whom Gods Destroy: Elements of Greek and Tragic Madness.* Princeton, NJ: Princeton University Press, 1995.

Palmer, D. J. "The Unspeakable in Pursuit of the Uneatable: Language and Action in *Titus Andronicus.*" *Critical Quarterly* 14 (1972): 320–39.

Parker, Robert. *Miasma: Pollution and Purification in Early Greek Religion.* Oxford: Clarendon Press, 1983.

Parten, Anne. "Falstaff's Horns: Masculine Inadequacy and Feminine Mirth in *The Merry Wives of Windsor.*" *Studies in Philology* 82, no. 2 (Spring 1985): 184–99.

Peristiany, J. G., ed. *Honour and Shame: The Values of Mediterranean Society.* Chicago: University of Chicago Press, 1966.

Peyré, Yves. "'Confusion Now Hath Made His Masterpiece': Senecan Resonances in *Macbeth.*" In *Shakespeare and the Classics,* edited by Charles Martindale and A. B. Taylor, 141–55. Cambridge: Cambridge University Press, 2004.

Pitt, Angela. *Shakespeare's Women.* Newton Abbot, England: David and Charles, 1981.

Pitt-Rivers, Julian. "Honour and Social Status." In *Honour and Shame: The Values of Mediterranean Society,* edited by J. G. Peristiany, 21–80. Chicago: University of Chicago Press, 1966.

Pliny the Elder. *Natural History.* Translated by H. Rackham. Vol. 8. Cambridge, MA: Harvard University Press, 1963.

Poole, Adrian. *Tragedy: Shakespeare and the Greek Example.* Oxford: Basil Blackwell, 1987.

Potter, Lois. "Shakespeare and the Art of Revenge." *Shakespeare Studies* 32 (1994): 29–54.

Prosser, Eleanor. *"Hamlet" and Revenge.* Stanford, CA: Stanford University Press, 1967.

Rackin, Phyllis. *Shakespeare and Women.* Oxford: Oxford University Press, 2005.

Rainolde, Richard. *The Foundation of Rhetoric.* 1563. Menston, England: Scolar Press, 1972.

Reid, Stephen. "In Defense of Goneril and Regan." *American Imago* 27, no. 3 (Fall 1970): 226–44.

Reynolds, John. *The Triumph of Gods Revenge against the crying and execrable sinne of murther.* 1639. Edited by Joan M. Walmsley. Lewiston, NY: Edwin Mellen Press, 2004.

Riefer, Marsha. "'Instruments of Some Mightier Member': The Constriction of Female Power in *Measure for Measure.*" *Shakespeare Quarterly* 35, no. 2 (Summer 1984): 157–69.

Roberts, Jeanne Addison. "Sex and the Female Tragic Hero." In *The Female Tragic Hero in English Renaissance Drama,* edited by Naomi Conn Liebler, 199–216. New York: Palgrave Macmillan, 2002.

———. *Shakespeare's English Comedy: "The Merry Wives of Windsor" in Context.* Lincoln: University of Nebraska Press, 1979.

Robertson, Karen. "Rape and the Appropriation of Progne's Revenge in Shakespeare's *Titus Andronicus,* or 'Who Cooks the Thyestean Banquet?'" In *Representing Rape in Medieval and Early Modern Literature,* edited by Elizabeth Robertson and Christine M. Rose, 213–237. New York: Palgrave Macmillan, 2001.

———. "A Revenging Feminine Hand in *Twelfth Night.*" In *Reading and Writing in Shakespeare,* edited by David M. Bergeron, 116–30. Newark: University of Delaware Press, 1996.

Rossiter, A. P. *Angel with Horns and Other Shakespeare Lectures.* Edited by Graham Storey. New York: Theatre Arts Books, 1961.

Rotunda, D. P. *Motif-Index of the Italian Novella in Prose.* Bloomington: Indiana University Press, 1942.

Ruff, Julius R. *Violence in Early Modern Europe.* Cambridge: Cambridge University Press, 2001.

Rushdie, Salman. *Shame.* New York: Picador, 1983.

Rutter, Carol Chillington. "Of Tygers' Hearts and Players' Hides." In *Shakespeare's Histories and Counter-Histories,* edited by Dermot Cavanagh, Stuart Hampton-Reeves, and Stephen Longstaffe, 182–98. Manchester: Manchester University Press, 2007.

Sachs, Hans. "The Measure in *Measure for Measure.*" In *The Design Within: Psychoanalytic Approaches to Shakespeare,* edited by Melvin D. Faber. New York: Science House, 1970.

Salingar, Leo. *Shakespeare and the Traditions of Comedy.* Cambridge: Cambridge University Press, 1974.

Saunders, Kate, ed. *Revenge.* Boston: Faber and Faber, 1991. First published 1990 by Virago Press.

Schafer, Elizabeth. *Ms-Directing Shakespeare: Women Direct Shakespeare.* New York: St. Martin's Press, 2000.

Schleiner, Louise. "Latinized Greek Drama in Shakespeare's Writing of *Hamlet.*" *Shakespeare Quarterly* 41, no. 1 (Spring 1990): 29–48.

Scott-Warren, Jason. "When Theaters Were Bear-Gardens; or, What's at Stake in the Comedy of Humors." *Shakespeare Quarterly* 54, no. 1 (2003): 63–82.

Sedgwick, Eve Kosofsky. *Between Men: English Literature and Male Homosocial Desire.* New York: Columbia University Press, 1985.

Seneca, Lucius Annaeus. *Seneca in Nine Volumes.* Translated by Frank Justus Miller. Vols. 8 and 9. Cambridge, MA: Harvard University Press, 1917.

Shakespeare, William. *Cymbeline.* Edited by J. M. Nosworthy. London: Methuen, 1955.

———. *Hamlet.* Edited by Ann Thompson and Neil Taylor. The Arden Shakespeare. London: Thomson Learning, 2006.

———. *Hamlet, The First Quarto, 1603.* Cambridge, MA: Harvard University Press, 1931.

———. *The History of King Lear* (The Quarto Text). In *The Norton Shakespeare, Based on the Oxford Edition,* edited by Stephen Greenblatt et al. New York: W. W. Norton and Company, 1997.

———. *Julius Caesar.* Edited by David Daniell. Surrey, England: Thomas Nelson and Sons, 1998.

———. *King Henry IV, Part 1.* Edited by David Scott Kastan. The Arden Shakespeare. London: Thomson Learning, 2002.

———. *King Henry V.* Edited T. W. Craik. London: Routledge, 1995.

———. *King Henry VI, Part 1.* Edited by Edward Burns. The Arden Shakespeare. London: Thomson Learning, 2000.

———. *King Henry VI, Part 2.* Edited by Ronald Knowles. Surrey, England: Thomas Nelson and Sons, 1999.

————. *King Henry VI, Part 3.* Edited by John D. Cox and Eric Rasmussen. The Arden Shakespeare. London: Thomson Learning, 2001.

————. *King John.* Edited by E. A. J. Honigmann. London: Methuen, 1951.

————. *King Richard II.* Edited by Charles R. Forker. The Arden Shakespeare. London: Thomson Learning, 2002.

————. *King Richard III.* Edited by Anthony Hammond. London: Methuen, 1981.

————. *Love's Labour's Lost.* Edited by H. R. Woudhuysen. Surrey, England: Thomas Nelson and Sons, 1998.

————. *Macbeth.* Edited by Kenneth Muir. London: Methuen, 1951.

————. *Measure for Measure.* Edited by J. W. Lever. London: Methuen, 1965.

————. *The Merchant of Venice.* Edited by John Russell Brown. London: Methuen, 1955.

————. *The Merry Wives of Windsor.* Edited by Giorgio Melchiori. Surrey, England: Thomas Nelson and Sons, 2000.

————. *Much Ado About Nothing.* Edited by Claire McEachern. The Arden Shakespeare: Thomson Learning, 2006.

————. *Othello.* Edited by E. A. J. Honigmann. Surrey, England: Thomas Nelson and Sons, 1997.

————. *Romeo and Juliet.* Edited by Brian Gibbons. London: Methuen, 1980.

————. *Titus Andronicus.* Edited by Jonathan Bate. London: Routledge, 1995.

————. *The Tragedy of King Lear.* In *The Norton Shakespeare: Based on the Oxford Edition,* edited by Stephen Greenblatt et al. New York: W. W. Norton and Company, 1997.

————. *Twelfth Night.* Edited by J. M. Lothian and T. W. Craik. London: Routledge, 1995.

————. *The Winter's Tale.* Edited by J. H. P. Pafford. London: Methuen, 1963.

Shand, G. B. "Gertred, Captive Queen of the First Quarto." In *Shakespearean Illuminations,* edited by Jay L. Halio and Hugh Richmond, 33–49. Newark: University of Delaware Press, 1998.

————. "Realising Gertrude: The Suicide Option." In *The Elizabethan Theatre XIII,* edited by A. L. Magnusson and C. E. McGee, 95–118. Toronto: P. D. Meany, 1994.

Shell, Marc. "The Wether and the Ewe: Verbal Usury in *The Merchant of Venice.*" *Kenyon Review,* n.s., 1, no. 4 (Autumn 1979): 65–92.

Showalter, Elaine. "Representing Ophelia: Women, Madness, and the Responsibilities of Feminist Criticism." In *Shakespeare and the Question of Theory,* edited by Patricia Parker and Geoffrey Hartman, 77–94. London: Routledge, 1985.

————. "Review Essay: Literary Criticism." *Signs* 1 (1975): 435–60.

Silber, Patricia. "The Unnatural Woman and the Disordered State in Shakespeare's Histories." *Proceedings of the PMR Conference* 2 (1977): 87–95.

Sillars, Stuart. *Painting Shakespeare: The Artist as Critic, 1720–1820.* Cambridge: Cambridge University Press, 2006.

Simkin, Stevie. *Early Modern Tragedy and the Cinema of Violence.* New York: Palgrave Macmillan, 2006.

————, ed. *Revenge Tragedy.* Houndmills, England: Palgrave Macmillan, 2001.

Slights, Camille Wells. *Shakespeare's Comic Commonwealths.* Toronto: University of Toronto Press, 1993.

Smith, Rebecca. "A Heart Cleft in Twain: The Dilemma of Shakespeare's Gertrude." In *The Woman's Part: Feminist Criticism of Shakespeare,* edited by Carolyn Ruth Swift Lenz,

Gayle Greene, and Carol Thomas Neely, 194–210. Urbana: University of Illinois Press, 1980.

Smith, William, ed. *A Dictionary of Greek and Roman Biography and Mythology.* 3 vols. New York: AMS Press, 1967.

Snyder, Susan. *The Comic Matrix of Shakespeare's Tragedies.* Princeton, NJ: Princeton University Press, 1979.

Solomon, Robert C. "Justice v. Vengeance: On Law and the Satisfaction of Emotion." In *The Passions of Law,* edited by Susan A. Bandes, 123–48. New York: New York University Press, 1999.

———. *A Passion for Justice: Emotions and the Origins of the Social Contract.* Reading, MA: Addison-Wesley Publishing Company, 1990.

Sorgenfrei, Carol Fisher. "Unsexed and Disembodied: Female Avengers in Japan and England." In *Revenge Drama in European Renaissance and Japanese Theatre,* edited by Kevin J. Wetmore, Jr., 45–73. New York: Palgrave Macmillan, 2008.

Spelman, Elizabeth. "Anger and Insubordination." In *Women, Knowledge, and Reality: Explorations in Feminist Philosophy,* edited by Ann Garry and Marilyn Pearsall, 263–73. Boston: Unwin Hyman, 1989.

Steadman, John M. "Falstaff as Actaeon: A Dramatic Emblem." *Shakespeare Quarterly* 14, no. 3 (Summer 1963): 230–44.

Steed, Maggie. "Beatrice in *Much Ado About Nothing.*" In *Players of Shakespeare 3,* edited by Russell Jackson and Robert Smallwood, 42–51. Cambridge: Cambridge University Press, 1993.

Stevenson, Kenneth W. *The Lord's Prayer: A Text in Tradition.* Minneapolis, MN: Fortress Press, 2004.

Stockton, Will. "'I Am Made an Ass': Falstaff and the Scatology of Windsor's Polity." *Texas Studies in Literature and Language* 49, no. 4 (Winter 2007): 340–60.

Stratford, Nicholas. *A Dissuasive from Revenge.* London: Richard Chiswell, 1684.

Stretton, Tim. *Women Waging Law in Elizabethan England.* Cambridge: Cambridge University Press, 1998.

Stuart, James. *Daemonologie, in Forme of a Dialogue.* Edinburgh: Robert Walde-graue, 1597.

Szymborska, Wisława. "The Poet and the World, Nobel Lecture 1996." In *Poems New and Collected, 1957–1997.* New York: Harcourt Brace and Company, 1998.

Taylor, Gary. "The War in *King Lear.*" *Shakespeare Survey* 33 (1980): 27–34.

Tenison, Eva Mabel. *Elizabethan England: Being the History of this Country "In Relation to all Foreign Princes."* Vol. 5. 1932. UK: Obscure Press, 2006.

Thomas, R. George. "Some Exceptional Women in the Sagas." *Saga-Book of the Viking Society* 13, no. 5 (1952–53): 307–27.

Thomas Aquinas. *Summa Theologica.* Translated by Fathers of the English Dominican Province. Vol. 3. Westminster, MD: Christian Classics, 1948.

Thomson, Leslie, ed. *Fortune: "All is but Fortune."* The Folger Shakespeare Library Exhibition. January 18–June 10, 2000. Seattle: University of Washington Press, 2000.

Thorndike, A. H. "The Relations of *Hamlet* to Contemporary Revenge Plays." *PMLA* 17 (1902): 125–220.

Toufic, Jalal. "If You Prick Us, Do We Not Bleed?" *Discourse: Berkeley Journal for Theoretical Studies in Media and Culture* 20, no. 3 (Fall 1998): 165–69.

The True Tragedie of Richard the Third. London: Thomas Creede, 1594.

Turner, Victor. "Social Dramas in Brazilian Umbanda: The Dialectics of Meaning." In *The Anthropology of Performance,* 33–71. New York: PAJ Publications, 1987.

Urkowitz, Steven. "Five Women Eleven Ways: Changing Images of Shakespearean Characters in the Earliest Texts." In *Images of Shakespeare: Proceedings of the Third Congress of the International Shakespeare Association, 1986,* edited by Werner Habicht, D. J. Palmer, and Roger Pringle, 292–304. Newark: University of Delaware Press, 1988.

Velz, John W. "Portia and the Ovidian Grotesque." In *The Merchant of Venice: New Critical Essays,* edited by John Mahon, 179–86. London: Routledge, 2002.

Vermigli, Peter Martyr. *The Common Places.* Translated by Anthonie Marten. London, 1583.

Virgil, *The Aeneid.* Translated by Allen Mandelbaum. Toronto: Bantam Books, 1961.

———. *The Aeneid.* In *P. Vergili Maronis: Opera,* edited by R. A. B. Mynors. Oxford: Oxford University Press, 1969.

Virgoe, Roger. "The Death of William de la Pole, the Duke of Suffolk." *Bulletin of the John Rylands Library* 47 (1964–65): 489–502.

Vives, Juan Luis. *The Office and Duty of an Husband.* Translated by Thomas Paynell. London: [1555?]. In *Daughters, Wives, and Widows: Writings by Men about Women and Marriage in England,* edited by Joan Larsen Klein. Urbana: University of Illinois Press, 1992.

Wall, Wendy. "*The Merry Wives of Windsor:* Unhusbanding Desire in Windsor." In *A Companion to Shakespeare's Works, vol. 3: The Comedies,* edited by Richard Dutton and Jean E. Howard, 376–92. Oxford: Blackwell, 2003.

Walter, Harriet. *Macbeth.* London: Faber and Faber, 2002.

Watson, Curtis Brown. *Shakespeare and the Renaissance Concept of Honor.* Princeton, NJ: Princeton University Press, 1960.

Webster, John. *The White Devil.* Edited by F. L. Lucas. New York: Macmillan, 1959.

Weil, Judith. "Visible Hecubas." In *The Female Tragic Hero in English Renaissance Drama,* edited by Naomi Conn Liebler, 51–69. New York: Palgrave Macmillan, 2002.

Westney, Lizette I. "Hecuba in Sixteenth-Century English Literature." *CLA Journal* 27, no. 4 (June 1984): 436–59.

Wheeler, Richard. *Shakespeare's Development and the Problem Comedies: Turn and Counter-Turn.* Berkeley and Los Angeles: University of California Press, 1981.

Whittier, Gayle. "Cordelia as Prince: Gender and Language in *King Lear.*" *Exemplaria* 1, no. 2 (Fall 1989): 367–99.

Williams, William Proctor. "*Titus Andronicus* in Washington, DC." *Shakespeare Newsletter* (Spring/Summer 2007): 1, 12, 14.

Williamson, Marilyn L. *The Patriarchy of Shakespeare's Comedies.* Detroit: Wayne State University Press, 1986.

Willis, Deborah. "'The Gnawing Vulture': Revenge, Trauma Theory, and *Titus Andronicus.*" *Shakespeare Quarterly* 53, no. 1 (2002): 21–52.

Wolf, Janet S. "'Like an Old Tale Still': Paulina, 'Triple Hecate,' and the Persephone Myth in *The Winter's Tale.*" In *Images of Persephone: Feminist Readings in Western Literature,* edited by Elizabeth T. Hayes, 32–44. Gainesville: University Press of Florida, 1994.

Woodbridge, Linda. "'Fire in Your Heart and Brimstone in Your Liver': Towards an Unsaturnalian *Twelfth Night.*" *Southern Review* 17 (November 1984): 270–91.

———. "Palisading the Body Politic." In *True Rites and Maimed Rites: Ritual and Anti-Ritual in Shakespeare and His Age,* edited by Linda Woodbridge and Edward Berry, 270–98. Urbana: University of Illinois Press, 1992.

———. "Payback Time: On the Economic Rhetoric of Revenge in *The Merchant of Venice*." In *Shakespeare and the Cultures of Performance,* edited by Paul Yachnin and Patricia Badir, 29–40. Aldershot, England: Ashgate, 2008.

Woolf, Rosemary. *The English Mystery Plays.* Berkeley and Los Angeles: University of California Press, 1972.

Wurmser, Léon. *The Mask of Shame.* Baltimore, MD: Johns Hopkins University Press, 1981.

Zeitlin, Froma I. "The Dynamics of Misogyny in the *Oresteia.*" *Arethusa* 11 (1978): 149–84.

———. *Playing the Other: Gender and Society in Classical Greek Literature.* Chicago: University of Chicago Press, 1996.

Zuckert, Michael. "The New Medea: On Portia's Comic Triumph in *The Merchant of Venice.*" In *Shakespeare's Political Pageant: Essays in Literature and Politics,* edited by Joseph Alulis and Vickie Sullivan, 3–36. Lanham, MD: Rowman and Littlefield, 1996.

Index

339